THE LIBRARY OF LITERATURE
UNDER THE GENERAL EDITORSHIP OF
JOHN HENRY RALEIGH
AND IAN WATT

5-95x

KING ARTHUR'S DEATH

THE LIBRARY OF LITERATURE

THE MIDDLE ENGLISH

Stanzaic Morte Arthur

AND *Alliterative Morte Arthure*

KING ARTHUR'S DEATH

The Middle English
Stanzaic Morte Arthur
and
Alliterative Morte Arthure

EDITED BY LARRY D. BENSON

The Bobbs-Merrill Company, Inc.
Indianapolis · New York

Library of Congress Cataloging in Publication Data

Benson, Larry Dean, 1929–   comp.
  King Arthur's death.

  (The Library of Literature)
  Bibliography: p.
  1. English poetry—Middle English (1100–1500)
2. Arthurian romances. I. Morte Arthur. 1974.
II. Le Morte Arthure. 1974. III. Title.
PR2064.B4   821'.1'08   73–13545
ISBN 0–672–61010–8 (pbk.)
ISBN 0–672–51453–2

For Cassandra and Gavin

Contents

Preface

The texts in this volume have been edited for readers who have had little or no training in Middle English. Except for an old and unsatisfactory edition (now long out of print) that contained a prose translation of the *Alliterative Morte Arthure* and a badly glossed edition of the *Stanzaic Morte Arthur,* the two romances in this volume have never been easily accessible to students who are not specializing in Middle English. The *Stanzaic Morte Arthur,* linguistically a relatively easy work, is available only in a diplomatic scholarly edition that presents formidable difficulties to the beginning student or casual reader. The *Alliterative Morte Arthure,* a more difficult poem, is partially available in well-annotated editions of selections (in the Owens' anthology and in Finlayson's edition, both listed in the Bibliography on p. xxxiv), but the whole original poem is accessible only in scholarly editions that make a difficult work almost impossible reading for all but advanced students. Yet these two romances are among the finest of our English medieval narrative poems; they deserve a wider readership simply for what they are, first-rate works of art. They are furthermore essential reading for the student of Malory, for the student of the Arthurian legend in England, and even for the reader who only wants a better understanding of medieval English narrative in the later Middle Ages.

The variety of Middle English in which these poems were written is not as difficult as may at first appear, and most of the initial difficulty is due to the reader's lack of familiarity with a relatively small number of words and a few syntactic peculiarities. The texts in this volume have been edited in such a way that a beginning student can read them on his own. The marginal glosses are designed to help him with the vocabulary, and the notes should clear up any syntactic difficulties. The student who reads these works with care will find that he has learned a good portion of the basic vocabulary necessary for further reading in Middle English texts. Consequently, when used as a first text in classes in Middle English, these poems can provide the student with an extensive body of Middle English, valuable in itself, that he can read even before he begins his formal study of the language, so that when he does begin he not only knows—at least unconsciously—much of the grammar and vocabulary that he needs for further study, he also has some idea of what he needs to know; he can bring to class his own questions about the varieties of Middle English and his own observations on the structure of the language.

The texts in this volume have not been "simplified" in any significant way. The language itself remains about the same as it is in the manuscripts. However, the spelling has been regularized (in somewhat the same way editors of Chaucer have regularized his spelling), and this makes them much easier to read. Middle English itself is not very difficult, but Middle English spelling is nearly impossible, especially in texts such as these, which are both preserved in unique manuscripts well removed in time and place from their original authors. The *Stanzaic Morte Arthur* survives in a manuscript (British Museum MS Harley 2252) produced in the late fifteenth century by two different scribes who wrote in two different dialects, neither of which was that of the author, who apparently composed his work about a century before. The *Alliterative Morte Arthure* survives in a manuscript (Lincoln Cathedral MS Thornton A 1, 17, now called Lincoln Cathedral MS 91) that was written about 1440 by Robert Thornton; his copy was evidently a West Midlands text, though there is reason to believe our poem was written in the East Midlands.*

It is no wonder that the language of the manuscripts is confused; each shows traces of at least two different dialects along with all the other difficulties that necessarily creep into vernacular texts in the process of transmission (the Winchester Manuscript of Malory's work, for example, shows that a number of lines were missing from Thornton's exemplar). Thus far, both poems have been edited only in more or less diplomatic editions that faithfully reproduce the confusion of the scribes. Such texts are essential for the advanced student, who must know and study the manuscripts' representation of the language (and the editions in this volume are not intended as substitutes for such texts). However, for the beginning reader, and often even for the relatively advanced student, a faithful representation of the manuscript forms is frequently a misrepresentation of the language itself. Every teacher of Middle English is painfully aware of what happens when students are necessarily taught to pronounce what they see on the page and then inevitably do pronounce what they see, thus producing a strange and wildly varying language that has only a remote connection with Middle English. Long study and much practice are necessary before a student can easily distinguish between significant and insignificant spelling variations or can tell when a later scribe has foisted a fifteenth-century sound change off on a fourteenth-century poet.

The spellings in these texts have been regularized in a manner somewhat different from other editions of Middle English works in the Bobbs-Merrill

* I have not regularized the titles, which are traditionally the *Alliterative Morte Arthure* (or *Morte Arthure*) and the *Stanzaic Morte Arthur* (or *Le Morte Arthur*). Both titles mean "Arthur's Death" and the variation between *Arthur* and *Arthure* has no significance.

Library of Literature series. Robert D. Stevick's *One Hundred Middle English Poems* and *Five Middle English Narratives* contain texts normalized to a variety of Middle English resembling Chaucer's, a procedure that proved impractical for the more northerly texts in this volume. The texts in *Middle English Poetry, An Anthology*, edited by Lewis J. and Nancy H. Owen, have been regularized in spelling although, because of the variety of texts they include, their method is slightly different from that employed in this volume. In general, I have tried to use one spelling for each form, with the spellings selected on the basis of their existence in the manuscripts, their ease of recognition for a modern reader, and their faithfulness in representing the sound probably used by, or at least understandable to, the author. In few cases have all three criteria been met; where I have had to make a choice between the three, I have chosen ease in recognition, preferring a small error in sound or a slight deviation from the form the author may have used to a major difficulty in understanding. This has resulted in giving both texts a slightly more Midlands cast than they may have originally had.

I have regularized the plural pronoun forms in the *Stanzaic Morte Arthur*, but beyond that I have not changed the grammatical forms (retaining both the *-eth* and *-es* endings of the third person present tense of the verbs), since many of these variations probably represent competing forms rather than a confused dialect. I have chosen the spellings *shall* and *sholde* rather than *sal* and *suld* (the more numerous forms in the *Alliterative Morte Arthure*); I have usually preferred ǫ to *a* in forms like *bǫld/bald*; I have used the modern spellings in most cases of variation of short vowels before *r*, such as *world/werld*, and in most cases of variation of short *e* and short *i* and short *u* and short *i*, and I have used the more modern forms in regularizing unstressed vowels (choosing *e* instead of *i* in inflectional endings and preferring *be-* to *bi-* in forms like *before/bifore*). I have generally used *-dg-*, *-tch-*, and *sh-* instead of the manuscript's *-gg-*, *-cch*, and *sch-*. The one case in which I have usually adopted a more archaic form is short French *a* plus an *n*, adopting the more common Modern English spelling of words like *giaunt* instead of the modern spelling *giant*. I have not aimed at complete consistency, since phonemes as well as grammatical forms were probably in competition. So were words; as the alliterations show, *Gawain* and *Wawain* were both acceptable forms of that knight's name, and so both forms have been retained. The idea is to produce a reasonably regular but not thoroughly anesthetized text.

Although the regularized spellings are intended as a guide to the pronunciation of these texts, I have not tried to use a phonemic alphabet of any sort, and in these texts, as in Modern English, the same sound may be represented in a variety of ways. I have retained five different spellings of /i/ and six different spellings of /e/. This obviously creates some initial difficulties in learning the correct pronunciation, a problem that would have been eliminated by a more purely phonemic alphabet, but I believe that these initial difficulties are more than compensated for by the ease in recognition this spelling allows and by the better preparation it provides for the student who intends to move from these texts to unregularized editions.

The occasional explanatory notes have been purposely kept to the minimum necessary for understanding the text, and the introduction has been kept as brief as possible. My hope is that the student will concentrate his full attention on the texts themselves and thereby be led to further study.

The edition of the *Stanzaic Morte Arthur* is based mainly on Bruce's text (see Bibliography for this and other editions mentioned below), which was read against a microfilm of the manuscript. I have made a very few minor emendations (indicated in the Textual Notes). The edition of the *Alliterative Morte Arthure* is based mainly on Brock's text, which was also read against a microfilm of the manuscript. I have made a good many emendations (the most important are listed in the Textual Notes), aside from the regularizing, which in both poems often involves new readings of the lines. The Textual Notes are very brief and, except for the important textual changes that they record, I have not been able to include a full discussion of the solutions I have adopted in the establishment and interpretation of the text. I hope it will be understood that I have omitted this information not out of any disrespect for the previous editors, including those whose work I have used to establish the readings, but because the considerable editorial apparatus this would require would have been out of place in an edition of this sort.

Several conjectured lines have been added to the *Alliterative Morte Arthure* and one to the stanzaic poem; they are indicated by brackets and are not counted in the numbering of lines.

I owe thanks to Gavin R. Benson, who worked hard on the mimeographed trial texts on which this volume is based; to Cassandra Benson, who also helped on that job; to Dr. Edward Tucker, who supplied helpful suggestions about the first of the trial editions; to the members of my Middle English class at Arizona State University at Tempe during the summer of 1970, who put up with the first trial edition; and to the members of English 2100 at Harvard during the spring term of 1971, who supplied valuable suggestions about the second. Fee Whitehall labored above and beyond the ordinary call of editorial duty, and her sharp eye saved these texts from many more errors and inconsistencies than they now contain.

L.D.B.

Lexington, Mass.
1972

Introduction

The romances in this volume are two of the best and most important of our surviving Middle English romances. Each deals with the last years and death of King Arthur, and yet in tone, style, characterization, and especially in plot the two poems are sharply contrasting works. They reveal two quite different aspects of the medieval Arthurian legend, and they exemplify the best of two distinct romance traditions.

The *Alliterative Morte Arthure* ranks just after the works of the *Gawain*-poet among the finest products of that late medieval literary movement that we call the "Alliterative Revival." It lacks the delicacy and balance of *Sir Gawain and the Green Knight,* but the vigor of its narrative, the epic sweep of its action, and its coolly realistic presentation of fourteenth-century warfare lend the poem an interest of its own. The King Arthur of this poem is neither the "somewhat childish" romance king who appears in *Sir Gawain* nor the helpless cuckold he so often seems in French romance. He is a warrior king, shifting his troops about, sending out skirmishers, and ever ready to do battle himself.

This is primarily a poem of battles, and there are no better accounts of late medieval warfare than we find in this poem. Nor are there any more sobering reminders that all was not heroic and romantic in this age. The poet's account of the siege of Metz (vv. 3032–43), with his description of the results of a medieval bombardment (from slings and catapults), reminds us all too sharply of more recent horrors. Yet our poet is finally more interested in the fates of men than of armies, and he has a keen eye for psychological facts. His description of Mordred's momentary repentance (ll. 3886–96) is a marvelous touch, unprecedented in Arthurian tradition (in which Mordred is never treated with such sympathetic understanding) and worthy of a place alongside some of the best passages in Chaucer. Each reader will find his own favorite passages, for the *Alliterative Morte Arthure* well deserves the high reputation it has among specialists, who, because of the difficulties of the text, have thus far constituted almost its only modern audience.

The *Stanzaic Morte Arthur* is a very different narrative. It is a brilliant condensation of the French prose romance (*La Mort Artu*) which, along with the *Stanzaic Morte Arthur* itself, was the source of Malory's last two tales, "The Tale of Lancelot and Guenevere" and "The Most Piteous Tale of the Mort

Arthur." Writing a century before Sir Thomas Malory completed his own *Morte Darthur*, the unknown English romancer achieved many of the virtues that we associate with Malory's later work and produced a relatively tight and fast-moving narrative. The French *Mort Artu* is a leisurely and complex narrative, characterized by an elaborate network of episodes and by a full treatment of the psychological and philosophical implications of the action. The author of the *Stanzaic Morte Arthur*, like most English romancers of his time, was less interested in psychological abstractions. He reduced the material he inherited from the French to about a fifth of its original length, producing a work that succeeds because of its lean and rapid narrative and that gains force because of its more obvious focus upon the actions themselves. Yet the author does not omit completely the psychologizing that characterized his French source. As any reader of Chaucer knows, the literature of the later fourteenth century, marked by a new interest in individual feelings, is often (as in *The Second Nun's Tale* or even parts of *Troilus*) what we might now call a sentimental literature ("Pitee runneth soon in gentle heart" is one of Chaucer's favorite sayings). Tears flow freely in this romance (as they do in the *Alliterative Morte Arthure*), but the compression of the narrative prevents the sentiment from becoming excessive. The poet's interest in the feelings of his characters humanizes them, just as his omission of the philosophical interest in Fortune, so important in the French, focuses the tragedy upon the characters themselves, and we feel that Lancelot, Guenevere, and Arthur are real people caught in a real web of tragic circumstance.

The *Stanzaic Morte Arthur*, though it has its admirers, has been neglected by readers even more than the alliterative poem, though its language offers fewer difficulties. It has appeared in none of the standard anthologies of Middle English literature since Brandl and Zippel's (which contained only a few stanzas) and has been little studied by scholars and critics. Yet, as the reader will see, it is a worthy companion to the *Alliterative Morte Arthure*.

Although these two romances deserve wider audiences primarily because of their literary value, they are also of great importance from the standpoint of literary history, because of the traditions they represent and because of their later influence. Most readers of English literature know the Arthurian legend only from the work (or works) of Sir Thomas Malory. Malory's great synthesis of earlier romances shaped the Arthurian legend for later English writers— for Spenser, for Milton, for Tennyson, for Mark Twain, for writers and readers of our own day; Malory's genius was such that almost all subsequent English treatments of Arthurian themes have been based on his work.

However, there was an English Arthurian tradition before Malory, and the two romances in this volume provide the best introduction to this tradition. One should say "traditions," for these two romances embody two distinct versions of the life and death of King Arthur. The *Alliterative Morte Arthure* is in the tradition of sober chronicle history, which stems ultimately from

Geoffrey of Monmouth's twelfth-century *Histories of the Kings of Britain*. Our poet, of course, used other sources as well, but his fondness for precise dates, his use of real place names, and his comparative lack of interest in the supernatural lend his poem the air of chronicle rather than romance. So does his lack of interest in matters of love and courtly manners. Honor is more important than courtesy in his poem; Gawain is a great warrior, not a famous courtier, and Lancelot is only a young and fierce knight, with no hint of interest in Guenevere (or Waynor, as she is called in this poem). Guenevere's desertion of Arthur seems more a political than an amatory act, and Arthur is infuriated rather than heartbroken at her betrayal.

The *Stanzaic Morte Arthur* represents a different tradition, more familiar to modern readers, one in which the emphasis is more romantic than historical. Arthur is the lord of the fictional Camelot (a place never mentioned in the alliterative poem), and his most important campaign is in Lancelot's legendary kingdom of Benwick rather than at Metz or Milan. When he goes to the Isle of Avalon, it is not because there are skilled surgeons there who try and fail to cure his wounds, as in the alliterative poem, but because the three strange ladies come to take him away in a magic boat. One can detect the skeleton of the historical tradition embedded in the plot of the *Stanzaic Morte Arthur*: while Arthur is engaged in a foreign war, Mordred, his steward, usurps his kingdom; Arthur returns, and in a final battle he and the traitor are both killed. This is the basic plot of both the stanzaic and alliterative poems. What the alliterative poet adds expands but does not essentially change the action. In the stanzaic poem, the tale of the love of Lancelot and Guenevere has been superimposed on the basic plot. The focus is shifted to the clash of loyalties and internal divisions within the Round Table itself; the significant foreign war is now that between Arthur's forces and Lancelot's, and Arthur's death is now due as much to the feud between Lancelot and Gawain as it is to Mordred's rebellion. Mordred is changed from the principal (and largely unmotivated) villain to simply one more element in the complex circumstances in which all the characters are trapped.

Sir Thomas Malory must have read a good many English romances before he turned to the French prose romances that were his main sources for the *Morte Darthur*. However, the only two English romances we can be sure he read are the two romances in this volume. Apparently Malory's first attempt to write an Arthurian romance of his own was what is now the second tale in the *Morte Darthur*, the "Tale of Arthur and the Emperor Lucius." This is a straightforward modernization, with relatively few changes, of the first half of the *Alliterative Morte Arthure*. As Vinaver has shown (in the introduction to his edition of Malory), Malory's adaptation of the alliterative poem had a profound influence on his style, and though he next turned to French sources, his experience with the alliterative rhythms of this romance is apparent throughout his later work.

The last romances Malory wrote were the last two tales in the *Morte Darthur*, "The Book of Sir Lancelot and Queen Guenevere" and "The Most Piteous Tale of the Morte Arthur." Though his principal source for these tales was the French *Mort Artu*, Malory again turned to English romance and drew on the *Stanzaic Morte Arthur*. When the English and French versions differed, he almost always preferred the English version, and occasionally he carried over into his own work the exact wording of the stanzaic romance. Probably the influence of the stanzaic poem is even deeper than this, since Malory's handling of his other French sources—the way in which he condensed and modified the plots—shows that he seems to have been following the example of the *Stanzaic Morte Arthur*.

We cannot be sure exactly where or when the two romances in this volume were composed. Probably both were written in the North Midlands area of England in the fourteenth century, the *Stanzaic Morte Arthur* around the middle of the century, the *Alliterative Morte Arthure* toward the end, probably around 1400 or so (see l. 3773, note). These, however, can be only guesses. All we can say for sure is that the unknown authors produced works of exceptional merit that have a unique importance for English literary history.

PRONUNCIATION

Any poem, whether medieval or modern, can be enjoyed most fully only when it is read aloud. Middle English narrative verse, which was written primarily for recitation rather than silent reading, especially needs oral presentation. The many "verse fillers" (set phrases such as "seemly to shew," "knightes ynow"), the repetitive nature of the style, and the frequent use of formulas can only annoy the reader who silently scans the page, demanding that narrative poetry show the same qualities as a tightly packed modern lyric. If one reads these poems aloud—and the reader is earnestly entreated to do so— he will come to appreciate some of the very same aspects of the style that he may at first deplore, and he will learn to value the rhythm that the "fillers," redundancies, and formulas allow.

In order to read these poems aloud (or even silently), the following rules of pronunciation should be observed and carefully practiced.

CONSONANTS   These should be pronounced like their modern equivalents, with these exceptions:

-gg- in words like *rigge* is pronounced like "-dg-" in modern "ridge." The spelling -*dg*- is also used for this sound. The doubled g in forms such as *dog/ dogges* is pronounced like the g in modern "dog."

-gh- in words like *knight* (where it precedes a *t*) has the sound of /X/ in German "ich" or Modern English "lickety-split," if you say it at that rate.

-gh at the end of words such as *sigh* or *bough* is not pronounced at all; it indicates only that the preceding vowel is long.

-gn at the end of words such as *sign* or *regn* is pronounced simply as *n*; it indicates that the preceding vowel is long.

h- in words of French derivation (e.g., *họst*) is usually silent. The reader need not try to distinguish between silent and pronounced *h*'s, but he should be aware of this fact in order to understand the alliterative patterns in the texts.

l, n, and *r* are all stronger than in Modern English and should be clearly pronounced. *r* should be slightly rolled.

CONSONANT COMBINATIONS   Aside from those consonants specified above, every consonant is clearly pronounced in Middle English, even those in combinations that no longer are pronounced in Modern English (though they may appear in Modern spelling).

-ld in words such as *wọlde* and *sholde* represents a combination of the sounds of *l* and *d*, as in Modern English "wild" or "bold," and the *l* is never silent, as in Modern English "should" and "would."

kn- in words such as *knight* represents a combination of the sounds of *k* and *n* such as can be heard in Modern English "jack-knife." The combination *gn-* does not appear in our text, though it is used in Middle English words such as *gnat,* in which both *g* and *n* are clearly pronounced.

wr- in words such as *wrīte* is a combination of the sounds of *w* and *r* and not simply the sound *r* as in Modern English.

wl- appears only in the word *wlonk* in our texts; the *w* and *l* are each clearly pronounced.

SHORT VOWELS   In general, the short vowels in this text are to be pronounced as they are in Modern English, with these exceptions:

a is pronounced like the sound in American "not" or "hot."

o is a short rounded sound, like the sound in British "hot."

e plus r as in *were* or *there* should be pronounced more like a short *a*, something like the th*ar* in "thar she blows." In these texts all short vowels followed by *r* have a tendency toward this sound.

e in inflectional endings such as *-es* and *-ed*, as in *brides* or *waited*, should probably be pronounced more like the vowel sound in Modern English "bit" than that in "but." That is, it probably represents the sound /ɪ/, which some Americans normally use in words like "wait*ed*" or "want*ed*." The *e* of inflectional endings must always be pronounced. Where it is not to be sounded, the *e* is not written: *wordes* has two syllables; *words* has one. If these *e*'s are not pronounced, the rhythm of the lines will be weakened.

Final *e* is often but not consistently pronounced in the stanzaic text. A final *e* that should be pronounced is marked with a dot below the letter: *riche̜*. The word *māke* (no dot under the *e*) has one syllable; the word *māke̜* (with a dot under the *e*) has two syllables. This final *-e*, when pronounced, has the sound called "schwah" /ə/, which we frequently use in Modern English when vowels are lightly stressed, as in the second syllable of "telephone" or the last syllable of "introduction."

LONG VOWELS   Most of the long vowels are represented by a variety of spellings. In pronouncing the Middle English examples given to illustrate the sounds, you should be aware that in Modern English we tend to diphthongize the long (or "tense") vowels, and you should guard against this in pronouncing Middle English.

"I," ī, y, -igh (when final), -ig- (when *n* follows)	These all represent /i/, as in Modern English "seat" /sit/. Note that the pronoun "I" is pronounced /i/.
ē, ee, ei, ey, -egh (when final), -eg- (when *n* follows)	These all represent /e/, the sound in Modern "late" /let/.
e̜, e̜e̜	These represent "open e" /æ:/, somewhat like the sound in Modern English "bag" /bæ:g/ as opposed to the sounds in "beg" /beg/ and "bait" /bet/. It is similar to the sound in Modern "hat" but lengthened and pronounced half-way between that sound /hæt/ and the sound in "hate" /het/.
ā, -au- (before *n*)	This represents the sound /a/, as in Modern English "father" /faðər/.
ō, oo, -ogh (when final)	These represent /o/, the sound in Modern "boat" /bot/.
o̜, o̜u	This is "open o" /ɔ/, the sound in most Americans' pronunciation of "ought" /ɔt/.
ou, ow, -ough (when final)	These represent /u/, the sound in Modern "boot" /but/.

DIPHTHONGS

ū, ew, eau	These represent /ɪu/, the sound in Modern "music" /mɪuzik/. In Middle English words like *rew*, the *r* must be rolled to produce this sound, though in such cases the sound may be pronounced simply as /u/, as in Modern "rue" /ru/.

ai, ay   These represent /aɪ/, the sound in Mod-
                                ern "bite" /baɪt/.
oi, oy   These represent /ɔɪ/, the sound in Mod-
                                ern "boy" /bɔɪ/.
ǫw, au, aw   These represent /au/, the sound in Mod-
                                ern "out" /aut/.

The spelling representations of the Middle English long vowels and diphthongs
can be summarized thus:

		Middle		Modern	
Spelling	Sound	English		English	
I	/i/	I (the pronoun)	/i/	"ee" in "see"	/si/
ī	/i/	rīde	/rid/	read	/rid/
y	/i/	my	/mi/	me	/mi/
-igh (final)	/i/	sigh	/si/	see	/si/
-ig- (followed by n)	/i/	sign	/sin/	seen	/sin/
ē	/e/	mē	/me/	may	/me/
ee	/e/	seen	/sen/	sane	/sen/
ei	/e/	receive	/risev/	re-save	/risev/
ey	/e/	they	/ðe/	they	/ðe/
-egh (final)	/e/	begh	/be/	bay	/be/
-eg- (followed by n)	/e/	regn	/ren/	rain	/ren/
ę	/æ:/	bęte	/bæ:t/	the sound in "bag"	/bæ:g/
ęę	/æ:/	pęęs	/pæ:s/	the sound in "bag"	/bæ:g/
ā	/a/	māke	/mak/	mock	/mak/
-au- (followed by n)	/a/	daun	/dan/	don	/dan/
ō	/o/	tō	/to/	toe	/to/
oo	/o/	doom	/dom/	dome	/dom/
-ogh (final)	/o/	slogh	/slo/	slow	/slo/
ǫ	/ɔ/	sǫ	/sɔ/	saw	/sɔ/
ǫu	/ɔ/	nǫught	/nɔXt/	nought	/nɔt/
ǫw	/au/	bǫw	/bau/	bough	/bau/
au	/au/	raught	/rauXt/	rout	/raut/
aw	/au/	saw	/sau/	sow	/sau/
ou	/u/	trouth	/truΘ/	truth	/truθ/
ow	/u/	now	/nu/	new	/nu/
-ough (final)	/u/	bough	/bu/	boo	/bu/
ū	/ɪu/	aventūre	/avɜntɪur/	the sound in "music"	/mɪusik/

Spelling	Sound	Middle English	Example	Modern English	Sound Equivalent
ew	/ɪu/	new	/nɪu/	the sound in "music"	/mɪusik/
eau	/ɪu/	beautee	/bɪute/	beauty	/bɪuti/
ai	/aɪ/	laik	/laɪk/	like	/laɪk/
ay	/aɪ/	day	/daɪ/	die	/daɪ/
oi	/oɪ/	toil	/toɪl/	toil	/toɪl/
oy	/oɪ/	boy	/boɪ/	boy	/boɪ/

Note: In these texts initial unstressed -e- (as in *besīde*, receive) is pronounced as in Modern English /bi-/, /ri-/.

SOME GRAMMATICAL NOTES

The main problems for the beginning reader of Middle English are those of accustoming himself to an unfamiliar word order and to a few unfamiliar grammatical forms. These problems are best solved by reading the texts and thus becoming familiar with the structure of Middle English, leaving the explanations of why it works that way for more advanced study. What follows is therefore not a grammar or even an outline of a grammar but simply a few notes on the more common distinctively Middle English forms that the reader will encounter. Since it is assumed that the reader will begin with the *Stanzaic Morte Arthur*, the examples (unless otherwise noted) are drawn from that poem.

NOUNS   Most Middle English nouns are inflected about the same way as Modern English nouns, with the exception of the singular dative:

	Singular	Plural
Nominative and Accusative:	herte	hertes
Dative:	herte, hertę	hertes
Genitive:	hertes	hertes

The singular dative case is that which may be used when the noun is the object of a preposition; when used in that way, the noun often has a final ę:

Noun as subject: Her *herte* nigh brast in twǫ ("Her heart nearly broke in two).

Object of Preposition: Shē lǫugh with *hertę* free ("She laughed with a noble heart).

This case is not always used when a noun follows a preposition (since the dative singular was disappearing in the fourteenth century); the noun may appear without an -*e* at all, or with an -*e* that is not pronounced. Since the final *e*'s that should be pronounced are marked in this text, this should not be a problem for the reader. (The reader will notice that the final -*e*'s that are pronounced are much more common in the *Stanzaic Morte Arthur* than in the Alliterative poem; this is because the stanzaic poem is a bit older than the alliterative work and because the optionally pronounced -*e* was more useful to a writer of a syllabically regular line. Note that final -*e* may also appear in other cases.

IRREGULAR NOUNS   There are more "irregular nouns" in Middle English than in Modern English, and the reader will encounter several nouns that have no distinctive form for the plural (like Modern English "sheep"). *Frēnd* ("friend" or "friends") is this sort of noun; the pronoun *other* also appears without a distinctive plural ending (so that *other* may stand for both "other" and "others").

There are also a few nouns that have no distinctive form for the possessive case. Most of these are proper names derived from the French:

In *Arthur* dayes ("In *Arthur's* days").

Some are survivals of older English inflectional systems:

Oure sweetę *Lādy* sāke ("Our sweet *Lady's* sake").
Of his *fader* land ("Of his *father's* land").

PRONOUNS   Although some Middle English texts (Chaucer's poems for example) have a system of pronouns differing from Modern English, in these texts the personal pronouns are the same as in Modern English, with the exception of *shō*, which is used for "she" in the *Alliterative Morte Arthure* (the stanzaic poem has *shē* throughout).

These texts preserve the distinction between the singular and plural second person pronouns. That is, *thou* and *thee* are used for addressing one person, *yē* and *you* for addressing two or more persons. In some varieties of Middle English (and occasionally in our texts) *yē* and *you* are the forms of respectful address, used to address one person in formal situations, while *thou* and *thee* are used to address one in a lower social class or one with whom the speaker is on terms of familiar intimacy.

For example, the earl's son who accompanies Lancelot to the tournament near the beginning of the *Stanzaic Morte Arthur* is very respectful to the great Lancelot and invariably addresses him with the formal plural pronouns:

Subject: "I drēde that *yē* bē hurt full sǫre" (I fear that you are sorely hurt).

Possessive: "Were it *your* will thider tō rīde" (If it were your will to ride thither).

Object: "And I myself will with *you* abīde" (And I myself will remain with you).

The earl's daughter aspires to be Lancelot's sweetheart, and she is—or hopes to be—on familiar terms with him. She and Lancelot use the singular when addressing one another:

Subject: "As *thou* art hardy knight and free" (As you are a strong and noble knight).

Possessive: "When thou may better spęke *thy* fill" (When you may better speak your fill).

Object: "Sith I of *thee* ne may have mǫre" (Since I may have no more of you).

This distinction between formal and familiar usages is not consistently maintained in these texts (very few Middle English authors consistently observe it), and there is not always a clear reason for the alternation between *yē* and *thou*. *Yē* is therefore sometimes used for the singular, sometimes for the plural. *Thou* is always singular.

Since in Modern English we seldom observe the difference between subject and object forms of these pronouns, the student should carefully note the Middle English distinction between the subject forms (*thou, yē*) and the object forms (*thee, you*). The form of the pronoun will often clarify the syntax of a clause.

ADJECTIVES   The *Stanzaic Morte Arthur* contains traces of the old inflection of the adjective: a final ę may be used for the plural forms, the singular objective forms, and for an adjective following a definite article or possessive form:

Subject: Yong Galehod was *good* in need (Young Galehod was a good man to have in times of need).

Object: As thou art man of *muchę* might (As you are a man of great strength).

Plural: Sǫ *blīthę* men they were that day (Such happy men they were that day).

In *rędde* armes that hē bǫre (In red arms that he bore).

After possessive: Oure *sweetę* Lādy sāke (Our sweet Lady's sake).

After definite article: Of all the world the *bestę* knight (The best knight in all the world).

These forms were disappearing in the fourteenth century and their use is by no means consistent; those which should be pronounced are indicated by the use of ę.

THE ABSOLUTE ADJECTIVE   In Middle English the adjective is often used alone to stand for a noun. This use of the absolute adjective is possible in Modern English ("*rich* and *poor* alike," "he's the *greatest*"), but it is far more common in Middle English:

> Such a *seemly* for tō see (Such a *seemly one* to see).
> That many a *bold* sithen abǫught (That many a *bold one* later paid for).
> The *wīse* sholde come (The *wise ones* should come).

VERBS   Both of our texts show considerable variation in the forms used for the verbs. This results from the use of alternate conjugations for the present tense, one a generally Midlands conjugation (of the sort usually employed by Chaucer), the other a more distinctively Northern set of forms:

	Midlands	*Northern*
I	come	come, comes
thou	comest	comes
hē, shē, it	cometh	comes
Wē, yē, they	comen, comę, come	comes

In general, both our poets show a preference for the Northern forms, but neither is consistent:

> How that your court *beginneth* tō spill (l. 23).
> Sir, your honour *beginnes* tō fall (l. 25).

This is probably because the two conjugations were competing forms in the North Midlands (in the way "dived" and "dove" are today competing forms for the past tense of the verb "dive"). *Tō bē* likewise has alternate forms of conjugation, both of which appear in these texts. Though the *bēs* forms on the right are more common in the North, the distinction between the two sets of forms is not entirely a matter of dialect. In general, the forms with *b-* (except for the third person plural *bē* and *bēn*) are most often used with a future sense and are best translated by "will be":

	"to be" forms	*"will be" forms*
I	am	bē
thou	art	bēs
hē, shē, it	is	bēs, bēth
Wē, yē, they	bē, bēn, aren, are	bēs

The distinction between "to be" and "will be" forms is not consistently observed (the "will be" forms were in competition with "will" and "shall," which finally became the ordinary means of expressing the future); however, the distinction appears frequently enough that the reader should be aware of it:

"to be": Hēre now *is* made a comsement (Here now is made a beginning).

"will be": That *bēth* nǫt finished many a yēre (That will not be finished for many a year).

INFINITIVES   Infinitives most commonly appear with the same form as in Modern English (as in "to go"). A few verbs appear with -*n* as an occasional sign of the infinitive: "To be" may be either *tō bē, bē,* or *bēn;* "to say" may appear as *sayn.* Occasionally verbs that end with a consonant will have a final *ę* as the sign of the infinitive: The Middle English verb meaning "to kill" may be *tō spill, tō spillę,* or *spillę.* Since both the final -*n* and the final -*ę* were disappearing in the fourteenth century, they are not consistently used and the uninflected form (like modern "to kill") is the most common. Occasionally in the *Alliterative Morte Arthure at* instead of *tō* is used as the sign of the infinitive:

Tō carry forth such a carl *at clǫse* him in silver.
(To carry forth such a churl *to enclose* him in silver.)

PRESENT PARTICIPLES   Both poets prefer the northerly form of the present participle ending, -*and.* Thus, for modern "flaming" these texts usually have *flāmand.* Just as we can add "-ing" to the stem of any verb to make a present participle ("come," "coming"), so Middle English speakers could add -*and* (*come, comand*). When the reader encounters a form with -*and,* he will usually find that substituting "-ing" for -*and* will provide a correct translation.

IMPERSONAL VERBS   Middle English frequently employs *impersonal verbs,* which usually appear without an expressed subject. The most common are *līke, rew,* and *think*:

Him līketh (It pleases him; i.e., he likes)
Him reweth (It pains him; i.e., he rues)
Him thinketh (It seems to him; i.e., he thinks)

MODAL VERBS   The modal verbs in Middle English (verbs such as *may* and *shall*) sometimes have meanings different from Modern English. *May* usually means "can, to be able." *Couth,* the preterite of *can,* sometimes means "could," but it is also used as a non-modal verb meaning "to know." *Will* and *shall* most often indicate the future, as they do in Modern English, but often *will* has the meaning of "to desire" and *shall* often means "must" or "has to" (meanings which are still faintly present in Modern English). *Dō* usually means "to cause." *Qught* is sometimes used as in Modern English, but often it is a non-modal verb meaning "possessed." In addition, Middle English has some modal verbs that have disappeared from Modern English, the most important of which is *gan.*

May ("can," "to be able")

    Present: Sāve my līfe nǫ lēchę *may* (No physician *can* save my life).

    Preterite: Tō slay Gawain yif that hē *might* (To slay Gawain, if he *could*).

Shall ("must," "have to")

    Present: Today I *shall* tō dęthę gǫ (Today I *must* go to death).

    Preterite: Well shē wiste shē *sholde* bē shent (She knew well she *had to* be lost).

Couth ("could, knew")

    "Could": And asked him yif hē *couth* them say (And asked him if he *could* tell them).

    "Knew": And Mordred that mikel *couth* of wrāke (And Mordred who *knew* much of trouble).

Will ("To desire, want")

    Present: Tō wit for whǫm yif yē *will* fonde (If you want to try to learn for whom).

    Preterite: For-why *wǫlde* men Launcelot behǫld (Because men *wanted* to see Lancelot).

Dō ("to cause")

    Present: Thus yong out of the world *dō* wend (*To cause* to go out of the world thus young).

    Preterite: Messengeres *did* hē gǫ and rīde (He *ordered* messengers to go and ride).

Qught ("owned, possessed")

    Of all that Uter *ǫught* (Of all that Uther *possessed*).

Gan ("did"—usually only an intensifier and sign of the past, like Modern *do* and *did*).

    Singular: The way tō court *gan* hē tāke (The way to court he *did* take).

    Plural: And soon there-in *gonne* they see (And soon therein they *did* see).

NEGATIVES   The usual forms of the negative particles are *ne* (not, nor), *nǫt* (not) and *nǫught* (in no way, not at all).

Ne can be translated as "not" when it appears with a modal or the verb "to be," since the usual form of negation for Modern English verbs of this sort is "is not," "may not," etc. With the other verbs, for the sake of a smoother translation, *ne* is best translated as "do not" or "did not":

Ne stood hē drēde (He *did not stand* in fear).

The negative *ne* is frequently attached to a few very common verbs (which begin with a vowel or *w*) to indicate negation:

nis (*ne* + *is*) "is not"
nere (*ne* + *were*) "were not"
nas (*ne* + *was*) "was not"
nill (*ne* + *will*) "will not" or "do not desire"
nolde (*ne* + *wolde*) "would not" or "did not desire"
not (*ne* + *wot*) "knows not"
niste (*ne* + *wiste*) "knew not"

DOUBLE NEGATIVES   The so-called "double negative" is very common and per-
fectly acceptable in Middle English. Neither in Middle English nor in Modern
is it ever the "equivalent of a positive"; it always indicates negation, simple
or emphatic:

Why *ne* may I *never* bē blīthe (Why can I never be happy)?
Hē *ne* might prōve it *never* more (He could never prove it).

WORD ORDER   Compared to Modern English, the word order of Middle
English verse is very free, and the reader may at first have some slight diffi-
culty in accustoming himself to this less rigid syntax. This is characteristic of
Middle English verse; Middle English prose is a good deal closer to Modern
English in this respect.

ADJECTIVES   With a few exceptions, adjectives in Modern English precede
the words they modify, as in "a good book" or "a pretty girl." In Middle
English the adjective often does come before the noun, but it can also follow
the noun it modifies:

With *shēldes brode* and *helmes sheen* (With *broad shields* and *bright
helmets*).
Then had the erl *sonnes two* (The earl then had *two sons*).

Occasionally an adjective is far removed from the noun it modifies:

Besauntes offered they hēre *bright* (They offered here *bright coins*).

OTHER MODIFIERS   Modifying phrases and adverbs are likewise often separated from the words they modify:

The sleeve *on his crest* was *there* (The sleeve was *there on his crest*).
All that *stiff* were *on steed* (All that were *bold on steeds*).

Relative clauses and appositives are often separated from the nouns they
modify. This is most frequent in the alliterative poem:

And there a *citee* hē set by assent of his lordes
That Caerlīon was called.
(And, with the assent of his lords, there he established a *city*
That was called Caerlīon).

PREPOSITIONS   Prepositions frequently follow the words they govern:

> There rich attīre lay *him before* (Where rich attire lay *before him*).
> Yē have gǫne *her til* (You have gone *to her*).

SUBJECTS AND OBJECTS   The normal Modern English declarative sentence order of subject-verb-object ("The boy sees the cat") is also common in Middle English, but that order is often changed, for reasons of rime or emphasis, to make the verb the last element in the clause. Middle English poets apparently regarded a clause that ends with a verb as more "elegant" and "poetic" than the subject-verb-object order characteristic of Modern English and Middle English prose. This fondness for ending a clause with a verb is responsible for many of the constructions that seem unusual to a modern reader. For example, the opening lines of the *Stanzaic Morte Arthur* are:

> Lǫrdinges that are lēf and dęre, *Listeneth* (*Listen,* lords who are beloved and dear)
> And I shall you *tell* (And I shall *tell* you)
> By ǫldę dayes what aunters *were* (About the adventures that *were* in the old days)
> Among our eldres that *befell* (That *befell* among our elders).

When the verb comes first in the clause it usually indicates either a question (as in Modern English) or a conditional clause:

> *Come* Arthur ever over the flood   (*If* Arthur ever *comes* over the sea),
> Thou mayst bē bǫld, it will bē bǫught   (You can be sure it will be paid for).

In most cases the general context will make the meaning of these unusual constructions clear (glosses are supplied where the syntax is not clear). The reader should remember that most of these forms are restricted to Middle English verse, in which they are used to add elegance and force to the language. A sympathetic reader (especially if he reads the poems aloud) will find that these devices often have exactly those effects.

VERSIFICATION AND STYLE

The two romances in this volume represent two distinct stylistic traditions. The *Alliterative Morte Arthure* belongs to the "Alliterative Revival," the literary movement that begins in the middle years of the fourteenth century and that includes such important writers as William Langland and the author of *Gawain and the Green Knight*. The *Stanzaic Morte Arthur* is written in the more common eight-syllable, four-beat line of English romance, a line that derives ultimately from French models. Despite its foreign source, this is a simpler, more popular style than that of the alliterative romance, and the author of the *Stanzaic Morte Arthur* probably intended his work for a somewhat wider and less sophisticated audience than the alliterative poet aimed for.

However, the author of the *Stanzaic Morte Arthur* selected an unusual and rather difficult stanza for his poem. It is an eight-line stanza riming *abababab*. There are variations from this, as there are from his normal eight-syllable line (the first stanza rimes *ababcbcb* and variant stanzas, such as ll. 361–67, do appear), but in general the poet adheres to this rime scheme, which requires two sets of four riming words for each full stanza. Such a stanza is easy enough for a lyric poet to handle (and it appears in a number of relatively short Middle English poems) but it raises real difficulties in a long narrative poem, and it is not surprising that no other romancer attempted to use it.

Our poet was able to use it successfully because he adopted a number of traditional devices that eased his task of handling this stanza. He uses a relatively limited set of stock rimes, some of them several times over. *Launcelot du Lāke*, for example, almost always rimes with *sāke, tāke, māke*, or *wāke*. The relatively rare word *neven* ("to name") almost invariably rimes with *hęven, steven* ("voice"), and *seven*. In addition to stock rimes such as these, the poet frequently uses imperfect rimes. In lines 528–35, for example, the word *līfe* rimes with *swīthe, kīthe*, and *blīthe*. This is not due to carelessness, for the same group of rimes appears several times in the poem. Nor does it seem to be due simply to including assonance within his definition of rime, since he also frequently rimes vowel sounds that are not exactly the same; he makes no clear distinction between open and close vowel sounds and he is willing to rime words such as *dęre* and *were*, as in the opening lines of the poem.

Such a use of rime has a definite advantage, not only for the poet but for the reader, since it helps to de-emphasize the rimes and to keep them from intruding too often upon the consciousness of the audience. As the reader will discover, the rimes remain well in the background and do not impede the narrative. That is not always the case in Middle English romance.

The sound texture of the *Stanzaic Morte Arthur* owes almost as much to alliteration as to rime. The earliest modern critic of this poem, the eighteenth-century bibliographer Humphrey Wanley, wrote that our poet "useth many Saxon or obsolete words, and very often delighted himself (as did the author of 'Piers Plowman') in the Chime of words beginning with the same letter as (that I may give one example) 'For well thee wist withouten ween.'" Examples of this delight in the chime of alliteration can be found in almost every stanza in the poem, beginning with the opening lines:

> Lǫrdinges that are lēf and dęre
> Listeneth and I shall you tell.

This fondness for alliteration and the frequent use of alliterative formulas (such as *wǫ and węle*) is not unusual among the authors of the riming romances, but the man who wrote the *Stanzaic Morte Arthur* seems particularly fond of the alliterative style, and one suspects that he could have cast his poem in the alliterative meter if he had so chosen.

In purely alliterative poems, such as the *Alliterative Morte Arthure*, there is no rime at the ends of the lines. Instead, each line falls into two half-lines which are united by alliteration—the identity (or near identity) of the initial sound of stressed syllables. In the first half-line most often two, but sometimes three, words will alliterate. In the second half-line usually only one word will alliterate. The alliteration always falls on a word that bears metrical stress; there are two (sometimes three) stressed words in the first half-line, and two (almost never three) in the second half-line. The number of unstressed syllables can vary considerably:

> Now grȩte glorīous Gód   through grǻce of Himsélven
> And the précious prayer   of His prīs Mōder
> Shéld us frǫ shǻmesdeede   and sinful workes,
> And gíve us grǻce tō gúīe   and góvern us hére
> In this wrétched wórld,   through vértuous líving
> That wē may káire til his cóurt,   the kíngdom of hȩven.

The reader need not worry too much about the metrical pattern; if he reads the lines aloud deliberately (but not too slow) with slight pauses at the ends of the half-lines and with attention to the sense, he will find that the stresses will fall where they should.

As shown by the lines above, the poet can take certain liberties with the alliterating sounds. *Sh-* can sometimes alliterate with *s-* and *w-* with *v-* (though these sounds may have been closer to one another than in Modern English). Moreover, it is a convention of this verse that any vowel sound can alliterate with any other vowel sound:

> Yē that lust has tō līthe   or loves for tō hēre
> Of elders of ǫlde tīme   and of their awk deedes . . .

Notice that only the important words (nouns, adjectives, verbs, and adverbs) bear the alliteration. The word "of" in the second line has no part in the alliterative scheme. Words like "of" (or "to" in the first line above) are not ordinarily stressed in speech, and such words are therefore not ordinarily stressed in alliterative poetry. That is why a reader can not go far wrong if he simply reads the lines with attention to the sense; he will almost never find himself stressing the wrong word.

One characteristic of the alliteration in the *Alliterative Morte Arthure* is the author's fondness for carrying one alliterating sound through several lines in a kind of *tour de force*:

> But they fit them fair,   thēse frek bernes,
> Fewters in freely   on feraunt steedes,
> Foines full felly   with flishand spęres,
> Freten off orfrayes   fast upon shēldes;
> Sǫ fęlę fay is in fight   upon the fēld lęved
> That ęch a furth of the firth   of red blood runnes.   (2139–2144)

The poet seems to have an endless stock of alliterating words, and if he stops at this point, it is probably not because he has run out of words beginning with *f*; only a couple of lines later he begins another series with *f*.

The alliterative style affects more than the meter. The poets of the Alliterative Revival used the traditional line of Anglo-Saxon poetry, which had disappeared from written records about two centuries before and was revived by a number of poets (mainly living in the West and North of England) in the fourteenth century. Evidently the style of alliterative poetry had been preserved by popular, unlettered poets who continued to compose and transmit poems by oral, non-written means from Anglo-Saxon times until well into the fourteenth century. Verse composed in this manner depends on a heavily formulaic language and a fixed, archaic poetic vocabulary. Even the casual reader of the *Alliterative Morte Arthure* will soon recognize how much of this old, formulaic style is preserved in the poems of the Alliterative Revival. Half-lines (especially second half-lines) tend to be used over and over in identical (or nearly identical) forms and the poet makes frequent use of the specialized vocabulary characteristic of alliterative poetry, with its many synonyms for "man" (*renk, bern, lēde, frēke, gōme, shalk,* etc.) or for the verb "go" (*graith, boun, ferk,* etc.) Much of the difficulty in a first reading of an alliterative poem is its use of this special poetic diction, consisting largely of words that are seldom encountered outside alliterative verse.

Although the ultimate background of the alliterative style is a popular, non-literary tradition, poems such as the *Alliterative Morte Arthure* are sophisticated works that were probably addressed to rather limited audiences that prized the verbal dexterity these poems display. The language was difficult even for the average listener in Middle English times, and the poets tended to prefer description and analysis to a rapidly moving plot such as we associate with more popular poetry. The *Stanzaic Morte Arthur*, with its emphasis on action, has a popular appeal quite different from that of the *Alliterative Morte Arthure*, in which the careful attention to the texture of events, to the description of armor and dress, to the niceties of feasting, to fine points of heraldry, and to the exact details of military campaigns reveals the interests of a leisured and aristocratic audience. The author expects his hearers to understand an occasional French phrase, to recognize his geographical references (at least the European ones), and to share with him an interest that goes beyond the action to the definition of the quality of the action and of the life it represents.

VOCABULARY

Difficult words are marked with a bubble (°) and glossed in the margins. Difficult constructions are marked with a dagger (†) and glossed in the notes. There is also a glossary at the end of the text which includes only the most common words (those which appear five times or more in either of these romances). These common words are glossed for the first three to five times they appear in each poem, usually three times if they differ from their modern English counterparts only in spelling and pronunciation (*bęte* for "beat"), five times if they have forms or meanings that do not appear in modern English (*frēke* meaning "man").

The vocabulary of the *Alliterative Morte Arthure* is more difficult than that of the *Stanzaic Morte Arthur*. The student should therefore read the stanzaic poem first. He will thus learn a good many of the words that reappear in the alliterative poem and will have accustomed himself to the Middle English vocabulary. He will also have recognized that there are regular relations between certain Middle English spellings and their modern forms. A Middle English *ę*, for example, is often related to the Modern English spelling *ea* and the sound /i/: *hęd*, "head"; *tręte*, "treat." Likewise, a Middle English *ǫ* is related to the spelling *oa* and the sound /o/ in Modern English: *brǫde*, "broad"; *lǫd*, "load"; *nǫble*, "noble"; *hǫme*, "home." Reading aloud will also help the student's understanding of words and constructions that look difficult on the page.

The reader will soon notice that both poets tend to use words rather more loosely than we expect in modern verse; the meaning of words necessary for purposes of rime or alliteration is often modified to suit the context, and a number of words meaning "strong" or "noble" seem almost devoid of meaning. Exact translation will therefore often be difficult; a word like *burlich*, "stately," can mean almost anything from "strong" to "noble" and can be used to describe everything from a sword to a pretty girl. This is a result of the formulaic character of both poems; the reader will soon become used to it, but he should not forget this method of handling vocabulary, since it serves as a reminder of the basically spoken character of this poetry and as a warning against attempting to read it as if it were compressed, highly polished lyric verse.

Proper names are not entered in the glossary (except for a few common place-names) and no attempt has been made to regularize them completely so that the same forms would be used in both poems. The only momentary difficulties will arise from the names used for Guenevere—*Gaynor* in the stanzaic poem, *Waynor* in the alliterative poem—and Gawain, who is always *Gawain* in the stanzaic poem but who is called both *Gawain* and *Wawain* in the alliterative poem. *Bedivere,* as he is called in the stanzaic poem, is *Bedvere* in the alliterative work.

Since the difficult common words are glossed for the first few times they appear, and the less common ones are always glossed in the margins, the student will probably not have to use the glossary very often. Instead, if he intends to continue his study of Middle English, he should use the glossary as a handy list of some of the most basic Middle English words, which he should learn before going on to more advanced texts. After reading the two poems in this volume, he might use the glossary to test his knowledge of the basic vocabulary.

SELECTED BIBLIOGRAPHY

EDITIONS

Edmund Brock, ed., *Morte Arthure, or The Death of Arthur.* Early English Text Society, Original Series, 8. London, New York, Toronto: Oxford University Press, New Edition, 1871; reprinted 1961.

This is the only full edition of the alliterative poem now in print; J.L.N. O'Loughlin has been preparing a new edition for some years. Brock's edition closely follows the manuscript, has a poor glossary, and has very few notes.

Erik Björkman, ed., *Morte Arthure.* Alt- und mittelenglische Texte, 9. New York and London: Carl Winters, 1915.

Now out of print, Björkman's edition is heavily emended but has a good glossary and full notes.

John Finlayson, *Morte Arthure.* York Medieval Texts. Evanston: Northwestern University Press, 1967.

This is the best available edition, though unfortunately it consists of extracts, amounting to a bit more than half of the poem. The glossary and notes are good, and Finlayson's introduction is full and helpful.

Lewis J. Owen and Nancy H. Owen, eds., "*The Alliterative Morte Arthure*: The Fall of Arthur," pp. 45–89, with commentary on pp. 371–375, in *Middle English Poetry: An Anthology.* The Library of Literature. Indianapolis and New York: Bobbs-Merrill, 1971.

This is an edition of lines 3206 to the end of the poem, with glosses on the page and literary comment.

J. D. Bruce, ed., *Le Morte Arthur: A Romance in Stanzas of Eight Lines.* Early English Text Society, Extra Series, 88. London, New York, Toronto: Oxford University Press, 1903; reprinted 1959.

This is the only edition in print; its glossary (except for a few common place names) is generally good, the notes skimpy, and the introduction now out of date.

S. B. Hemingway, ed., *Le Morte Arthur*. New York: Riverside Press, 1912.
Now out of print, Hemingway's text differs little from Bruce's but has somewhat fuller notes.

TRANSLATIONS

Andrew Boyle, tr., *Morte Arthur: Two Early English Romances*, with an Introduction by Lucy A. Patton. Everyman's Library. London: J. M. Dent, and New York: E. P. Dutton, 1912. Reprinted 1936.
Now out of print, this volume contains a usually reliable prose translation of the *Alliterative Morte Arthure* and a poor edition of the *Stanzaic Morte Arthur*.

John Gardner, tr., *The Alliterative Morte Arthure, The Owl and The Nightingale and Five Other Middle English Poems*. Carbondale, Ill.: University of Southern Illinois Press, 1971.
Contains a vigorous, rather free, translation of the alliterative poem.

R. S. Loomis and R. Willard, eds., *Medieval English Verse and Prose*. New York: Appleton-Century-Crofts, 1948.
This volume contains a vigorous verse translation of selections drawn from line 3151 to the end of the *Alliterative Morte Arthure*.

Richard L. Brengle, ed., *Arthur: King of Britain*. New York: Appleton-Century-Crofts, 1964.
This volume contains a prose translation of selections from the *Stanzaic Morte Arthur* and reprints the Loomis and Willard translation of the *Alliterative Morte Arthure*.

ANALOGUES

Both Loomis and Willard's *Medieval English Verse and Prose* and Brengle's *Arthur: King of Britain* contain translations of analogous Arthurian romances. In addition, see:

Geoffrey of Monmouth, *Histories of the Kings of Britain*, trans. Sebastian Evans. Everyman's Library. London: J. M. Dent, and New York: E. P. Dutton, 1903; revised and with a new Introduction by Charles W. Dunn, 1958.
A good translation with an excellent introduction.

TEXTUAL STUDIES

E. V. Gordon and Eugène Vinaver, "New Light on the Text of the Alliterative *Morte Arthure*," *Medium Aevum*, VI (1937), 81–98.
A study of the text in relation to the then recently discovered Winchester

Manuscript of Malory; the notes to Vinaver's edition of Malory, listed below, contain further observations and suggested emendations.

Angus McIntosh, "The Textual Transmission of the Alliterative *Morte Arthure*," in *English and Medieval Studies Presented to J. R. R. Tolkien,* eds. Norman Davis and C. L. Wrenn (London: Allen & Unwin, 1962), pp. 231–40.

J. L. N. O'Loughlin, "The Middle English Alliterative *Morte Arthure*," *Medium Aevum,* IV (1935), 153–68.

INFLUENCE ON MALORY

E. T. Donaldson, "Malory and the Stanzaic *Le Morte Arthur*," *Studies in Philology,* XLVII (1950), 460–72.

Eugène Vinaver. *The Works of Sir Thomas Malory,* Second Edition. (Oxford: Clarendon, 1967). Pp. 1366–1406 and 1585–1663.

R. H. Wilson, "Malory, the Stanzaic Morte Arthur, and the *Mort Artu*," *Modern Philology,* XXXVII (1939–40), 125–38.

GENERAL CRITICISM

Richard A. Wertime, "The Theme and Structure of the *Stanzaic Morte Arthur*," *PMLA,* LXXXVII (1972), 1075–82.

This is the only published critical study aside from brief treatments in general books, such as Dieter Mehl's *The Middle English Romances of the Thirteenth and Fourteenth Centuries.* (New York: Barnes and Noble, 1969). Pp. 186–93.

William Matthews, *The Tragedy of Arthur.* Berkeley and Los Angeles: University of California Press, 1960.

This is the only full study of the alliterative poem and should be consulted by the serious student. For a slightly different conception of the tragic meaning of the poem, see L. D. Benson, "The Alliterative *Morte Arthure* and Medieval Tragedy," *Tennessee Studies in Literature,* XI (1966), 75–87, and for yet another view see Robert M. Lumiansky, "The Alliterative *Morte Arthure,* the Concept of Medieval Tragedy, and the Cardinal Virtue Fortitude," *Medieval and Renaissance Studies,* ed. John M. Headley (Chapel Hill: University of North Carolina Press, 1968), pp. 95–118.

See also Introduction and bibliography in Finlayson's edition.

BIBLIOGRAPHY

For full bibliographies of these poems see Helaine Newstead, "Arthurian Legends," in J. Burke Severs, ed., *A Manual of the Writings in Middle English: 1050–1500,* Fascicule 1, I. *Romances,* by Mortimer J. Donovan, *et al.* (New Haven: The Connecticut Academy of Arts and Sciences, 1967).

Stanzaic Morte Arthur

LE MORTE ARTHUR

†Lordinges that are lēf and dęre
   Listeneth, and I shall you tell,
By oldę dayes what aunters were
   Amǫng our eldres that befell;
In Arthur dayes, that nǫble king,
   Befell aunters ferly fęle,
And I shall tell of their ending,
   That mikel wiste of wǫ and węle.

The knightes of the Tāble Round,
10   The Sangrail when they had sǫught,
Aunters they before them found
   Finished and tō endę brǫught;
Their enemīes they bętte and bound
   For gold on līfe they left them nǫught.
Four yēre they lived sound,
   When they had thēse workes wrǫught.

Til on a tīme that it befell
   The king in bed lay by the queen;
Of °aunters they began tō tell,   *adventures*
20   Many that in that land had been:
"Sir, °yif that it were your will,   *if*
   Of a wonder thing I °wǫlde you °męne,   *would/tell*
How that your court beginneth tō °spill   *become empty*
   Of doughty knightes °all bydēne;   *completely*

1-16 Lords, who are beloved and dear, listen and I shall tell you about
the old days, what adventures there were that happened among our
elders; in the days of Arthur, that noble king, wondrously many adventures happened, and I shall tell of the end of those knights who
knew much of woe and joy.
The Knights of the Round Table, when they had sought the Holy
Grail, they finished and brought to an end those adventures that they
found before them. They beat and bound their enemies; for no gold
(as ransom) did they leave them alive. Four years they lived in health
when they had wrought these deeds.

"Sir, your honour beginnes tō fall,
    That wont was wīde in world tō °spręde,   *spread*
Of Launcelot and other all,
    That ever sǫ doughty were in deed."
"Dāme, there tō thy counsēl I call:
30   What were best for such a need?"
"°Yif yē your honour hǫlde shall,   *if*
    A tournament were best tō °bēde,   *announce*

"°For-why that °aunter shall begin   *because/*
                                          adventure
    And bē spǫke of on every sīde,
†That knightes shall there worship win
    Tō deed of armes for tō rīde.
Sir, lettes thus your court °nǫ blinne,   *not cease*
    But live in honour and in °prīde."   *admiration*
"°Certes, dāmę," the king said then,   *certainly*
40   "This °ne shall nǫ lenger abīde."   *shall no longer*

A tournament the king °let bēde   *commanded to*
                                          be announced
    At Winchester °sholde it bē;   *should*
Young Galehod was good in need;
    The °chēftain of the °cry was hē,   *chieftain/*
                                          company
With knightes that were °stiff on steed,   *strong on horses*
    That lādīes and maidens might see
Whǫ that bestę were of deed,
    Through doughtīness tō have the °gree.   *prize*

Knightes armę them °bydēne   *at once*
50   Tō the tournament tō rīde,
With °shēldes °brǫde and helmes °sheen   *shields/broad/*
                                          bright
    Tō win °gręte honour and °prīde.   *great/admiration*
Launcelot °left with the queen,   *remained*
    And °sēke hē lay that °ilkę °tīde;   *sick/same/time*
For lovę that was them between,
    Hē made °enchęsoun for tō abīde.   *occasion (excuse)*

The king sat upon his steed,
    And forth is went upon his way;
Sir Agravain for such a need,
60   At hǫme °beleft, for °sooth tō say,   *remained/truth*

35-36 That knights shall win honor there by riding to do deeds of arms.

For men tǫld in many a °thēde   *nation*
    That Launcelot by the queen lay;
For tō tāke them °with the deed,   *in the act*
    Hē awaites bǫth night and day.

Launcelot forth °wendes hē   *goes*
    Untō the chāmber tō the queen,
And set him down upon his knee
    And °salūes there that lādy °sheen   *salutes/bright*
"Launcelot, what °dostou hēre with mē?   *dost thou*
70   The king is went and the court °bydēne;   *as well*
I °drēde wē shall discovered bē   *dread*
    °Of the love is us between.   *by*

"Sir Agravain at hǫme is hē;
    Night and day hē waites us twǫ."
"Nay," hē said, "my lādy °free,   *noble*
    I °ne think nǫt it shall bē sǫ;   *do not think*
I come tō tāke my °lęve of thee,   *leave*
    Out of court ęre that I gǫ."
"†Yā, swīthę that thou armed bē,
80   For thy dwelling mē is full wǫ."

Launcelot tō his chāmber °yēde   *went*
    There rich attīre lay him before,
†Armed him in nǫble weed,
    Of that armour gentylly was shore.
Sword and °shēld were good at need   *shield*
    In many °batailes that hē had bǫre,   *battles*
And horsed him on a grey steed
    King Arthur had him °geve before.   *given*

Hǫldes hē nǫne highę way,
90   The knight that was hardy and °free,   *noble*
But hāstes bǫth night and day
    Fast tōward that °riche citee   *great city*
(Winchester it °hight, for °sooth to say)   *is called/truth*
    °There the tournament °sholde bē;   *where/should*
King Arthur in a castle lay,
    Full much there was of °gāme and glee.   *pleasure*

<hr/>

79-80 Indeed, arm yourself quickly, for your remaining here is painful to
    me.
83-84 Armed himself in a noble material (*weed*) from which his armor
    was nobly (*gentylly*) fashioned (*shore*).

†For-why wǫlde men Launcelot behǫld,
　And hē °ne wǫlde nǫt himselfe shǫw — *did not want to*
With his shouldres °gan hē fǫld — *did*
100　And down hē hanged his °hęd full lǫw, — *head*
†As hē ne might his limmes wēld;
　°Keeped hē nǫ bugle blǫw; — *i.e., had no trumpeteer*
Well hē seemed as hē were ǫld,
　°For-thy ne °couth him nǫ man knǫw. — *therefore/could*

The king stood on a °towr °on hight; — *tower/on high*
　Sir Ēwain °clēpes hē that °tīde: — *calls/time*
"Sir Ēwain, °knǫwestou any wight — *knowest thou in any way*
　This knight that rīdes hēre besīde?"
Sir Ēwain °spękes wordes °right — *speaks/directly*
110　†(That ay is hende is nǫt tō hīde):
"Sir, it is some ǫldę knight
　Is come tō see the °yonge knightes rīde." — *young*

†They behēld him bǫth anǫn
　A stoundę for the steedes sāke;
His horse °stomeled at a stǫne — *stumbled*
　°That all his body there-with °gan shāke; — *so that/did*
The knight then °braundished °īch a bǫne, — *shook/every*
　As hē the brīdle up °gan tāke; — *did*
There-by °wiste they bǫth °anǫn — *knew/immediately*
120　That it was Launcelot du Lāke.

King Arthur then °spękes hē — *speaks*
　Tō Sir Ēwain thēse wordes °right: — *directly*
"Well may Launcelot °hǫlden bē — *considered*
　Of all the world the bestę knight,
Of °beautee and of °bountee, — *beauty/generosity*
　And °sithe is nǫne sǫ much of might, — *since there is no one*
At every deedę best is hē,
　†And sithe hē nǫlde it wiste nǫ wight,

"Sir Ēwain, will wē °dǫn him °bīde; — *make/wait*
130　Hē °weenes that wē knǫw him nǫught." — *supposes*

97 Because men wanted to see Lancelot.
101 As if he could not control his limbs.
110 That which is courteous should not be hidden.
113-14 Immediately (*anǫn*) they both looked at him for a while (*a stoundę*) because they wanted to admire the horse.
128 And since he wants no one to know it.

"Sir, it is better °let him rīde,   *to let*
 And let him °dōn as hē hath thǫught; *do*
Hē will bē hēre °nęr besīde,   *nearby*
 °Sithe hē thus °fer °hider hath °sǫught; *since/far/ hither/come*
Wē shall knǫw him by his deed
 And by the horse that hē hath brǫught."

An °erl °wonned there besīde,   *earl/dwelled*
 The Lǫrd of Ascolot was °hight; *called*
Launcelot °gan °thider rīde,   *did/thither*
140 And said hē will there dwell all night;
They received him with °grętę °prīde; *great/pomp*
 A richę °soper there was °dight; *supper/prepared*
His nāmę °gan hē °hęle and hīde, *did/conceal*
 And said hē was a °strāngę knight. *foreign*

Then had the °erlę sonnes twǫ,   *earl*
 That were nǫble knightes °māked new. *newly made*
†In that tīme was the manner sǫ,
 When yongę knightes sholde shēldes shew,
Til the first yēre were agǫ
150 Tō bęre armes of ǫne hew,
Ręd or whīte, yellow or °blō;   *blue*
 There-by men °yongę knightes knew. *young*

As they sat at their °soper,   *supper*
 Launcelot tō the °erl spāke there: *earl*
"Sir, is hēre any °bacheler   *young knight*
 That tō the tournament will fare?"
"I have twǫ sonnes that mē is °dęre, *dear*
 And now that ǫne is °sēke full sǫre, *sick*
†Sǫ that in company hē were,
160 Mīne other son I °wǫlde were there." *would*

†"Sir, and thy son will thider right,
 The °lenger I will him abīde, *longer*
And help him there with all my might,
 That him nǫne harmę shall betīde."

147-50 At that time it was the custom that, when young knights were to show their shields for the first time, they should bear arms all of one color [without any heraldic device] until the first year had passed. [This was not the case in actual life.]
159 Providing that he had company.
161 Sir, if your son wants to go directly there.

"Sir, thee seemes a noble knight,
   °Courtais and °hende, is not tō hīde;   *courteous/polite*
°At morrow shall yē dīne and °dight,   *in the morning/*
   °Tōgeder I °rede well that yē rīde."   *prepare*
                                             together/advise

"Sir, of one thing I will you °minne,   *say*
170   And beseech you for tō °speed,   *succeed*
°Yif hēre were any armour in   *if*
   That I might borrow it °tō this deed."   *for*
"Sir, my son līeth °sēke hēre-in;   *sick*
   Tāke his armour and his steed;
For my sonnes men shall you °ken,   *know*
   Of rēd shall bē °your bothes weed."   *both your*
                                           garments

Th'erl had a doughter that was him dere;
   °Mikel Launcelot shē behēld;   *much*
Her °rōde was rēd as blossom on °brēre   *cheek/briar*
180   Or °flowr that springeth in the °fēld;   *flower/field*
Glad shē was tō sit him °ner,   *near*
   The noble knight under °shēld;   *shield*
†Weeping was her moste cheer,
   So mikel on him her herte gan hēlde.

Up then rose that maiden still,
   And tō her chāmber went shē °tho;   *then*
Down upon her bed shē fell,
   That nigh her °herte °brast in two.   *heart/broke*
Launcelot °wiste what was her °will,   *knew/desire*
190   †Well hē knew by other mo;
Her brōther °clēped hē °him til,   *called/to him*
   And tō her chāmber °gonne they go.   *did*

Hē sat him down for the maidens sāke,
   Upon her °bedde °there shē lay;   *bed/where*
°Courtaisly tō her hē spāke,   *courteously*
   For tō comfort that faire °may.   *maid*
In her armes shē °gan him tāke,   *did*
   And thēse wordes gan shē say:
†"Sir, but yif that yē it māke,
200   Sāve my līfe no °lēche °may."   *physician/can*

[183-84] Her heart was so firmly set on him that she was most often seen
    weeping.
[190] He knew well by other signs in addition to her weeping.
[199] Unless you do it (save my life).

"Lādy," hē said, "thou °moste let;   *must stop*
   †For mē ne gif thee nǫthing ill;
In another °stęde mīne herte is set;   *place*
   It is nǫt at mīne ǫwnę will;
In °erthe is nǫthing that shall mē °let   *earth/prevent*
   Tō bē thy knight loud and still;
Another tīme wē may bē met
   When thou may better °spęke thy fill."   *speak*

"°Sithe I of thee °ne may have mǫre,   *since/can not*
210   As thou art hardy knight and °free,   *noble*
In the tournament that thou °wǫlde °bęre   *would/bear*
   Some sign of mīne that men might see."
"Lādy, thy sleeve thou shalt °of-shęre;   *cut off*
   I will it tāke for the love of thee;
†Sǫ did I never nǫ lādīes ęre,
   But ǫne that mǫst hath loved mē."

°On the morrow when it was day,   *In the morning*
   They dīned and māde them °yare,   *ready*
And then they went forth on their way,
220   °Tōgeder as they brethern were.   *together*
They met a °squīer by the way   *squire*
   That from the tournament °gan fare,   *did travel*
And asked him °yif he °couth them say   *if/could*
   Which party was the bigger there.

"Sir Galahod hath folk the mǫre,
   For sooth,° lǫrdinges, as I you tell,   *lords*
But Arthur is the °bigger there;   *i.e., more powerful*
   Hē hath knightes °stiff and °fell;   *stout/fierce*
They are bǫld and °brēme as °bǫre,   *fierce/boar*
230   Ēwain, and Bors, and Līonel."
Th'erles son tō him spāke there:
   "Sir, with them I °ręde wē dwell."   *advise*

Launcelot spāke, as I you °ręde;   *tell*
   "°Sithe they are men of gręte valour,   *since*
How might wē amǫng them °speed,   *succeed*
   °There all are °stiff and strǫng in °stour?   *where/stout/battle*
°Help wē them that hath mǫst need;   *let us help those*
   °Again the best wē shall well °doure;   *against/endure*

---

202 Do not make yourself sick for my sake.
215 I never did so for any lady before this.

°And wē might there dō any deed,   *if*
240   It wǫlde us turn tō mǫre honour."

Launcelot spękes in that °tīde   *time*
    As knight that was hardy and °free: *noble*
"Tōnight °without I °ręde wē °bīde   *outside/advise/*
    The °press is gręte in that citee."   *remain*
                         crowd
"Sir, I have an aunt hēre besīde,
    A lādy of °swīthę gręte beautee;   *very great beauty*
Were it your will °thider tō rīde,   *thither*
    Glad of us then wǫlde shē bē."

°Thǫ tō the castle °gonne they fare,   *then/did*
250   Tō the lādy fair and bright;
Blīthę was the lādy there
    That they wǫlde dwell with her that night;
Hāstely was their °soper °yare   *supper/ready*
    Of °męte and drink richly °dight.   *food/prepared*
°On the morrow °gonne they dīne and fare,   *In the morning/*
    Bǫth Launcelot and that other knight.   *did*

When they come intō the °fēld,   *field*
    Much there was of °gāme and play;   *pleasure*
A whīle they °hōved and behēld   *paused*
260   How Arthurs knightes rǫde that day.
Galehodes party began tō °hēld,   *draw back*
    On foot his knightes are led away.
Launcelot—°stiff was under shēld—   *stout*
    °Thinkes tō help, °yif that hē °may.   *intends/if/can*

Besīde him cǫme then Sir Ēwain,
    °Brēme as any wīldę °bǫre;   *fierce/boar*
Launcelot springes him °again   *against*
    In °ręddę armes that hē bǫre;   *red*
A dint hē gāve with °mikel main;   *much force*
270   Sir Ēwain was unhorsed there,
That all men °wēnd hē had been slain,   *supposed*
    Sǫ was hē wounded °wonder sǫrè.   *very painfully*

Sir Bors thǫught nǫthing good,
    When Sir Ēwain unhorsed was;
Forth hē springes °as hē were °wōde,   *as if/crazy*
    Tō Launcelot, °withouten lęęs,   *without lies*
                         (I tell it)

Launcelot hit him on the hood,
    The °nexte way tō ground hē °chẹse;   *closest/went*
Was nọne sọ °stiff °again him stood;   *stout/against*
280   Full thin hē māde the thickest °press.   *crowd*

Sir Līonel began tō °teen,   *mourn*
    And hāstely hē made him °boune;   *ready*
Tō Launcelot with °hertẹ keen,   *heart*
    Hē rọde with helm and °swordẹ brown;   *shining sword*
Launcelot hit him, as I °ween,   *suppose*
    Through the helm intō the °crown,   *skull*
That ever after it was seen
    Bọth horse and man there °yēde adown.   *went*

The knightes °gadered tōgeder there   *gathered together*
290   And °gonne with °craft their counsēl tāke;   *did/skill*
Such a knight was never ẹre
    But it were Launcelot du Lāke;
But, for the sleeve on his crest was there,
    For Launcelot wọlde they him nọt tāke,
For hē bọre never nọne such before,
    °But it were for the queenes sake.   *except*

"Of Ascolot hē never was
    That thus well °bẹres him tōday!"   *bears himself*
Ector said, °withouten lẹẹs,   *without lies*
300   What hē was hē wọlde °assay.   *test*
A nọble steed Ector °him chẹse,   *chose for himself*
    And forthẹ rīdes glad and gay;
Launcelot hē met amid the °press,   *crowd*
    Between them was nọ chīldes play.

Ector smọte with °hertẹ good   *heart*
    Tō Launcelot that °ilkẹ tīde;   *very time*
Through helm intō his °hẹd it °yōde   *head/went*
    That °nighẹ lost hē all his prīde.   *nearly*
Launcelot hit him on the hood
310   That his horsẹ fell and hē besīde.
†Launcelot blīndes in his blood;
    Out of the °fēld full fast gan rīde.   *field*

³¹¹ Lancelot is blinded by his own blood.

Out of the fēld they °rīden thọ   *ride then*
   Tō a forest high and °họre.   *hoar*
†When they come by them ọne twọ,
   Off his helm hē tākes there.
"Sir," hē said, "°mē is full wọ;   *(it) is very sad to*
   I °drēde that yē bē hurt °full sọre."   *me [I am very sad]*
                                                dread/very
"Nay," °hē said, "it is nọt sọ,   *painfully*
320   †But fain I wọlde at rest wē were."   *i.e., Launcelot*

"Sir, mīne aunt is hēre besīde,
   °There wē bọthẹ were all night;   *where*
Were it your will thider tō rīde,
   Shē will us help with all her might,
And send for °lēches this °ilkẹ tīde,   *physicians/*
   Your woundes for tō °hẹle and °dight;   *very time*
                                              heal/prepare
And I myself will with you abīde,   *(dress)*
   And bē your servaunt and your knight."

Tō the castle they took the way,
330   Tō the lādy fair and °hende.   *courteous*
She sent for °lēches, as I you say,   *physicians*
   That °wonned bọth °fer and °hende,   *lived/far/near*
But by the °morrow that it was day,   *morning*
   In bed hē might himself nọt °wend;   *turn*
Sọ sọrẹ wounded there hē lay
   That well nigh had hē sọught his end.

°Thọ King Arthur with °mikel °prīde   *then/much/*
   Called his knightes all him by,   *pomp*
And said a month hē wọlde there bīde,
340   And in Winchester līe.
°Heraudes hē °did gọ and rīde   *heralds/caused*
   Another tournament for tō °cry;   *to*
                                              announce
"This knight will bē hēre besīde,
   For hē is wounded bitterly."

When the °lettres mādẹ were,   *letters*
   The °heraudes forth with them °yēde,   *heralds/went*
Through °Yngland for tō fare,   *England*
   Another tournament for tō °bēde;   *announce*

315 When they came alone by themselves (them two alone).
320 But I wish we were at a resting place.

Bade them °busk and māke them °yare,   *hasten/ready*
350 All that °stiff were on steed.   *stout*
 Thus thēse °lettres sentẹ were   *letters*
  Tō °thọ that doughty were of deed.   *those*

 Til on a tīme that it befell
  An °heraud comes by the way   *herald*
 And at the castle a night gan dwell
  °There as Launcelot wounded lay,   *where*
 And of the tournament gan tell
  That °sholdẹ come on the Sunday;   *should*
 Launcelot sighes wonder still
360 And said: "Alas and wẹle-away!

                 honor/
                admiration
 "When knightes win °worship and °prīde,
                adventure
  Some °aunter shall họld mē away,   *(chance*
                happening)
 As a coward for tō abīde.
  This tournament, for sooth tō say,
 For mē is māde this °ilkẹ tīde;   *very time*
  Thọugh I °sholde dīe this °ilkẹ day,   *should/very*
 °Certes, I shall thider rīde."   *certainly*

                physician/
 The °lēche answered °alsọ soon   *immediately*
  And said: "Sir, what have yē °thọught?   *intended*
370 All the craft that I have dōne
                believe/not at
  I °ween it will you help °right nọught.   *all*
 There is nọ man under the moon,
  By Him that all this world hath wrọught,
 Might sāve your life °tō that tīme come   *if the time*
                should come
  That yē upon your steed were brọught!"

 "°Certes, thọugh I dīe this day,   *certainly*
  In my bed I will nọt līe;
 Yet had I °lēver dō what I °may   *rather/can*
  Than hēre tō dīe thus cowardly!"
                physician/
380 The °lēche °anọn then went his way   *immediately*
  And wọlde nọ °lenger dwell him by;   *longer*
 His woundes °scrived and still hē lay,   *broke open*
  And in his bed hē swooned °thrīe.   *thrice*

 The lādy wept as shē were °wōde,   *crazy*
  When shē saw hē °dẹde wọlde bē;   *dead*

Th'erles son with sorry mood
  The °lēche again °clēpes hē   *physician/calls*
And said: "Thou shalt have °yiftes good   *gifts*
  °For-why that thou wilt dwell with mē."   *providing*
390 Craftily then staunched hē his blood
  And of good comfort bade him bē.

The °heraud then went on his way   *herald*
  At °morrow when the day was light,   *morning*
°Also swīthe as ever hē may,   *as quickly*
  Tō Winchester that ilke night;
He °salūed the king, for sooth tō say   *saluted*
  (By him sat Sir Ēwain the knight),
†And sithe hē told upon his play
  What hē had °herde and seen with sight: *heard*

400 "Of all that I have seen with sight,
  †Wonder thought mē never more
Than mē did of a °fooled knight   *foolish*
  That in his bed lay wounded sore;
†Hē might not heve his hed up-right
  For all the world have wonne there;
For anguish that hē °ne rīde might   *could not ride*
  All his woundes °scrived there."   *broke open*

Sir Ēwain then spekes wordes °free,   *noble*
  And tō the kinge said hē there:
410 "°Certes, no coward knight is hē;   *certainly*
  Alas, that hē °nere hole and fere!   *is not healthy and sound*
Well I °wot that it is hē   *know*
  †That wē all of unhorsed were.
The tournament is best let bē,
  Forsooth, that knight may not come there."

There tournament was then no more,
  But thus departeth all the °press;   *company*
Knightes took their °leve tō fare;   *leave*
  °Īchon his owne way °him chese.   *Each one/went*
420 Tō Camelot the king went there,
  °There as Queen Gaynor was;   *where*

398 And then he told them about his amusements.
401 Never a greater wonder did it seem to me.
404-05 He could not have lifted up his head, even if by doing so he could
  have won the whole world.
413 By whom all of us were unhorsed.

Hē °wēnd have found Launcelot there;   *expected to*
    Away hē was, °withouten lēēs.   *without lies*
                                                              (I tell it)

Launcelot °sǫre wounded lay;   *painfully*
    Knightes sǫught him full wīde;
Th'erles son night and day
    Was °alway him besīde.   *always*
Th'erl himself, when hē rīdę °may,   *can*
    Brǫught him hǫme with °mikel °prīde   *much/pomp*
430 And māde him bǫth °gāme and play   *pleasure*
    Til hē °might bǫthę °gǫ and rīde.   *could/walk*

Bors and Līonel then swǫre,
    And °at the king their °lęve took there,   *from/leave*
Again they wǫlde come never mǫre,
    Til they °wiste where Launcelot were.   *knew*
Ector went with them there
    Tō °seech his °brōder that was him dęre.   *seek/brother*
Many a land they °gonne through fare   *did*
    And sǫught him bǫthę °fer and nęr.   *far and near*

440 Til on a tīme that it befell
    That they come by that ilkę way,
And at the castle at °męte °gonne dwell,   *food/did*
    °There as Launcelot wounded lay.   *where*
Launcelot they saw, as I you tell,
    Walk on the walles him tō play;
On knees for joy all they fell,
    So blīthę men they were that day.

When Launcelot saw °thǫ ilkę three   *those*
    That hē in worldę loved best,
450 A merrīer meeting might nǫ man see,
    And °sithe hē led them tō rest.   *then*
Th'erl himself, glad was hē
    That hē had gotten such a guest;
Sǫ was the maiden fair and free
    That all her love on him had cast.

When they were tō soper °dight   *prepared*
    †Bōrdes were set and clǫthes spredde;

---

457 Boards were set and (table-) cloths spread. [The boards are set on
    trestles to form tables. Permanently assembled tables were still rare at
    this time.]

Th'erles doughter and the knight
    °Tōgeder was set, as hē them bade;   *together*
460 Th'erles sonnes that both were °wight,   *strong*
    Tō serve them were never sad,
And th'erl himself with all his might,
    Tō māke them both °blīthe and glad.   *happy*

But Bors ever in mind hē thought
    That Launcelot had been wounded sore:
†"Sir, were it your will tō hele it nought
    But tell where yē thus hurte were?"
"By Him That all this world hath wrought,"
    Launcelot himselfe swore,
470 "The °dint shall bē full °dere bought,   *blow/dearly*
    °Yif ever wē may meet us more!"   *if*

Ector ne līked that °no wight,   *not a bit*
    The wordes that hē °herde there;   *heard*
For sorrow hē lost both strength and might;
    The colours chānged in his °lēre.   *face*
Bors then said thēse wordes °right: *directly*
    "Ector, thou may māke °īvel cheer;   *evil (sour)*
                                                            expression
For sooth, it is no coward knight
    That thou art °of ymanased hēre."   *menaced by*

480 "Ector," hē said, "°were thou it were   *was it you who*
    That wounded mē thus wonder sore?"
Ector answered with °simple cheer: *innocent*
                                                            expression
    "Lord, I ne °wiste that yē it were;   *knew*
A dint °of you I had there;   *from*
    Feeled I never none so sore."
Sir Līonel by God then swore
    †That "Mīne will seen bē ever more!"

Sir Bors then answerd °as tīte   *quickly*
    As knight that wīse was under °weed: *garment*
490 "I °hope that none of us was °quīte;   *suppose/free*
                                                            (of wounds)
    I had one that tō ground I °yēde;   *went*
Sir, your °brōder °shall yē not °wīte;   *brother/must/*
                                                            blame
    Now knowes either others deed;

---

466 Sir, would it be your desire not to conceal it.
487 My wound will be seen forevermore.

Now know yē how Ector can smīte,
    Tō help you when yē have need."

Launcelot °lough with herte free   *laughed*
    That Ector māde so °mikel sīte: *much lament*
"Brōther, nothing °drēde thou thee,   *dread*
    For I shall bē both °hole and °quīte.   *healthy/free (of harm)*
500 Though thou have sore wounded mē,
    There-of I shall thee never °wīte,   *blame*
But ever the better love I thee,
    Such a dint that thou can smīte."

Then upon the °thridde day,   *third*
    They took their °leve for tō fare;   *leave*
Tō the court they will away,
    For hē will dwell a whīle there:
"Greet well my lord, I you pray,
    And tell my lādy how I fare,
510 And say I will come when I may,
    †And biddeth her long nothing sore."

They took their leve, °withouten lees,   *without lies (I tell it)*
    And °wightly went upon their way;   *stoutly*
Tō the court the way they °chese,   *went*
    °There as the Queen Gaynor lay.   *where*
The king tō the forest is,
    With knightes him for tō play;
Good spāce they had °withouten press   *without a crowd*
    Their °errand tō the queen tō say.   *message*

520 They kneeled down before the queen,
    The knightes that were wīse of °lore,   *learning*
And said that they had Launcelot seen
    And three dayes with him were,
And how that hē had wounded been,
    And °sēke hē had °līe full sore: *sick/lain*
"°Ere ought long yē shall him °seen;   *before much longer/see*
    Hē bade you longe nothing sore."

The queen °lough with herte free,   *laughed*
    When shē °wiste hē was °on līfe: *knew/alive*

511 And tell her not to long sorely for me.

530 "Ọ, worthy God, what °wẹle is mē!   *joy*
    †Why ne wiste my lọrd it alsọ swīthe!"
Tō the forest rọde thēse knightes three,
    Tō the king it tō °kīthe;   *make known*
Jēsū Crīst then thankes hē,
    †For was hē never of word sọ blīthe.

Hē °clēped Sir Gawain him °nẹr,   *called/near*
    And said: "Certes, that was hē
That the rẹd armes bọre,
    But now hē lives, °wẹle is mē!"   *joy*
540 Gawain answerd with mīldẹ °cheer,   *expression*
    As hē that °ay was °hende and free: *ever/courteous*
"Was never °tīthandes mē sọ dẹre,   *tidings*
    But sọre °mē lọnges Launcelot tō see."   *I yearn*

°At the king and at the queen   *from*
    Sir Gawain took his lẹve that tīde,
And °sithe at all the court °bydēne,   *then/together*
    And °buskes him with mikel °prīde,   *hastens/display*
°Til Ascolot, withouten °ween,   *to/doubt*
    °Alsọ fast as hē might rīde;   *as*
550 Til that hē have Launcelot seen,
    Night ne day ne will hē bīde.

°By that was Launcelot °họle and °fere   *by that time/ healthy/sound*
    °Buskes him and mākes all °yare;   *hastens/ready*
His lẹve hath hē tākẹ there;
    The maiden wept for sọrrow and care:
"Sir, °yif that your willes were,   *if it were your wish*
    °Sithe I of thee ne may have mọre,   *since*
Some thing yē wọlde °belẹve me hēre,   *leave*
    Tō look on when °mē lọngeth sọre."   *I yearn*

560 Launcelot spāke with hertẹ free,
    For tō comfort that lādy °hende: *courteous*
"Mīne armour shall I lẹve with thee,
    And in thy brōthers will I °wende;   *go*
Look thou ne lọnge nọt after mē,
    For hēre I may nọ °lenger °lende;   *longer/remain*

531 If only my husband knew this quickly!
535 He was never so happy because of a word.

Long tīme ne shall it nought bē
    That I ne shall either come or °sende."   *send word*

Launcelot is °redy for tō rīde,   *ready*
    And on his way hē went forth °right;   *directly*
570 Sir Gawain come after on a °tīde,   *time*
    And askes after such a knight.
They received him with grete prīde
    (A riche soper there was °dight),   *prepared*
And said, in herte is nought tō hīde,
    Away hē was for °fourtenight.   *a fortnight*

Sir Gawain gan that maiden tāke
    And sat him by that sweete °wight,   *creature*
And spāke of Launcelot du Lāke;
    In all the world °nas such a knight.   *was not*
580 The maiden there of Launcelot spāke,
    Said all her love was on him °lighte: *alighted*
"For his °lēman hē hath mē tāke;   *sweetheart*
    †His armour I you shewe might."

"Now dāmesel," hē said °anon,   *immediately*
    "And I am glad that it is so;
Such a °lēman as thou hast one,   *sweetheart*
    In all this world ne bē no °mo.   *more (i.e., better)*
There is no lādy of flesh ne bone
    In this worlde so °thrīve or °thro,   *excellent/strong*
590 Though her herte were steel or stone,
    †That might her love holde him fro.

"But, dāmesel, I beseech thee,
    His shēlde that yē wolde mē °shew;   *show*
Launcelotes yif that it bē
    By the coloures I °it knew."   *would know it*
The maiden was both hende and free,
    And led him tō a chāmber new;
Launcelotes shēld shē let him see,
    And all his armour forth shē drew.

600 °Hendely then Sir Gawain   *courteously*
    Tō the maiden there hē spāke:

583 I could show you his armor.
591 That could withhold her love from him.

"Lādy," hē said, "°withouten laine,   *without conceal-*
   †This is Launcelotes shēld du Lāke.   *ment (truly)*
Dāmesel," hē said, "I am °full fain   *very pleased*
   That hē thee wǫlde °tō lēman tāke   *as a sweetheart*
And I with all my might and main
   Will bē thy knight for his sāke."

Gawain thus spāke with that sweete °wight   *creature*
   What his will was for tō say.
610 Til hē was tō bed °ydight,   *prepared*
   About him was °gāme and play.   *pleasure*
Hē took his lęve °at erl and knight   *from*
   On the morrow when it was day,
And °sithen at the maiden bright,   *then*
   And forth hē went upon his way.

Hē °niste where that hē °might,   *did not know/*
   Ne where that Launcelot wǫlde °lende,   *could go*
For when hē was out of sight,   *stay*
   Hē was full °īvel for tō find.   *evil (i.e.,*
620 Hē tākes him the way °right.   *difficult)*
   And tō the courtę gan hē °wend;   *directly*
Glad of him was king and knight,   *go*
   For hē was bǫth °courtais and hende.   *courteous*

Then it befell upon a tīde,
   The king stood by the queen and spāke:
Sir Gawain standes him besīde;
   †Īchon til other their mǫne gan māke,
How lǫng they might with °bāle abīde   *suffering*
   The coming of Launcelot du Lāke;
630 In the court was little prīde,
   Sǫ sǫre they sighed for his sāke.

"Certes, yif Launcelot were °on līfe,   *alive*
   Sǫ lǫng °frǫ court hē °nǫlde nǫt bē."   *away from/*
Sir Gawain answerd °alsǫ swīthe: *would not*
   "There-of nǫ wonder °thinketh mē;   *quickly*
The fairest lady that is on līfe   *it seems to me*
   °Til his lēman chǫsen hath hē;   *as his sweetheart*

---

[603] This is Lancelot du Lake's shield. [The poet uses the older form of
   the genitive phrase. See Introduction, p. xv.]
[627] Each complained to the other.

Is nǫne of us but wǫlde bē blīthe
    Such a °seemly for tō see."

seemly (i.e.,
lovely) one

640 The King Arthur was full blīthe
    Of that °tīthinges for tō °lęre,

tidings/learn

  And asked Sir Gawain °alsǫ swīthe

quickly

    What maiden that it were.
  "Th'erles dǫughter," hē said °as swīthe,

quickly

    Of Ascolot, as yē may °hēre,

hear

  There I was mādę glad and blīthe;
    His shēld the maiden shewed mē there."

The queen then said wordes nǫ °mǫ,

more

    But tō her chāmber °soon shē °yēde,

immediately/
went

650 And down upon her bed fell sǫ
    That nigh of wit she wǫldę °wēde.

go mad

  "Alas," shē said, "and węle-a-wǫ,
    †That ever I ǫught līfe in lēde!
  The bestę body is lost mē frǫ
    That ever in °stour bestrǫdę steed."

battle

Lādīes that about her stood,
    That wiste of her °privitee,

private affairs

  Bade her bē of comfort good;
    Let nǫ man such °semblaunt see.

outward
appearance

660 A bed they mādę with sǫrry mood,
    Therein they brǫught that lādy free;
  Ever shē wept as shē were °wōde;

crazy

    Of her they had full gręte °pitee.

pity

Sǫ sǫre °sēke the queen lay,

sick

    Of sǫrrow might shē never °let,

stop

  Til it fell upon a day
    Sir Līonel and Ector yēde
  Intō the forest, them tō play,
    That flowred was and °braunched sweet,

had sweet
branches

670 And as they wentę by the way,
    With Launcelot °gonne they meet.

did

What wonder was though they were blīthe,
    When they their master saw with sight!

653 That I ever had life in this nation (i.e., that I was ever born).

On knees they felle °alsǫ swīthe,   *quickly*
    And all they thanked God all-might;
Joy it was tō see and °līthe   *hear*
    The meeting of the nǫble knight.
And °sithe hē frained alsǫ swīthe: *then he quickly asked*
    "How fares my lādy bright?"

680 Then answered the knightes free,
    And said that shē was sēke full sǫre:
"Grǫte dole it is tō °hēre and see,   *hear*
    Sǫ mikel shē is in sǫrrow and care;
The king a sǫrry man is hē,
    In court for that yē come nǫ mǫre;
°Dęde hē °weenes that yē bē,   *dead/supposes*
    And all the court, bǫth less and mǫre.

"Sir, were it your will with us tō fare,
    For tō spęke with the queen,
690 †Blīthe I wǫt well that shē were
    Yif that shē had you ǫnes seen.
The king is mikel in sǫrrow and care,
    And sǫ is all the court °bydēne;   *as well*
°Dęde they °ween well that yē are   *dead/suppose*
    From court for yē sǫ lǫng have been."

Hē °grauntes them at that ilkę °sīthe   *grants/time*
    Hǫme that hē will with them rīde;
Therefore the knightes were full blīthe
    And °busked them with mikel prīde   *hastened*
700 Tō the court alsǫ swīthe;
    Night ne day they °nǫlde abīde;   *would not*
The king and all the court was blīthe
    The °tīdandes when they °herde that tīde.   *tidings/heard*

The king stood in a °towr on high,   *tower*
    Besīdes him standes Sir Gawain;
Launcelot when that they °sigh   *saw*
    Were never men on °molde so °fain.   *earth/glad*
They ran as °swīthe as ever they might   *quickly*
    Out at the gātes him °again;   *against (i.e., toward)*
710 Was never °tīdandes tō them sǫ °light;   *tidings/joyful*
    The king him kissed and knight and °swain.   *young man*

690-91 I know well she would be happy if she could see you but once.

Tō a chāmber the king him led;
  †Fair in armes they gonne him fǫld,
And set him on a richę bed,
  That °spredde was with a clǫth of gold;   *spread*
Tō serve him there was nǫ man sad,
  †Ne dight him as himselfę wǫlde
Tō māke him bǫth blīthe and glad,
  And sithę aunters hē them tǫld.

720 Three dayes in court hē dwelled there
       That hē ne spāke nǫt with the queen,
     Sǫ muchę press was ay them nęr;
       The king him led and court bydēne.
     The lādy, bright as blossom on °brēre,   *briar*
       Sǫre shē lǫnged him tō °sēn;   *see*
     Weeping was her °mǫstę cheer,   *most (frequent)*
                                                     expression
       Thǫugh shē ne durst her tō nǫ man °męne.   *speak*

     Then it fell upon a day
       The king gan on hunting rīde,
730 Intō the forest him tō play,
       With his knightes by his sīde.
     Launcelot lǫng in beddę lay;
       With the queen hē thǫught tō bīde;
     Tō the chāmber hē took the way
       And °salūes her with mikel prīde.   *salutes*

     First hē kissed that lādy sheen,
       And °salūes her with hertę free,   *salutes*
     And sithe the lādīes all bydēne;
       For joy the tęres ran on their °blee.   *face(s)*
740 "Węle-away," then said the queen,
       "Launcelot, that I ever thee see!
     The love that hath us °bē between,   *been*
       That it shall thus departed bē!

     "Alas, Launcelot du Lāke,
       Sithe thou hast all my hertę in °wōld,   *(your)*
                                                     possession
     Th'erles dǫughter that thou wǫlde tāke
       Of Ascolot, as men mē tǫld!
     Now thou lęvest for her sāke
       All thy deed of armes bǫld;

---

713 They embraced him gently.
717 But served him whatever he wanted.

750 I may wǫfully weep and wāke
        †In clay til I bē clongen cǫld!

     "But, Launcelot, I beseech thee hēre,
        Sithe it °needelinges shall bē sǫ,   *of necessity*
     That thou never mǫre °diskēre   *reveal*
        The love that hath been betwix us twǫ,
     †Ne that shē never bē with thee sǫ dęre,
        Deed of armes that thou bē frǫ,
     That I may of thy body hēre,
        Sithe I shall thus belęve in wǫ."

760 Launcelot full still then stood;
        His herte was °hęvy as any stǫne;   *heavy*
     Sǫ sǫrry hē °wex in his °mood,   *grew/mind*
        †For rewth him thǫught it all tō-torne.
     †"Mādāme," hē said, "For Cross and °Rood,   *cross*
        What °betǫkeneth all this °mǫne?   *means/moan*
     By Him that bǫught mē with His blood,
        Of thēse °tīdandes knǫw I nǫne.   *tidings*

     "But by these wordes °thinketh mē   *it seems to me*
        Away yē wǫldę that I were;
770 Now have good day, my lādy free,
        For sooth, thou seest mē never mǫre!"
     Out of the chāmber then wendes hē;
        °Now whether his herte was full of wǫ!   *Now (consider)*
                                                                  whether
     The lādy swoones °sīthes three;   *times*
        Almost shē slew herselfę there.

     Launcelot tō his chāmber °yēde,   *went*
        There his ǫwn attīre in lay,
     Armed him in a nǫble weed,
        Though in his herte were little play;
780 Forth hē sprang as spark of °glēde,   *live coal*
        With sǫrry cheer, for sooth tō say;

---

751 Until I am clasped in cold clay (i.e., dead and buried).
756-59 May she never be so dear to you that you give up performing
    deeds of arms; since I must remain alone in sorrow, I would at least
    like to hear of your deeds of prowess.
763 Because of his sorrow it seemed to him that all was lost.
764 [In the expression "Cross on (or and) rood," which is used fre-
    quently in this poem, the word "cross" is probably a metathesis of
    "cors"—body, as in line 2880, where "Cors on rood" does appear.]

Up hē °worthes upon his steed,   *gets*
    And tō a forest hē wendes away.

°Tīthinges come intō the hall   *tidings*
    That Launcelot was upon his steed;
Out then ran the knightes all,
    Of their wit as they wǫlde °wēde;   *run mad*
Bors de Gawnes and Līonel
    And Ector that doughty was of deed,
790 Followen him on horses °snell,   *swift*
    Full loudę gonne they °blǫw and °grēde.   *blow horns/cry*

There might nǫ man him ǫvertāke;
    Hē rǫde intō a forest green;
Muchę °mǫne gonne they māke,   *moan*
    The knightes that were bǫld and keen.
"Alas," they said, "Launcelot du Lāke,
    That ever °sholdestou see the queen!"   *you should have seen*
And her they cursed for his sāke,
    That ever love was them between.

800 They ne wiste never where tō fare,
    Ne tō what land that hē °wǫlde;   *would go*
Again they went with sighing sǫre,
    The knightes that were keen and bǫld;
The queen they found in swooning there,
    Her comely tresses all unfǫld;
They were sǫ full of sǫrrow and care,
    There was nǫne her comfortę wǫlde.

The king then hāstes him for his sāke,
    And hǫme then cǫme that ilkę day,
810 And asked after Launcelot du Lāke,
    And they said: "Hē is gǫne away."
The queen was in her bed all nāked,
    And sǫre sēke in her chāmber lay;
So muchę mǫne the king gan māke,
    There was nǫ knight that °lust tō play.   *wanted*

The king clēpes Gawain that day,
    And all his sǫrrow tǫld °him til: *to him*
"Now is Launcelot gǫne away,
    And come, I wǫt, hē never will."

820 Hē said: "Alas and węle-away,"
    Sighed sọre and °gāve him ill;   *made himself*
                                              sick
"The lọrd that wē have loved alway,
    In court why °nill hē never dwell?"   *will not*

Gawain spękes in that tīde,
    And tō the king said hē there:
"Sir, in this castle shall yē bīde,
    Comfort you and māke good cheer,
And wē shall bọth °gọ and rīde,   *walk*
    In allę landes °fer and nęr;   *far and near*
830 Sọ °prively hē shall him nọt hīde   *secretly*
    °Through hap that wē ne shall of him °hēre." *by chance/*
                                                hear

Knightes then sọught him wīde;
    Of Launcelot might they nọt °hēre,   *hear*
Til it fell upon a tīde,
    Queen Gaynor, bright as blossom on °brēre, *briar*
Tō °męte is set that ilkę tīde,   *food*
    And Sir Gawain sat her nęr,
And upon that other sīde
    A Scottish knight that was °her dęre.   *dear to her*

840 A °squīer in the court hath °thọught   *squire/intended*
    That ilkę day, yif that hē might,
With a poison that hē hath wrọught
    Tō slay Gawain, yif that hē might;
In °frūt he hath it forthę brọught   *fruit*
    And set before the queenę bright;
An apple °ọverest lay °on loft,   *uppermost/above*
    There the poison was in °dight.   *prepared*

For hē thọught the lādy bright
    Wọlde the best tō Gawain °bēde;   *offer*
850 But shē it gāve tō the Scottish knight,
    For hē was of an °uncouthe stęde.   *foreign place*
There-of hē °ęte a little °wight;   *ate/bit*
    Of °tręsoun took there nọ man heed;   *treason*
There hē lost bọth main and might
    And dīed °soon, as I you °ręde.   *immediately/tell*

They °niste nọt what it might °bemęne,   *knew/mean*
    But up him °stert Sir Gawain   *leaped*

And °sithen all the court bydēne,   *then*
   And ọver the bōrde they have him °drayn.   *drawn*
860 "Wẹle-away," then said the queen,
   "Jēsū Crīst, what may I °sayn?   *say*
Certes, now will all men ween
   Myself that I the knight have slain."

°Trīacle there was anọn forth brọught;   *medicine*
   The queenẹ °wēnd tō sāve his līfe;   *hoped*
But all that might help him nọught,
   For there the knight is °dẹde as swīthe.   *dead*
So grẹtẹ sọrrow the queen then wrọught,
   Grẹte dole it was tō see and °līthe: *hear*
870 "Lọrd, such °sītes mē have sọught!   *misfortunes*
   Why ne may I never bē blīthe?"

Knightes °dōn nọne other might   *could do nothing else*
   But burīed him with °dole ynow   *much sorrow*
At a chapel with °richẹ light,   *i.e., expensive candles*
   In a forest by a °clough;   *ravine*
A richẹ tōmb they °did bē dight,   *had prepared*
   A crafty clerk the lettres °drow,   *drew*
How there lay the Scottish knight
   That queen Gaynor with poison °slogh.   *slew*

880 After this a tīme befell
   Tō the court there cọme a knight;
His brōder hē was, as I you tell,
   And Sir Mador for sooth hē °hight;   *was called*
Hē was an hardy man and °snell   *active*
   In tournament and eek in fight,
And mikel loved in court tō dwell,
   For hē was man of muchẹ might.

Then it fell upon a day
   Sir Mador went with mikel prīde
890 †Intō the forest, him for tō play,
   That flowred was and braunched wīde;
Hē °fand a chapel in his way,   *found*
   As hē cāme by the °cloughes sīde,   *ravine's*

890-91 To amuse himself (he went) into the forest, which was in flower
  and had wide branches overhead.

There his owne brōder lay,
    †And there at mass hē thought tō abīde.

A riche tōmb °hē °fand there dight   *very fair*
    With lettres that were °fair ynow;   *found*
A whīle hē stood and °redde it right;   *read*
    Grete sorrow then tō his herte °drow;   *drew*
900 Hē fand the nāme of the Scottish knight
    That Queen Gaynor with poison °slogh.   *slew*
There hē lost both main and might,
    And over the tōmb hē fell in °swough.   *swoon*

Of swooning when hē might awāke,
    His herte was °hevy as any °lede;   *heavy/lead*
Hē sighed for his brōthers sāke;
    Hē ne wiste what was beste °rede.   *counsel*
The way tō court gan hē tāke,
    Of nothing ne stood hē °drēde;   *in dread*
910 A loude cry on the queen gan māke,
    In challenging of his brōthers °dede.   *death*

The king full sore then gan him drēde,
    For hē might not bē °again the right;   *against*
The queen of wit wolde nighe °wēde,   *run mad*
    †Though that shē aguilte had no wight.
Shē °moste there °beknow the deed   *must/confess*
    Or fīnd a man for her tō fight,
For well shē wiste tō dethe shē °yēde,   *would go*
    †Yif shē were on a quest of knightes.

920 Though Arthur were king the land tō °wēld,   *rule*
    Hē might not bē °again the right;   *against*
A day hē °took with °spere and shēld   *set/spear*
    Tō fīnd a man for her tō fight,
That shē shall either tō dethe her °yēld   *yield*
    †Or put her on a quest of knightes;   *i.e., Mador and*
' There-tō °both their handes uphēld   *Gaynor*
    And trewly °their trouthes plight.   *pledged their*
                                         words

895 And there he intended to abide at mass (to hear a mass).
915 Although she had no touch of guilt.
919 If she were judged by the knights [i.e., a court composed of the
    knights of the Round Table].
925 Or submit herself to a judgment by knights.

When they in certain had set a day
    And that quarrel undertāke,
930 The word sprang °soon through °ẹch countree   *immediately/*
    What sọrrow that Queen Gaynor gan māke;   *each*
Sọ at the last, shortly tō say,
    Word cọme tō Launcelot du Lāke,
There as hē sēke ywounded lay;
    Men tọld him °họlly all the °wrāke,   *wholly/trouble*

How that Queen Gaynor the bright
    Had slain with grẹte °trẹsoun   *treason*
A swīthẹ nọble Scottish knight
    At the mẹte with strọng °poisoun;   *poison*
940 Therefore a day was tāken right
    That shē sholde fīnd a knight full °boun   *ready*
For her sāke for tō fight
    †Or elles bē brent without ransoun.

When that Launcelot du Lāke
    Had °herde °họlly all this °fare,   *heard/*
Grẹte sọrrow gan hē tō him tāke,   *completely/affair*
    For the queen was in such care,
†And swọre tō venge her of that wrāke,
    That day °yif that hē livand were;   *if he were living*
950 †Then pained hē him his sọrrows tō slāke
    And wex as brēme as any bọre.

Now lẹve wē Launcelot there hē was,
    With the °ermīte in the forest green,   *hermit*
And tell wē forth of the cāse
    That °toucheth Arthur, the king sọ keen.   *concerns*
Sir Gawain on the morn tō counsēl hē °tās,   *takes*
    And °mōrned sọrẹ for the queen;   *mourned*
Into a °towr then hē him has   *tower*
    And ordained the best there them between.

960 And as they in their talking stood
    Tō ordain how it best might bē,

---

943 Or else be burned without rescue.
948 And swore to avenge her for that trouble.
950-51 He exerted himself to ease his sorrow and grew as fierce as any
    wild boar.

A fair river under the towr °yōde,   *went*
    †And soon there-in gonne they see
A little bọte of shāpe full good
    Tō them-ward with the streme gan tē;
There might nọne fairer sail on flood
    Ne better °forged as of tree.   *made of wood*

When King Arthur saw that sight,
    Hē wondred of the rich °apparail   *furnishings*
970 That was about the bọte °ydight;   *arranged*
    So richly was it covered °sanzfail,   *without fail*
                                                                (i.e., indeed)
    †In manner of a vọut with clọthes ydight
    All °shīnand as gold as it gan sail.   *shining*
Then said Sir Gawain the goodẹ knight:
    "This bọte is of a rich °entail."   *fashion*

"For sooth, sir," said the king thọ,
    "Such ọnẹ saw I never ẹre;
Thider I rẹde now that wē gọ;
    Some adventūres shall wē see there,
980 And yif it bē within dight sọ
    As without, or gayer mọre,
I dare °sāvely say there-tō   *safely*
    †Begin-will aunters ẹre ọught yare."

Out of the °towr adown they went,   *tower*
    The King Arthur and Sir Gawain;
Tō the bọte they °yēde withoutẹ stint,   *went without*
                                                                delay
    They twọ alọne, for sooth tō °sayn;   *say*
And when they come there as it °lente,   *remained*
    They behēld it °fast, is nọt tō °laine;   *carefully/hide*
990 A clọth that ọver the bọte was bent
    Sir Gawain lift up, and went in °bain.   *both*

' When they were in, °withouten lẹẹs,   *without lies*
                                                                (truly)
    Full richly arrayed they it °fand,   *found*
And in the middes a fair bed was
    For any king of °Cristen land.   *Christian*

963-65 And immediately they saw in the river a well-made little boat that
    drew toward them with the current.
972 Fashioned from cloth in the shape of a vault.
983 Adventures will begin very soon.

Then as swīthe, ęre they wǫlde °sęse,   *cease*
    The coverlet lift they up with hand;
A dęde woman they °sigh there was,   *saw*
    The fairest maid that might bē fand.

1000 Tō Sir Gawain then said the king:
    "For sooth, dęth was too °unhende,   *discourteous*
When hē wǫlde thus fair a thing
    Thus yonge out of the world °dō wend;   *make go*
For her °beautee, without °lęęsing,   *beauty/lying*
    †I wǫlde fain wite of her kind,
What shē was, this sweet °dęrling,   *darling*
    And in her līfe where shē gan °lende."   *live*

Sir Gawain his °eyen then on her cast   *eyes*
    And behēld her °fast with hertę free,   *carefully*
1010 Sǫ that hē knew well at the last,
    That the Maid of Ascolot was shē,
Which hē some tīme had wooed fast
    His ǫwnę °lēman for tō bē,   *sweetheart*
But shē answerd him ay in hāste
    Tō nǫne but Launcelot wǫlde shē °tē.   *draw*

Tō the king then said Sir Gawain thǫ:
    "Think yē nǫt on this °endres day,   *other day*
When my lādy the queen and wē twǫ
    Stood tōgeder in your play,
1020 Of a maid I tǫld you thǫ,
    That Launcelot loved °paramour ay?"   *as a lover / forever*
"Gawain, for sooth," the king said thǫ,
    "When thou it saidest well think I may."

"For sooth, sir," then said Sir Gawain,
    "This is the maid that I of spāke;
Mǫst in this world, is nǫt tō °laine,   *hide*
    Shē loved Launcelot du Lāke."
"Forsooth," the king then °gan tō sayn,   *did say*
    "Mē reweth the dęth of her for his sāke;
1030 †The enchęsoun wǫlde I wite full fain;
    For sǫrrow I °trow dęth gan her tāke."   *believe*

1005 I would like to know about her family lineage.
1030 I would very much like to know the cause.

Then Sir Gawain, the goode knight,
  Sought about her withoute °stint   *delay*
And fand a purse full °rich aright,   *richly arrayed*
  With gold and °perles that was °ybent;   *pearls/banded*
All empty seemed it nought tō sight;
  That purse full soon in hand hē °hent;   *seized*
A letter there-of then out hē °twight;   *took*
  †Then wite they wolde fain what it ment.

1040 What was there writen wite they wolde,
  And Sir Gawain °it took the king,   *gave it to the king*
And bade him open it that hē sholde.
  So did hē soon, withoute °leesing;   *lying*
Then fand hē when it was unfold
  Both the end and the beginning
(Thus was it writen as mèn mē told)
  Of that fair maidens dying:

"Tō King Arthur and all his knightes
  That °longe tō the Round Tāble,   *belong*
1050 °That courtais been and most of mightes   *who are courteous*
  Doughty and noble, °trew and stāble,   *true*
And most worshipful in alle fightes,
  Tō the needful helping and profitāble,
The Maid of Ascolot °tō rightes   *by right (justly)*
  Sendeth greeting, °withouten fāble;   *without lying (truly)*

"Tō you all my plaint I māke
  Of the wrong that mē is wrought,
But nought in manner tō °undertāke   *claim*
  That any of you sholde mend it ought,
1060 But only I say for this sāke,
  That, though this world were °through sought, *searched through*
†Men sholde nowhere fīnd your māke,
  All noblesse tō fīnd that might bē sought.

"Therefore tō you tō understand
  That for I °trewly many a day   *truly*
Have loved °lēlīest in land,   *most loyally*
  †Dęth hath mē fette of this world away;

1039 Then they wanted to know what it said.
1062-63 Men would nowhere find your equal, though they searched out
    all the nobleness in the world.
1067 Death has fetched me away from this world.

Tō °wite for whom, yif yē °will fonde,   *know/wish to*
    That I so long for in langour lay,   *discover*
1070 Tō say the sooth will I not °wonde,   *delay*
    †For gaines it nought for tō say nay.

"Tō say you the soothe tāle,
    For whom I have suffred this wo,
I say dēth hath mē tāke with °bāle,   *suffering*
    For the noblest knight that may go;
Is none so doughty dintes tō °dēle,   *deal out*
    So °rēal ne so fair there-tō;   *royal*
But so churlish of manners in fēld ne hall,
    Ne know I none of °frēnd ne fo.   *friend nor foe*

1080 "Of fo ne frēnd, the sooth tō say,
    So °unhende of thewes is there none;   *discourteous in manners*
His gentilness was all away,
    All churlish manners hē had in °wone;   *(his) possession*
For no thing that I °coude pray,   *could*
    Kneeling ne weeping with °rewful mone,   *pitiful moan*
Tō bē my lēman hē said ever nay,
    And said shortly hē wolde have none.

"°Forthy, lordes, for his sāke   *Therefore*
    I took tō herte grete sorrow and care,
1090 So at the last dēth gan mē tāke,
    So that I might live no more;
For trewe loving had I such °wrāke   *pain*
    †And was of bliss ybrought all bare;
All was for Launcelot du Lāke,
    Tō wite wīsely for whom it were."

When that King Arthur, the noble king,
    Had °redde the letter and °ken the nāme,   *read/learned*
Hē said tō Gawain, without leesing,
    That Launcelot was gretly tō blāme,
1100 And had him won a °reprōving,   *reproof*
    For ever, and a wicked fāme;
Sithe shē dīed for grete loving,
    That hē her refūsed it may him shāme.

1071 For denying it gains nothing.
1093 And was made bare of all bliss (i.e., made unhappy).

Tō the king then said Sir Gawain:
  †"I gabbed on him this ender day,
That hē lǫnged, when I gan sayn,
  With lādy other with some other maye.
But sooth then said yē, is nǫt tō °laine,   *hide*
  †That hē nǫlde nǫt his lovę lay
1110 In sǫ lǫw a plāce in vain,
  But on a prīs lādy and a gay."

"Sir Gawain," said the king thǫ,
  "What is now thy bestę rędè?
How may wē with this maiden dō?"
  Sir Gawain said: "°Sǫ God mē speed,   *As God may save me*
Yif that yē will assent there-tō,
  †Worshipfully wē shull her lędè
Intō the °palais and bury her sǫ   *palace*
  As °falles a dūkes dǫughter in-deed."   *befits*

1120 There-tō the king assented soon;
  Sir Gawain °did men soon bē °yare,   *commanded/ ready*
†And worshipfully, as fell tō dōn,
  Intō the °palais they her bǫre.   *palace*
The king then tǫld, withoutę °lǫne,   *concealment*
  Tō all his barons, less and mǫre,
How Launcelot °nǫlde nǫt graunt her boon,   *would not grant her plea*
  Therefore she dīed for sǫrrow and care.

Tō the queen then went Sir Gawain
  And gan tō tell her all the cāse:
1130 "For sooth, mādāme," hē gan tō °sayn,   *say*
  †"I yēld me guilty of a trespās.
I °gabbed on Launcelot, is nǫt tō °laine,   *lied about/hide*
  †Of that I tǫld you in this plāce;
I said that his °bidding bain   *lover (ready at his bidding)*
  The dūkes dǫughter of Ascolot was.

1105-07 I lied about him the other day when I said that he belonged to
  a lady or to some other maid.
1109-11 That he would not waste his love in so low a place (a mere
  maiden) but would rather love some noble and gay lady.
1117 We shall honorably take her.
1122 And honorably, as was fitting to do.
1131 I confess myself guilty of an offense.
1133 Concerning what I told you in this place.

"Of Ascolot that maiden free
   I said you shē was his lēman;
†That I sọ gabbed it reweth mē,
   And all the sooth now tell I can;
1140 †Hē nọlde her nọt, wē mowe well see;
   For-thy dẹde is that whīte as swan;
This letter there-of warrant will bē;
   She °plaineth on Launcelot tō °ẹchẹ man."   *complains about/ every*

The queen was °wrọth as wind,   *angry*
   And tō Sir Gawain said shē then:
"For sooth, sir, thou were too unkīnd
   †Tō gabbẹ sọ upon any man,
°But thou haddest wiste the sooth in mīnd,   *unless you knew*
   Whether that it were sooth or nọne;
1150 Thy courtaisy was all behīnd
   †When thou thọ sawes first began.

     honor/damaged greatly
"Thy °worship thou °undidest grẹtlich,
   °Such wrọng tō wīte that goodẹ knight;   *so wrongly to blame*
†I trow that hē ne aguilt thee never much
   Why that thou ọughtest with nọ right
Tō gabbe on him sọ vilainlich,
   Thus behīnd him, out of his sight.
†And, sir, thou ne wọst nọt right wīselich
   What harm hath falle there-of and might.

1160 †"I wēnd thou haddest bē stable and trew
   And full of all courtaisy,
But now mē think thy manners new;
   They °bēn all turned tō °vilainy,   *are/churlishness*
Now thou on knightes mākest thy °glewe   *tricks*
   Tō liē upon them for envy;
Whọ that thee °worshippeth, it may them rew;   *honors*
   Therefore, °devoied my company!"   *leave*

1138 It pains me that I so lied.
1140-41 He did not want her, as we can well see, and therefore that
   maiden, as white as a swan, is dead.
1147 To lie so about any man.
1151 When you first began to say those words.
1154-56 I believe that he never wronged you so much that you ought to
   lie about him so unjustly and so churlishly.
1158-59 And, sir, you do not know right wisely (i.e., do not realize) what
   harm has and could yet come from what you said.
1160 I supposed that you had been (were) stable and true.

Sir Gawain then °slyly went away;   *wisely*
    Hē °sigh the queen °agrēved sǫre;   *saw/sorely*
                          aggrieved
1170 Nǫ mǫre tō her then wǫlde hē say,
    †But trowed her wrath have ever mǫre.
The queen then, as shē nigh °wōde were,   *crazy*
    Wringed her handes and said: "Węle-away!
Alas! in world that I was °bǫre!   *born*
    That I am wretched well say I may!"

"Herte, alas! Why were thou °wōde   *crazy*
    Tō °trowe that Launcelot du Lāke   *believe*
Were sǫ false and °fikel of mood   *fickle*
    Another lēman than thee tō tāke?
1180 Nay, certes, for all this worldes good,
    He nǫlde tō mē have wrǫught such °wrāke!"   *pain*

(At this point one leaf from the manuscript has been lost; evidently it told of the burial of the Maid of Ascolot and of the queen's distress, the material in chapters 74 and 78 of the French *Mort Artu*, our poet's source. Probably not more than ninety lines are missing, but I follow the line-numbering in Bruce's edition.)

Tō find a man for her tō fight
    †Or elles yēld her tō bē brent;
1320 If shē were on a °quest of knightes   *judgment*
    †Well shē wiste she sholde bē shent;
Thǫugh that shē aguilt had nǫ wight,
    Nǫ lenger līfe might her bē lent.

The king then sighed and °gāve him ill,   *made himself ill*
    And tō Sir Gawain then hē yēde,
Tō Bors de Gawnes and Līonel,
    Tō Ector that doughty was in deed,
And asked if any °were in will   *intended*
    Tō help him in that mikel need.
1330 The queen on knees before them fell,
    That nigh out of her wit shē yēde.

1171 But expected to have her wrath forevermore.
1319 Or else surrender herself to be burned at the stake.
1321-23 She knew well that she must be put to death shamefully; although she had no touch of guilt, she could no longer be granted life.

The knightes answerd with little pride—
   Their hertes was full of sǫrrow and wǫ—
Said: "All wē saw and sat besīde
   The knight when shē with poison °slogh,   *slew*
And sithe, in herte is nǫt tō hīde,
   Sir Gawain ǫver the bōrde him °drow;   *drew*
°Again the right wē will nǫt rīde,   *against*
   Wē saw the sooth °verily ynow."   *very truly*

1340 The queenė wept and sighed sǫre;
   Tō Bors de Gawnes went shē thǫ,
On knees before him fell shē there,
   That nigh her hertė °brast in twǫ;   *burst*
"Lǫrd Bors," shē said, "thīne °ǫre!   *mercy*
   Tōday I shall tō dėthė gǫ,
°But yif thy worthy will were   *unless*
   Tō bring my līfe out of this wǫ."

Bors de Gawnes stillė stood,
   And °wrǫthe away his °eyen went;   *angrily/eyes*
1350 †"Mādāme," hē said, "By Cross on °Rood,   *cross*
   Thou art well worthy tō bē brent!
The nǫblest body of flesh and blood,
   That ever was yet in erthė °lente,   *remained*
For thy will and thy wicked °mood,   *mind*
   Out of our company is went."

Then shē wept and °gāve her ill,   *made herself sick*
   And tō Sir Gawain then shē yēde;
On knees down before him fell,
   That nigh out of her wit shē yēde;
1360 "Mercy!" she crīed loud and shrill,
   "Lǫrd, as I nǫ guilt have of this deed,
°Yif it were thy worthy will   *(I ask) if it*
   Tōday tō help mē in this need?"

Gawain answerd with little prīde;
   His hertė was full of sǫrrow and wǫ:
"Dāme, saw I nǫt and sat besīde
   The knight when thou with poison °slogh?   *slew*

1350 [See note on line 764.]

And sithe, in herte is nǫt tō hīde,
   Myself ǫver the bōrde him °drow.   *drew*
1370 Again the right will I nǫt rīde;
   I saw the sooth °very ynow."   *very truly*

Then shē went tō Līonel,
   That ever had been her ǫwnę knight;
On knees adown before him fell,
   That nigh shē lostę main and might.
"Mercy," shē crīed loud and shrill,
   "Lǫrd, as I ne have °aguilt nǫ °wight,   *of guilt/bit*
°Yif it were thy worthy will   *(I ask) if it*
   For my līfe tō tāke this fight?"

1380 †"Mādāme, how may thou tō us tāke
   And wǫt thyself sǫ witterly
That thou hast Launcelot du Lāke
   Brǫught out of ower company?
Wē may sigh and mǫning māke
   When wē see knightes keen in °cry;   *company*
By Him That mē tō man gan °shāpe,   *create*
   Wē are glad that thou it °abye!"   *suffer*

Then full sǫre shē gan °her drēde;   *fear for herself*
   Well shē wiste her līfe was °lorn;   *lost*
1390 Loudę gan shē weep and °grēde,   *cry*
   And Ector kneeles shē beforn:
"For Him That on the °rood gan °spręde   *cross/spread*
   And for us bǫre the crown of thorn,
Ector, help now in this need,
   Or, certes, tōday my līfe is lorn!"

†"Mādāme, how may thou tō us tāke,
   Or how sholde I for thee fight?
Tāke thee now Launcelot du Lāke,
   That ever has been thīne ǫwnę knight.
1400 My dęrę brother, for thy sāke
   I ne shall him never see with sight!
Cursed bē hē that the °batail tāke   *battle*
   Tō sāve thy līfe again the right!"

1380-81 Madame, how can you come to us when you know so well.
1396 [See 1380.]

There wolde no man the batail tāke;
　　The queen went tō her chāmber so;
Sọ dolefully °mọne gan shē māke,   *moan*
　　That nigh her hertẹ brast in twọ;
For sọrrow gan shē shiver and quāke,
　　And said: "Alas and wẹle-a-wọ!
1410　Why °nadde I now Launcelot du Lāke?   *do I not have*
　　All the court nọlde mē nọt °slọ!   *slay*

"°Īvel have I °beset the deed,   *evilly (i.e.,*
                                                                     uselessly)/used
　　That I have °worshipped sọ many a knight,   *honored*
[And I have nọ man in my need]
　　For my love dare tāke a fight.
Lọrd, King of allẹ °thēde,   *nations*
　　That all the world shall °rẹde and °right,   *advise/direct*
†Launcelot Thou sāve and heed,
　　Sithe I ne shall never him see with sight."

The queenẹ wept and °gāve her ill;   *made herself*
                                                                     sick
1420　When shē saw the fīre was yare,
Then °mōrned shē full still.   *mourned*
　　Tō Bors de Gawnes went shē there,
Besọught him, yif it were his will,
　　Tō help her in her mikel care;
In swooning shē before him fell;
　　The wordes might shē spẹke nọ mọre.

When Bors saw the queen sọ bright,
　　Of her hē °haddẹ grẹte pitee;   *had*
In his armes hē hēld her up-right,
1430　Bade her of good comfort bē:
"Mādāme, °but there come a better knight   *unless*
　　That wọlde the °batail tāke for thee,   *battle*
I shall myselfẹ for thee fight,
　　Whīle any līfe may last in mē."

Then was the queenẹ wonder blīthe,
　　That Bors de Gawnes wọlde for her fight,
†That nẹr for joy shē swooned swīthe,
　　But as that hē her hēld up-right;

────────────────────────────
1417 May you save and care for Lancelot.
1437-38 Because of her joy she promptly almost fainted, except that he
　held her upright.

Tō her chamber hē led her blīthe,
1440   Tō lādīes and tō maidens bright,
And bade shē sholde it °nǫ man kīthe,   *tell no man of it*
    Til hē were armed and °rędy dight.   *ready*

Bors, that was bǫld and keen,
    Clēped all his other knightes,
And tooken counsēl them between,
    The bestę that they °couthe and °might,   *knew how/could (do)*
How that hē hath °hight the queen   *promised*
    That ilkę day for her tō fight
Against Sir Mador, full of °teen,   *anger*
1450   Tō sāve her līfe, yif that hē might.

The knightes answerd with wǫ and °wrāke   *pain*
    And said they wistę °witterly   *certainly*
That "Shē hath Launcelot du Lāke
    Brǫught out of °ower company.   *our*
†Nis nǫne that nǫlde this batail tāke
    Ęre shē had any vilainy,
But wē will nǫt sǫ glad her māke,
    †Before wē ne suffer her tō bē sǫrry."

Bors and Līonel the knight,
1460   Ector, that doughty was of deed,
Tō the forest then went they right
    Their °orisons at the chapel tō °bēde   *prayers/offer*
Tō our Lǫrd God, all full of might,
    †That day sholde lēne him well tō speed,
A grāce tō vanquish the fight;
    Of Sir Mador they had gręte drēde.

As they cāme by the forest sīde,
    Their °orisons for tō māke,   *prayers*
The nǫblest knight then saw they rīde
1470   That ever was in ęrthę °shāpe;   *created*
His °lorēme °lęmed all with prīde;   *reins/gleamed*
    Steed and armour all was °blāke;   *white*

1455-56 There is no one who would have refused this battle before her
    behavior became criminal.
1458 Before we allow her to be sorry. [The "ne" is omitted in translation.
    See Introduction, p. xv.]
1464-65 That He might grant him (Bors) success, give him the grace to
    win the battle.

His nāme is nǫught tō °hęle and hīde: *conceal*
   Hē hight Sir Launcelot du Lāke!

What wonder was though they were blīthe,
   When they their māster see with sight!
On knees fell they as swīthe,
   And thanked all tō God All-might.
Joy it was tō °hēre and °līthe   *hear/listen to*
1480 The meeting of the nǫble knight;
And after hē asked alsǫ swīthe:
   "How now fares my lādy bright?"

Bors then tǫld him all the right,
   It was nǫ lenger for tō hīde,
How there dīed a Scottish knight,
   At the °męte the queen beside: *meal*
"Tōday, sir, is her dęth all dight,
   It may nǫ lenger bē tō bīde,
And I for her have tāke the fight.

1490 "Sir Mador, strǫng thǫugh that hē bē,
   I °hǫpe hē shall well prōve his might."   *expect*
"Tō the court now wend yē three
   And °recomfort my lādy bright;   *comfort*
But look yē spęke nǫ word of mē;
   I will come as a °strānge knight."   *foreign*

Launcelot, that was mikel of might,
   Abīdes in the forest green;
Tō the courte went thēse other knightes
   For tō °recomfort the queen.   *comfort*
1500 Tō māke her glad with all their might
   Gręte joy they māde them between;
†For-why shē ne sholde drēde nǫ wight,
   Of good comfort they bade her °bēn.   *be*

Bōrdes were set and clǫthes spredde;
   The king himself is gǫne tō sit;
The queen is tō the tāble led,
   With cheekes that were wan and wet;

1502 So that she should fear nothing.

Of sorrow were they never unsad;
   Might they neither drink ne ęte;
1510 The queen of dęthe was sǫre °adredde,   *afraid*
   That grimly tęres gan shē let.

And as they were at the °thriddę mese,   *third course*
   The king and all the court bydēne,
Sir Mador all rędy was,
   With helm and shēld and hauberk sheen;
Amǫng them all before the °dēse,   *dais (raised*
   Hē blǫweth out upon the queen   *platform)*
Tō have his right withouten lęęs,
   As were the °covenantes them between.   *agreements*

1520 The king looked on all his knightes;
   Was hē never yet sǫ wǫ;
Saw hē never ǫne °him dight   *prepare himself*
   Against Sir Mador for tō gǫ.
Sir Mador swǫre by Goddes might,
   As hē was man of hertę °thrǫ,   *fierce*
But yif hē hāstely have his right
   Amǫng them all hē sholde her °slǫ.   *slay*

Then spāke the king of mikel might,
   That ay was courtais and hende:
1530 "Sir, let us ęte and sithen us dight;
   This day nis nǫt yet gǫne tō the end.
Yet might there comę such a knight,
   Yif Goddes will were him tō send,
Tō findę thee thy fill of fight
   Ęre the sun tō groundę wend.

Bors then °lǫugh on Līonel;   *laughed*
   Wiste nǫ man of their hertes word;
His chāmber anǫn hē wendes til,
   Withoute any other word,
1540 Armed him at all his will,
   With helm and hauberk, °spęre and sword;   *spear*
Again then comes hē full still
   And set him down tō the bōrde.

The °tęres ran on the kinges knee   *tears*
   For joy that hē saw Bors °adight;   *prepared*

Up hē rǫse with hertę free
  And Bors in armes °clippes right,   *embraces*
And said: "Bors, God °foryēld it thee,   *reward you for it*
  In this need that thou wǫlde fight;
1550 †Well acquītest thou it mē
  That I have °worshipped any knight!"   *honored*

Then as Sir Mador loudest spāke
  The queen of tręsoun tō °becall,   *accuse*
Comes Sir Launcelot du Lāke,
  °Rīdand right intō the hall.   *riding directly*
His steed and armour all was °blāke,   *white*
  His vīsor over his °eyen °fall;   *eyes/fallen*
Many a man began tō quāke;
  °Adrēde of him nigh were they all.   *afraid*

1560 Then spāke the king, mikel of might,
  That hendę was in °īch a sīthe: *every occasion*
"Sir, is it your will tō °light,   *alight*
  Ęte and drink and māke you blīthe?"
Launcelot spāke as a °strängę knight: *foreign*
  "Nay, sir," hē said as swīthe,
"I herde tell hēre of a fight;
  I come tō sāve a lādyes līfe.

"Īvel hath the queen °beset her deedes   *employed*
  That shē hath worshipped many a knight,
1570 And shē hath nǫ man in her needes
  That for her līfe dare tāke a fight.
†Thou that her of tręsoun grēdes
  Hāstely that thou bē dight;
Out of thy wit thǫugh that thou °wēdes,   *run mad*
  Tōday thou shalt prōve all thy might."

Then was Sir Mador alsǫ blīthe
  As fowl of day after the night;
Tō his steed hē went that sīthe,
  As man that was of muchę might.
1580 Tō the fēld then rīde they swīthe;
  Them followes both king and knight,

1550 Well do you repay me for it.
1572-73 You who accuse her of treason, quickly see that you are ready to
fight.

The batail for tō see and °līthe;   *hear*
   Saw never nǫ man strǫnger fight!

Unhorsed were bǫthe knightes keen,
   They °metten with sǫ muche main,   *met*
And sithe they fǫught with swordes keen,
   Bǫth on foot, the sooth tō °sayn.   *say*
In all the batailes that Launcelot had been,
   †With hard acountres him again,
1590 In pointe had hē never been
   Sǫ nigh-hand for tō have been slain.

There was sǫ wonder strǫng a fight,
   †Q foot nǫlde nǫuther flee ne found,
From °lǫwe noon til lāte night,   *low noon (about*
   But °given many a wǫful wound.   *ten a.m.)*
Launcelot then gāve a dint with might;   *they give*
   Sir Mador falles at last tō ground;
"Mercy!" crīes that nǫble knight,
   For hē was sēke and sǫre unsound.

1600 Thǫugh Launcelot were brēme as bǫre,
   Full sternely hē gan up stand;
†Q dint wǫlde hē smīte nǫ mǫre;
   His sword hē threw out of his hand.
Sir Mador by God then swǫre:
   "I have fǫught in many a land,
With knightes bǫth less and mǫre,
   And never yet ęre my match I fand;

"But, Sir, a prayer I wǫlde māke,
   For thing that yē love mǫst on līfe,
1610 And for Our Sweete °Lady sāke,   *Lady's (i.e.,*
   Your nāme that yē wǫlde mē °kīthe."   *Virgin Mary's)*
Launcelot gan his vīsor up tāke,   *tell*
   And hendely him shewed that sīthe;
When hē saw Sir Launcelot du Lāke,
   Was never man on °molde sǫ blīthe.   *earth*

1589 With hard encounters (attacks) against him.
1593 Neither would flee nor advance a single foot.
1602 He would not strike one more blow.

"Lọrd," then said hē, "Wẹle is mē,
  †Mīne avauntement that I may māke
That I have stande ọne dint of thee,
  And fọughten with Launcelot du Lāke;
1620 My brōthers dẹth forgiven bē
  Tō the queen for thy sāke."
Launcelot him °kist with hertẹ free,   *kissed*
  And in his armes gan him up tāke.

King Arthur then loudẹ spāke
  Amọng his knightes tō the queen:
"°Yā, yonder is Launcelot du Lāke,   *yea*
  Yif I him ever with sight have seen!"
They rīden and °ronne then for his sāke,   *run*
  The king and all his knightes keen;
1630 In his armes hē gan him tāke;
  The king him °kist and court bydēne.   *kissed*

Then was the queenẹ glad ynow,
  When shē saw Launcelot du Lāke,
That nigh for joy she fell in °swough,   *swoon*
  °But as the lọrdes her gan up tāke.   *except that*
The knightes allẹ wept and °lọughe   *laughed*
  For joy as they tōgeder spāke;
With Sir Mador, withouten wọ,
  Full soon °acordement gonne they māke.   *reconcilement*

1640 It was nọ lenger for tō abīde
  But tō the castle they rọde as swīthe,
With °trompes and with mikel prīde,   *trumpeters*
  That joy it was tō hēre and °līthe;   *listen to*
Thọugh Sir Mador might nọt °gọ ne rīde,   *walk*
  Tō the court is hē brọught that °sīthe,   *time*
And knightes upon īch a sīde
  Tō māke him bọth glad and blīthe.

The °squīers then were tāken all,   *squires*
  And they are °put in hardẹ pain,   *i.e., tortured*

1617-18 That I may make the boast that I have stood one blow from you.
[Compare Priamus' words to Gawain in the *Alliterative Morte Arthure*, ll. 2646–49.]

1650 °Which that had served in the hall   *those who*
    When the knight was with poisun slain.
  †There hē graunted among them all
    (It might no lenger bē tō °laine)   *hide*
How in an apple hē °did the gall,   *put the poison*
    And had it °thought tō Sir Gawain.   *intended*

When Sir Mador herde all the right,
    That no guilt had the lādy sheen,
For sorrow hē lost main and might
    And on knees fell before the queen.
1660 Launcelot then him hēld up right,
    For love that was them between;
He °kist both king and knight   *kissed*
    And sithen all the court bydēne.

The °squīer then was °dōne tō shende,   *squire/put to death*
    As it was bothe law and right,
°Drawen and °honged and °for-brende,   *drawn/hanged/burned*
    Before Sir Mador, the noble knight.
In the °castel they gonne forth °lende,   *castle/remain*
    The Joyous Gard then was it °hight;   *called*
1670 Launcelot, that was so hende,
    They honoured him with all their might.

A tīme befell, sooth tō °sayn,   *say*
    The knightes stood in chāmber and spāke,
Both Gaheriet and Sir Gawain,
  †And Mordred, that mikel couthe of wrāke.
"Alas!" then said Sir Agravain,
    "How false men shall wē us māke?
And how long shall wē °hele and laine   *conceal and hide*
    The tresoun of Launcelot du Lāke?

1680 "Well we °wote, withouten ween,   *know, without doubt*
    The king Arthur our °eme sholde bē,   *uncle*
And Launcelot līes by the queen;
    Again the king traitour is hē,
And that wote all the court bydēne,
    And īche day it hēre and see;

1652 One among all the squires there admitted.
1675 And Mordred, who knew much of trouble-making.

Tō the king wē sholde it °mẹne,   *tell*
  Yif yē will dō by the counsēl of mē."

"Well wọte wē," said Sir Gawain,
  "That wē are of the kinges kin,
1690 And Launcelot is sọ mikel of main
  That suchẹ wordes were better °blinne.   *stopped*
Well wọt thou, brōther Agravain,
  Thereof sholde wē but harmes win;
Yet were it better tō hẹle and laine
  Than war and wrāke thus tō begin.

"Well wọt thou, brōther Agravain,
  Launcelot is hardy knight and °thrọ;   *fierce*
King and court had oft been slain
  °Nadde hē been better than wē mọ,   *had he not*
1700 And sithen might I never sayn
  The love that has been between us twọ;
Launcelot shall I never °betrayn,   *betray*
  Behīnd his back tō bē his fọ.

"Launcelot is kinges son full good,
  And theretō hardy knight and bọld,
†And sithen, and him need bestood,
  Many a land °wọlde with him họld.   *i.e., be his ally*
Shed there sholde bē mikel blood
  For this tāle, yif it were tọld;
1710 Sir Agravain, hē were full wōde,
  That such a thing beginnẹ wọlde."

Then °thus-gātes as the knightes stood,   *in this manner*
  Gawain and all the other press,
In cọme the king with mīldẹ mood;
  Gawain then said: "Fellọwes, °pẹẹs!"   *be still*
The king for wrath was nighẹ wōde
  For tō witẹ what it was;
Agravain swọre by Cross and °Rood: *cross*
  "I shall it you tell withoutẹ lẹẹs."

1720 Gawain tō his chāmber went;
  †Of this tāle nọlde hē nọught hēre;

1706 And, moreover, if he had need.
1721 He did not want to hear any of this tale.

Gaheriet and Gaheries of his assent,
   With their brōther went they there;
Well they wiste that all was °shent,   *lost*
   And Sir Gawain by God then °swēre: *did swear*
"Hēre now is māde a °comsement   *commencement*
                               (beginning)
   That °bēth nǫt finished many a yēre."   *will not be*

Agravain tǫld all bydēne
   Tō the king with °simple cheer,   *innocent*
                             expression
1730 How Launcelot °ligges by the queen,   *lies*
   And sǫ has dōne full many a yēre,
   And that wǫt all the court bydēne
      And īchę day it see and hēre:
"And wē have false and traitours been
   That wē ne wǫlde never tō you °diskēre."   *discover (reveal)*

"Alas!" then said the kingę there,
   "Certes, that were grętę pitee;
†Sǫ as man nadde never yet mǫre
   Of beautee ne of °bountee,   *generosity*
1740 Ne man in world was never yet ęre
   Of sǫ mikel nǫbilitee.
Alas, full grętę dole it were
   In him sholde any tręsoun bē!

"But sithe it is sǫ, withouten fail,
   Sir Agravain, sǫ God thee ręde,
What were now thy best counsēl,
   For tō tāke him °with the deed?   *in the act*
Hē is man of such °apparail,   *accomplishments*
   Of him I have full mikel drēde;
1750 All the court nǫlde him assail
   Yif hē were armed upon his steed."

"Sir, yē and all the court bydēne
   Wendeth tōmorrow on hunting right,
And sithen send word tō the queen
   That yē will dwell °without all night,   *outside (the*
                             court)
And I and other twelve knightes keen
   Full °prively wē shall us dight;   *secretly*
Wē shall him have °withouten ween   *doubtless*
   Tōmorrow ęre any day bē light."

1738 No man ever had more.

1760 On the morrow with all the court bydēne
          The king gan on hunting rīde,
       And sithen hē sent word tō the queen
          That hē wǫlde all night out abīde.
       Agravain with twelve knightes keen
          °Atte hǫme beleft that ilkę tīde   *at home*
                                                              remained
       Of all the day they were nǫt seen,
          Sǫ °privily they gonne them hīde.   *secretly*

       Thǫ was the queenę wonder blīthe
          That the king wǫlde at the forest dwell;
1770 Tō Launcelot shē sent as swīthe
          And bade that hē sholde come °her til.   *to her*
       Sir Bors de Gawnes bęgan tō °līthe,   *listen*
          †Thǫugh his herte līked ill;
       "Sir," hē said, "I wǫlde you °kīthe   *tell*
          A word, °yif that it were your will.   *i.e., if you please*

       "Sir, tōnight I rędę yē °dwell;   *remain (here)*
          I drēde there bē some tręsoun dight
       °With Agravain, that is sǫ °fell,   *by/fierce*
          That waites you bǫth day and night.
1780 †Of all that yē have gǫne her til,
          Ne grēved mē never yet nǫ wight,
       Ne never yet gāve mīne herte tō ill,
          Sǫ mikel as it dōth tōnight."

       "Bors," hē said, "hǫldę still;
          Such wordes are nǫt tō kīthe;
       I will wend my lādy til,
          Some new tīthandes for tō līthe;
       †I ne shall nǫught but wite her will;
          Look yē make you glad and blīthe;
1790 Certainly I °nill nǫt dwell,   *will not remain*
          But come again tō you all swīthe."

       †For-why hē wēnd have comen soon,
          For tō dwell had hē nǫt thǫught,

       ¹⁷⁷³ Although it ill pleased his heart.
       ¹⁷⁸⁰⁻⁸³ Of all the nights that you have gone to her, none ever bothered
          me in any way or made my heart so sick as this one does tonight.
       ¹⁷⁸⁸ I shall do nothing but find out what she wants.
       ¹⁷⁹² Because he expected to come back immediately.

Nǫne armour hē °did him upon   *put upon himself*
   But a rǫbe all °singlē wrǫught;   *uniquely made*
In his hand a sword he °fōne,   *grasped*
   †Of trẹsoun dredde hē him right nǫught;
There was nǫ man under the moon
   Hē wēnd with harm durst him have sǫught.

1800 When hē cǫme tō the lādy sheen
   Hē °kist and °clipped that sweetẹ °wight;   *kissed/em-
braced/creature*
For sooth, they never wǫldẹ °ween   *expect*
   That any trẹsoun was there dight;
Sǫ mikel love was them between
   That they nǫt departẹ might;
Tō bed hē gǫeth with the queen,
   And there hē thǫught tō dwell all night.

†Hē was nǫt busked in his bed,
   Launcelot in the queenes °bowr,   *bower (bedroom)*
1810 Come Agravain and Sir Mordred,
   With twelvẹ knightes °stiff in stour;   *bold in battle*
Launcelot of trẹsoun they °begredde,   *accused*
   Calld him false and kinges traitour,
And hē sǫ strǫngly was °bestedde,   *set upon*
   There-in hē had nǫne armour.

"Wẹle-away," then said the queen,
   "Launcelot, what shall °worthe of us twǫ?   *become*
The love that hath been us between,
   Tō such ending that it sholde gǫ!
1820 °With Agravain, that is sǫ keen,   *by*
   That night and day hath been our fǫe,
Now I wǫt, withouten ween,
   That all our °wẹle is turned tō wǫ!"   *joy*

"Lādy," hē said, "thou must °blinne;   *stop*
   †"Wīde I wǫt thēse wordes bēth rīfe;
But is hēre any armour in
   That I may have tō sāve my līfe?"

1797-99 He had absolutely no fear of treason (betrayal); he supposed
   there was no man on earth who would dare attempt to do him harm.
1808 He had hardly gotten in his bed.
1825 I know that this news will be widely told.

"Certes, nay," shē said then,
   †"This aunter is sǫ wonder strīfe
1830 That I ne may tō nǫne armour win
   Helm ne hauberk, sword ne knīfe."

Ever Agravain and Sir Mordred
   Calld him °recrēant false knight,   *perjured*
Bade him rīse out of his bed,
   For hē °moste °needes with them fight.   *must/*
                                           by necessity
In his rǫbe then hē him °cledde,   *clad*
   Thǫugh hē nǫne armour gettę might;
Wrǫthly out his sword hē °gredde;   *drew*
   The chāmber door hē °set up right.   *stood close to*

1840 An armed knight before in went
   And wēnd Launcelot well tō slǫ,
But Launcelot gāve him such a dint,
   That tō the groundę gan hē gǫ;
The other all again then °stent;   *stopped*
   After him °durste follow nǫ mǫ;   *dared*
Tō the chāmber door hē °sprent   *leaped*
   And °clasped it with °barres twǫ.   *locked/two bars*

The knight that Launcelot has slain,
   His armour fand hē fair and bright;
1850 Hāstely hē hath °them °off-drayn   *the armor/*
                                          drawn off
   And there-in himselfę dight.
"Now knǫw thou well, Sir Agravain,
   Thou prisouns mē nǫ mǫre tōnight!"
Out then sprang hē with mikel main,
   Himself against them all tō fight.

Launcelot then smǫte with hertę good;
   Wite yē well, withouten lęęs,
Sir Agravain tō dęthę °yōde,   *went*
   And sithen all the other press;
1860 Was nǫne sǫ strǫng that him withstood,
   °By hē had māde a little °ręse,   *by the time/*
                                          attack
But Mordred fled as hē were wōde,
   Tō sāve his life full fain hē was.

1829-30 Our luck is so very bad that I can get to no armor.

Launcelot tō his chămber °yōde,   *went*
  Tō Bors and tō his other knightes;
Bors, armed, before him stood;
  Tō °beddę yet was hē nǫt dight.   *bed*
The knightes for °fęre was nighę wōde,   *fear*
  Sǫ were they °dreched all that night;   *disturbed by dreams*
1870 But blīthę °wexed they in their mood   *grew*
  When they their master saw with sight.

"Sir," said Bors, the hardy knight,
  "After you have wē thǫught full lǫng;
Tō beddę durst I mē nǫt dight,
  For drēde yē had some aunter strǫng;
Our knightes have °bē dreched tōnight   *been disturbed by dreams*
  That some nāked out of beddę sprǫng,
For-thy wē were full sǫre affright,
  Lest some tręsoun were us amǫng."

1880 "Yā, Bors, drēdę thee nǫ wight,
  But bēth of hertę good and bǫld,
And swīthe awāken up all my knightes
  And look which willę with us hǫld;
Look they bē armed and rędy dight,
  For it is sooth that thou mē tǫld;
Wē have °begonne this ilkę night   *begun*
  That shall bring many a man full cǫld."

Bors then spāke with °drēry mood: *dreary*
  "Sir," hē said, "sithe it is sǫ,
1890 Wē shall bē of hertes good,
  After the węle tō tāke the wǫ."
The knightes °sprent as they were wōde,   *leaped*
  And tō their °harnēs gonne they gǫ;   *harness (equipment)*
At the morrow armed before him stood
  An °hundreth knightes and squīers mǫ.   *hundred*

When they were armed and rędy dight,
  °A softę pās forth gonne they rīde,   *at a gentle pace*
As men that were of mikel might,
  Tō a forest there besīde.
1900 Launcelot °arrayes all his knightes,   *arranges in formation*
  And there they °lodgen them tō bīde,   *lodge*
Til they herde of the lādy bright,
  What aunter of her sholde betīde.

Mordred then took a way full °gain,   *direct*
    And tō the forest went hē right,
His aunters tǫld, for sooth tō sayn,
    That were befallen that ilkę night.
"Mordred, have yē that traitour slain,
    Or how have yē with him dight?"
1910 "Nay, sir, but dęde is Agravain,
    And sǫ are all our other knightes."

When it herde Sir Gawain,
    That was sǫ hardy knight and bǫld:
"Alas! Is my brōther slain?"
    Sǫre his herte began tō °cǫlde: *grow cold*
"I warned well Sir Agravain,
    Ęre ever yet this tāle was tǫld,
Launcelot was sǫ much of main
    Against him was °strǫng tō hǫld."   *i.e., difficult*

1920 It was nǫ lenger for tō bīde;
    King and all his knightes keen
Took their counsēl in that tīde,
    What was best °dō with the queen.   *to do*
It was nǫ lenger for tō bīde;
    That day °forbrent sholde shē bēn.   *burned to death*

The fīre then māde they in the fēld;
    There-tō they brǫught that lādy free;
All that ever might °wēpen wēld   *weapon*
    About her armed for tō bē.
1930 Gawain, that stiff was under shēld,
    Gaheriet, ne Gaheries ne wǫlde nǫt see;
In their chāmber they them hēld;
    Of her they haddę gręte pitee.

The king Arthur that ilkę tīde
    Gawain and Gaheries for sent;
Their answers were nǫt for tō hīde;
    †They ne wǫlde nǫt bē of his assent;
Gawain wǫlde never bē nęr besīde
    There any woman sholde bē °brent;   *burned*
1940 Gaheriet and Gaheries with little prīde,
    All unarmed thider they went.

1937 They would not agree with him.

†A squīer gan tho tīthandes līthe,
  That Launcelot tō court hath sent;
Tō the forest hē went as swīthe,
  There Launcelot and his folk was °lente,   *stayed*
Bade them come and °hāste blīthe: *hasten quickly*
  "The queen is ledde tō bē brent!"
And they tō horse and armes swīthe,
  And īch one before other °sprent.   *leaped*

1950 The queen by the fīre stood,
  †And in her smok all redy was;
Lordinges was there many and good,
  And grete powēr, withouten lees;
Launcelot sprent as hē were wōde;
  Full soone parted hē the press;
Was none so stiff before him stood
  °By hē had made a little °rese.   *By the time/ attack*

There was no steel stood them again,
  Though fought they but a little °stound;   *time*
1960 Lordinges that were much of main,
  Many good were brought tō ground;
Gaheriet and Gaheries both were slain
  With many a doleful dethes wound;
The queen they took, withoute laine,
  And tō the forest gonne they °found.   *go*

The tīthinges is tō the kinge brought,
  How Launcelot has °tān away the queen: *taken*
"Such wo as there is wrought!
  Slain are all our knightes keen!"
1970 Down hē fell and swooned oft;
  Grete dole it was tō hēre and °seen;   *see*
So ner his herte the sorrow sought,
  †Almost his life wolde no man ween.

"Jēsū Crīst! What may I sayn?
  In erthe was never man so wo;

1942-43 A squire whom Lancelot has sent to court heard that news.
1951 [The smock is a loose, usually white, simple sleeveless dress over
  which the other garments were put; the counterpart of a modern slip,
  though it would usually show beneath the vest, sleeves, cloaks, and
  such that were put over it.]
1973 Almost no one expected him to live.

Such knightes as there are slain,
  In all this world there is no mo.
Let no man telle Sir Gawain
  Gaheriet his brother is dede him fro,
1980 But wele-away, the °rewful reyne,   *pitiful kingdom*
  That ever Launcelot was my fo!"

Gawain gan in his chāmber him hold;
  Of all the day hē nolde not out go;
A squīer then the tīthandes told;
  What wonder though his herte were wo?
"Alas," hē said, "My brōther bold,
  †Were Gaheriet bē dede mē fro?"
So sore his herte began tō °colde,   *grow cold*
  Almost hē wolde himselfe slo.

1990 The squīer spāke with drēry mood
  Tō °recomfort Sir Gawain: *comfort*
†"Gaheriet ailes nought but good;
  Hē will soon come again."
Gawain sprent as hē were wōde
  Tō the chāmber there they lay slain;
The chāmber floor all ran on blood
  And clothes of gold were over them °drayn.   *drawn*

A cloth hē °heves then °upon height;   *lifts/up high*
  What wonder though his herte were sore,
2000 So dolefully tō see them dight,
  That ere so doughty knightes were!
When hē his brōther saw with sight,
  A word might hē speke no more;
There hē lost both main and might
  And over him fell in swooning there.

Of swooning when hē might awāke,
  The hardy knight, Sir Gawain,
By God hē swore and loude spāke,
  As man that muche was of main:
2010 "Betwix mē and Launcelot du Lāke,
  °Nis man on erthe, for sooth tō sayn,   *There is no man*

1987 Can it be that Gaheriet is dead and away from me?
1992 Nothing but good ails Gaheriet (i.e., he is all right).

Shall °trewes set and pęęs make ... truce
  Ęre either of us have other slain!"

A squīer that Launcelot tō court had sent
  Of the tīthandes gan hē līthe;
Tō the forest is hē went
  And tọld Launcelot alsọ swīthe
How lọrdinges that were rich of rent,
  °Fęlę good had lost their līfe, ... many
2020 Gaheriet and Gaheries sọught their end;
  But then was Launcelot nọthing blīthe.

"Lọrd," hē said, "What may this °bēn? ... be
  Jēsū Crīst! What may I sayn?
The love that hath betwixt us been!
  †That ever Gaheriet mē was again!
Now I wọt for all bydēne
  A sọrry man is Sir Gawain;
†Accordement thar mē never ween
  Til either of us have other slain."

2030 Launcelot gan with his folk forth wend,
  With sọrry herte and drēry mood.
Tō queenes and countesses °fęlę hē send ... many
  And grętę lādīes of gentle blood,
That hē had oft their landes defend
  And fọughten when them need bestood.
°Īchon her powēr him °lend ... each one/ granted
  And mādę his party stiff and good.

Queenes and countesses that richę were
  Send him erles with gręte °meynē; ... company
2040 Other lādīes that °might nọ mọre ... could (send)
  Sent him barons or knightes free.
Sọ mikel folk tō him gan fare
  °Hidous it was his họst tō see; ... hideous (frightening)
Tō the Joyous Gard went hē there
  And hēld him in that strọng citee.

2025 That ever Gaheriet was against me! [Launcelot apparently thinks
  Gaheriet fought against him.]
2028 I may never expect reconciliation.

Launcelotes herte was full sǫre
    For the lādy fair and bright;
A dāmesel hē °did bē yare,   *commanded to*
    In rich apparail was shē dight,   *be ready*
2050 Hāstely in messāge for tō fare
    Tō the king of mikel might,
†Tō prōve it false—what might hē mǫre?—
    But profferes him therefore tō fight.

The maiden is rędy for tō rīde,
    In a full rich apparailment
Of °samīte green, with mikel prīde,   *silk*
    That wrǫught was in the Orīent;
A dwarf sholde wendę by her sīde;
    Such was Launcelotes °commaundement;   *command*
2060 Sǫ were the mannēres in that tīde,
    When a maid on messāgę went.

Tō the castle when shē cǫme,
    In the °palais gan shē light;   *palace*
Tō the king her °errand shē saidę soon   *message*
    (By him sat Sir Gawain the knight),
Said that līes were said him upon;
    Trew they were by day and night;
Tō prōve it as a knight sholde °dōn   *do*
    Launcelot profferes him tō fight.

2070 The king Arthur spękes there
    Wordes that were keen and thrǫ:
†"Hē ne might prōve it never mǫre,
    But of my men that hē wǫlde slǫ.
By Jēsū Crīst," the king swǫre
    And Sir Gawain then alsǫ,
†"His deedes shall bē bǫught full sǫre,
    But yif nǫ steel nill in him gǫ!"

2052-53 To prove the accusation false—what more could he do?—he
offers himself to fight. [Lancelot offers to take part in a judicial duel
of the sort he previously fought to prove Guenevere's innocence of
the charge of poisoning.]
2072-73 Even if he could not prove it he would slay some of my men.
2076-77 He will pay dearly for his deeds unless no steel (sword) will go
in him.

The maiden hath her answer;
   Tō the Joyous Gard gan shē rīde;
2080 Such as the kinges wordes were
   Shē tǫld Launcelot in that tīde.
Launcelot sighed wonder sǫre,
   Tęres from his eyen gan glīde.
Bors de Gawnes by God then swǫre:
   "In middes the fēld wē shall them bīde!"

Arthur wǫlde nǫ lenger abīde,
   But hāstes him with all his might.
Messengeres °did hē °gǫ and rīde,   *commanded/ walk*
   That they ne sholde let for day ne night,
2090 Throughout Yngland °by īch a sīde,   *on every side*
   Tō erlę, baron, and tō knight,
Bade them come that ilkę tīde,
   With horsę strǫng and armour bright.

†Thǫugh the knight that were dędę them frǫ,
   Thereof was all their mikel care,
Three hundreth they mādę mǫ,
   Out of castle ęre they wǫlde fare,
Of Yngland and Īreland alsǫ,
   Of Wāles and Scottes that bestę were,
2100 Launcelot and his folkes tō slǫ
   With hertes brēme as any bǫre.

When this hǫst was all °boun,   *ready*
   It was nǫ lenger for tō bīde,
Raises spęre and °gonfanoun,   *banner*
   As men that were of mikel prīde;
With helm and shēld and hauberk °brown,   *shining*
   Gawain himself before gan rīde
Tō the Joyous Gard, that richę °town,   *fortified place*
   And set a °sēge on ęch a sīde.   *siege*

2110 About the Joyous Gard they lay
   Seventeen weekes and well mǫre,
Til it fell upon a day
   Launcelot hǫmę bade them fare:

2094-95 Although their great sorrow was for the knight that was dead and
away from them.

"°Brẹke your sēge! Wendes away!   *break*
    You tō slay grẹte pitee it were."
Hē said: "Alas and wẹle-away,
    That ever began this sọrrow sọre!"

Ever the king and Sir Gawain
    °Calld him false °recrēant knight,   *called/perjured*
2120 And said hē had his brethren slain,
    And traitour was by day and night,
Bade him come and prōve his main
    In the fēld with them tō fight.
Launcelot sighed, for sooth tō sayn;
    Grẹte dole it was tō see with sight.

Sọ loud they Launcelot gonne °ascry,   *call at*
    †With vois and hidous hornes bēre,
Bors de Gawnes standes him by,
    And Launcelot mākes °īvel cheer.   *a sour face*
2130 "Sir," hē said, "wherefore and why
    Sholde wē thēse proudẹ wordes hēre?
Mē think yē fare as cowardly
    †As wē ne durst nọ man nighe nẹr.

"Dight wē us in rich array,
    Bọth with spẹre and with shēld,
As swīthe as ever that wē may,
    And rīde wē out intō the fēld.
Whīle my līfe lastẹ may,
    This day I ne shall my °wēpen yēld;   *weapon*
2140 Therefore my līfe I dare well °lay   *wager*
    Wē twọ shall māke them all tō °hēld."   *withdraw*

"Alas," °quọd Launcelot, "Wọ is mē,   *said*
    That ever sholde I see with sight
Again my lọrd for tō bē,
    The nọble king that mādē mē knight!
Sir Gawain, I beseechẹ thee,
    As thou art man of muchẹ might,
†In the fēld let nọt my lọrd bē,
    Ne that thyself with mē nọt fight."

2127 With voices and hideous braying of horns.
2133 As if we dared approach no man.
2148-49 Do not let my lord (Arthur) be in the field of battle and see that
    you yourself do not fight with me.

2150 It may no lenger for tō bīde,
  But °busked them and māde all °boun;   *hastened/ready*
 When they were rędy for tō rīde,
  They raised spęre and °gonfanoun;   *banner*
 When thēse hǫstes gan °sāmen glīde,   *together*
  With °vois and °hidous hornes °soun,   *voice/hideous/*
 Gręte pitee was on either sīde,   *sound*
  So °fęlę good there were laid down.   *many*

 Sir Līonel with muchę main,
  With a spęre before gan found;
2160 Sir Gawain rīdes him again,
  Horse and man hē bǫre tō ground,
 That all men wēnd hē had been slain;
  Sir Līonel had such a wound
 Out of the fēld was hē °drayn,   *drawn*
  For hē was sēke and sǫre unsound.

 In all the fēld that ilkę tīde
  Might nǫ man stand Launcelot again,
 †And sithen as fast as hē might rīde
  Tō sāve that nǫ man sholde bē slain.
2170 The king was ever nęr besīde
  And °hew on him with all his main,   *hewed*
 And hē sǫ courtais was that tīde
  †Ǫ dint that hē nǫlde smīte again

 Bors de Gawnes saw at last,
  And tō the king then gan hē rīde,
 And on his helm hē hit sǫ fast
  That nęr °hē lost all his prīde;   *i.e., Arthur*
 †The steedę rigge under him brast,
  That hē tō groundę fell that tīde;
2180 And sithen wordes loud °hē cast,   *i.e., Bors*
  With Sir Launcelot tō chīde:

 "Sir, °shaltou all day °suffer sǫ   *shalt thou/*
  That the king thee assail,   *allow*

2168-69 And yet he rode about as fast as he could to see that no man
 should be slain.
2173 He would not strike one blow in return.
2178 The steed's back broke under him.

†And sithe his herte is so thro,
   Thy courtaisy may not avail?
Batailes shall there never bē mo,
   °And thou wilt dō by my counsēl: *if*
Giveth us lēve them all tō slo,
   For thou hast vanquished this batail."

2190 "Alas," °quod Launcelot, "Wo is mē,   *said*
   That ever sholde I see with sight
Before mē him unhorsed bē,
   The noble king that māde mē knight!"
Hē was then so courtais and free
   That down of his steed hē °light;   *alighted*
The king there-on then horses hē,
   And bade him flee, yif that hē might.

When the king was horsed there,
   Launcelot lookes hē upon,
2200 How °courtaisy was in him more   *courtesy*
   Than ever was in any man.
Hē thought on thinges that had been ere;
   The teres from his eyen ran;
Hē said, "Alas," with sighing sore,
   "That ever yet this war began!"

The partīes °arn withdrawen away,   *are*
   Of knightes were they °wexen thin;   *grown*
On morrow on that other day
   Sholde the batail °eft begin;   *again*
2210 They dight them on a rich array
   And parted their hostes both °in twinne;   *in two*
Hē that began this wretched play,
   What wonder though hē had grete sin?

Bors was brēme as any bore,
   And out hē rode tō Sir Gawain;
For Līonel was wounded sore,
   °Venge his brother hē °wolde full fain.   *avenge/eagerly*
                                                     desired
Sir Gawain gan again him fare,
   As man that muche was of main;

2184-85 And (do you not see) that his heart is so fierce that your courtesy
   cannot avail?

2220 Either through other body bọre
         That well nẹr were they bọthẹ slain.

      Bọth tō ground they fell °in fẹre;   *together*
         Therefore were fẹlẹ folk full wọ.
      The kinges party rẹdy were
         Away tō tāke them bọthẹ twọ.
      Launcelot himself come nẹr,
         Bors rescūes hē them frọ;
      Out of the fēld men him bẹre;
         So were they wounded bọthẹ twọ.

2230 Of this batail were tō tell
         A man that it well understood,
      How knightes under saddles fell
         And sitten down with sọrry mood;
      Steedes that were bọld and °snell   *fast*
         Amọng them °wāden in the blood;   *wade*
      But by the tīme of ēven-bell
         Launcelot party the better stood.

      Of this batail was nọ mọre,
         But thus departen they that day;
2240 Folk their frēndes họme led and bọre,
         That slain in the fēldes lay.
      Launcelot gan tō his castle fare,
         The batail vanquished, for sooth tō say;
      There was dole and weeping sọre;
         Amọng them was nọ chīldes play.

      Intō all landes north and south
         Of this war the word sprọng,
      And yet at Rōme it was °full couthe   *well known*
         In Yngland was such sọrrow strọng;
2250 There-of the Pọpe had grẹtẹ °rewth;   *pity*
         A letter hē °sēled with his hand: *sealed*
      But they accorded well in °trewth   *truth*
         †Enterdīte hē wọlde the land.

      Then was a bishop at Rōme,
         Of Rochester, withouten lẹẹs;

2253 He would place the land under interdict. [This would deny the
     Sacraments of the Church to everyone in the country.]

Til Yngland hē, the °messāge, cǫme,   *messenger*
   Tō Carlīsle there the king was;
The Pǫpes letter out hē °nǫme,   *took*
   In the °palais, before the °dēse,   *palace/dais*
                                (high table)
2260 And bade them dō the Pǫpes °doom   *judgment*
   And hǫld Yngland in rest and pęęs.   *(decree)*

°Redde it was before all bydēne,   *read*
   The letter that the Pǫpe gan māke,
How hē must have again the queen
   And accord with Launcelot du Lāke,
Māke a pęęs them between
   For ever mǫre, and trewes māke,
Or Yngland enterdīted sholde bēn
   And turn tō sǫrrow for their sāke.

2270 The king again it wǫlde nǫt bēn,
   Tō dō the Pǫpes °commaundement,   *command*
Blīthely again tō have the queen;
   Wǫlde hē nǫt that Yngland were °shent;   *destroyed*
But Gawain was of herte sǫ keen
   That tō him wǫlde hē never assent
Tō māke accord them between
   Whīle any līfe were in him °lente.   *remained*

Through the °sent of all bydēne,   *assent*
   Gan the king a letter māke;
2280 The bishop °in messāge yēde between   *as a messenger*
   Tō Sir Launcelot du Lāke,
And asked if hē wǫlde the queen
   Courtaisly tō him °betāke,   *entrust*
Or Yngland enterdīte sholde bēn
   And turn tō sǫrrow for their sāke.

Launcelot answerd with gręte favour,
   As knight that hardy was and keen:
"Sir, I have °stand in many a °stour,   *stood/battle*
   Bǫth for the king and for the queen;
2290 †Full cǫld had been his bestę towr
   Yif that I nadde myselfę been;

2290-91 His strongest castles would have been destroyed if I had not been
with him.

Hē °quītes mē with little honour,   *repays*
    That I have served him all bydēne."

The bishop spāke withoutę fail,
    Though hē were nǫthing °afrǫught: *afraid*
"Sir, think that yē have vanquished many a batail,
    Through grāce that God hath for you wrǫught;
Yē shall dō now by my counsēl;
    Think on Him That you dęrę bǫught;
2300 Women are °fręle of their °entail;   *frail/character*
    Sir, lettes nǫt Yngland gǫ tō nǫught!"

"Sir Bishop, °castelles for tō hǫld,   *castles*
    Wite you well, I have nǫ need;
I might bē king, yif that I wǫlde,
    †Of all Benwick, that richę °thēde,   *nation*
Rīde intō my landes bǫld,
    With my knightes stiff on steed;
The queen, yif that I tō them °yǫlde,   *yield*
    Of her līfe I have gręte drēde."

2310 †"Sir, by Mary, that is maiden flowr,
    And by God That all shall ręde and right,
Shē ne shall have nǫ dishonour;
    There-tō my °trowth I shall you °plight,   *pledged word/*
                                         pledge
But bǫldly brǫught intō her bowr,
    Tō lādīes and tō maidens bright,
And hǫlden in well mǫre honour
    Than ever shē was by day or night."

"Now, yif I graunt such a thing,
    That I deliver shall the queen,
2320 Sir Bishop, say my lǫrd, the king,
    Sir Gawain and them all bydēne,
That they shall °māke mē a sēkering,   *give me assurance*
    A °trews tō hǫlde us between."   *truce*

Then was the bishop wonder blīthe
    That Launcelot gāve him this answer;
Til his palfrey hē went as swīthe,
    And til Carlisle gan hē fare.

2305 [Benwick is Bayonne (or Beune), a city in southwestern France.]
2310 Sir, by Mary, who is the flower of maidens (the best of virgins).

Tīthandes soon were °dōne tō līthe,   *i.e., announced*
   Which that Launcelotes wordes were;
2330 The king and court was all full blīthe;
   †A trews they set and sēkered there.

Through the assent of all bydēne
   A °sēker trews there they wrǫught;   *sure truce*
Thǫugh Gawain were of hertę keen,
   There-against was hē nǫught,
Tō hǫld a trewes them between,
   Whīle Launcelot the queen hǫme brǫught;
†But cordement thar him never ween
   Ęre either other herte have sǫught.

2340 A °sēker trews gonne they māke   *sure truce*
   And with their °sēles they it °band;   *seals/bound*
There-tō they three bishoppes gonne tāke,
   The wīsest that were in all the land,
And sent tō Launcelot du Lāke;
   At Joyous Gard then they him °fand;   *found*
The lettres there they him °betāke,   *deliver*
   And there-tō Launcelot °hēld his hand.   *i.e., pledged himself*

The bishoppes then went on their way,
   Tō Carlīsle there the king was;
2350 Launcelot shall come °that other day,   *the next day*
   With the lādy proud in press.
Hē dight him in a rich array,
   Wite yē well, withouten lęęs;
An hundreth knightes, for sooth tō say,
   The best of all his hǫst hē °chęse.   *chose*

Launcelot and the queen were °cledde   *clad*
   In rǫbes of a richę °weed,   *material*
Of °samīte whīte, with silver °shredde,   *silk/trimmed*
   Ivory saddle and whītę steed,
2360 °Sambūes of the sāmę °thręd,   *saddle-cloths/ thread*
   †That wrǫught was in the hęthen thēde;

2331 They set a truce and pledged themselves to it there.
2338-39 But he may never expect reconciliation until one of us has sought
  (with a sword) the other's heart.
2361 That was made in the heathen nations [the Orient, from which silk
  came].

Launcelot her brīdle led,
  In the °rōmaunce as wē rẹde.

romance (French book)

The other knightes °everychọne,
  In °samīte green of °hẹthen land,
And in their °kirtels rīde alọne,
  And īchẹ knight a green garland;
Saddles set with richẹ stọne;
  Īchon a braunch of olīve in hand;
2370 All the fēld about them shọne;
  The knightes rọde full loud °singand.

every one
silk/heathen
gowns (i.e., without armor)

singing

Tō the castle when they come
  In the palais gonne they °light;
Launcelot the queen off her palfrey °nọme;
  They said it was a seemly sight.
The king then °salūes hē full soon,
  As man that was of muchẹ might;
Fair wordes were there °fọne,
  But weeping stood there many a knight.

alight

took

salutes

taken

2380 Launcelot spāke, as I you °mẹne,
  Tō the king of mikel might:
"Sir, I have thee brọught thy queen,
  And sāved her līfe with the right,
As lādy that is fair and sheen,
  And trew is bọth day and night;
If any man sayes shē is nọt °clẹne,
  I proffer mē therefore tō fight."

tell

clean (i.e., sexually pure)

The king Arthur answeres there
  Wordes that were keen and °thrọ:
2390 "Launcelot, I ne wēnd never mọre
  That thou wọlde mē have wrọught this wọ;
So dẹre as wē °sāmen were,
  °There-under that thou was my fọ;
†But nọught-for-thy mē rewes sọre
  That ever was war betwixt us twọ."

fierce

together
i.e., despite this

Launcelot then answerd hē,
  When hē had listened lọng:

2394 But nevertheless it sorely pains me.

†"Sir, thy wǫ thou wītest mē,
   And well thou wǫst it is with wrǫng;
2400 I was never °fer from thee   *far*
   When thou had any sǫrrow strǫng;
†But līers listenes thou tō līe,
   Of whǫm all this word out sprǫng."

Then bespāke him Sir Gawain,
   That was hardy knight and free:
"Launcelot, thou may it nǫt °withsayn   *deny*
   That thou hast slain my brethern three;
For-thy shall wē prōve our main
   †In fēld whether shall have the gree.
2410 Ēre either of us shall other °slayn,   *slay*
   Blīthe shall I never bē."

Launcelot answerd with hertę sǫre,
   Thǫugh hē were nothing °afrǫught: *afraid*
"Gawain," hē said, "Thǫugh I were there,
   Myself thy brethern °slogh I nǫught;   *slew*
Other knightes fęle there were
   That sithen this war dęre °han bǫught."   *have*
Launcelot sighed wonder sǫre;
   †The tęres of his eyen sǫught.

2420 Launcelot spāke, as I you męne,
   Tō the king and Sir Gawain:
"Sir, shall I never of °cordement ween,   *reconcilement*
   That wē might frēndes bē again?"
Gawain spāke with hertę keen,
   As man that muchę was of main:
†"Nay, cordement thar thee never ween
   Til ǫne of us have other slain!"

"Sithe it never may betīde
   That pęęs may bē us between,
2430 May I intō my landes rīde,
   Sāfely with my knightes keen?

---

²³⁹⁸⁻⁹⁹ Sir, you blame your troubles on me, and you well know you do so
   wrongfully.
²⁴⁰² You listen to liars lying.
²⁴⁰⁹ (To see) who should have the prize on the field (of battle).
²⁴¹⁹ The tears ran from his eyes.
²⁴²⁶ Nay, you may never expect reconciliation.

Then will I hēre nǫ lenger bīde,
  But tāke lęve of you all bydēne;
Where I wend in worldę wīde,
  Yngland will I never °sēn."   *see*

The king Arthur answerd there—
  The tęres from his eyen ran—
"By Jēsū Crīst," hē there swǫre,
  That all this world wrǫught and wǫn,
2440 Intō thy landes when thou wilt fare,
  †Thee shall let nǫ livand man."
Hē said, "Alas!" with sighing sǫre,
  "That ever yet this war began!"

"Sithe that I shall wend away,
  And in mīne ǫwnę landes °wonne,   *dwell*
May I sāfely wonne there ay,
  That yē with war nǫt come mē on?"
Sir Gawain then said: "Nay,
  By Him That mādę sun and moon,
2450 Dight thee well as ever thou may,
  For wē shall after come full soon."

Launcelot his lęve hath tāken there;
  It was nǫ lenger for tō bīde;
His palfrey fand hē rędy yare,
  Māde him rędy for tō rīde;
Out of the °castel gonne they fare;   *castle*
  Grimly tęres let they glīde;
There was dole and weeping sǫre;
  At the parting was little prīde.

2460 Tō the Joyous Gard, the richę °town,   *fortified place*
  Rǫde Launcelot, the nǫble knight;
Busked them and māde all boun,
  As men that were of muchę might.
With spęre in hand and °gonfanoun   *banner*
  (°Let they neither day ne night)   *delayed*
†Tō an hāven hight Kerlīoun;
  Rich galleys there they fandę dight.

2441 No living man shall stop you.
2466 [Caerleon, on the river Usk in South Wales.]

Now are they shipped on the flood,
  Launcelot and his knightes hende;
2470 °Wederes had they fair and good   *weathers (winds)*
  Where their will was for tō wend,
Tō an hāven there it stood,
  †As men were lēvest for tō lende;
Of Benwick blīthe was their mood,
  When Jēsū Crīst them thider °send.   *sent*

Now are they arrīved on the strand;
  Of them was fęle folk full blīthe;
Gręte lordes of the land,
  Again him they come as swīthe,
2480 †And fellen him tō foot and hand;
  For their lord they gonne him kīthe,
At his doomes for tō stand,
  And at his lawes for tō līthe.

Bors māde hē king of Gawnes,
  As it was both law and right;
Līonel māde king of Fraunce,
  By ǫldę tīme °Gawle hight;   *Gaul*
All his folk hē gan °avaunce   *advance*
  And landes gāve tō īch a knight,
2490 And °stored his casteles for °all chaunce,   *supplied/every emergency*
  For mikel hē °hǫped mǫre tō fight.   *expected*

Ector hē crownes with his hand,
  Sǫ says the book withouten lęęs,
Māde him king of his °fader land,   *father's*
  And prince of all the richę press,
Bade nǫthing him sholde withstand,
  But hǫld him king, as worthy was,
For there nǫ mǫre himself wǫlde °fǫnde   *try (to do)*
  Til hē °wiste tō live in pęęs.   *knew (he could)*

2500 Arthur will hē nǫ lenger abīde
  Night and day his herte was sǫre;
Messengēres °did hē °gǫ and rīde   *commanded/walk*
  Throughout Yngland tō fare,

2473 Where the men were most eager to stay.
2480-83 And knelt and kissed Lancelot's foot and hand and acknowledged
  him to be their lord, and (promised) to obey his decrees and to heed
  his laws.

Tō erles and barons on īch a sīde,
  Bade them busk and māke all yare,
On Launcelot landes for tō rīde,
  Tō °bren and °slee and māke all bare.   *burn/slay*

°At his knightes all bydēne   *from*
  The king gan his counsēl tāke,
2510 And bade them ordain them between
  Whọ beste steward were for tō māke,
The °rēmẹ for tō sāve and °yēme,   *realm/control*
  And bestẹ were for Britaines sāke;
Full mikel they drēde them all bydēne,
  That ālīens the land wọlde tāke.

The knightes answerd, withoutẹ lẹẹs,
  And said, for sooth, that sọ them thọught
That Sir Mordred the °sēkerest was   *most trustworthy*
  Thọugh men the °rēme throughoutẹ sọught,   *realm*
2520 Tō sāve the rēme in trews and pẹẹs.
  Was a book before him brọught;
Sir Mordred they °tō steward chẹse;   *as*
  †That many a bọld sithen abọught.

It was nọ lenger for tō bīde,
  But buskes them and māde all boun;
When they were rẹdy for tō rīde,
  They raised spẹre and °gonfanoun;   *banner*
Forth they went with mikel prīde
  Til an hāven hight °Kerlīoun,   *Caerlion*
2530 And °graithes by the landẹ sīde   *prepare*
  Galleys grẹte of °fẹle fasoun.   *many fashions*

Now are they shipped on the sẹ
  And wenden ọver the water wīde;
'Of Benwick when they mightẹ see,
  With grẹtẹ °rout they gonne up rīde;   *company*
Withstood them neither stọne ne tree,
  But °brent and °slogh on īch a sīde;   *burned/slew*
Launcelot is in his best citee;
  There hē batail will abīde.

2523 Many a bold one later paid for that.

2540 Launcelot clēpes his knightes keen,
        His erles and his barons bǫld;
     Bade them ordain them between,
        Tō wite their will, what they wǫlde,
     Tō rīde again them all bydēne
        Or their worthy walles hǫld,
     For well they wiste, withouten ween,
        For nǫ °fantysē Arthur nǫlde fǫld.   *fantasy*

     Bors de Gawnes, the nǫble knight,
        Sternly spękes in that °stound: *time*
2550 "Doughty men, °that yē bē dight,   *(see) that*
        °Foundes your worship for tō °fǫnde   *prepare/test*
     With spęre and shēld and armes bright,
        Again your fǫmen for tō °founde;   *go*
     King and dūke, erl and knight,
        Wē shall them °bęte and bring tō ground!"   *beat*

     Līonel spękes in that tīde,
        That was of °warrę wīse and bǫld: *war*
     "Lǫrdinges, yet I ręde wē bīde
        And our worthy walles hǫld;
2560 Let them °prik with all their prīde,   *spur*
        Til they have caught bǫth hunger and cǫld;
     Then shall wē out upon them rīde,
        And °shręd them down as sheep in fǫld."   *cut*

     Sir Bangdemagew, that bǫldę king,
        Tō Launcelot spękes in that tīde:
     "Sir, courtaisy and your suffering
        †Has wākend us wǫ full wīde;
     Avīse you well upon this thing;
        Yif that they over our landes rīde,
2570 All tō nǫught they might us bring,
        Whīle wē in hǫles hēre us hīde."

     Galyhod, that ay was good,
        Tō Launcelot hē spękes there:
     "Sir, hēre are knightes of kinges blood,
        That lǫng will nǫt droop and °dare;   *crouch from fear*

     2567 Has brought great woe to us.

Give mē lẹve, for Cross on °Rood,   *cross*
    With my men tō them tō fare;
Though they bē worse than outlawes wōde,
    I shall °them slee and māke full bare."   *slay and plunder*
                                                                       them

2580 Of °North-Gāles were brethern seven,   *North Wales*
        °Ferly mikel of strength and prīde;   *wondrously*
                                                                       great
      †Not full fẹlẹ that men coude neven
        °Better durst in batail bīde;   *dare better*
      And they said with ọnẹ °steven: *voice*
        "Lọrdinges, how lọng will yē chīde?
      Launcelot, for Goddes love in Hẹven,
        With Galyhod forth let us rīde!"

      Then spāke the lọrd that was sọ hende,
        Himself, Sir Launcelot du Lāke:
2590 "Lọrdinges, a whīle I rẹde wē °lende   *remain*
        And our worthy walles °wāke;   *watch*
      A messāge will I tō them send,
        A trews between us for tō °tāke;   *offer*
      My lọrd is sọ courtais and hende
        That yet I họpe a pẹẹs tō māke.

      "Though wē might with °worship win,   *honor*
        Of °a thing mīne herte is sọre: *one*
      This land is full of folk °full thin,   *i.e., starving*
        Batailes have māde it full bare;
2600 Wite yē well it were grẹtẹ sin
        Cristen folk tō °slee thus mọre;   *slay*
      With mīldẹness wē shall begin
        And God shall °wisse us well tō fare."   *direct*

      And at this assent all they were,
        And set a °watch for tō °wāke,   *guard/watch*
      Knightes brēme as any bọre
        And °derf of drēde as is the drāke;   *fearsome as the*
                                                                       dragon
      A dāmesel they did bē yare,
        And hāstely gonne her lettres māke;
2610 A maid sholde on the messāge fare,
        A trews between them for tō °tāke.   *offer*

²⁵⁸² Not very many that men could name.

The maid was full sheen tō °shew,   *be seen*
   Upon her steed when shē was set;
Her °parail all of ǫnę hew,   *apparel*
   Of a green velvet;
In her hand a °braunch °new,   *branch/i.e.,*
                                                 green
   For-why that nǫ man sholde her let;
°There-by men messengēres knew,   *By that (i.e.,*
                                        green branch)
   In hǫstes when that men them met.

2620 The king was °loked in a fēld,   *lodged*
   By a river brǫde and °dregh;   *wide*
A whīle she °hōved and behēld,   *paused*
   °Paviliouns that were pight on high;   *tents that were*
                                         pitched
Shē saw there many comely °telde,   *tents*
   †With pommels bright as goldes bee;
On ǫnę hung the kinges shēld;
   That pavilioun shē drew her nigh.

The kinges banner out was set;
   That pavilioun shē drew her °nęr;   *nearer*
2630 With a knight full soon shē met,
   Hight Sir Lucan de Botteler;
Shē °hailsed him and hē her °grette,   *saluted/greeted*
   The maid with full mīld cheer;
Her errand was not for tō let;
   Hē wiste shē was a messengēr.

Sir Lucan down gan her tāke
   And in his armes forth gan lęde;
Hendely tō her hē spāke,
   †As knight that wīse was under weed:
2640 "Thou comest from Launcelot du Lāke,
   The best that ever strǫde on steed;
Jēsū, for his °Mōderes sāke,   *Mother's*
   Give thee grāce well tō speed!"

Fair was °pight upon a °plain   *pitched/open*
                                                 meadow
   The pavilioun in rich apparail;

2625 With knobs on the tent poles bright as golden rings.
2639 Like a knight who was wise in his armor. [The phrase "wise under
    weed" has little real meaning and conveys only the idea of a "good
    knight."]

The king himself and Sir Gawain
    Comely sitten in the hall;
The maiden kneeled the king again,
    Sọ lọw tō groundẹ gan shē fall;
2650 Her lettres were nọt for tō laine;
    They were °yredde amọng them all.   *read*

Hendely and fair the maiden spāke,
    †Full fain of spēche shē wọlde bē speed:
"Sir, God sāve you all from wọ and wrāke,
    And all your knightes in richẹ weed;
You greetes well Sir Launcelot du Lāke,
    That with you hath been ever at need;
A twelve-month trews hē wọldẹ tāke,
    Tō live upon his ọwnẹ °lēde,   *country*

2660 "And sithen, yif yē māke an °hest,   *promise*
    Hē will it °họld with his hand   *i.e., swear*
Between you for tō mākẹ pẹẹs,
    Stābely ever for tō stand;
Hē will °rap him on a rẹse   *hasten in a rush*
    Mīldly tō the Họly Land,
There tō live, withouten lẹẹs,
    Whīle hē is man livand."

The king then clēped his counsēl,
    His doughty knightes all bydēne;
2670 First hē said, withouten fail:
    "Mē think it were best tō °sēn;   *see (about this)*
Hē were a fool, withouten fail,
    †Sọ fair forwardes for tō flēme."
The king the messengēr thus did °assail: *i.e., address*
    "It were pity tō set war us between."

"Certes, nay!" said Sir Gawain,
    "Hē hath wrọught mē wọ ynow,
Sọ traitourly hē hath my brethern slain,
    All for your love, sir; that is °trouth!   *truth*
2680 Tō Yngland will I nọt turn again
    Til hē bē hanged on a bough;

²⁶⁵³ She was very eager to succeed by her speech (by means of her
    speech).
²⁶⁷³ To flee (turn down) such fair offers.

While mē lasteth might or main,
    There-tō I shall fīnd °pēple ynow."   *people*

The king himself, withouten lęęs,
    And īch a lǫrd, is nǫt tō laine,
All they spāke tō havę pęęs,
    But himselfę, Sir Gawain;
Tō batail hath hē māde his °hest,   *promise*
    Or elles never tō °turn again.   *return*
2690 They māde them rędy °tō that ręse;   *for that attack*
    †Therefore was fęlę folk unfain.

The king is comen intō the hall,
    And in his royal °see him set;   *seat (i.e., throne)*
Hē māde a knight the maiden call,
    Sir Lucan de Botteler, withouten °let: *delay*
"Say tō Sir Launcelot and his knightes all,
    Such an °hest I have him °hette,   *promise/*
                                        promised
†That wē shall wend for nǫ wall,
    Til wē with mightes ǫnes have met."

2700 The maid had her answer;
    With drēry herte shē gan her dight;
Her fair palfrey °fand shē yare,   *found*
    And Sir Lucan led her thider right.
Sǫ through a forest gan shē fare
    And hāsted her with all her might,
There Launcelot and his knightes were,
    In Benwick the °brough with °bēmes bright.   *castle/trumpets*

Now is shē went within the wall,
    The worthy dāmesel fair in weed;
2710 Hendely shē cāme intō that hall;
    A knight her took down off her steed.
Amǫng the princes proud in °palle   *costly cloth*
    Shē °took her lettres for tō ręde;   *offered*
There was nǫ counsēl for tō call,
    But rędyly buskes them tō that deed.

As folkes that °prestę were tō fight,   *eager*
    From fēldę wǫlde they never flee;

2691 Many people were not eager for it.
2698 That we shall turn aside for no obstacle (be deterred in no way).

But by the morrow that day was light,
　　†About besēged was all their fee;
2720　†Ĭchon them rayed in all rightes;
　　Neither party thọught tō flee.

Ẹrly as the day gan spring,
　　The °trompets upon the walles went;   *trumpeters*
There might they see a wonder thing,
　　Of °teldes rich and many a tent.   *rich dwellings*
Sir Arthur then, the comely king,   *(tents)*
　　With his folkes there was lente,
Tō give assaut, without lẹẹsing,
　　With °alblasters and bọwes bent.   *cross-bows*

2730　Launcelot all °forwondered was   *amazed*
　　Of the folk before the wall;
　　†But hē had rather knọwen that rẹse
　　Out had run his knightes all.
He said: "Princes, °bēth in pẹẹs,   *be still*
　　For follīes °fẹlẹ that might befall;   *many*
Yif they will nọt their sēgẹ °sẹse,   *cease*
　　†Full sọre I họpe forthink them shall."

Then Gawain, that was good at every need,
　　°Graithed him in his good armour,   *prepared*
2740　And stiffly °stert upon a steed,   *leaped*
　　That sēker was in ilk a °stour;   *battle*
Forth hē sprang as spark on °glēde,   *live coal*
　　Before the gātes °again the towr;   *next to*
Hē bade a knight come °kīthẹ main,   *prove his*
　　A °course of war for his honour.   *strength*
                                                               joust

Bors de Gawnes °buskes him boun,   *makes himself*
　　Upon a steed that sholde him bẹre,   *ready*
With helmẹ, shēld, and hauberk brown,
　　And in his hand a full good spẹre;
2750　Out hē rọde °a grẹte randoun;   *at a rapid pace*
　　†Gawain kydde hē coude of war;

2719 All their holdings were besieged.
2720 Each one arranged himself correctly (for battle).
2732-33 But he would rather have known about that attack than to have
　　had all his knights rush out.
2737 I suppose they will regret it sorely.
2751 Gawain proved he knew of war.

Horse and man both bore hē down,
    Such a dint hē gāve him there.

Sir Līonel was all rędy then,
    And for his brōther was wonder wǫ;
Rędyly with his steed out ran,
    And wēnd Gawain for tō slǫ.
†Gawain him kept as hē well can,
    As hē that ay was keen and thrǫ;
2760 Down hē bore both horse and man,
    And every day some served hē sǫ.

And sǫ mǫre than half a yēre,
    As lǫng as they there °layn,   lay (remained)
Every day men might see there
    Men wounded and some slain;
But how that ever in world it were,
    Such grāce had Sir Gawain,
Ever hē passed °hǫle and °clēre;   whole/clear
    There might nǫ man stand him again.   (of any wound)

2770 Then it befell upon a tīde,
    Sir Gawain, that was hende and free,
Hē māde him rędy for tō rīde,
    Before the gātes of the citee;
Launcelot of tręsoun hē °becrīed,   accused
    That hē had slain his brethern three;
That Launcelot might nǫ lenger abīde,
    °But hē ever a coward sholde bē.   unless

The lǫrd that gręte was of honour,
    Himself, Sir Launcelot du Lāke,
2780 Above the gātes upon the towr,
    Comely tō the king hē spāke:
"My lǫrd, God sāve your honour!
    Mē is wǫ now for your sāke,
Against thy kin tō stand in stour,
    But °needes I °moste this batail tāke."   must
                                                by necessity/

Launcelot armed him full well,
    For sooth, had full gręte need,

<hr>
2758 Gawain protected himself as he well knows how.

Helme, hauberk, and all of steel,
   And stiffly stert upon a steed;
2790 †His harnes lacked hē never a dele;
   Tō warre wanted him no weed,
Ne wēpen with all tō °dele;   *deal*
   Forth hē sprang as spark on °glēde,   *live coal*

Then it was warned fast on high,
   How in world that it sholde fare,
That no man sholde come them nigh,
   †Til the tone dede or yōlden were.
Folk withdrew them then by;
   Upon the fēld, was brode and bare,
2800 The knightes met, as men it °sigh   *saw*
   How they set their dintes sore.

Then had Sir Gawain such a grāce—
   An holy man had °bodden that boon—   *granted that gift*
When hē were in any plāce
   There hē sholde batail dōn,
His strength sholde °wax in such a °spāce,   *grow/space of*
                                          time
   From the °under-tīme til noon,   *about 9 a.m.*
                                        (undern)
And Launcelot forbore for that cāse;
   Again twenty strokes hē gāve not one.

2810 Launcelot saw there was no succour;
   †Needes moste hē his ventūre abīde;
Many a dint hē gan well endūre
   Til it drew near the noone tīde;
Then hē °straught in that stour   *straightened up*
   And gāve Gawain a wounde wīde;
The blood all covered his colour
   And hē fell down upon his sīde.

°Thorough the helm intō the hede   *through*
   Was hardy Gawain wounded so
2820 †That unnethe was him līfe leved;
   On foot might hē no ferther go;

²⁷⁹⁰⁻⁹¹ He lacked not a bit of equipment; he lacked no garment (armor)
    for war.
²⁷⁹⁷ Until one of them was dead or had surrendered.
²⁸¹¹ By necessity he had to wait his chance.
²⁸²⁰ That life was hardly left to him.

But °wightly his sword about he wāved,   *stoutly*
 For ever hē was bọth keen and thrọ.
Launcelot then °him lyand lẹved;   *left him lying*
 For all the world hē nọlde him slọ.   *(there)*

Launcelot then him drew °on dryghe,   *back*
 His sword in his handẹ °drayn,   *drawn*
And Sir Gawain crīed loud on high:
 "Traitour and coward, come again,
2830 When I am họle and gọing on high;
 Then will I prōve with might and main;
 †And yet a thou wọldest nighe mē nigh,
 Thou shalt well wite I am nọt slain!"

"Gawain, whīle thou mightest stiffly stand,
 Many a strọke tōday of thee I stood,
And I forbọre thee in every land,
 †For love and for the kinges blood;
When thou art họle in hẹrte and hand,
 I rẹde thee turn and chānge thy °mood;   *mind*
2840 Whīle I am Launcelot and man livand,
 God shēlde mẹ from °workes wōde!"   *mad deeds*

"But have good day, my lọrd the king,
 And your doughty knightes all;
Wendeth họme and lẹve your warring;
 Yē win nọ worship at this wall;
And I wọlde my knightes outẹ bring,
 I wọt full sọre rew it yē shall;
My lọrd, therefore think on such thing,
 How fẹlẹ folk therefore might fall."

2850 Launcelot, that was much of main,
 Bọldly tō his citee went;
His goodẹ knightes there-of were fain
 And hendely him in armes °hent.   *took*
The °tother party thọ took Sir Gawain;   *other*
 They °wesh his woundes in his tent;   *washed*
Ẹre ever hē °covered might or main,   *recovered*
 †Unnẹthe was him the līfẹ lente.

2832 And yet, if you would come near me.
2837 Because of love (for you) and because you are the king's kinsman. [Gawain is Arthur's nephew.]
2857 Hardly any life remained in him.

A °fourtenight, the sooth tō say,   *fortnight*
  Full passing sēke and unsound
2860 There Sir Gawain °on lēching lay   *in medical care*
  Ęre hē were hǫle all of his wound.
Then it befell upon a day,
  Hē māde him rędy for tō °wǫnde;   *go*
Before the gāte hē took the way,
  And asked batail in that °stound: *time*

"Come forth, Launcelot, and prōve thy main,
  Thou traitour that hast tręsoun wrǫught;
My three brethern thou hast slain
  And falsely them tō groundę brǫught;
2870 Whīle mē lasteth might or main,
  This quarrel lęvę will I nǫught,
Ne pęęs shall there never bē seen,
  Ęre thy sīdes bē °thorough sǫught."   *pierced*
                  through

Then Launcelot thǫught it nǫthing good,
  And for thēse wordes hē was full wǫ;
Above the gātes then hē yōde,
  And tō the king hē saidę sǫ:
"Sir, mē rewes in my °mood   *mind*
  That Gawain is in hertę sǫ thrǫ;
2880 †Whǫ may mē wīte, for Cors on Rood,
  Thǫugh I him in batail slǫ?"

Launcelot busked and māde him boun;
  Hē will bǫldly the batail abīde,
With helmę, shēld, and hauberk brown,
  Nǫne better in all this worldę wīde,
With spęre in hand and °gonfanoun,   *banner*
  His nǫble swordę by his sīde;
Out hē rǫde °a gręte randoun,   *at a rapid pace*
  When hē was rędy for tō rīde.

2890 Gawain grippes a full good spęre,
  And in hē glīdes glad and gay;
†Launcelot kydde hē coude of war,
  And ēven tō him hē tākes the way;

2880 Who can blame me, by the Body on the Cross.
2892 Lancelot proved he knew about war.

Sọ stoutly they gan tōgeder bẹre
   That marvēl it was, sooth tō say;
With dintes sọrẹ gan they °dẹre,   *injure*
   And deepẹ woundes °dẹlten they.   *dealt*

When it °was nighed nẹr-hand noon,   *was nearly noon*
   Gawaines strength gan tō °incrẹse;   *increase*
2900 So bitterly hē hewed him upon,
   That Launcelot all °for-wēry was;   *tired out*
Then tō his sword hē grippes anọn,
   And sithe that Gawain will not °sẹse,   *cease*
Such a dint hē gāve him ọne,
   That many a richẹ °rewed that rẹse.   *rued that attack*

†Launcelot stert forth in that stound,
   And sithe that Gawain will nọt °sẹse,   *cease*
The helm, that was rich and round,
   The nọble sword °rọve that °rẹse;   *cut/attack*
2910 Hē hit him upon the oldẹ wound
   That ọver the saddle down hē went,
And grisly grọned upon the ground,
   And there was good Gawain °shent.   *put to shame*

Yet Gawain, swooning there as hē lay,
   Gripped tō him bọth sword and shēld;
"Launcelot," hē said, "soothly tō say,
   And by Him That all this world shall °wēld,   *wield (control)*
While mē lasteth līfe tōday,
   Tō thee mē shall I never yēld;
2920 But dō the worst that ever thou may,
   I shall defend mē in the fēld."

Launcelot then full stillẹ stood,
   As man that was much of might:
"Gawain, mē rewes in my °mood   *mind*
   Men họld thee sọ noble a knight.
†Weenestou I were sọ wōde
   Against a feeble man tō fight?
I will nọt now, by Cross on Rood,
   Nor never yet did by day nor night.

2906 Lancelot leaped forth at that moment.
2926 Do you think I would be so mad?

2930 "But have good day, my lord the king,
      And all your doughty knightes bydēne;
Wendeth home and lẹve your warring,
      For hēre yē shall nọ worship win.
Yif I wọlde my knightes outẹ bring,
      I họpe full soon it sholde bē seen;
But, good lọrd, think upon a thing,
      The love that hath °us bē between."   *been between us*

After was it monthes twọ,
      As °freely folk it understand,   *noble*
2940 Ẹre ever Gawain might rīde or gọ,
      Or had foot upon erthe tō stand.
The thirdẹ tīme hē was full thrọ
      Tō dō batail with herte and hand;
But then was word comen them tō
      That they moste họme tō Yngland.

Such messāge was them brọught,
      There was nọ man that thọught it good.
The king himself full soon it thọught—
      Full muchẹ mōrned hē in his mood
2950 That such trẹsoun in Yngland sholde bē wrọught—
      That hē moste °needes ọver the flood.   *of necessity (go)*
They brokẹ sēge and họmeward °sọught;   *went*
      And after they had much angry mood.

That false traitour, Sir Mordred,
      †The kinges soster son hē was
And eek his own son, as I rẹde
      (Therefore men him for steward chẹse),
Sọ falsely hath hē Yngland led,
      Wite you well, withouten lẹẹs,
2960 †His emes wife wọlde hē wed,
      That many a man rewed that rẹse.

°Fẹstes made hē many and fẹle,   *feasts*
      And grẹte giftes hē gāve alsọ;

2955-56 He was the king's sister's son and also the king's own son, as I
    say. [Mordred was the product of an incestuous union between Arthur
    and his own sister. Though little is made of it in this poem, Arthur's
    fall is partly a consequence of his own sin.]
2960 He wanted to wed his uncle's wife. [Thus Mordred intends to com-
    mit incest, made worse since Guenevere is also his father's wife.]

They said with him was joy and wẹle,
  And in Arthurs tīme but sọrrow and wọ;
And thus gan right tō wrọngẹ gọ;
  All the counsēl, is nọt tō hẹle,
Thus it was, withouten mọ,
  Tō họld with Mordred in land with wẹle.

2970 Falsẹ lettres hē māde bē wrọught,
  And caused messengēres them tō bring,
That Arthur was tō groundẹ brọught
  And chēse they moste another king.
All they said as them thọught:
  "Arthur loved nọught but warring
And such thing as himselfẹ sọught;
  Right sọ hē took his ending."

†Mordred let cry a parlement;
  The °pēple gan thider tō come,   *people*
2980 And họlly through their assent
  They māde Mordred king with crown.
At Canterbury, fer in Kent,
  A °fourtenight hēld the °fẹste in town,   *fortnight/feast*
And after that tō Winchester hē went;
  †A richẹ brīde-āle hē let māke boun.

In sommer, when it was fair and bright,
  His faders wīfe then wọlde hē wed
And her họld with main and might,
  And sọ her bring as brīde tō bed.
2990 She prayd him of lẹve a °fourtenight—   *fortnight*
  The lādy was full °hard bestedde—   *hard pressed*
Sọ tō London shē her °dight,   *went*
  †That shē and her maidens might be cledde.

The queen, whīte as lily flowr,
  With knightes fẹlẹ of her kin,
Shē went tō London tō the towr
  And °sperred the gātes and dwelled therein.   *barred the gates*

2978 Mordred had a parliament announced.
2985 He had a rich bridal feast prepared.
2993 So that she and her maidens could be clad. [That they could buy
  new clothes for the wedding.]

Mordred chānged all his colour;
   Thider hē went and wǫlde nǫt °blinne;
3000 There-tō hē māde many a °showr,
   But the walles might hē never win.

The Archebishop of Canterbury thider yōde
   And his cross before him brǫught;
Hē said: "Sir, for Crīst on Rood,
   What have yē now in all your thǫught?
Thy faders wīfe, whether thou bē wōde,
   Tō wed her now mayst thou nǫught.
°Come Arthur ever ǫver the flood,
   †Thou mayst bē bǫld, it will be bǫught!"

3010 "Ā, °nīcę clerk," then Mordred said,
   †"Trowest thou tō warn mē of my will?
By Him That for us suffred pain,
   Thēse wordes shalt thou līke full ill!
With wīldę horse thou shalt bē °drayn
   And hanged high upon an hill!"
The bishop tō flee then was fain,
   And suffred him his follīes tō fulfill.

Then hē °him cursed with book and bell
   At Canterbury, fer in Kent.
3020 Soon, when Mordred herde thereof tell,
   Tō °seech the bishop hath hē sent;
The bishop durst nǫ lenger dwell,
   But gold and silver hē hath °hent;
There was nǫ lenger for tō °spell,
   But tō a wildernesse hē is went.

The worldes węle there hē will forsāke;
   †Of joy keepeth hē never mǫre,
But a chapel hē °lettę make
   Between two highę °holtes hǫre;
3030 Therein °węred hē the clǫthes black,
   In wood as hē an °ermīte were;
Often gan hē weep and wāke
   For Yngland that had such sǫrrows sǫre.

stop
shower (of arrows)

if Arthur comes

foolish clergyman

drawn apart

i.e., excommunicated him

seek

seized

talk

commanded to be built
gray woods
wore
hermit

3009 You can be sure it will be paid for.
3011 Do you expect to forbid me my desire?
3027 He cares no more for joy.

Mordred had then °līen full long,   *lain (in siege)*
    But the towr might hē never win,
With strengthe ne with stoure strong
    Ne with none other °kinnes gin;   *sort of trick*
His fader °dredde hē ever among;   *dreaded*
    †Therefore his bāle hē nill not blinne;
3040 Hē °wēnd tō warn them all with wrong   *expected to deny*
    The kingdom that hē was crowned in.   *them*

Forth tō Dover gan hē rīde,
    All the °costes well hē °kend;   *coasts/knew*
Tō erles and tō barons on ilk a sīde
    Grēte giftes hē gāve and lettres sent
And °forset the se on ilk a sīde   *blockaded*
    With bolde men and bowes bent;
Fro Yngland, that is brode and wīde,
    His owne fader hē wolde °defend.   *deny (entry)*

3050 Arthur, that was mikel of might,
    With his folk come over the flood,
An hundreth galleys that were well dight
    With barons bold and high of blood;
Hē wēnd tō have landed, as it was right,
    At Dover, there him thought full good,
And there hē °fand many an hardy knight   *found*
    That stiff in stour again him stood.

Arthur soon hath tāke the land
    †That him was lēvest in tō lende;
3060 His fele fomen that hē there °fand   *found*
    Hē wēnd before had been his °frēnd;   *friends*
The king was wroth and well-nigh wōde,
    And with his men hē gan up wend;
So strong a stour was upon that strand
    That many a man there had his end.

Sir Gawain armed him in that stound;
    Alas! Too long his hede was bare;
Hē was sēke and sore unsound;
    His woundes grēved him full sore.

3039 Therefore he will not stop his evil deeds.
3059 Which he liked best to dwell in.

3070   Qne hit him upon the olde wound
      With a °tronchon of an °ore;   *handle/oar*
  There is good Gawain gone tō ground,
      That spēche spāke hē never more.

  Bolde men, with bowes bent,
      Boldly up in botes yōde,
  And rich hauberkes they °rīve and °rent   *cut/tear*
      That through-out brast the °redde blood.   *red*
  °Grounden glaives through them went;   *sharpened spears*
      °Tho gāmes thought them nothing good;   *those*
3080 †But by that the stronge stour was stent,
      The stronge stremes ran all on blood.

  Arthur was so much of might
      Was there none that him withstood;
  Hē hewed on their helmes bright
      That through their °brēstes ran the blood.   *breasts*
  By then ended was the fight;
      The false were °felld and some were fled   *felled (struck down)*
  Tō Canterbury all that night
      Tō warn their master, Sir Mordred.

3090   Mordred then māde him boun,
      And boldly hē will batail abīde
  With helme, shēld, and hauberk brown;
      So all his °rout gan forthe rīde;   *troop*
  †They them met upon Barendown,
      Full °erly in the morrow tīde;   *early*
  With °glaives grete and gonfanoun,   *spears*
      Grimly they gonne tōgeder rīde.

  Arthur was of rich array
      And hornes blewe loud °on hight,   *on high*
3100 And Mordred cometh glad and gay,
      As traitour that was false in fight.
  They fought all that longe day
      Til the night was nighed nigh;
  Who had it seen well might say
      That such a stour never hē °sigh.   *saw*

3080 But by the time that strong battle was ended.
3094 [Barlam Down, in Kent.]

Arthur then fǫught with hertę good;
   A nǫbler knight was never nǫne.
Through helmes intō hęde °it yōde   *i.e., a sword*
   †And sterred knightes both blood and bǫne.
3110 Mordred for wrath was nighę wōde,
   Called his folk and said tō them °ǫne: *alone*
"°Relēve you, for Cross on Rood!   *recover*
   Alas! This day sǫ soon is gǫne!"   *yourselves*

Fęlę men līeth on bankes bare,
   †With brightę brandes through-oute borne;
Many a doughty dęde was there,
   And many a lǫrd his līfe hath °lorne.   *lost*
Mordred was full of sǫrrow and care;
   At Canterbury was hē upon the morn;
3120 And Arthur all night hē dwelled there;
   His °freely folk lay °him beforn.   *noble/before*
                                       him

°Ęrly on the morrow tīde   *early*
   Arthur bade his hornes blǫw,
And called folk on every sīde,
   And many a dęde burīed on a rǫw,
In pittes that was deep and wīde;
   †On īch an hępe they laid them lǫw,
Sǫ all that ever gǫn and rīde
   Some by their markes men might knǫw.

3130 Arthur went tō his dinner then,
   His freely folk him followed fast,
But when hē °fand Sir Gawain   *found*
   In a ship lay dęde by a mast,
Ęre ever hē °covered might or main,   *recovered*
   An hundreth tīmes his herte °nigh brast.   *nearly broke*

They laid Sir Gawain upon a °bēre,   *bier*
   And tō a castle they him bǫre,
And in a chapel amid the °quēre   *choir*
   That bǫld baron they burīed there.

3109 And stirred the blood and bones of knights.
3115 Driven through with bright swords.
3127-29 They made a mound over each body (on which markers were
   set), so that all that walked or rode by could know some of them
   by their markers.

3140 Arthur then chānged all his cheer;
    What wonder though his herte was sǫre!
    His °soster son, that was him dęre,   *sister's son (i.e.,*
        Of him sholde hē hēre never mǫre.   *nephew)*

    Sir Arthur hē wǫlde nǫ lenger abīde;
        Then had hē all manner of īvil rest;
    †Hē sǫught ay forth the southę sīde,
        And tōward Wāles went hē west.
    At Salisbury hē thǫught tō bīde,
        At that tīme hē thǫught was best,
3150 And call tō him at °Whitsuntīde   *Pentecost*
        Barons bǫld tō battail °prest.   *eager*

    Untō him cāme many a doughty knight,
        For wīde in world thēse wordes sprǫng,
    That Sir Arthur had all the right,
        And Mordred warred on him with wrǫng.
    Hidous it was tō see with sight;
        Arthures hǫst was brǫde and lǫng,
    And Mordred, that mikel was of might,
        With grętę giftes made him strǫng.

3160 †Soon after the fęste of the Trinitee,
        Was a batail between them set,
    That a stern batail there sholde bē;
        For nǫ °lēde wǫlde they it let;   *man*
    And Sir Arthur māketh gāme and glee,
        †For mirth that they sholde bē met;
    And Sir Mordred cāme tō the countree
        †With fęlę folk that fer was fette.

    At night when Arthur was brǫught in bed
        (Hē sholde have batail upon the morrow),
3170 †In strǫngę swevenes hē was bestedde,
        That many a man that day sholde have sǫrrow.
    Him thǫught hē sat in gold all cledde,
        As hē was comely king with crown,

3146 He went ever forth by the south side (of England).
3160 [The Feast of the Trinity is the first Sunday after Pentecost.]
3165 For mirth that they should meet in battle.
3167 With many folk that were brought (fetched) from afar.
3170 He was beset with strong (painful) dreams.

Upon a wheel that full wīde °spredde,   *spread*
  †And all his knightes tō him boun.

The wheel was °ferly rich and round;   *wondrously*
  In world was never nǫne half sǫ high;
Thereon hē sat richly crowned,
  With many a °besaunt, brooch, and °bee;   *coin*
                                                               (Byzantine)/ring
3180 Hē looked down upon the ground;
  A black water there under him hē °see,   *saw*
With dragons fęlę there lay unbound,
  That nǫ man durst °them nighę nigh.   *come near them*

†He was wonder fęrde tō fall
  Amǫng the °fēndes there that fǫught.   *fiends*
°The wheel ǫver-turned there with-all   *The wheel then*
                                                               turned
  †And everich by a limm him caught.
The king gan loudę cry and call,
  †As marred man of wit unsaught;
3190 His chāmberlains wāked him there with-all,
  And °wōdely out of his sleep hē °raught.   *madly/roused*

All nightę gan hē wāke and weep,
  With drēry herte and sǫrrowful °steven,   *voice*
And °against the day hē fell on sleep.   *near day (-light)*
  About him was set °tapers seven.   *candles*
Him thǫught Sir Gawain him did °keep,   *await*
  With mǫ folk than men can °neven,   *name*
By a river that was brǫde and deep;
  All seemed āngeles cǫme from hęven.

3200 The king was never yet sǫ fain,
  His °soster son when that he °sigh: *sister's son/saw*
"Welcome," hē said, "Sir Gawain,
  And thou might live, well were mē.
Now, lēvę frēnd, withouten laine,
  What are thǫ folk that follow thee?"
"Certes, sir," hē said again,
  "They bīde in bliss °there I mot bē.   *where I may be*

3175 And all his knights stood (ready) by him.
3184 He was strangely afraid of falling.
3187 And each (of the dragons) caught him by a limb.
3189 Like a troubled man with a disturbed mind.

"Lordes they were, and lādīes hende
  †This worldes līfe that han forlorn;
3210 Whīle I was man on līfe tō °lende,   *remain*
  †Against their fon I fought them forn;
Now fīnd I them my °moste frēnd;   *greatest friends*
  They bless the tīme that I was born;
They asked leve with mē tō wend,
  Tō meet with you upon this morn.

"A °monthe-day of trewes moste yē tāke   *month's truce*
  And then tō batail bē yē °bain;   *ready*
†You cometh tō help Launcelot du Lāke,
  With many a man mikel of main;
3220 Tō-morn the batail yē moste forsāke,
  Or elles, certes, yē shall bē slain."
The king gan woefully weep and wāke,
  And said, "Alas, this °rewful regne!"   *pitiful kingdom*

Hāstely his clothes on him hē did,
  And tō his lordes gan hē sayn:
†"In stronge swevenes I have been stedde,
  That glad I may not for no gāmes gay.
Wē moste untō Sir Mordred send
  †And fonde tō tāke another day,
3230 Or trewly this day I mon bē shend;
  This know I in bed as I lay."

"Go thou, Sir Lucan de Botteler,
  That wīse wordes hast °in wōld,   *in (your) power*
And look that thou tāke with thee hēre
  Bishoppes fele and barons bold;
Forth they went °all in a fēre,   *all together*
  In trewe bookes as it is told,
Tō Sir Mordred and his lordes, there they were,
  And an hundreth knightes all °untold.   *uncounted
                                                           (inumerable)*

3240 The knightes that were of grete valour,
  Before Sir Mordred as they stood,

<hr>

3209 Who have lost this world's life.
3211 I fought for them against their foes.
3218 Lancelot du Lake is coming to help you.
3226 I have been beset by strong (painful) dreams.
3229-30 And try to set another day (for the battle), or truly this day I
  must be put to shame.

They greeten him with gręte honour,
   As barons bǫld and high of blood:
"Right well thee greetes King Arthur,
   And prayeth thee with mīldę mood,
†A monthę-day tō stint this stour,
   For His love That dīed on Rood."

Mordred, that was bǫth keen and bǫld,
   Māde him brēme as any bǫre at bay,
3250 And swǫre by Judas that Jēsūs sold:
   "Such °sawes are nǫt now tō say;   *speeches*
†That hē hath hight hē shall it hǫld;
   The °tǫne of us shall dīe this day;   *one*
And tell him trewly that I tǫld:
   I shall him °mar, yif that I may."   *injure*

"Sir," they said, "withouten lęęs,
   †Thǫugh thou and hē tō batail boun,
Many a rich shall rew that ręse,
   By all bē dęlt upon this down,
3260 Yet were it better for tō sęse,
   And let him bē king and bęre the crown,
And after his dayes, °full drēdeless,   *without doubt*
   †Yē tō wēlde all Yngland, towr and town."

Mordred thǫ stood still a whīle,
   And wrǫthly up his eyen there went,
And said: "Wiste I it were his will
   Tō give mē Cornwall and Kent!
Let us meet upon yonder hill
   And talk tōgeder with good °entent;   *intent*
3270 Such °forwardes tō fulfill   *agreements*
   There-tō shall I mē soon assent.

"And yif wē may with spēches speed,
   With trewę trouthes of °entail,   *good character*
†Hǫld the bǫde-word that we bēde,
   Tō give mē Kent and Cornwall,

3246 To delay this battle for a month.
3252 He must hold to what he has promised.
3257-59 Though, if you and he were to prepare for battle, many a powerful (knight) would rue that attack, by the time all (blows) were
   dealt on this down.
3263 You (will be allowed) to rule all England, (every) castle and town.
3274 Keep the agreements that we have made.

Trewe love shall there leng and lende,
  †And certes, forwardes yif wē fail,
Arthur tō stert upon a steed
  Stiffly for tō dō batail."

3280 "Sir, will yē come in such manner,
  With twelve knightes or fourteen,
Or elles all your strength °in fēre,   *together*
  With helmes bright and hauberkes sheen?"
"Certes, nay," then said hē there,
  "Other work thou °thar nǫt ween,   *need not expect*
But bǫth our hǫstes shall nighę nęr,
  And wē shall talkę them between."

They took their lęve, withouten lęęs,
  And wightly upon their way they went;
3290 Tō King Arthur the way they chęse,
  There that hē sat, within his tent:
"Sir, wē have proffered pęęs,
  Yif yē will there-tō assent;
Give him your crown after your dayes
  And in your līfe Cornwall and Kent.

"Tō his behest yif yē will hǫld
  And your trouth trewly there-tō plight,
Māketh all rędy your men bǫld,
  With helmę, sword, and hauberk bright;
3300 Yē shall meet upon yon °molde,   *ground*
  That either hǫst may see with sight,
And yif your forward fail tō hǫld,
  There is nǫ °boot but for tō fight."   *remedy*

But when Arthur herde this °neven,   *said*
  Trewly there-tō hē hath sworn,
And arrayed him with batailes seven,
  With brǫde banners before him borne;
They °lēmed bright as any °leven   *gleamed/flash*
  When they sholde meet upon the morn.   *of lightning*
3310 There lives nǫ man under hęven
  A fairer sight hath seen beforn.

3277-78 And certainly, if we fail to keep our promises, let Arthur leap
  upon a steed.

But Mordred many men had mọ;
   Sọ Mordred, that was mikel of main,
Hē had ever twelve against him twọ,
   Of barons bọld tō batail °bain.   *ready*
Arthur and Mordred—bọth were thrọ—
   Sholde meetẹ bọth upon a plain;
The wīse sholde comẹ tō and frọ,
   Tō māke accord, the sooth tō sayn.

3320 Arthur in his herte hath °cast,   *i.e., considered*
   And tō his lọrdes gan hē say:
"To yonder traitour have I nọ trust,
   But that hē will us falsely betray,
Yif wē may nọt °our forwardes faste.   *i.e., agree on our terms*
   And yē see any wēpen °drayn,   *drawn*
Presseth forth as princes °preste,   *eager*
   That hē and all his họst bē slain."

Mordred, that was keen and thrọ,
   His freely folk hē said toforn:
3330 "I wọt that Arthur is full wọ
   That hē hath thus his landes °lorn;   *lost*
With fourteen knightes and nọ mọ
   Shall wē meet at yonder thorn;
Yif any trẹsoun between us gọ,
   †That brọdẹ banners forth bē borne."

Arthur with knightes fully fourteen
   Tō that thorn on foot they foundẹ,
With helmẹ, shēld, and hauberk sheen;
   Right sọ they trotted upon the ground.
3340 But as they accorded sholde have been,
   An adder °glọde forth upon the ground;   *glided*
Hē °stang a knight, that men might °sēn   *stung/see*
   That hē was sēke and full unsound.

Out hē °brayed with a swordẹ bright;   *drew*
   Tō kill the adder had hē thọught.
When Arthur party saw that sight,
   Freely they tōgeder sọught;

³³³⁵ Let broad banners be borne forth (as a signal to attack).

There was nǫ thing withstand them might;
They wēnd that tresoun had been wrǫught;
3350 That day dīed many a doughty knight,
And many a bǫld man was brǫught tō nǫught.

Arthur °stert upon his steed;   *leaped*
Hē saw nǫ thing him withstand might;
Mordred out of wit nẹr yēde,
And wrǫthly intō his saddle hē °light;   *leaped*
Of accord was nǫthing tō bēde,
†But fewtered speres and tōgeder sprent;
Full many a doughty man of deed
Soon there was laid upon the °bente.   *ground*

3360 Mordred °ymarred many a man,   *injured*
And bǫldly hē gan his batail abīde;
Sǫ sternly out his steedẹ ran,
Many a °rout hē gan through rīde.   *company*
Arthur of batail never °blanne   *ceased*
Tō dẹlẹ woundes °wicke and wīde,   *wicked*
Frǫ the morrow that it began
Til it was nẹr the nightes tīde.

There was many a spẹrẹ sprent,
And many a thrǫ word they spāke;
3370 Many a brand was bǫwed and bent,
And many a knightes helm they brāke;
Richẹ helmes they °rǫve and °rente;   *cut/tore*
The richẹ °routes gan tōgeder °raike,   *companies/rush*
An hundreth thousand upon the °bente;   *ground*
The bǫldest ẹre ēven was made right meek.

†Sithe °Britain out of Troy °was sǫught   *Brutus/came*
And māde in Britain his ǫwnẹ °wonne,   *dwelling*
, Such wonders never ẹre was wrǫught,
Never yet under the sun.

3357 [*Fewtered*: placed spears against the "fewter," the spear rest on the saddle, into which the spear would be placed when the knight prepared to attack.]
3376 [Brutus, here mistakenly called "Britain," is the legendary Trojan who, according to Geoffrey of Monmouth's *Histories of the Kings of Britain* (Book I), conquered what is now England (from a race of giants) and founded the nation to which he gave his name.]

3380 By ēven lẹved was there nọught
    That ever °sterred with blood or bọne,   *stirred*
But Arthur and twọ that hē thider brọught,
    And Mordred was lẹved alọne.

The °tọne was Lucan de Botteler,   *one*
    That bled at many a bāleful wound,
And his brōder, Sir Bedivere,
    Was °sēly sēke and sọre unsound.   *wondrously*
Than spāke Arthur thēse wordes there:
    "Shall wē nọt bring this thēf tō ground?"
3390 A spẹre he gripped with °fellẹ cheer,   *fierce expression*
    And °felly they gan tōgeder founde.   *fiercely*

Hē hit Mordred amid the brēste
    And out at the backẹ bọne him bọre;
There hath Mordred his līfe lost,
    That spēchẹ spāke hē never mọre;
Then keenly up his arm hē cast
    And gāve Arthur a woundẹ sọre,
Intō the hẹde through the helm and crest,
    That three tīmes hē swooned there.

3400 Sir Lucan and Sir Bedivere
    Between them twọ the king uphēld;
Sọ forthẹ went thọ three °in fēre,   *together*
    And all were slain that lay in fēld.
The doughty king that was them dẹre
    For °sọre might nọt himselfẹ °wēld;   *pain/wield (move)*
Tō a chapel they went in fēre;
    °Of boot they saw nọ better °bēld.   *for a remedy/ comfort*

All night they in the chapel lay,
    By the sẹ sīde, as I you neven,
3410 Tō Mary mercy cryand aye,
    With drēry herte and sorrowful steven,
And tō her °lēve Son gonne they pray: *dear*
    "Jēsū, for thy nāmes seven,
°Wisse his sọul the rightẹ way,   *teach (direct)*
    That hē °lēse nọt the bliss of Hẹven."   *lose*

As Sir Lucan de Botteler stood,
    Hē sigh folk upon plaines °hīe;   *hasten*

Bolde barons of bone and blood
    †They reft them of besaunt, brooch, and bee;
3420 And tō the king again they yōde
    Him tō warn with wordes °slee.   *sly (wise)*

Tō the king spāke hē full still,
    Rewfully as hē might then °roun: *speak*
"Sir, I have been at yon hill,
    There fęle folk drawen tō the down;
I °not whether they will us good or ill;   *know not*
    I ręde wē busk and māke us boun,
Yif it were your worthy will
    That wē wendę tō some town."

3430 "Now, Sir Lucan, as thou °redde,   *advised*
    Lift mē up, whīle I may last."
Both his armes on him hē °spredde,   *spread*
    With all his strength tō hold him fast.
The king was wounded and °forbledde,   *bled to death*
    And swooning on him his eyen hē cast;
· Sir Lucan was °hard bestedde;   *hard beset*
    Hē hēld the king °tō his own herte brast.   *until*

When the king had swooned there,
    By an °auter up hē stood;   *altar*
3440 Sir Lucan, that was him dęre,
    Lay dędę and °fomed in the blood.   *foamed*
His boldę brōder, Sir Bedivere,
    Full mikel °mōrned in his mood;   *mourned*
For sorrow hē might not nighe him nęr,
    But ever weeped as hē were wōde.

The king turned him there hē stood,
    Tō Sir Bedivere with wordes keen:
"Have Excaliber, my swordę good,
    A better brand was never seen;
3450 Go, cast it in the saltę flood,
    And thou shalt see wonder, as I ween;
°Hīe thee fast, for Cross on Rood,   *hasten*
    And tell mē what thou hast there seen."

3419 They (the folk in line 3417) robbed the bold barons (in line 3418)
    of coins, brooches, and rings.

The knight was bọthẹ hende and free;
   Tō sāve that sword hē was full glad,
†And thọught: "Whether I better bē,
   Yif never man it after had?
And I it cast intō the sẹ,
   Of °molde was never man sọ mad."   *earth*
3460 The sword hē hid under a tree,
   And said: "Sir, I did as yē mē bade."

"What saw thou there?" then said the king,
   "Tell mē now, yif thou can."
"Certes, sir," hē said, "nọthing
   But watres deep and °wawes wan."   *pale waves*
"Ā, now thou hast brọke my bidding!
   Why hast thou dō sọ, thou falsẹ man?
Another °bọde thou must mē bring."   *message*
   Then carefully the knight forth ran,

3470 And thọught the sword yet hē wọlde hīde
   And cast the °scauberk in the flood: *scabbard*
"Yif any °aventūres shall betīde,   *adventures*
   Thereby shall I see tọkenes good."
Intō the sẹ hē let the scauberk glīde;
   A whīle on the land hē there stood;
Then tō the king hē went that tīde
   And said: "Sir, it is dōne, by the °Rood."   *cross*

"Saw thou any wondres mọre?"
   "Certes, sir, I saw nọught."
3480 "Ā, falsẹ traitour!" hē said there,
   "Twīce thou hast mē trẹsoun wrọught;
That shall thou rewẹ °sēly sọre,   *wondrously*
   †And, bē thou bọld, it shall bē bọught."
The knight then crīed, "Lọrd, thīne °ọre!"   *mercy*
   And tō the swordẹ soon hē sọught.

†Sir Bedivere saw that boot was best,
   And tō the goodẹ sword hē went;
Intō the sẹ hē it cast;
   Then might hē see what that it ment.

3456 And thought, "Would I be any better."
3483 And, you can be sure, it must be paid for.
3486 Sir Bedivere saw that remedy (i.e., course of action) was best.

3490 There cāme an hand withouten rest,
    Out of the water, and fair it °hent,   *seized*
And °braundished as it sholde °brast,   *shook/break*
    And sithe, °as glęm, away it °glent.   *like a gleam/ glided*

Tō the king again went hē there
    And said: "°Lēve sir, I saw an hand;   *dear*
Out of the water it cāme all bare
    And thrīce °braundished that richę brand."   *shook*
"Help mē, soon that I were there."
    Hē led his lǫrd untō that strand;
3500 A richę ship, with mast and °ǫre,   *oar*
    Full of lādīes there they fand.

The lādīes, that were fair and free,
    Courtaisly the king gan they °fǫnge;   *take*
And ǫne that brightest was of °blee   *complexion*
    Weeped sǫre and handes °wrang.   *wrung*
"Brōder," shē said, "wǫ is mē!
    †Frǫ lēching hastou bē too lǫng;
°I wǫt, that grętly grēveth mē,   *I know (i.e., indeed)*
    For thy paines are full strong."

3510 The knight cast a rewful °roun,   *speech*
    There hē stood, sǫre and unsound,
And said: "Lǫrd, °whider are yē boun?   *whither are you bound?*
    Allas! Whider will yē frǫ mē found?"
The king spāke with sǫrry °soun: *sound*
    "I will wend a little stound
Intō the vāle of Aveloun,
    A whīle tō hęle mē of my wound."

When the ship from the land was brǫught,
    Sir Bedivere saw of them nǫ mǫre.
3520 Through the forest forth hē sǫught
    On hilles and °holtes hǫre.   *hoary (gray) forests*
Of his līfe °rǫught hē right nǫught;   *reckoned*
    All night hē went weeping sǫre;
°Against the day hē fand there wrǫught   *before daybreak*
    A chapel between twǫ holtes °hǫre.   *hoary*

3507 You have been too long away from medical attention.

Tō the chapel hē took the way,
   There hē might see a wonder sight;
Then saw hē where an ermīte lay,
   Before a tōmb that was new dight,
3530 And covered it was with marble gray,
   And with richę lettres °rayled aright;   *rightly adorned*
There-on an °hęrse, soothly tō say,   *bier (hearse)*
   With an hundreth °tāpers light.   *candles*

Untō the ermīte went hē there
   And asked whǫ was burīed there.
The ermīte answerd swīthę yare:
   "Thereof can I tell nǫ mǫre;
About midnight were lādīes hēre,
   In world ne wiste I what they were;
3540 This body they brǫught upon a °bēre   *bier*
   And burīed it with woundes sǫre.

†"Besauntes offred they hēre bright,
   I hǫpe an hundreth pound and mǫre,
And bade mē pray bǫth day and night
   For him that is burīed in °thēse moldes hǫre   *this hoary*
                                    (gray) ground
Untō our Lādy bǫth day and night
   That shē his sǫul help sholde."
The knight °redde the lettres aright;   *read*
   For sǫrrow hē fell untō the °folde.   *ground*

3550 "Ermīte," hē said, "without lęęsing,
   Hēre līeth my lǫrd that I have lorn,
Bǫld Arthur, the bestę king
   That ever was in Britain born.
Give mē some of thy clǫthing,
   For Him That bǫre the crown of thorn,
And °lęve that I may with thee °lenge,   *grant/stay*
   While I may live, and pray °him forn."   *for him*

The hǫly ermīte wǫlde nǫt °wǫnde;   *delay*
   Some tīme Archebishop hē was,
3560 That Mordred °flēmed out of land,   *put to flight*
   And in the wood his °wonning chęse;   *dwelling*

3542 They offered here bright coins (Byzantine coins).

Hē thanked Jēsū all of his °sound   *good fortune*
   That Sir Bedivere was comen in pęęs;
Hē received him with herte and hand,
   Tōgeder tō dwell, withouten lęęs.

When Queen Gaynor, the kinges wīfe,
   Wiste that all was gǫne tō °wrāke,   *ruin*
Away shē went, with lādīes fīve,
   At Aumsbury, a nun her for tō māke.
3570 There-in shē lived an hǫly līfe,
   In prayers for tō weep and wāke;
Never after shē °coude bē blīthe;   *could*
   There °węred shē clǫthes °whīte and black.   *wore/i.e., a*
                                                    nun's habit

When this tīdinges was tō Launcelot brǫught,
   What wonder though his herte were sǫre?
His men, his frēndes, tō him sǫught,
   And all the wīse that with him were.
Their galleys were all rędy wrǫught;
   They busked them and māde yare;
3580 Tō help Arthur was their thǫught
   And māke Mordred of bliss full bare.

Launcelot had crowned kinges seven,
   Erles fęle and barons bǫld;
The number of knightes I can nǫt °neven,   *tell*
   The squīers too fęlę tō bē tǫld;
†They lēmed light as any leven;
   The wind was as °themselvę wǫlde;   *they desired*
Through the grāce of God of Hęven,
   At Dǫver they took hāven and °hǫld.   *protection*

3590 There herde tell Launcelot in that town,
   †In land it is nǫt for tō laine,
How they had fǫught at Barendown
   And how burīed was Sir Gawain,
And how Mordred wǫlde bē king with crown,
   And how either of them had other slain,
And all that were tō batail boun,
   At Salisbury lay dęde upon the plain.

3586 They gleamed as bright as any lightning.
3591 The news is not to be concealed.

Also in lande °herde it kīthe   *he heard it said*
    That māde his herte wonder sore:
3600 Queen Gaynor, the kinges wīfe,
    Much had lived in sorrow and care;
Away shē went with lādīes fīve,
    In land they °wiste not whider where,   *knew not where*
†Dolven dede or tō bē on līfe;
    That māde his °mōrning much the more.   *mourning*

Launcelot clēped his kinges with crown;
    Sir Bors stood him ner besīde;
Hē said: "Lordinges, I will wend °tōforn,   *before (onward)*
    And by thēse bankes yē shall abīde
3610 Untō fifteen dayes at the morn.
    †In land whatsoever us betīde
Tō herken what lord his līfe hath lorn,
    Look yē rappe you not up tō rīde."

There had hē neither °roo ne rest,   *peace*
    But forth hē went with drēry mood,
And three dayes hē went °ēven west   *straight*
    As man that °coude neither īvel nor good.   *knew*
Then sigh hē where a towr °by west   *on the west*
    †Was bigged by a burnes flood;
3620 There hē hoped it were best
    †For tō get him some līves stood.

As hē cāme through a cloister clēre—
    Almost for weeping hē was mad—
Hē sigh a lady bright of °lēre,   *complexion*
    In nunnes clothing was shē cledde;
Thrīce shē swooned swiftly there,
    So stronge paines shē was in °stedde   *placed*
That many a nun then nighed her ner,
    And tō her chāmber was shē led.

3630 "Mercy, mādāme," they said all,
    "For Jēsū, That is King of bliss,

3604 Whether dead and buried or living.
3611-13 Whatever may happen to us in this land (as we go) to hear what
    lord has lost his life, see that you do not rush to ride out (to help us).
3619 Was built by the flood of a stream.
3621 In order to get himself some support for life (i.e., food).

Is there any °brīde in bowr or hall   *maiden*
  Hath wrathed you?" Shē said: "Nay, īwis."
Launcelot tō her gan they call,
  The abbess and the other nunnes, īwis,
They that °wonned within the wall.   *dwelt*
  In counsēl there then said shē thus:

"Abbess, tō you I °knǫwlech hēre   *acknowledge*
  That through this ilkę man and mē,
3640 For wē tōgeder han loved us dęre,
  All this sǫrrowful war hath bē;
My lǫrd is slain, that hath nǫ peer,
  And many a doughty knight and free;
Therefore for sǫrrow I dīed nęr,
  As soon as I ever gan him see.

"When I him °see, the sooth tō say,   *saw*
  All my herte began tō °cǫlde;   *grow cold*
That ever I sholde abīde this day,
  Tō see sǫ many barons bǫld
3650 Sholde for us bē slain away!
  †Our will hath bē too sǫre bǫught sǫld;
But God, That all mightes may,
  Now hath mē set where I will hǫld.

"°Yset I am in such a plāce   *set*
  †My sǫulę hęle I will abīde,
Til God send me some grāce,
  Through mercy of his woundes wīde,
That I may dō sǫ in this plāce,
  My sinnes tō amend this ilkę tīde,
3660 After tō have a sight of His fāce,
  At Doomes-day on His righte sīde.

"Therefore, Sir Launcelot du Lāke,
  For my love now I thee pray,
My company thou ay forsāke,
  And tō thy kingdom thou tāke thy way,
And keep thy °rēme from war and wrāke,   *realm*
  And tāke a wīfe with her tō play,

3651 Our desire has been too painfully bought and paid for. [We have
   suffered because of our lust.]
3655 I will await the healing of my soul.

And love well then thy °worldes māke;   *worldly mate*
   God give you joy tōgeder, I pray!

3670 "Untō God I pray, Allmighty King,
   Hē give you tōgeder joy and bliss;
But I beseech thee in allę thing
   That never in thy līfe after this
Ne come tō mē for nǫ °sokering,   *comfort*
   Nor send mē °sǫnde, but dwell in bliss;   *message*
I pray tō God Everlasting
   Tō graunt mē grāce tō mend my °misse."   *sins*

"Now, sweet mādāme, that wǫlde I nǫt dō
   Tō have all the world °untō my meed;   *as my reward*
3680 Sǫ untrew find yē mē never mǫ;
   †It for tō dō Crīst mē forbēde!

"Forbēde it God that ever I sholde
   †Against you work sǫ gręte unright,
°Sinne wē tōgeder upon this °molde   *since/earth*
   Have led our līfe by day and night!
Untō God I give a °hest tō hǫld: *promise*
   That sāme °destainy that you is dight   *destiny*
I will °receive in some house bǫld   *i.e., receive*
                                                         monkhood
   Tō °plęse hēreafter God Allmight.   *please*

3690 "Tō °plęse God all that I may   *please*
   I shall hēreafter °dō mīne entent,   *make my intent*
And ever for you specīally pray,
   Whīle God will mē līfe °lente."   *grant*
"Ā, wilt thou sǫ," the queen gan say,
   "Fulfill this forward that thou has °ment?"   *said*
Launcelot said: "Yif I said nay,
   I were well worthy tō bē °brent."   *burned*

"Brent tō bēn worthy I were,
   Yif I wǫlde tāke nǫne such a līfe,
3700 Tō bīde in °penaunce, as yē dō hēre,   *penance*
   And suffer for God sǫrrow and strīfe;

3681 Christ forbid me to do it.
3683 To do so great a wrong against you.

†As wē in līking lived in fēre,
  By Mary, Mōder, maid, and wīfe,
Til God us depart with dẹthes dẹre,
  Tō penaunce I yēld mē hēre as blīthe.

"°All blyve tō penaunce I will mē tāke,   *quickly*
  As I may find any ermīte
That will mē receive for Goddes sāke,
  Mē tō clọthe with black and whīte."
3710 The sọrrow that the °tọne tō the °tother gan māke   *one/other*
  Might nọne erthely man see it.
"Mādāme," then said Launcelot du Lāke,
  "Kiss mē, and I shall °wend as-tīte."   *go quickly away*

"Nay," said the queen, "that will I nọt;
  Launcelot, think on that nọ mọre;
†Tō abstain us wē moste have thọught
  Frọ such wē have delīted in ẹre.
Let us think on Him That us hath bọught,
  And wē shall °plẹse God therefore.   *please*
3720 Think on this world, how there is nọught,
  But war and strīfe and batail sọre."

What helpeth lenger for tō °spell?   *speak*
  With that they gan depart in twain;
But nọne erthely man coude tell
  The sọrrow that there began tō bēn;
Wringing their handes and loud they yell,
  As they never mọre sholde blinne,
And sithe in swoon bọth down they fell;
  †Whọ saw that sọrrow ever might it mẹne.

3730 But lādīes then, with °mōrning cheer,   *mourning*
  Intō the chāmber the queen they bọre,
And all full busy māde them there
  Tō °cover the queen of her care.   *recover*
But many alsọ that with Launcelot were,
  They comfort him with rewful care;
When hē was covered, hē took his °gẹre   *gear (equipment)*
  And went from thence withouten mọre.

3702 Since we lived together in pleasure.
3716-17 We must be determined to abstain from what we once delighted
  in.
3729 He who saw that sorrow could tell of it forever.

His herte was hẹvy as any °lẹde,   *lead*
  †And lēver hē was his līfe have lorn.
3740 Hē said: "Rightūous God, what is my rẹde?
  Alas, °forbọre, why was I born?"   *misbegotten*
                                                    (creature)
Away hē went, as hē had fled,
  Tō a forest that was him beforn;
His life fain hē wọlde have lẹved;
  His rich attīre hē wọlde °off-torn.   *have torn off*

All night gan hē weep and °wring   *wring his hands*
  And went about as hē were wōde;
Ẹrly, as the day gan spring,
  Thọ sigh hē where a chapel stood;
3750 A bell herde hē rewfully ring;
  Hē °hīed him then and thider yōde;   *hastened*
A prēst was rẹdy for tō sing,
  And mass hē herde with drēry mood.

The Archebishop was ermīte there,
  †That flēmed was for his workes trew;
The mass hē sang with sighing sọre,
  †And oft hē chānged hīde and hew;
Sir Bedivere had sọrrow and care
  †And oft mōrned for thọ workes new;
3760 After mass was mōrning mọre,
  When ẹch of them other knew.

When the sọrrow was to the end,
  The bishop took his habit there
†And welcomed Launcelot as the hende,
  And on his knees down gan hē fare:
"Sir, yē bē welcome as our frēnd,
  Untō this °bigging in bankes bare;   *building*
Were it your will with us tō lende
  This ọnẹ night, yif yē may nọ mọre!"

3770 When they knew him at the last,
  Fair in armes they gan him fọld,

3739-40 And he would rather have lost his life. He said: "Righteous God,
  what should I do?"
3755 Who was put to flight for his true (loyal) deeds.
3757 And often his skin and hue changed. [The Archbishop's complexion
  changes from emotion.]
3759 And often mourned for those recent deeds [Mordred's treachery
  and Arthur's death].
3764 And welcomed Lancelot as a courteous person should do.

And sithe hē asked freely fast
    Of Arthur and of other bǫld;
An hundreth times his herte nẹr brast,
    Whīle Sir Bedivere the tāle tǫld.
Tō Arthures tōmb hē °cast;   *went*
    †His careful corāge wexed all cǫld.

Hē threw his armes tō the °walle,   *walls*
    That richẹ were and bright of °blee;
3780 Before the ermīte hē gan down fall
    And comely kneeled upon his knee;
Then hē °shrǫve him of his sinnes all,   *confessed himself*
    And prayd hē might his brōder bē,
Tō servẹ God in bowr and hall,
    That might-full King of mercy free.

The hǫly bishop °nǫlde nǫt blinne,   *would not refuse*
    But blīthẹ was tō °dō his boon;   *fulfill his request*
Hē received him with wẹle and °winne,   *rejoicing*
    And thanked Jēsū trew in °trōne,   *throne*
3790 And °shrǫve him there of his sin,   *absolved*
    As clẹne as hē had never dōne nǫne;
And sithe hē kiste him cheek and chin
    †And an habit there did him upon.

His grẹtẹ hǫst at Dǫver lay,
    And wēnd hē sholde have come again,
Til after befell upon a day,
    Sir Līonel, that was mikel of main,
With fifty lǫrdes, the sooth tō say,
    Tō seek his lǫrd hē was full fain;
3800 Tō London hē took the rightẹ way;
    Alas, for wǫ! There was hē slain.

Bors de Gawnes wǫlde nǫ lenger abīde
    But busked him and māde all boun,
And bade all the hǫst hǫmeward rīde—
    God send them wind and °weder round!   *ample wind*
Tō seek Launcelot will hē rīde;
    Ector and hē dīverse wayes yōde,

3777 His sorrowful heart grew cold.
3793 And he put a monastic habit on him.

And Bors sought forth the weste sīde,
  †As hē that coude neither īvel nor good.

3810 Full erly in a morrow tīde
  In a forest hē fand a well;
Hē rode ever forth by the river sīde,
  Til hē had sight of a chapel;
There at mass thought hē abīde;
  Rewfully hē herde ring a bell;
There Launcelot hē fand with mikel prīde,
  And prayd hē might with him there dwell.

Ere the half yēre were comen tō the end,
  There was comen of their fellowes seven,
3820 Where īchon had sought their frēnd,
  With sorrowful herte and drēry °steven;   *voice*
Had none never will away tō wend,
  When they °herde of Launcelot neven,   *heard tell of*
                                                     Lancelot
But all tōgeder there gan they lende,
  As it was Goddes will of heven.

°Holich all tho seven yēres   *wholly*
  Launcelot was prēst and mass song,
In penaunce and in dīverse prayers;
  That līfe him thought nothing long;
3830 Sir Bors and his other °fēres   *companions*
  On bookes °redde and belles °rong.   *read/rang*
†So little they wex of lin and lēres
  Them tō know it was °strong.   *difficult*

†It fell again an ēven-tīde
  That Launcelot °sēkened sēly sore.   *sickened*
                                                   wondrously
The bishop hē clēped tō his sīde,
  And all his fellows less and more;
Hē said: "Brethern, I may no lenger abīde;
  My bāleful blood of līfe is bare;
3840 †What boot is it tō hele and hīde?
  My foul flesh will tō erthe fare.

3809 Like one who knew neither evil nor good (i.e., in a daze).
3832 They grew so thin in loin and countenance.
3834 It happened toward one evening-time.
3840 What good is it to conceal and hide it?

"But, brethern, I pray you tōnight,
　Tōmorrow, when yē fīnd mē dẹde,
†Upon a bēre that yē will mē dight,
　And tō Joyous Gard then mē lẹde;
For the love of God Almight,
　Bury my body in that °stẹde;　　　　　　　　　*place*
†Some tīme my trouth there-tō I plight;
　Alas! Mē forthinketh that I sọ did!"

3850　"Mercy, sir," they said all three,
　　"For His love That dīed on Rood;
Yif any īvel have grēved thee,
　　It is but °hẹvyness of your blood;　　　　　*heaviness*
Tōmorrow yē shall better bē;
　　When were yē but of comfort good?"
Merrily spāke all men but hē,
　　But straight untō his bed hē yōde.

And clēped the bishop him until,
　†And shrọve him of his sinnes clẹne,
3860 Of all his sinnes loud and still,
　　And of his sinnes much did hē °mẹne;　　　*speak*
There hē received with goodẹ will
　　°God, Maryes Son, maiden clẹne.　　　　　*i.e., received*
　　　　　　　　　　　　　　　　　　　　　the Sacrament
Then Bors of weeping had never his fill;
　　Tō bed they yēde then all bydēne.

A little whīle before the day,
　As the bishop lay in his bed,
A laughter took him there hē lay,
　That all they were right sọre °adredde;　　　*frightened*
3870 They wākened him, for sooth tō say,
　　And asked yif hē were hard °bestedde;　　　*pressed*
Hē said: "Alas, and wẹle-away!
　　Why ne had I lenger thus °bē led?　　　　　*been led (in*
　　　　　　　　　　　　　　　　　　　　　dreams)

"Alas! Why nighed yē mē nigh
　Tō awākẹ mē in word or steven?
Hēre was Launcelot bright of blee
　With āngeles thirty thousand and seven;

3844 That you will place me on a bier.
3848-49 Once I pledged my word to that; Alas! I repent that I did so!
3859 And cleansed himself of his sins by confession.

Him they bǫre up on high;
　　Against him ǫpened the gātes of hęven;
3880　Such a sight right now I see,
　　Is nǫne on erthe that might it neven."

"Sir," they said, "for Cross on Rood,
　　Dōth such wordes clęne away.
Sir Launcelot aileth nǫthing but good;
　　Hē shall bē hǫle by °prīme of day."　　　　　　*the first hour*
Candle they light and tō him yōde,
　　And fand him dęde, for sooth tō say,
Ręd and fair of flesh and blood,
　　Right as hē in sleeping lay.

3890　"Alas!" said Bors, "That I was born!
　　That ever I sholde see this in-deed!
The bestę knight his līfe hath lorn
　　That ever in stour bestrǫdę steed!
Jēsū, That crowned was with thorn,
　　In hęven his sǫul foster and feed!"
Untō the fifth day at the morn
　　They left nǫt for tō sing and rędę,

And after they māde them a °bēre,　　　　　　　*bier*
　　The bishop and thēse other bǫld,
3900　And forth they went, all in fēre,
　　Tō Joyous Gard, that richę °hǫld;　　　　　　*stronghold*
In a chapel, °amiddes the quēre,　　　　　　　*amid the choir*
　　A grāve they māde as they wǫlde,
And three dayes they °wāked him there,　　　*watched*
　　In the castel with cares cǫld.

Right as they stood about the °bēre　　　　　　*bier*
　　And tō burying him sholde have brǫught,
In cāme Sir Ector, his brōder dęre,
　　That seven yēre afore had him sǫught.
3910　Hē looked up into the quēre;
　　Tō hēre a mass then had hē thǫught;
†For that they all ravished were
　　They knew him and hē them nǫught.

3912-13 Because they were all in a religious ecstasy, they neither knew
　　him nor did he know them.

Sir Bors both wept and sang,
  †When they that faire fast unfold;
There was none but his handes °wrang,
  The bishop nor none of the other bold.   *wrung*
Sir Ector then thought long;
  What this corpse was fain wite hē wolde;
3920 An hundreth times his herte °nigh sprang,   *nearly broke*
  By that Bors had him the tāle told.

Full hendely Sir Bors tō him spāke,
  And said: "Welcome, Sir Ector, īwis;
Hēre līeth my lord Launcelot du Lāke,
  For whom that wē have mōrned thus."
Then in armes hē gan him tāke,
  The dede body tō °clipp and kiss,   *embrace*
And prayed all night hē might °him wāke,   *watch by him*
  For Jēsū love, King of bliss.

3930 Sir Ector of his wit ner went,
  Wallowed and °wrang as hē were wōde;   *wrung his hands*
So wofully his mone hē °ment   *said*
  His sorrow °minged all his °mood;   *confused/mind*
When the corpse in armes hē °hent,   *seized*
  The teres out of his eyen yōde;
At the last they might no lenger stent,
  But burīed him with drēry mood.

Sithen on their knees they kneeled down—
  Grete sorrow it was tō see with sight:
3940 "Untō Jēsū Crīst I ask a boon,
  And tō his Mōder, Mary bright:
Lord, as thou mādest both sun and moon,
  And God and Man art most of might,
Bring this soul untō Thy °trōne,   *throne*
  †And ever Thou rewdest on gentle knight."

Sir Ector °tent not tō his steed,   *paid no attention*
  Wheder hē wolde °stint or run away,   *stand still*

3915 When they closely embrace that fair one (Ector, who is Bors'
    brother).
3945 If ever You had pity on a noble knight.

†But with them all tō dwell and lẹde,
   For Launcelot all his life tō pray.
3950 On him did hē °ermītes weed,   *hermit's*
   And tō their chapel went their way;
A fourtenight on foot they yēde,
   Ẹre they họme come, for sooth tō say.

When they cāme tō Aumsbury,
   Dẹde they found Gaynor the queen,
With °rodes fair and rẹd as cherry,   *cheeks*
   And forth they bọre her them between,
And burīed her with mass full merry
   By Sir Arthur, as I you mẹne;
3960 Now hight their chapel Glastonbury,
   An abbey full rich, of °order clẹne.   *pure (monastic)*
                                             order

Of Launcelot du Lāke tell I nọ mọre,
   But thus belẹve thēse ermītes seven.
And yet is Arthur burīed there,
   And Queen Gaynor, as I you neven,
With monkes that are right of lọre;
   They rẹde and sing with mildẹ steven:
"Jēsū, That suffred woundes sọre,
   Graunt us all the bliss of hẹven!"
                         Amen

3948 But decided to dwell with them all and lead his life there.

Explicit le Morte Arthur
(Here ends the Death of Arthur)

Alliterative Morte Arthure

MORTE ARTHURE

Hēre beginnes Morte Arthure. In Nomine Patris et
Filii et Spiritus Sancti. Amen pur Charite. Amen.

†Now grẹte glorīous God   through grāce of Himselven
And the precīous prayer   of his °prīs Mōder
Shēld us frọ shāmesdeede   and sinful workes
And give us grāce tō guīe   and govern us hēre
In this wretched world,   through virtūous living
That wē may kaire til his court,   the kingdom of hẹven
When our sọules shall part   and sunder frọ the body
Ever tō beld and tō bīde   in bliss with Himselven;
And wisse mē tō warp out   some word at this tīme
10 That nọther void bē ne vain   but worship til Himselven
Plẹsand and profitāble   tō the pople that them hēres.

    Yē that °lust has tō °līthe   or loves for tō °hēre   *desire/listen/ hear*
Of elders of ọlde tīme   and of their °awke deedes,   *strange*
How they were °lēle in their °law   and loved God Almighty   *loyal/religion*
°Herkenes mē °hendely   and họldes you stille,   *hearken/ courteously*
And I shall tell you a tāle   that °trew is and nọble   *true*
Of the °rēal °renkes   of the Round Tāble   *royal/men*
That °chēf were of chivalry   and °chēftains nọble   *chief/chieftains*
Bọth °wary in their workes   and wīse men of armes,   *skilled*
20 Doughty in their dōings   and °dredde ay shāme,   *dreaded*
Kīnd men and °courtais   and °couth of court °thewes,   *courteous/ skilled/manners*

1-11 Now (may the) great glorious God,   by the grace of Himself
   And the precious prayer   of His excellent Mother,
   Shield us from shameful deeds   and sinful acts
   And give us grace to guide   and govern us here
   In this wretched world,   that, through virtuous living,
   We may go to His court,   the Kingdom of heaven,
   When our souls must part   and separate from the body,
   Ever to dwell and to remain   in bliss with Himself;
   And teach me to utter   some words at this time
   That will be neither empty nor vain   but worshipful to Himself,
   Pleasing and profitable   to the people that hear them.

How they wǫn with war   °worshippes many,   *honors*
°Slogh Lūcīus the °lithere   that lǫrd was of Rōme,   *slew/wicked*
And conquered that °kingrik   through craftes of armes;   *kingdom*
†Herkenes now hiderward   and hēres this story!

When that the King Arthur   by conquest had °wonnen   *won*
Casteles and kingdomes   and °countrees many,   *countries*
And hē had °covered the crown   of that °kith riche   *recovered/*
                                                               country
†Of all that Uter in °erthe   °ǫught in his tīme: *earth/owned*
30 Argayle and Orkney   and all thēse °oute-īles,   *outer-isles*
Īreland °utterly,   °as Ōcēan runnes,   *entirely/where*
                                                               the
†Scāthel Scotland by skill   hē skiftes as him līkes
And Wāles °of war   hē wǫn °at his will,   *by/to*
Bǫthe Flaunders and Fraunce   free °til himselven,   *to*
Holland and Hainault   they hēld of him °bǫthen,   *both*
†Burgoigne and Brabaunt   and Bretain the less,
Guīenne and Gothland   and Greece the rich,
Bayonne and Bourdeaux   hē °belded full fair,   *dwelt in*
Touraine and Toulouse   with °towres full high,   *towers*
40 Of Poitīers and Prōvence   hē was prince hǫlden;
Of Valence and Vīenne,   of valūe sǫ nǫble,
Of °Overgne and Anjou,   thǫse °erldoms rich,   *Auvergne/*
                                                               earldoms
By conquest full crūel   they °knew him for lǫrd   *acknowledged*
Of Navarre and Norway   and Normandy °eek   *also*
†Of Almaine, of Estriche,   and other ynow;
Denmark hē °dressed   all by °drēde of himselven   *directed/dread*
†Frǫ Swynne untō Swetherwike,   with his sword keen!

When hē thēse deedes had dōne,   hē dubbed his knightes,
†Devīsed dūcherīes and dęlt   in dīverse °rewmes,
50 Māde of his °cosins   kinges annointed   *relatives*
In °kithes °there they covēt   crownes tō °bęre.   *countries/*
                                                               where/bear
When hē thēse °rewmes had ridden   and °rewled the °pople,   *realms/ruled/*
                                                               people
Then rested that °rēal   and hēld the Round Tāble;   *royal (one)*

---

25 Harken (listen) now hither (to me) and hear this history.
29 [Uter: Uther Pendragon, Arthur's father.]
32 Harmful Scotland he skillfully rules as it pleases him. [Scotland and
England were often at war in the fourteenth century; hence "harmful"
Scotland.]
36 Burgundy, Brabant, and Little Britain (i.e., Brittainy). [All areas of
what is now France.]
45 Of Germany, of Austria, and many others.
47 From Swynn (an arm of the North Sea near Zeeland) to Sweden
(Swetherwike); i.e., the whole extent of Denmark.
49 Created and gave out dukedoms in diverse realms.

°Sujourns that °sẹson   tō °solāce himselven   *sojourns/season/ please*
†In Bretain the brọdder,   as him best °līkes;   *pleases*
°Sithen went intō Wāles   with his °wyes all,   *then/men*
Sways intō Swaldīe   with his °snell houndes   *swift*
For tō hunt at the hartes   in thọse high landes,
In Glamorgan with glee   °there °gladship was ever,   *where/gladness*
60 And there a °citee hē set,   by assent of his lọrdes *city*
That Caerlīon was called,   with °cūrīous walles,   *skillfully made*
On the rich river   that runnes sọ fair,
†There hē might semble his sorte   tō see when him liked.
Then after at Carlīsle   a °Christenmass hē họldes,   *Christmas*
This °ilk °kidd conquerour   and hēld him for lọrd   *same/famous*
†With dūkes and douspeeres   of dīverse °rewmes,   *realms*
†Erles and erchevesques   and other ynow,
†Bishoppes and bachelers   and bannerettes nọble
That bowes tō his banner,   °busk when °him līkes.   *go/it pleases him*
70 But on the Christenmass-day   when they were all °sembled, *assembled*
That °comlich conquerour   commaundes himselven   *comely*
That °ilk a lọrd °sholde °lenge   and nọ °lẹve tāke   *each/should/ remain/leave*
Tō the °tende day fully   were tāken tō the end.   *tenth*
Thus on °rēal array   hē hēld his Round Tāble   *royal*
With °semblaunt and solāce   and °selcouthe mẹtes;   *splendor/rare foods*
Was never such °nọblay   in nọ mannes tīme   *nobleness*
†Māde in mid-winter   in °thọ West Marches!   *those*

But on the °New-Yēre day,   at the noon °ēven,   *New Year's/ exactly*
†As the bọld at the bōrde   was of brẹd served,
80 Sọ cọme in °sodēnly   a senatour of Rōme,   *suddenly*
With sixteen knightes in a °suīte,   °sewand him °ọne; *company/ following/alone*
Hē °salūed the soveraign   and the °sale after   *saluted/hall*
°Ilk a king after king,   and māde his °inclīnes;   *each/bows*

---

55 In Britain the broader (i.e., Great Britain).
63 Where he might assemble his troop to see when it pleased him.
66 [*Douspeeres:* originally Charlemagne's twelve peers, but here simply "high noblemen."]
67 Earls and archbishops and many others.
68 Bishops and young knights (*bachelors*) and noble senior knights (*bannerets*). [A banneret was a knight entitled to bear his own banner; a bachelor ranked somewhat lower and was either a newly made knight or a young man about to be knighted.]
77 [West Marches: the countries bordering on Wales.]
79 As the bold men at the table were served with bread. [On the absolute adjective, see Introduction (p. xv). The bread is the first course (since the other food was heaped upon it), and the first course is the traditional time for the arrival of a messenger; cf. *Sir Gawain and the Green Knight*, vv. 116–32.]

Gaynor in her degree   hē °grētte as °him līked   *greeted/it*
†And sinn again tō the gōme   hē gāve up his needes: *pleased him*
"Sir Lūcīus Īberīus,   the Emperour of Rōme,
°Salūes thee as °subjet,   under his °sēle rich;   *salutes/subject/seal*
It is °crēdans, Sir King,   with crūel wordes;   *credentials*
†Trow it for nọ troufles,   his targe is tō shew!
90 Now in this New-Yēres Day,   with nọtarīes sign,
   I māke thee summons in °sale   tō °sew for thy landes,   *hall/plead*
   That on °Lamass Day   there bē nọ °let °founden   *August 1/hindrance/found*
   That thou bē °rẹdy at Rōme   with all thy Round Tāble   *ready*
   °Appẹre in his presence   with thy °prīs knightes   *appear/excellent*
   At °prīme of the day,   °in pain of your līves,   *first hour/on*
   In the °kidd Capitoil   before the king °selven   *famous/himself*
   When hē and his senatours   °bēs set as °them līkes,   *are/it pleases them*
   Tō answer °ọnly   why thou occūpīes the landes   *alone*
   That ọwe homāge of ọld   °til him and his elders,   *to*
100 Why thou has ridden and °raimed   and °ransound the pople   *robbed/ransomed*
   And killed down his °cosins,   kinges annointed;   *kinsmen*
   There shall thou give reckoning   for all thy Round Tāble,
   Why thou art rebel tō Rōme   and °rentes them with-họldes!   *revenue*
   °Yif thou thēse summons °withsit,   hē sendes thee thēse wordes: *if/resist*
   Hē shall thee seek ọver the °sẹ,   with sixteen kinges,   *sea*
   †Brin Bretain the brọde   and britten thy knightes
   And bring thee buxomly as a bẹste   with brēthe where him līkes,
   That thou ne shall route ne rest   under the hẹven rich
   Thọugh thou for reddour of Rōme   run tō the erthe!
110 For if thou flee intō °Fraunce   or °Frīsland other,   *France/Frisia*
   Thou shall be fetched with force   and °ọverset forever!   *overthrown*
   Thy °fader made °fewtee   wē fīnd in our °rolles,   *father/fealty/records*
   In the °regestrē of Rōme,   whọ-sọ right lookes;   *registry*
   Withouten mọre °troufling   the tribūte wē ask   *trifling*
   †That Jūlīus Cẹsar wọn   with his °gentle knightes!"   *noble*

---

85 And then (he bowed) again to the man (Arthur) and delivered his message.

89 Think it not a trifle, his shield (armorial device) is to be seen (hereon).

106-09 Burn Britain the broad (Great Britain) and beat down your knights; And with anger bring you compliantly as a beast where he pleases; And you shall not sleep nor rest under the rich heaven, though for fear of Rome you run to the earth (i.e., into a hole, like a hunted animal)!

115 [The Romans claim title to Britain on the basis of Caesar's conquest, as recorded in chronicles based ultimately on Book V of Geoffrey of Monmouth's *Histories of the Kings of Britain*.]

†The king blushed on the berne   with his brǫde eyen,
That full brēmly for brēthe   brent as the glēdes,
Cast colours as the king   with crūel °lātes   *features*
Looked as a līon   and on his lip bītes.
120 The Rōmanes for °radness   rusht to the °erthe,   *fear/earth*
For °fęrdness of his fāce   as they °fey wēre;   *fear/fated to die*
°Couched as kennetes   before the king selven;   *crouched like
                                                                 hounds*
Because of his countenaunce   confūsed °them seemed!   *they seemed*

Then °covered up a knight   and crīed full loud: *got up (on his
                                                                 knees)*
"King, crowned °of kind,   °courtais and nǫble,   *by nature/
                                                                 courteous*
°Misdō nǫ messanger   for °mensk of thyselven,   *harm/honor*
°Sēnn wē are in thy °manrēde   and mercy °thee beseekes;   *since/power/
                                                                 beseech you*
Wē °lenge with Sir Lūcīus,   that lǫrd is of Rōme,   *belong*

That is the °marvēloustest man   than on °molde °lenges;   *most marvelous/
                                                                 earth/lives*
130 †It is lēlful til us   his līking til work;
Wē come at his commaundment;   have us excūsed."

Then carpes the conquerour   crūel wordes:
"Hā! °crāvand knight,   a coward °thee seemes!   *craven/you seem*
†There is some segge in this sale,   and hē were sǫre grēved
Thou durst nǫt for all Lumbardy   look on him ǫnes!"

"Sir," says the senatour,   "°Sǫ Crīst °mot mē help,   *as/may*
The °vout of thy visāge   has wounded us all!   *expression*
Thou art the lordlīest °lēde   that ever I on looked.   *man*
By looking, withouten °lęęs,   a līon °thee seemes!"   *lies/you seem*

140   "Thou has mē summoned," °quǫd the king,   "and said what   *said*
                                                    thee līkes.
For sāke of thy soveraign   I suffer thee the mǫre;
°Sēnn I crowned was in °kith   with °crisom annointed,   *since/country/
                                                                 holy oil*
Was never crēatūre tō mē   that °carped sǫ large!   *talked so big*
But I shall tāke counsēl   °at kinges annointed   *from*
Of dūkes and °douspeeres   and °doctours nǫble,   *high noblemen/
                                                                 theologians*
Of peeres of the °parlement,   prēlātes and other   *parliament*

Of the °richest °renkes   of the Round Tāble;   *most powerful/
                                                                 men*
Thus shall I tāke °avīsement   of valīant °bernes,   *advice/men*

116-17 The king looked on the man with his large eyes, which burned
    very fiercely like coals because of (his) anger.
130 It is loyal (our duty) for us to do his pleasure.
134-35 There is a certain man in this hall, and he was sorely grieved that
    you dared not look on him once for all Lombardy (as a reward)!

°Work °after the wit   of my wīse knightes.   *do/according to*

150 Tō °warp wordes in wāste   nǫ °worship it wēre,   *utter/honor*

°Ne wilfully in this wrath   tō °wreken myselven.   *nor/avenge*

°Forthy shall thou °lenge hēre   and lodge with thēse lǫrdes   *therefore/remain*

This seven-night in °solāce   tō °sujourn your horses,   *pleasure/rest*

Tō see what līfe that wē °lede   in thēse °lǫw landes."   *lead/humble*

For by the °rēaltee of Rōme,   that °richest was ever,   *royalty/most powerful*

Hē commaundes Sir Kayous,   "Tāke °keep tō thǫse lǫrdes   *care of*

Tō °stightel °thǫ stern men   as their stāte °askes,   *arrange/those/ requires*

That they bē °herbered in hāste   in thǫse °high chāmbres,   *lodged/noble chambers*

°Sithen °sittandly in °sale   served thereafter,   *then/suitably/ hall*

160 That they find nǫ °faute   of food tō their horses,   *lack*

†Nǫther wīne ne wax   ne welth in this erthe;

†Spare for nǫ spīcery,   but spend what thee līkes

That there bē °largess on loft   and nǫ lack founden;   *generosity*

†If thou my worship wait,   wye, by my trewth,

Thou shall have gersoms full grete   that gain shall thee ever!"

†Now are they herbered in high   and in hǫst hǫlden,

Hāstily with °hende men   within these °high walles.   *courteous/noble*

†In chāmbers with °chimpnees   they °chāngen their °weedes,   *chimneys/ change/clothes*

And °sithen the chaunceller   them fetched with chevalry   *then*
                                                         nǫble;

170 Soon the senatour was set   as him well °seemed,   *befit*

†At the kinges ǫwn bōrde;   twǫ knightes him served,

Singulere, soothly,   as Arthur himselven,

Richly on the right hand   at the Round Tāble.

By °resoun that the Rōmans   were sǫ °rich hǫlden,   *reason/powerful*

As of the °rēalest blood   that °regned in erthe.   *most royal/ reigned*

†There come in at the first course,   before the king selven,

°Bǫrehevedes that were bright,   °burnisht with silver   *boar-heads/ adorned*

---

161 Neither wine nor wax (candles) nor wealth on this earth.

162 Don't save money on spices, but spend what you please.

164-65 If you guard my honor, man, by my pledged word, you shall have
very great rewards that will profit you forever.

166 Now are they nobly lodged and regarded as guests.

168 [Chambers with chimneys are heated rooms, a luxury at this time.]

171-72 At the king's own table (a place of honor); two knights served
him alone (singly), in truth, as (was done for) Arthur himself.

176 [The elaborate feast that follows might actually have been served in
a royal household of the late fourteenth century. Menus for royal
feasts are printed in *Two Fifteenth-Century Cookery-Books*, ed.
Austin, EETS, o.s., 91 (London, 1888; reprinted 1964).]

†All with taught men and towen   in togges full rich,
Of sank rēal in suīte,   sixty at ǫnes;

180 †Flesh flourisht of fermison,   with frumentee nǫble,
There-tō wīld tō wāle,   and winlich briddes,
°Pācockes and plǫvers   in platters of gold   *peacocks*
°Pigges of °pork despīne   that pastūred never;   *piglets / porcupine*
Sithen herons in °hedoyne   °hęled full fair,   *plumage / concealed*
†Gręte swannes full swīthe   in silveren chargeours,
°Tartes of °Turky,   tāste when them līkes;   *pies / Turkey*
°Gumbaldes °graithly,   full grācīous tō tāste;   *Beef pies / readily*
†Sēnn bǫwes of wīld bǫres   with the brawn lēched,
Bernakes and botoures   in batterd dishes,

190 Thereby °braunchers in °bręd,   better was never, *young hawks / bread*

With °brēstes of °barrowes   that bright wēre tō °shew; *breasts / pigs / be seen*

°Sēnn come there °sēwes °sēre   with solāce thereafter, *then / stews / various*
†Ownde of azūre all ǫver   and ardaunt them seemed,
Of ilk a lēche the lowe   launched full high,
That all °lēdes might līke   that looked them upon; *men*
Then crānes and curlewes   craftily °rǫsted,   *roasted*
°Connīes in °cretoyne   coloured full fair,   *rabbits / milk and spices*

°Fesauntes °enflourished   in °flāmand silver,   *pheasants / adorned / flaming*
†With darīelles endorded   and daintīes ynow;

200 †Then Claret and Crēte   clergīally rennen
With condethes full cūrīous   all of clęne silver,
°Osay and Algarde   and °other ynow   *Alastian and Spanish wines / many others*
Rhēnish wīne and Rochelle,   richer was never,
°Vernāge of Venice,   virtūous, and Crēte,   *white wine*
In faucetes of fīne gold,   °fǫnde whǫ-sǫ līkes;   *to try*
†The kinges cup-bōrd   was clǫsed in silver,
In gręte gobletes overgilt,   glorīous of hew;

178-79 All with men trained and taught, in very rich clothes, all of royal
    blood in a troop, sixty together.
180-81 Flesh fattened in season, with noble frumentee (a dish made of
    wheat), along with wild (game) to choose, and pleasant birds.
185 Very many large swans on silver platters.
188-89 Then shoulders of wild boars, with the lean meat sliced, barnacle
    geese and bitterns in pastry-covered dishes (i.e., baked in pies).
193-94 Wavy with azure-colored sauce all over, and they appeared to be
    flaming; from each slice the flame leaped very high.
199 With pastries glazed with egg yolks and many (other) dainties.
200-01 Then Claret and Cretan wine were cunningly made to flow by
    conduits that were skillfully made, all of pure silver.
206-07 The king's cup-board was enclosed in silver and with great jewels
    gilded over, glorious of hue [i.e., a cabinet for storing cups, which
    were often very valuable, as in this case.]

There was a °chēf butler,   a °chevalēr nǫble   *chief/chevalier*
Sir Kayous the °courtais,   that of the cup served;   *courteous*
210 Sixty °cuppes of °suīte   for the king selven,   *cups/a set*
Crafty and °cūrīous,   °cǫrven full fair,   *skillfully made/*
                                                                       carved
In °ever-ilk a party pight   with precīous stǫnes,   *each part adorned*
†That nǫne enpoison sholde gǫ   privily there-under
But the bright gold for brēthe   sholde brist all tō pēces,
Or else the venom sholde void   through virtūe of the stǫnes;
And the conquerour himselven,   so °clęnly arrayed,   *handsomely*
In colours of °clęne gold °cledde,   with his knightes,   *pure/clad*
Dressed with his dīadem   on his °dēse rich,   *dais*
For hē was deemed the doughtīest   that dwelled in erthe.

220   Then the conquerour kīndly   °carped tō thǫse lǫrdes,   *spoke*
°Rehēted the Rōmans   with °rēal °spēche: *cheered/royal/*
                                                                       speech
"Sirs, °bēs knightly of countenaunce   and comfortes   *be*
                              yourselven;
†Wē knǫw nǫught in this countree   of cūrīous mętes;
In thēse °barrain landes   breedes nǫne other;   *barren*
†Forthy, withouten feining,   enforce you the mǫre
Tō feed you with such °feeble   as yē before fīnd."   *poor food*

       "Sir," says the senatour,   "°Sǫ Crīst °mot mē help,   *as/may*
There °regned never such °rēaltee   within °Rōme walles!   *reigned/royalty/*
                                                                       Rome's
There °ne is prēlāte °ne pǫpe   ne prince in this erthe   *is no/nor*
230 That hē ne might bē well °payed   of these °prīs °mętes!"   *pleased/*
                                                                       excellent/foods

       After their °węlth they °wesh   and went untō chāmber,   *wealth/washed*
This °ilk °kidd conquerour   with °knightes ynow;   *same/famous/*
                                                                       many knights
Sir Gawain the worthy   Dāme °Waynor hē °lędes,   *Gaynor/leads*
Sir Owghtreth on °tother sīde,   of Turry was lǫrd.   *the other*
Then spīces °unsparely   they °spended thereafter,   *unsparingly/*
                                                                       expended
°Malvesy and Muskadell,   thǫse marvēlous drinkes,   *malmsey and*
                                                                       muscatel

213-15 So that if any poison should go secretly under them (i.e., in the
    cup), the bright gold would burst all to pieces with anger, or else
    the poison should empty (lose its power) by means of the virtue of
    the precious stones. [The virtues (powers) of precious stones were
    commonplace in the Middle Ages. See *English Medieval Lapidaries*,
    eds. Evans and Serjeantson, EETS, o.s., 190 (London, 1932; re-
    printed 1960).]
223 In this country we know nothing of skillfully prepared foods.
225 Therefore, without pretending (that you are enjoying it), force
    yourself all the more.

†Raiked full rāthely   in rosset cuppes
Til all the rich on rǫw,   Rōmans and other.
But the soveraign soothly,   for °solāce of himselven,   °*pleasure*
240 Assigned tō the senatour   certain lǫrdes
Tō °lęde tō his °leverē,   when hē his °lęve askes,   °*lead/assigned*
                                                                          °*place/leave*
With mirth and with melody   of °minstralsy nǫble.   °*musicians*

     Then the conquerour tō counsēl   °kaires thereafter   °*goes*
With lǫrdes of his °lēgeaunce   that tō himself °lǫnges   °*allegiance/belong*
Tō the Gīauntes °Towr   jollily hē wendes   °*tower*
With justices and judges   and °gentle knightes.   °*noble*

     Sir Cador of Cornwall   tō the king °carpes,   °*speaks*
Laugh °on him lovely   with °līkand °lātes: °*at/pleasing/*
                                                                          features
"I thank God of that °thrǫ   that thus us °thrętes!   °*trouble/threatens*
250 You must be °trailed, I °trow,   °but yif yē °tręt better!   °*dragged/believe/*
                                                                          unless/treat
The lettres of Sir Lūcīus   °lightes mīne °herte.   °*lighten/heart*
Wē have as °losels lived   many lǫng day   °*wastrels*
With °delītes in this land   with lǫrdshippes many   °*delights*
And °forlitened the °lōs   that wē are °laited.   °*lessened/praise/*
                                                                          esteemed
I was abāshed, by our Lǫrd,   °of our best °bernes,   °*by/men*
For gręte dole of disūse   of deedes of armes.
Now wākenes the war!   Worshipped bē Crīst!
And wē shall win it again   by °wightness and strength!"   °*vigor*

     "Sir Cador," °quǫd the king,   "thy counsēl is nǫble;   °*said*
260 But thou art a marvēlous man   with thy merry wordes!
†For thou countes nǫ cāse   ne castes nǫ further,
But hurles forth upon °hęved,   as thy °herte thinkes;   °*head/heart*
†I moste tręte of a trews   touchand thēse needes,
Talk of these °tīthandes   that °teenes mīne herte.   °*tidings/grieves*
Thou sees that the emperour   is angerd a little;
It seemes by his °sandesman   that hē is sǫre °grēved;   °*messenger/*
                                                                          grieved
His senatour has summond mē   and said what him līked,
°Hethely in my hall,   with °heinous wordes,   °*scornfully/*
                                                                          hateful
In °spēche despīsed mē   and spared mē little;   °*speech*
270 I °might nǫt °spęke for spīte,   sǫ my herte trembled!   °*could/speak*
Hē asked me tyrauntly   tribūte of Rōme,

237-38 Went round very quickly in russet-colored (i.e., gold) cups, to all
       the powerful ones in turn, Romans and others.
261 You take account of no circumstances, nor consider (the matter)
    any further.
263 I must bargain for a truce (with you, Cador) concerning this mes-
    sage.

That °teenfully °tint was   in tīme of mīne elders,   *sorrowfully/lost*
There ālīenes, in absence   of all men of armes,
°Coverd it of commouns,   as cronīcles telles.   *obtained*
I have tītle tō tāke   tribūte of Rōme;
Mīne auncestres were emperours   and °ought it themselven,   *owned*
†Belin and Bremin   and Bawdewyne the third;
They occūpīed the empīre   eight score winters,
°Ilkon °eier after other,   as old men telles;   *each one/heir*

280 They °covered the Capitol   and cast down the walles,   *seized*
Hanged of their °hedesmen   by °hundrethes at °ones;   *head men/*
                                                                       hundreds/once
†Sēnn Constantīne, our kinsman,   conquered it after,
That °eier was of °Yngland   and emperour of Rōme,   *heir/England*
Hē that conquered the cross   by craftes of armes,
That Crīst was on crūcifīed,   That King is of °heven.   *heaven*
Thus have wē evidence tō ask   the emperour the sāme,
That thus °regnes at Rōme,   what right that hē claimes."   *reigns*

Then answerd King Aungers   tō Arthur himself:
"Thou ought tō bē °overling   over all other kinges,   *overlord*
290 For wīsest and worthyest   and °wightest of handes,   *strongest*
The knightlyest of counsēl   that ever crown bore.

I dare say for Scotland   that wē °them scāthe limped;   *suffered harm*
                                                                       from them
When the Rōmans °regned   they °ransound our elders   *reigned/*
                                                                       ransomed
And rode in their rīot   and ravished our wīves,
Withouten °resoun or right   °reft us our goodes;   *reason/bereft*
                                                                       us of
And I shall māke my avow   °devōtly tō Crīst   *devoutly*
†And tō the holy vernācle,   virtūous and noble,
Of this grete °vilany   I shall bē °venged °ones,   *villainy/*
                                                                       avenged/once

277 [In Book III of Geoffrey's *Histories* we are told that, long before
Caesar came to Britain, Belinus and Brennius conquered and ravaged
Rome. This is, of course, not historical.]

282 [According to Geoffrey (Book V, chapter 6), Constantine was the
son of a Roman Senator and a British Princess, and he succeeded to
the kingship of Britain. Then he overthrew the Emperor Maxentius
and became Emperor. According to legend, his mother, Helen, discovered the True Cross. Arthur claims kinship with Constantine
because of his supposed British mother. Constantine actually did
proclaim himself Caesar while in York, but he was never king of
Britain and was not of British descent.]

297 [The vernacle (Veronica) is the handkerchief with which St. Veronica wiped the face of Christ on His way to the Crucifixion. Mirac-
ulously, the image of His face was preserved on the handkerchief,
which still survives. The cult of the Veronica was especially strong in
the fourteenth century; Pope John XXII granted an indulgence of
10,000 days for a prayer to the Veronica, and its legend had an
important part in the popular romances about Titus and Vespasian.]

On yon venomous men   with valīant knightes!
300 I shall thee further of defence   °fostred ynow   *well trained*
Twenty thousand men   within twǫ months
°Of my wāge tō wend   where-sǫ thee līkes,   *at my expense*
†Tō fight with thy fǫmen   that us unfair lędes!"

Then the °burlich °berne   of °Bretain the little   *stately/man/ Brittany*
Counsēls Sir Arthur   and of him °congee °beseekes   *leave/beseeches*
Tō answer the ālīenes   with °austeren wordes,   *bold*
Tō entīce the emperour   tō tāke ǫver the mountes.
Hē said: "I māke mīne avow   verily tō Crīst,
And tō the hǫly °vernācle,   that °void shall I never   *Veronica/retreat*
310 For °radness of nǫ Rōman   that °regnes in erthe,   *fear/reigns*
But ay bē °rędy in array   and at °ęrest founden;   *ready/the first*
Nǫ mǫre °dout the dintes   of their °derf °wēpens   *fear/strong/ weapons*
Than the dew that is dank   when that it down falles;
Ne nǫ mǫre °shoun for the °swap   of their sharp swordes   *shunt/sweep*
Than for the fairest °flowr   that on the °folde growes!   *flower/ground*
I shall tō °batail thee bring   of °brenyed knightes   *battle/armored*
Thirty thousand by °tāle,   °thrifty in armes,   *count/prosperous*
Within a month-day,   intō °what march   *whatever country*
That thou will soothly assign,   when thyself līkes."

320   "Ā! Ā!" says the Welsh king,   "Worshipped bē Crīst!
Now shall wē °wręke full well   the wrath of our elders!   *avenge*
In West Wāles, īwis,   such wonders they wrǫught
That all for °wandreth may weep   that on that war thinkes.   *sorrow*
I shall have the °avauntward   °witterly myselven,   *vanguard/ certainly*
Til that I have vanquisht   the Vīscount of Rōme,
That wrǫught mē at Viterbō   a °vilany °ǫnes,   *villainy/once*
As I past in pilgrimāge   by the °Pount Tremble.   *Pontremoli*
Hē was in °Tuskānē that tīme   and took °of our knightes,   *Tuscany/some of*
†Arrest them unrightwīsly   and ransound them after.
330 I shall him sūrely ensūre   that °saghtel shall wē never   *be reconciled*
Ęre wē sadly assemble   by °ourselven ǫnes   *ourselves alone*
†And dęle dintes of dęth   with our derf wēpens!
And I shall °wāge tō that war   of worshipful knightes,   *bring at my expense*
Of °wightest of Welshland   and of the West Marches,   *strongest*
Twǫ thousand in °tāle,   horsed on steedes,   *number*
Of the °wightest °wyes   in all yon West Landes!"   *strongest/men*

---

303 To fight with your foes, who treat us unfairly.
329 Arrested them unjustly and afterwards held them for ransom.
332 And deal blows of death with our strong weapons.

Sir Ēwain fitz Urīen   then °ęgerly °fraines,   *eagerly/asks*

Was °cosin to the conquerour,   °corāgēous himselven: *kinsman/*
                                                               courageous

"Sir, °and we wiste your will   wē °wǫlde work thereafter;   *if we knew/*
                                                               would

340 Yif this °journee sholde hǫld   or bē °ajourned further,   *journey/*
                                                               adjourned

Tō rīde on yon Rōmans   and °rīot their landes,   *ravage*

Wē °wǫlde shāpe us therefore,   tō ship when you līkes."   *would prepare*

"°Cosin," °quǫd the conquerour,   "Kīndly thou askes   *kinsman/said*

Yif my counsēl accord   tō conquer yon landes.

By the °kalendes of °Jūny   wē shall encounter ǫnes   *first day/June*

With full crūel knightes,   °sǫ Crīst °mot mē help!   *as/may*

Theretō I māke mīne avow   °devōtly tō Crīst   *devoutly*

And tō the hǫly °vernācle,   virtūous and nǫble;   *Veronica*

†I shall at Lamass tāke lęve   tō lenge at my large

350 In Lorraine or Lumbardy,   whether mē lēve thinkes;

°Merk untō °Meloine   and mīne down the walles   *go/Milan*

Bǫth of °Pētersand and of °Pīs   and of °the Pount Tremble;   *Pietrasanta/*
                                                               Pisa/Pontremoli

In the Vāle of Viterbō   °vitail my knights,   *victual*

°Sujourn there six weekes   and °solāce myselven,   *sojourn/refresh*

Send °prikers tō the °prīs town   and plant there my °sēge   *riders/excellent/*
                                                               siege

°But if they proffer mē the °pęęs   by prōcess of tīme."   *unless/peace*

"°Certes," says Sir Ēwain,   "And I °avow after,   *certainly/vow*

°And I that °hathel may see   ever with mīne °eyen   *if/man/eyes*

That occupīes thīne heritāge,   the empīre of Rōme,

360 I shall °aunter mē ǫnes   his °ęgle tō touch   *adventure/*
                                                               eagle-standard

That borne is in his banner   of bright gold rich,

And °rāse it from his rich men   and °rīve it °in sonder,   *snatch/cut/*
                                                               asunder

†But hē bē rędily rescūed   with rīotous knightes.

I shall °enforce you in the °fēld   with fresh men of armes, *reinforce/field*

Fifty thousand folk   upon fair steedes,

On thy °fǫmen tō °founde   °there thee fair thinkes,   *foemen/go/*
                                                               where

In Fraunce or in °Frīsland,   fight when thee līkes!"   *Frisia*

"By our Lǫrd," quǫd Sir Launcelot,   "Now °lightes mīne   *lightens*
                                                    herte!

I °lowe God of this love   thēse lǫrdes has avowed!   *praise*

370 Now may °less men have °lęve   tō say what them līkes,   *lesser/leave*

349-50 At Lamastide (August 1) I shall take my leave, to remain freely
    in Lorraine (in France) or Lombardy (in Italy), whichever seems
    preferable to me.
363 Unless he (the eagle) is quickly rescued by vigorous knights.

And have nǫ °letting by law;   but listenes these wordes: *hindrance*
I shall bē at °journee   with °gentle knightes   *the day's fight/ noble*
On a °jamby steed   full jollily °graithed,   *active/equipped*
†Ęre any journee begin   tō joust with himselven
Amǫng all his gīauntes,   °genivers and other,   *Genoese*
Strīke him °stiffly °frǫ his steed   with °strenghe of mīne   *stoutly/from/ strength*
                                    handes,
†For all the steren in stour   that in his stale hōves!
Bē my retinūe arrayed,   I °reck it but a little   *reckon*
Tō māke route intō Rōme   with rīotous knightes.
380 †Within a seven-night day,   with six scǫre helmes,
I shall bē seen on the °sę,   sail when thee līkes."   *sea*

    Then laughes Sir Lot   and all on loud °męles: *speaks*
"Mē līkes that Sir Lūcīus   lǫnges °after sǫrrow;   *for*
Now hē °wilnes the war   his °wandreth beginnes;   *desires/sorrow*
It is our °wērdes tō °wręke   the wrath of our elders!   *fates/avenge*
I māke mīne avow tō God   and tō the hǫly °vernācle: *Veronica*
†And I may see the Rōmans   that are sǫ rich hǫlden,
Arrayed in their rīotes   on a round fēld,
I shall °at the reverence   of the Round Tāble   *for*
390 †Rīde through all the rout,   ręreward and other,
Rędy wayes tō māke   and renkes full rowm,
Runnand on ręd blood,   as my steed rushes!
Hē that followes my °fare   and first comes after   *route*
Shall fīnd in my fare-way   many °fey °lęved!"   *dead/left*

    Then the conquerour kindly   comfortes these knightes,
°Alowes them grętly   their lǫrdly °avowes: *praises/vows*
"°Allwēldand God   °worship you all!   *All-ruling/honor*
And let mē never want you,   whīles I in world regn;
My °mensk and my °manhēd   yē maintain in erthe,   *honor/manhood*
400 Mīne honour all utterly   in other kinges landes;
My °węle and my worship   of all this world rich,   *prosperity*
Yē have knightly conquered   that tō my crown °lǫnges.   *belongs*
°Him thar bē °fęrd for nǫ fǫes   that °swilk a folk lędes,   *he need/afraid/ such*

---

374 Before any day's fight (the major battle) begins, to joust with himself
    (Lucius).
377 Despite the strong (ones) in battle that remain in his troop.
380 Within a week from today with 120 knights.
387-88 If I can see the Romans, who are considered so powerful, arrayed
    in their riotous groups on a broad field.
390-91 Ride through all the company, rear guard and the rest, to make
    a ready way and plenty of room for men (who come after me).

But ever fresh for tō fight in °fēld when him līkes.	*field*
I °account nǫ king that under Crīst lives;	*take account of*
Whīles I see you all sound, I °set by nǫ mǫre."	*depend on*

†When they trustily had tręted they trumped up after,	
Descended down with a °daunce of dūkes and °erles.	*group (dance)/ earls*
Then they °sembled tō °sale and °souped °als swīthe,	*assembled/hall/ dined/quickly*
410 All this seemly °sorte, with °semblaunt full nǫble.	*company/ splendor*
Then the °roy °rēal °rehētes thēse knightes	*king/royal/cheers*
With reverence and °rīot of all his Round Tāble	*riotous amusement*
Til seven dayes was gǫne. The senatour askes	
Answer tō the Emperour with °austeren wordes.	*bold*
After the °Ēpiphany, when the purpose was tāken	*January 6*
Of peeres of the °parlement, prēlātes and other,	*parliament*
The king in his counsēl, °courtais and nǫble,	*courteous*
°Ūters the ālīenes and answers himselven:	*brings out*
"Greet well Lūcīus, thy lǫrd, and °laine nǫt thēse wordes;	*conceal*
420 If thou bē °lēgemen °lēle, let him °wite soon	*liege-man/loyal/ know*
I shall at °Lamass take lęve and lodge °at my large	*August 1/freely*
In °delīte in his landes with °lǫrdes ynow,	*delight/many lords*
°Regne in my °rēaltee and rest when mē līkes;	*reign/royalty*
By the river of Rhōne hǫld my Round Tāble,	
†Fang the fermes in faith of all thǫ fair rewmes	
°For all the menāce of his might and °maugree his eyen!	*despite/curses to*
And °merk °sithen ǫver the °mountes intō his °main landes,	*go/then/ mountains/strong*
Tō °Miloine the marvēlous and mīne down the walles;	*Milan*
In Lorraine ne in °Lumbardy °lęve shall I °nǫther	*Lombardy/ leave/neither*
430 °Nǫkine lēde upon līfe that there his lawes °yēmes;	*No kind of man/ keeps*
And turn intō °Tuskānē when mē tīme thinkes,	*Tuscany*
Rīde all thǫse °rowm landes with °rīotous knightes.	*spacious/vigorous*
Bid him māke rescūes for °mensk of himselven,	*honor*
And meet mē for his °manhēd in thǫse °main landes!	*manhood/strong*
I shall bē founden in Fraunce, °fraist when him līkes!	*to try*
The first day of °Feveryer in thǫse fair marches!	*February*
Ęre I bē fetched with force or forfeit my landes,	
The flowr of his fair folk full °fey shall bē °lęved!	*dead/left*
I shall him °sēkerly ensūre under my °sēle rich	*certainly/seal*
440 Tō °sēge the °citee of Rōme within seven winter	*besiege/city*

---

407 When they had confidently discussed (this business), they blew on
   trumpets afterwards (as a signal that the council was concluded).
425 Seize the revenues, in faith, of all those fair realms.

And that sọ °sēkerly °ensēge   upon °sēre halves   *securely/ besiege/all sides*
That many a senatour shall sigh   for sāke of mē °ọne!   *alone*
My summons are certifīed   and thou art full °served   *provided*
†Of cundit and crēdens;   kaire where thee līkes.
†I shall thy journee engist,   enjoin them myselven,
°Frọ this plāce tō the port   there thou shall pass ọver: *from*
Seven days tō Sandwich   I set °at the large;   *freely*
Sixty mīle on a day,   the sum is but little!
Thou °moste speed at the spurs   and spare nọt thy °fọle;   *must/foal*
450 †Thou wendes by Watling Street   and by nọ way °elles;   *else*
†There thou nightes on night   needes moste thou lenge;
Bē it forest or °fēld,   °found thou nọ further;   *field/go*
Bīnd thy °blonk by a °busk   with thy brīdle ēven,   *horse/bush*
†Lodge thyselven under linde   as thee lēfe thinkes;
There °ọwes nọne ālīenes   tō °ayer upon nightes,   *ought/wander*
With such a °ribawdous °rout   tō rīot thyselven.   *ribald/company*
Thy līcense is °limit   in presence of lọrdes,   *limited*
†Bē now lọth or lēfe,   right as thee thinkes,
For bọth thy līfe and thy °limm   °ligges thereupon,   *limb/lie*
460 Thọugh Sir Lūcīus had °laid thee   the lọrdship of Rōme,   *laid on you*
For bē thou founden a foot   withoute the °flood marches   *edge of the sea*
After the °aughtende day   when °undern is rungen,   *eighteenth/ nine a.m.*
†Thou shall bē hẹveded in hīe   and with horse drawen,
And sēnn hīely be hanged,   houndes tō gnawen!
The rent ne red gold   that untō Rōme °lọnges   *belongs*
Shall nọt rẹdily, °renk,   °ransoun °thīne ọne!"   *man/ransom/ you alone*

"Sir," says the senatour,   "°Sọ Crīst °mot mē help,   *as/may*
°Might I with worship   °win away ọnes   *could/go*
I °sholde never for Emperour   that on erthe °lenges   *should/remains*
470 °Eft untō Arthur   °ayer on such °needes;   *again/go/a message*
But I am °singely hēre   with sixteen knightes;   *singly*
I °beseek you, sir,   that wē may °sound pass.   *beseech/safely*
If any unlawful °lēde   °let us by the way,   *man/hinder*
Within thy līcense, lọrd,   thy °lōs is °inpaired."   *fame/impaired*

444 With safe-conduct and credentials; go where you please.
445 I shall assign the resting-places for your journey, order them myself.
450 [*Watling Street*: the old Roman road leading from the southern coast by way of London to Cardigan in Wales.]
451 Wherever you are caught by night you must by necessity remain.
454 Lodge yourself under trees, wherever it seems good to you.
458 Whether (my order) is now hateful or pleasing (to you).
463-64 You shall be speedily beheaded and torn apart by horses, and then quickly hanged for dogs to gnaw.

"Care, nọt," °quọd the king,   "Thy °cundit is knọwen   *said/safe conduct*
°Frọ Carlīsle tō the °cọste   there thy °cogge lenges;   *from/coast/ship*
Thọugh thy coffers were full,   crammed with silver,
Thou might bē °sēker of my °sēle   sixty mile further."   *secure/seal*

　　They °enclīned tō the king   and °congee they asked,   *bowed/leave*
480 °Kaires out of Carlīsle,   catches on their horses;   *go*
Sir Cador the °courtais   °kend them the wayes,   *courteous/taught*
Tō Catrik them conveyed   and tō Crīst them °bekenned.   *entrusted*
Sọ they sped at the spurres   they °sprangen their horses, *exhausted*
Hīres them °hackenayes   hāstily thereafter.   *horses*
Sọ for °reddour they °ridden   and rested them never,   *fear/rode*
°But yif they lodged under °linde   °whīles them the light   *Unless/tree/ when*
　　　　　　　　　failed;
But ever the senatour forsooth   °sọught at the °gainest.   *went/nearest (way)*
†By the sevende day was gọne   the citee they rẹched.
Of all the glee under God   sọ glad were they never
490 †As of the sound of the °sẹ   and Sandwich belles.   *sea*
Withouten more °stunting   they shipped their horses;   *stopping*
°Wēry tō the °wan sẹ   they went all at ọnes.   *weary/pale*
With the men of the °wāle   they weighed up their °ankers   *gunwale/anchors*
And fled at the °fore °flood;   °in Flaunders they rọwed   *first/high tide/to*
And through Flaunders they °found,   as them fair thọught, *went*
°Til Aachen in °Almaine,   in °Arthur landes;   *to/Germany/ Arthur's*
°Gọs by Mount Goddard   full °grēvous wayes,   *they go/grievous*
And sọ intō Lumbardy,   °līkand tō shew.   *pleasant to be seen*
They turn through °Tuskānē   with towres full high;   *Tuscany*
500 †In pris appairelles them   in precīous weedes.   *Sunday/Sutri/ rest*
The °Sononday in °Sutere   they °sujourn their horses
And seekes the saintes of Rōme   by assent of knightes;
Sithen °prikes to the °palais   with °portes sọ rich,   *spur/palace/ gates*
°There Sir Lūcīus lenges   with °lọrdes ynow;   *where/many lords*
°Loutes tō him °lovely   and lettres him °bēdes   *bow/lovingly/ offers*
Of °crēdens enclọsed   with °knightlich wordes.   *credentials/ knightly*

　　Then the Emperour was °ẹger   and °enkerly °fraines;   *eager/ardently/ asks*
The answer of Arthur   hē askes him °soon,   *immediately*
†How hē arrayes the rewm   and rewles the pople,

---

488 By the time the seventh day was gone they reached the city.
490 [Sandwich is the port from which the Romans will take ship.]
500 Hastily dress themselves in precious garments.
509 How he orders the realm and rules the people.

510 °Yif hē bē rebel tō Rōme, what right that hē claimes; *if*
"Thou sholde his sceptre have °sesed and sitten °aboven *seized/above*
For reverence and °rēaltee of Rōme the noble; *royalty*
°By certes thou was my °sandesman and senatour of Rōme, *because/ messenger*
Hē sholde for °solempnitee have served thee himselven." *solemnity*

"That will hē never for no °wye of all this world rich *man*
°But who may win him of war, by °wightness of handes; *except/strength*
Many °fey shall be first upon the fēld °leved, *dead/left*
Ere hē °appere in this plāce, proffer when thee līkes. *appears*
I say thee, sir, Arthur is thīne °enmy forever, *enemy*
520 And °ettles tō bē °overling of the empīre of Rōme, *intends/overlord*
That all his auncestres °ought °but Uter himselven. *owned/except*
Thy °needes in this New Yēre I °notified myselven *message/made known*
Before that noble of nāme and °nīne sum of kinges; *nine in all*
In the most rēal plāce of the Round Tāble
†I summond him solemnly on-seeand his knightes;
°Sēnn I was formed, in faith, so °ferd was I never, *since/feared (afraid)*
In all the plāces °there I passed of princes on erthe. *where*
I °wolde forsāke all my °suīte of °seignoury of Rōme *would/following/ lordship*
Ere I eft tō that soveraign were sent on such °needes! *message*
530 Hē may bē chosen °chēftain, °chēf of all other *chieftain/chief*
Both by chaunces of armes and chevalry noble,
For wīsest and worthyest and °wightest of handes. *strongest*
Of all the wyes that I °wot in this world rich— *know*
The knightlīest crēatūre in Cristendom °holden *considered*
Of king or of conquerour crowned in erthe,
Of countenaunce, of °corāge, of crūel °lātes, *courage/ expressions*
The comlyest of knighthood that under Crīst lives!
Hē may bē spoken °in dispens despīser of silver, *in his expenditures*
That no more of gold gives than of grete stones,
540 No more of wīne than of water that of the well runnes,
Ne of °welth of this world °but worship alone. *wealth/except for*
Such countenance was never knowen in no °kith riche *country*
As was with this conquerour in his court holden;
I counted at this Cristenmass of kinges annointed,
°Hole ten at his tāble that tīme with himselven. *ten in all*
Hē will °warray, īwis, bē ware yif thee līkes; *make war*
°Wāge many wight men and watch thy °marches, *pay/borders*
That they bē redy in array and °at erest founden, *at the earliest time*

525 I summoned him solemnly (to appear in Rome) with his knights looking on.

For °yif hē °reche untō Rōme,   hē ransouns it forever.   *if/reach*
550 †I rede thou dress thee therefore   and draw no let longer;
Be °sēker of thy °soudēours   and send tō the mountes; *sure/mercenaries*
By the quarter of this °yēre,   °and him °quert stand, *year/if/health*
Hē will °wightly in a whīle   on his wayes °hīe."   *stoutly/hasten*

"By °Ester," says the Emperour,   "I °ettle myselven *Easter/intend*
Tō °hostay in °Almaine   with armed knightes;   *lead a host/*
                     Germany
Send °frekly intō Fraunce,   that flowr is of rewmes, *boldly*
°Fonde tō °fette that °frēke   and forfeit his landes, *try/fetch/man*
For I shall set °keepers,   full °cunnand and noble, *guards/cunning*
Many gīaunt of °Gene,   jousters full good,   *Genoa*
560 Tō meet him in the mountes   and martyr his knightes,
Strīke them down in °straites   and °stroy them forever. *narrow places/*
                     destroy
†There shall upon Goddard   a °garret bē °rered   *watch-tower/*
                     reared
That shall bē °garnisht and °keeped   with good men of *furnished/*
               armes, *watched*
And a °becon aboven tō °brin   when them līkes,   *beacon/burn*
That none °enmy with host   shall enter the mountes. *enemy*
†There shall on Mount Bernard   bē °belded another, *built*
†Busked with bannerettes   and bachelers noble.
In at the °portes of Pāvīa   shall no prince pass   *gates*
Through the perilous plāces   for my °prīs knightes." *excellent*

570 Then Sir Lūcīus lordlich   lettres hē sendes
Anon intō the Orīent   with °austeren knightes   *bold*
†Til Ambyganye and Orcage   and Alisaundere eek
Tō Inde and tō Ermonye,   as Eufrātēs runnes,
Tō Asīa and to Afrīke,   and Europe the large,
†Tō Irritaine and Elamet,   and all those °oute iles,
Tō Arraby and Ēgypt,   °til erles and other   *to*
That any erthe occūpīes   in those °este marches   *eastern countries*
Of °Damaske and °Damīet,   and dūkes and erles. *Damascus/*
                     Damietta
†For drēde of his daungēr   they dressed them soon;

550 I advise you to prepare yourself for this and delay no longer.
562 [*Goddard*: Mt. Goddard, in the Alps.]
566 [*Mount Bernard*: at the St. Bernard pass, in the Alps.]
567 Equipped with noble bachelors and bannerets (see note on line 68).
572-73 To Ambyganye and Orcage and Alexandria as well, to India and
  to Armenia, where the Euphrates runs (Ambyganye and Orcage are
  apparently in the East).
575 Hyrcania (*Irritaine*) and Elam (*Elamet*) and all those outer isles.
  Hyrcania and Elam are not islands but countries in Asia.
579 For fear of his displeasure they prepared themselves immediately.

580 Of Crēte and of °Capadōs   the honourāble kinges
     Come at his commaundement   °clęnly at'ǫnes;
     Tō °Tartary and Turkey   when °tīthinges is comen
     They turn in by °Thēbay,   tyrauntes full hūge,
     †The flowr of the fair folk   of °Amazonnes landes;
     All that °failes on the fēld   bē forfeit forever.
     Of °Babylon and °Baldake   the °burlich knightes
     °Boyes with their baronāge   bīdes nǫ lǫnger;
     †Of Perse and of Pamphile   and Preter John landes
     °Ęch prince with his powēr   °appertlich °graithed;
590 The °Sowdan of °Surry   assembles his knightes
     °Frǫ °Nīlus to Nazareth,   numbers full hūge;
     Tō °Garyere and tō Galilee   they °gader all at °ǫnes,
     The °sowdanes that were °sēker   °soudēours tō Rōme;
     They °gadered ǫver the Greekes Sę   with °grēvous °wēpens,
     In their gręte galleys,   with °glitterande °shēldes;
     †The King of Cyprus on the sę   the Sowdan abīdes,
     With all the °rēales of Rhodes   arrayed with him °ǫne;
     They sailed with a °sīde wind   ǫver the salt strandes,
     °Sodēnly the °Sarazenes,   as themselvę līked;
600 Craftyly at °Cornett   the kinges are arrīved,
     °Frǫ the citee of Rōme   sixty mīle °large.
     °By that the Greekes were °graithed,   a full gręte number,
     The mightīest of Macedone,   with men of °thǫ marches,
     †°Pulle and Prūssland,   °presses with other,
     The °lēge-men of Lettow   with °lēgīons ynow.
     Thus they °semble in °sortes,   summes full hūge;
     The °sowdanes and °sarazenes   out of °sēre landes
     The °Sowdan of °Surry   and sixteen kinges
     At the citee of Rōme   assembled at ǫnes.

Cappadocia (in Turkey)
completely
China/tidings
Thebes
land of the Amazons
are lacking
Cairo/Bagdad/stately
knaves

each/openly/prepared
Sultan/Syria
from/Nile
Gadara/gather/once
sultans/trusty/mercenaries
gathered/grievous/weapons
glittering/shields

royal (ones)/alone
ample
quickly/Saracens
Corneto
from/away
By this time/prepared
those
Apulia hastens
liege-men/many troops
assemble/companies
sultans/saracens/various
Sultan/Syria

584 [The land of the Amazons was thought to be in Africa.]
588 From Persia and Pamphilia and the lands of Prester John [Prester
    John was thought to be a Christian ruler living somewhere in the
    Orient. In *The Travels of Sir John Mandeville* (a famous fourteenth-
    century book of fictitious travels, presented as a true account), Prester
    John is said to be the emperor of India, allied by marriage to the
    great Khan of China. The legend was probably based on reports of
    Christian communities (such as the Nestorian Christians) which
    actually did exist in the East.]
596 The King of Cyprus awaits the Sultan on the sea. [For the word
    order, see Introduction, p. xv.]
604-05 [*Prūssland*: Prussia; *Lettow*: Lithuania. Prussia and Lithuania
    were still pagan in the fourteenth century.]

610   Then °ishews the Emperour,   armed °at rightes   *issues/
                                                                                 completely*

Arrayed with his Rōmans   upon rich steedes;

Sixty gīauntes before,   engendered °with °fēndes,   *by/fiends*

With witches and °warlaws,   tō watchen his tentes   *warlocks*

°Aywere where hē wendes   wintres and °yēres.   *anywhere/years*

Might nǫ °blonkes them °bęre,   those °bustous churles,   *horses/bear/wild*

But °coverd cameles of towrs,   enclǫsed in mailes;   *camels covered with towers*

Hē °ayeres out with ālīenes,   hǫstes full hūge   *goes*

°Ēven intō °Almaine,   that Arthur had wonnen,   *directly/ Germany*

Rīdes in by the river   and rīotes himselvę,

620 And °ayeres with a hūge will   all thǫse high landes;   *goes*

All °Westfāle by war   hē winnes as him līkes,   *Westphalia*

Drawes in by °Danūby   and dubbes his knightes,   *Danube*

In the countree of °Coloine   castelles °ensēges   *Cologne/ besieges*

†And sujourns that sęsoun   with sarazenes ynow.

     †At the ūtas of Hillary   Sir Arthur himselven   *famous/ commanded*

In his °kidd counsēl   °commaunde the lǫrdes:

"°Kaire to your countrees   and °semble your knightes,   *go/assemble*

†And °keepes mē at Constantīne,   °clęnlich arrayed,   *await/ completely*

Bīdes mē at Barflēte   upon the blīthe °stręmes   *streams*

630 Bǫldly °within bǫrde,   with your best °bernes;   *aboard (ships)/ men*

I shall °menskfully you meet   in thǫse fair marches."   *honorably*

     Hē sendes forth °sodēnly   sergēauntes of armes   *quickly*

Tō all his mariners in rǫw   tō °arrest him shippes;   *commandeer*

Within sixteen dayes   his fleet was assembled,

At Sandwich on the sę,   sail when him līkes.

In the °palais of York   a °parlement hē hǫldes   *palace/ parliament*

With all the peeres of the rewm,   prēlātes and other;

And after the °pręching,   in presence of lǫrdes,   *preaching*

The king in his counsēl   °carpes thēse wordes: *speaks*

640 "I am in purpose tō pass   perilous wayes,

Tō °kaire with my keen men   tō conquer yon landes,   *go*

†Tō outraye mīne enmy,   yif aventūre it shew,

That occūpīes mīne heritāge,   the empīre of Rōme.

I set you hēre a soveraign,   assent °yif you līkes,   *if*

That is my °sib, my °sister son;   Sir Mordred himselven   *relation/sister's son*

---

624 And sojourns that season with many saracens.
625 At the Octave of St. Hillary's day (i.e., a week after January 24).
628-29 [Constantīne (the Peninsula of Cotentin) and Barflēte (Barfleur) are on the coast of Normandy.]
642 To outrage my enemy, if a chance should appear.

Shall bē my °leutenant,   with °lordshippes ynow   *lieutenant / sufficient authority*

Of all my °lēle °lēge-men   that my landes °yēmes."   *loyal / liege-men / possess*

Hē carpes tō his °cosin then,   in counsēl himselven;   *kinsman*

"I māke thee °keeper, Sir Knight,   of °kingrikes many,   *guardian / kingdoms*

650 Wardēn worshipful,   tō °wēld all my landes,   *wield (rule)*

That I have wonnen of war   in this world rich.

I °will that Waynor, my wīfe,   in worship bē holden,   *desire*

That her want no °wele   ne welth that her līkes;   *prosperity*

Look my °kidd casteles   bē °clenlich arrayed,   *famous / completely equipped*

There shō may sujourn herselve   with °seemlich bernes;   *seemly*

†Fonde my forestes bē frithed,   of frēndship for ever,

That none warray my wīld   but Waynor herselven,

And that in the sesoun   when grees is assigned,

That shō tāke her solāce   in certain tīmes.

660 Chaunceller and chāmberlain   chānge as thee līkes,

Auditours and officers,   ordain them thyselven,

Both °jurees and judges,   and justices of landes;   *juries*

Look thou °justify them well   that injury °workes.   *do justice to / do*

If mē bē °destained tō dīe   at °Drightens will,   *fated / God's*

I charge thee my °sektour,   chēf of all other,   *executor*

Tō minister my °mobles   for °meed of my soul   *goods / reward*

Tō °mendinauntes and °misese   in mischēf fallen.   *mendicants / those in misery*

Tāke hēre my testament   of °tresure full hūge;   *treasure*

As I °traist upon thee,   betray thou mē never!   *trust*

670 As thou will answer before   the °austeren Judge   *austere*

That all this world °winly   °wisse as Him līkes,   *pleasantly / directs*

Look that my last will   bē °lēly °perfourned!   *loyally / performed*

†Thou has clenly the cūre   that tō my crown longes

Of all my wordles °wele   and my wīfe °eek;   *prosperity / as well*

Look thou keep thee so °clēre   there bē no °cause founden   *clear / complaint*

When I tō °countree come,   if Crīst will it °thōle;   *country / allow*

°And thou have grāce goodly   tō govern thyselven,   *if*

I shall crown thee, knight,   king with my handes."

Then Sir Mordred full mīldly   °meles himselven,   *speaks*

680 Kneeled tō the conquerour   and carpes thēse wordes:

656-59 See that my forests are preserved (from poachers), in friendship
     forever, that no one be allowed to hunt the game except for Guen-
     evere herself, and even she is to hunt only at the season when the
     game are fat enough to be hunted, so that she will take her pleasure
     at fixed times. [Arthur's concern for the protection of his game is not
     surprising in a century when (as shown by *Sir Gawain and the Green
     Knight*) hunting was of great importance to the aristocracy.]
673 You are completely in charge of all that belongs to my crown.

"I °beseek you, sir,   as my °sib lord, — *beseech/related by blood*
That yē will for charitee   °chēse you another, — *choose*
For if yē put mē in this °plitt,   your °pople is deceived; — *plight/people*
Tō prēsent a °prince estāte   my power is simple; — *princely*
When other of °war-wisse   are worshipped hēreafter, — *cunning in warfare*
Then may I, forsooth,   °bē set but at little. — *be little regarded*
Tō °pass in your presence   my purpose is tāken — *travel*
And all my °pervēance °appert   for my prīs knightes." — *provisions/ready*

"Thou art my °nevew full °ner,   my °nurree of old, — *nephew/near/nursling*
690   That I have °chastīed and °chosen,   a chīld of my chāmber; — *disciplined/praised*
For the °sibreden of mē,   forsāke not this office; — *blood relationship to*
°That thou ne work my will,   thou °wot what it °menes." — *if/know/means*

Now hē tākes his leve .   and lenges no longer
†At lordes, at lēge-men   that leves him behīnden;
And °sēnn that °worthiliche °wye   went untō chāmber — *then/worthy/man*
For tō comfort the queen   that in care lenges.
Waynor °waikly   °weepand him kisses, — *weakly/weeping*
Talkes to him tenderly   with °teres ynow; — *tears*
"I may °wērye the wye   that this war mōved, — *curse*
700   That °warnes mē worship   of my °wedde lord; — *denies/wedded*
All my °līking of līfe   out of land wendes, — *pleasure*
And I in langour am left,   °lēve yē, forever! — *believe*
Why ne might I, dere love,   dīe in your armes,
Ere I this °destainy of dole   sholde °drīe °by mīne one!" — *destiny/suffer/alone*

"Grēve thee not, Gaynor,   for Goddes love of heven,
Ne °grouch not my °ganging;   it shall tō good turn! — *grudge/going*
Thy °wandrethes and thy weeping   woundes mīne herte; — *sorrows*
I may not °wīte of this wo   for all this world rich; — *depart (turn aside from)*
I have māde a °keeper,   a knight of thīne °owen, — *guardian/own*
710   °Overling of Yngland,   under thyselven, — *overlord*
And that is Sir Mordred,   that thou has °mikel praised, — *much*
Shall bē thy °dictour, my °dere,   tō dō what thee līkes." — *spokesman/dear*

Then hē tākes his leve   °at lādīes in chāmber, — *from*
Kissed them °kīndlich   and tō Crīst °beteches; — *kindly/entrusts (them)*
And then °shō swoones full °swīthe   when hē his sword — *she/quickly/asked for*
                                          °asked,
Sways in a swooning,   °swelte as shō wolde! — *as if she would die*

694 From lords, from liege-men, whom he leaves behind.

Hē °pressed tō his palfrey,   in presence of lordes,   *hastened*
°Prikes of the °palais   with his prīs knightes   *spurs from/*
                                                                          palace
With a rēal °rout   of the Round Tāble,   *company*
720 °Sought tōward Sandwich;   °shō sees him no more.   *went/she*

    †There the grete were gadered   with galīard knightes,
    °Garnished on the green fēld   and °graitheliche arrayed;   *drawn up/*
                                                                          suitably
    Dūkes and °douspeeres   daintely rīdes,   *high noblemen*
    Erles of Yngland   with archers ynow.
    †Shīrrēves sharply   shiftes the commouns,
    Rewles before the rich   of the Round Tāble,   *the soldiers from*
                                                                          each country
    Assignes °ilk a countree   tō certain lordes,
    In the south on the se bank   sail when them līkes.
    Then barges them °buskes   and tō the bank rowes,   *prepare*
730 Bringes °blonkes °on bōrde   and °burlich helmes   *horses/aboard/*
                                                                          stately
    Trusses in °tristly   °trapped steedes,   *securely/equipped*
    Tentes and other °tooles,   and °targes full rich,   *siege-engines/*
                                                                          shields
    °Cabanes and °cloth-sackes   and cofferes full noble,   *cabins/sacks of*
                                                                          clothes
    °Hackes and °hackeneys   and horses of armes;   *kind of horse*
    Thus they stow in the stuff   of full °steren knightes.   *stern*

    When all was shipped that sholde,   they °shunt no °lenger,   *hold back/longer*
    But °unteld them °tīte,   as the tīde runnes;   *untied/quickly*
    †Cogges and crayers   then crosses their mastes,
    At the commaundement of the king   °uncovered at ones;   *unfurled (sails)*
740 †Wightly on the wāle   they wīe up their ankers,   *handsome/waves*
    By wit of the watermen   of the °wāle °ythes.   *men/bow/coil*
    °Frēkes on the °forestaine   °faken their cābles   *small ships/*
    In °floynes and °fercostes   and Flemish shippes,   *merchantmen*
    °Titt sailes tō the top   and turnes the luff,   *pull*
    Standes upon °steerbōrd,   °sterenly they °songen.   *starboard/*
                                                                          sternly/sang
    The prīs shippes of the port   °prōven their deepness,   *test*
    And °foundes with full sail   over the °fawe °ythes;   *go/variegated/*
                                                                          waves
    °Holly withouten harm   they °hāle in °botes,   *wholly/haul/*
                                                                          boats
    Shipmen sharply   °shutten their °portes,   *shut/portholes*
750 †Launches lede upon luff   latchen their deepes,

---

721 There the great (ones) were gathered with jolly knights.
725-26 Sheriffs (the chief administrative officers of the counties) sharply
    move the common soldiers about, give orders (to their men) before
    the powerful (men) of the Round Table.
738 Large ships and small boats then hoist their sails.
740 Stoutly on the gunwale they weigh up their anchors.
750 Launch the lead on the luff (the bow) to measure the depth of the
    water.

Lookes to the °lode-stern   when the light failes,   *North Star*
Castes courses by craft   when the cloud rīses
°With the needle and the stone   on the night tīdes.   *i.e., with a*
                                                                        compass
For drēde of the dark night   they °drechèd a little   *slowed down*
†And all the steren of the streme   streken at ones.

    The king was in a grēte °cogge   with knightes full many,   *ship*
In a °cabane enclosed,   °clenlich arrayed;   *cabin/completely*
Within on a rich bed   restes a little,
And with the °swogh of the se   in °swefning he fell.   *swaying/*
                                                                        dreaming
760 °Him dremed of a dragon,   drēdful tō behold,   *he dreamed*
Come °drīvand over the deep   tō °drenchen his pople,   *driving/drown*
°Ēven °walkand   out the West landes,   *directly/walking*
°Wanderand unworthyly   over the °wāle °ythes;   *wandering/*
                                                                        handsome/waves
†Both his hed and his hals   were holly all over
Oundèd of azūre,   ēnamelled full fair;
His shoulders were shāled   all in clene silver
Shredde over all the shrimp   with shrinkand pointes;
His °wōmb and his winges   of wonderful °hewes,   *belly/hues*
In marvēlous mailes   hē mounted full high.
[His tail was °tōtattered,   with °tonges full hūge;]   *serrated/tongues*
770 Whom that hē touchèd   hē was °tint forever!   *lost*
His feet were °flourished   all in fīne sāble   *decorated*
[And his clawes were enclosed   with clene gold;]
And such a venomous °flaire   °flow from his lippes   *flame/flowed*
The °flood of the °flawes   all on fīre seemed!   *sea/flames*

    †Then come out of the Orīent,   ēven him againes,
A black bustous bere   aboven in the cloudes,
With ech a paw as a post   and paumes full hūge
With pikes full perilous,   all plīand them seemed;
Lothen and lothly,   lockes and other,
All with lutterd legges,   lokkerd unfair,
780 Filtered unfreely,   with fomand lippes;
The foulest of figūre   that formèd was ever!

---

755 And all the stern men of the stream (sailors) struck sail at once.
764-67 Both his head and his neck were completely covered all over with
    waves of azure, enamelled (colored) very fair; his shoulders were all
    covered with scales of pure silver that clothed the monster with
    shrinking points (i.e., like mail).
774-80 Then came out of the East, directly against him, a wild, black bear
    above in the clouds, with each paw as big as a post, and palms very
    huge, with very perilous claws that seemed all curling; hateful and
    loathly, his hair and the rest, with legs all bowed, covered with ugly
    hair that was churlishly matted, with foaming lips.

He °baltered, he °blēred, hē braundished thereafter; *danced about/ grimaced*

Tō batail hē °bounes him with °bustous clawes; *prepares himself/wild*

Hē °rōmed, hē °rọred, that °rogged all the erthe, *bellowed/ roared/rocked*
Sọ rūdely hē rapped it tō rīot himselven!

†Then the dragon on dregh dressed him againes
And with his °duttes him drọve °on dregh by the °welken; *blows/afar/sky*
Hē fares as a °faucon, °frekly hē strīkes; *falcon/boldly*
Bọth with feet and with fīre hē fightes at ọnes.
790 The °bẹre in the batail the bigger him seemed, *bear*
And bītes him bọldly with bāleful tuskes;
Such buffetes hē him °rẹches with his brọde °klokes, *reaches to (gives)/claws*
His °brēste and his °brayell was bloody all ọver. *breast/waist*
Hē °ramped sọ rūdely that all the erthe rīves, *struck with his claws*
°Runnand on rẹd blood as rain of the hẹven! *running*
Hē had °wēried the °worm by wightness of °strenghe *wearied/ serpent/strength*
Ne were it nọt for the wīld fīre that hē him with defendes.

Then wanders the °worm away tō his heightes, *serpent*
Comes glīdand frọ the cloudes and °coupes full °ēven, *strikes/directly*
800 Touches him with his talōnes and °tẹres his °rigge, *tears/back*
Betwix the taile and the top ten foot °large! *long*
†Thus hē brittened the bẹre and brọught him ọ līve,
Let him fall in the flood, °fleet where him līkes. *float*
†Sọ they thring the bọld king binne the ship-bōrde,
That nẹr hē bristes for bāle on bed where hē ligges.

Then °wāknes the wīse king, °wēry °fortravailed, *wakens/weary*
Tākes him twọ philosophers that followed him ever,
†In the seven scīence the °sutelest founden, *most subtle*
The cunningest of °clergy under Crīst knọwen; *book learning*
810 Hē tọld them of his torment that tīme that hē sleeped:
"°Dreched with a drāgon and such a °derf bẹste, *harassed/dire/ beast*
Has māde mē full wēry, as °wisse mē Our Lọrd; *direct*
†Ẹre I mon swelt as swīthe, yē tell mē my swefen!"

786 Then the dragon went toward him from afar.
802 Thus he beat down the bear and killed him (*o līve*: out of life).
804-05 These dreams so oppress the king aboard the ship that he nearly
  bursts for pain on the bed where he lies.
808 [*Seven sciences*: the seven liberal arts (grammar, rhetoric, logic,
  which were the *trivium*, and arithmetic, geometry, astronomy, music,
  which were the *quadrivium*); these were the basis of medieval edu-
  cation.]
813 Before I must die quickly, interpret my dream for me!

"Sir," said they °soon then,   thēse sāge philosophers,   *immediately*
"The drāgon that thou °drẹmed of,   sọ drēdful tō shew,   *dreamed*
That cọme °drīvand ọver the deep   tō °drenchen thy °pople,   *driving/drown/*
                                                                    people
Soothly and certain   thyselven it is,
That thus sailes ọver the sẹ   with thy °sēker knightes.   *trusty*
The coloures that were casten   upon his °clēre winges   *clear (shining)*
820 May bē thy °kingrikes all,   that thou has right wonnen,   *kingdoms*
And the tattered tail,   with °tonges sọ hūge,   *tongues*
Betọkens this fair folk   that in thy fleet wendes.
The bẹre that °brittened was   aboven in the cloudes   *beaten down*
Betọkenes the tyrauntes   that tormentes thy °pople   *people*
Or °elles with some gīaunt   some °journee shall happen,   *else/day's fight*
In singular °batail   by yourselve °ọne;   *battle/alone*
And thou shall have the victory,   through help of Ọur Lord,
As thou in thy visīon   was ọpenly shewed.
Of this drēdful °drẹme   ne drēde thee nọ mọre,   *dream*
830 Ne care nọt, sir conquerour,   but comfort thyselven
And thēse that sailes ọver the sẹ   with thy sēker knightes."

With °trumpes then °tristly   they trussen up their sailes   *trumpet calls/*
                                                                    boldly
And rọwes ọver the rich sẹ,   this °rout all at ọnes;   *company*
The comly °cọste of Normandy   they catchen full ēven   *coast*
And blīthely at °Barflēte   thēse bọld are arrīved,   *Barfleur*
And fīndes a fleet there   of frēndes ynow,
The flowr and the fair folk   of fifteen rewmes,
For kinges and capitaines   °keeped him fair,   *awaited*
As hē at Carlīsle commaunded   at Cristenmass himselven.

840   °By they had tāken the land   and tentes up °rẹred,   *by the time/*
                                                                    reared
Comes a Templar °tīte   and °touched tō the king;   *quickly/told*
"Hēre is a tyraunt besīde   that tormentes thy pople,
A grẹte gīaunt of °Gene,   engendered °of fēndes;   *Genoa/by fiends*
Hē has °freten of folk   °mọ that fīve °hundreth,   *devoured/more/*
                                                                    hundred
†And als fẹlẹ fauntekins   of free-born chīlder.
This has been his sustenaunce   all this seven winteres,
And yet is that sot nọt sad,   sọ well him it līkes!
†In the countree of Constantīne   nọ kīnd has hē lẹved
Withouten kidd casteles,   enclọsed with walles,
850 That hē ne has clẹnly distroyed   all the °knāve °childer,   *male/children*
And them carrīed tō the crāg   and clẹnly devoured.

---

⁸⁴⁵ And as many infants of noble children.
⁸⁴⁸ He has left no one living in the country around Cotentin (a penin-
  sula on the coast of Normandy).

The duchess of °Bretain   tōday has hē tāken,   *Brittany*
Besīde °Reines as °shō rǫde   with her rich knightes,   *Rennes/she*
Led her tō the mountain   there that °lēde lenges   *man*
Tō līe by that lady   ay whīles her līfe lastes.
Wē followed °o ferrome   mǫ than fīve hundreth   *from afar*
Of bernes and of °burgēs   and bachelers nǫble,   *townsmen*
But hē °covered the crāg;   shō crīed sǫ loud   *got to*
°The care of that crēatūre   °cover shall I never!   *(Because of)/*
                                                                  recover
860   Shō was the flowr of all Fraunce   or of fīve rewmes,
And ǫne of the fairest   that formed was ever,
The °gentilest °jowell   ajudged °with lǫrdes   *most noble/*
                                                                  jewel/by
Frǫ °Gene untō °Gerone   by Jēsū of hęven!   *Genoa/Gironne*
Shō was thy wīfes °cosin,   °knǫw it if thee līkes,   *relative/*
                                                                  acknowledge
Comen of the richest   that °regnes in erthe;   *reigns*
As thou art °rightwīse king,   °rew on thy pople   *righteous/have*
                                                                  pity
And °fǫnde for tō °venge them   that thus are rebūked!"   *endeavor/avenge*

   "Alas," says Sir Arthur,   "Sǫ lǫng have I lived!
†Had I witten of this,   well had mē chēved.
870   Mē is nǫt fallen fair   but mē is foul happened
That thus this fair lādy   this °fēnd has destroyed!   *fiend*
†I had lēver than all Fraunce   this fifteen winter
I had been before that frēke   a furlǫng of way
When hē that lādy had °laght   and led tō the mountes;   *siezed*
I had left my līfe   ęre shō had harm °limped.   *suffered*
But wǫlde thou °ken mē tō that crāg   there that °keen lenges,   *show/keen one*
I wǫlde kaire tō that cǫste   and carp with himselven,
Tō °tręte with that tyraunt   for °tręsoun of landes   *treat/treason*
And tāke °trews for a tīme   til it may °tīde better."   *truce/betide*

880   †Sir, see yē yon °fǫrland   with yon twǫ fīres?   *promontory*
There °filsnes that fēnd,   °fraist when thee līkes,   *lurks/try*
Upon the crest of the crāg   by a cǫld well
That enclǫses the cliff   with the °clēre strandes;   *clear (shining)*
There may thou fīnd folk   °fey withouten number,   *dead*
°Mǫ °florines, in faith,   than Fraunce is in after,   *more/coins*
And mǫre °tręsure °untrewly   that traitour has °getten   *treasure/*
                                                                  dishonestly/gotten
Than in Troy was, as I °trow,   that tīme that it was wonnen."   *believe*

---

869 Had I known of this, it would have been well for me.
872-73 I would give the revenues of all France for the past fifteen years
    to have been even a furlong from that man.
880 [The promontory is Mont-Saint-Michel, on which—according to this
    story—Arthur founds the famous monastery to commemorate his vic-
    tory.]

Then °rōmes the rich king   for °rewth of the pople,   *bellows/pity*
°Raikes right tō a tent   and restes nǫ °lenger;   *goes/longer*
890 Hē °welteres, hē °wresteles,   hē wringes his handes;   *writhes/wrestles*
There was nǫ wye of this world   that °wiste what hē °mened.   *knew/meant*
Hē calles Sir Kayous   that of the cup served
And Sir Bedvere the bǫld   that bǫre his °brand rich: *sword*
"Look yē after ēven-song   bē armed °at rightes   *completely*
On °blonkes by yon °buscaile,   by yon blīthe strǫmes,   *horses/brush*
For I will pass in pilgrimāge   privily hēreafter,
In the tīme of °souper,   when lǫrdes are served,   *dinner*
For tō seeken a saint   by yon salt strǫmes,
In Saint Michel mount,   there mirācles are shewed."

900   After ēven-song   Sir Arthur himselven
Went tō his °wardrǫpe   and °warp off his °weedes   *wardrobe/ threw/clothes*
Armed him in a °aketoun   with °orfrayes full rich;   *padded jacket/ gold embroidery*
°Aboven, on that, a °jerin   of Ācres out ǫver;   *above/leather jacket*
Aboven that a °gesseraunt   of gentle mailes,   *coat of mail*
†A jupon of Jerodīne   jāgged in shrǫdes;
Hē °braides on a °bacenett   burnisht of silver   *draws/helmet*
The best that was in Bāsel,   with °bordours rich;   *borders*
The crest and the °coronal   enclǫsed sǫ fair   *diadem*
With claspes of °clēre gold,   °couched with stǫnes;   *clear (shining)/ set*
910 The °vēsar, the °aventail,   ēnamelled sǫ fair,   *visor/moveable face guard*
°Void withouten vīce,   with windowes of silver;   *devoid of defects*
His glōves °gaylich gilt   and °grāven at the hemmes   *gayly/engraved*
With °graines and °gobelets,   glorīous of hew.   *seed pearls/ jewels*
†Hē brāces a brǫde shēld   and his brand askes,
°Bouned him a brown steed   and on the °bente °hōves;   *went to/ground/ waits*
Hē °stert til his stirrup   and strīdes °on loft,   *leaped/aloft*
Straines him stoutly   and stirres him fair,
°Brǫches the bay steed   and tō the °busk rīdes,   *spurs/bush*
And there his knightes him °keeped   full clǫnlich arrayed.   *awaited*

920   Then they rǫde by that river   that runned sǫ °swīthe,   *swiftly*
There the °rindes °ǫver-rǫches   with rēal boughes;   *trees/reach over*
The rǫe and the reindeer   reckless there runnen,

⁹⁰⁵ [A gipon (*jupon*) is a sleeveless cloth garment worn over the armor;
    Arthur's is *jagged in shrǫdes*—with fashionable scallopings at the
    edges. *Jerodine* is apparently a kind of cloth.]
⁹¹⁴ He puts on the arm straps (*braces*) of a broad shield and asks for
    his sword.

In °ranes and in °rōsers   tō °rīot themselven;   *bushes/rose bushes/amuse*
The °frithes were °flourisht   with flowres full many,   *woods/flowered*
With °faucons and °fesauntes   of °ferlich hewes;   *falcons/pheasants/ wondrous*
All the fowles there flashes   that flīes with winges,
For there °gāled the °gouk   on °grēves full loud;   *sang/cuckoo/ groves*

With °alkine °gladship   they gladden themselven;   *all sorts of/ gladness*
Of the nightingāle nǫtes   the noises was sweet;
930 They °thrēped with the °throstels   three hundreth at ǫnes!   *debated/thrushes*
That °whate °swowing of water   and singing of birds,   *swift/sound*
It might salve him of sǫre   that sound was never!

Then °ferkes this folk   and on foot lightes,   *go*
†Fastenes their fair steedes   o ferrom between;
And then the king keenly   commaunded his knightes
For tō bīde with their °blonkes   and °boun nǫ further;   *horses/go*
"For I will seek this saint   by myselve ǫne
And °męle with this māster man   that this mount °yēmes,   *speak/possesses*
†And sēnn shall yē offer,   either after other
940 °Menskfully °at Saint Michel,   full mighty with Crist."   *honourably/to*

The king °covers the crāg   with °cloughes full high,   *gets to/ravines*
Tō the crest of the cliff   hē clīmbes on loft,
Cast up his °umbrere   and keenly hē lookes,   *visor*
Caught of the cǫld wind   tō comfort himselven.
Twǫ fires hē fīndes   flāmand full high;
The °fourtedęle a furlǫng   between them hē walkes;   *quarter of*
The way by the °well-strandes   hē wanderd him ǫne   *welling water*
Tō °wite of the °warlaw,   where that hē lenges.   *learn/warlock*
Hē °ferkes tō the first fīre   and ēven there hē fīndes   *goes*
950 A wēry wǫful widow   wringand her handes,
And °grētand on a grāve   grisly tęres,   *weeping*
°New merked on °molde,   sēnn mid-day it seemed.   *newly made (the grave)/ground*
Hē °salūed that sǫrrowful   with °sittand wordes   *saluted/fitting*
And °fraines after the °fēnd   fairly thereafter.   *asks/fiend*

Then this wǫful °wīfe   °unwinly him greetes,   *woman/ unhappily*
°Coverd up on her knees   and °clapped her handes,   *got/clasped*
Said: "Careful, °careman,   thou carpes too loud!   *man*
May yon °warlaw °wite,   hē °warrays us all!   *warlock/know/ attacks*
°Wēryd °worth the °wight ay   that thee thy wit °rēved,   *cursed/be/man/ stole*

934 They tie their horses with a good distance between them.
939 And afterwards you shall make your offerings, each after the other.

960 That °mās thee tō °waife hēre   in thēse wīld lākes!   *makes/wander*
    I warn thee, for worship,   thou °wilnes after sorrow!   *desire*
    °Whider °buskes thou, berne?   unblessed thou seemes!   *whither/go*
    °Weenes thou tō °britten him   with thy °brand rich?   *expect/beat*
                                                                        down/sword
    †Were thou wighter than Wāde   or Wawain either,
    Thou winnes nǫ worship,   I warn thee before.
    †Thou sained thee unsēkerly   tō seek tō thēse mountes;
    Such six were too simple   tō semble with him ǫne,
    For, and thou see him with sight,   thee serves nǫ herte
    Tō saine thee sēkerly,   sǫ seemes him hūge.
970 Thou art °freely and fair   and in thy first flowres,   *noble*
    But thou art °fey, by my faith,   and that mē °forthinkes!   *fated to die/*
                                                                        grieves
    Wēre °such fifty on a fēld   or on a fair erthe,   *fifty such (as you)*
    The °frēke wǫlde with his fist   fell you at ǫnes.   *man*
    Lǫ! Hēre the duchess °dęre—tōday was shō tāken—   *dear*
    Deep °dolven and dęde,   °diked in °moldes.   *buried/buried/*
                                                                        ground
    †Hē had murthered this mīld   by mid-day were rungen,
    Withouten mercy on °molde,   I °nǫt what it °ment;   *ground/knew*
                                                                        not/meant
    Hē has forced her and °fīled   and shō is °fey °lęved;   *defiled/dead/left*
    Hē slew her °unslēly   and slit her tō the nāvel.   *crudely*
980 And hēre have I °baumed her   and burīed thereafter.   *embalmed*
    For °bāle of the °bootless,   blīthe bē I never!   *sorrow/helpless*
                                                                        (one)
    Of all the frēndes shō had   there followed nǫne after
    But I, her foster °mōder,   of fifteen winter.   *mother*
    Tō °ferk off this °fǫrland   °fǫnde shall I never,   *go/promontory/*
                                                                        endeavor
    But hēre bē founden on fēld   til I bē fey lęved."

        Then answers Sir Arthur   tō that ǫld °wīfe: *woman*
    "I am comen frǫ the conquerour,   courtais and gentle,
    As one of the °hathelest   of Arthure knightes,   *most manly*
    Messenger tō this° mix,   for °mendement of the pople,   *dung/*
                                                                        amendment
990 Tō °męle with this māster man   that hēre this mount °yēmes,   *speak/possesses*
    Tō tręte with this tyraunt   for °tręsure of landes   *treasure*
    And tāke °trew for a tīme,   °tō better may °worthe."   *truce/until/be*

964 [*Wade*: A figure in Germanic legend and the hero of a now lost
    English romance.]
966-69 You crossed yourself unsafely (i.e., started out wrong) to go to
    these mountains; six such as you would be too weak to attack him
    alone, for, if you see him with sight (of your eyes), you will not have
    the heart to cross yourself securely, so huge does he seem.
976 He had murdered this mild one by the time that midday (bell) was
    rung.

"Yā, °thir wordes are but wāste,"   quod this °wīfe then,   *these/woman*
"For both landes and °lythes   °full little by hē settes;   *nations/he / thinks little of*
Of rentes ne of rẹd gold   °reckes hē never,   *reckons*
For hē will °lenge out of law,   as himself thinkes,   *live outside the law*

Withouten līcense of °lēde,   as lọrd in his °ọwen.   *prince/own (right)*
But hē has a °kirtle on,   keeped for himselven,   *gown*
That was spunnen in Spain   °with speciāl °birdes   *by/maidens*
1000 And sithen °garnisht in Greece   full °graithely tōgeders;   *sewn/readily*
It is °hīded all with °hēre,   °họlly all ọver   *covered/hair/ wholly*
And borderd with the °bẹrdes   of °burlich kinges,   *beards/stately*
°Crisped and combed   that °kempes may knọw   *curled/warriors*
Īch king by his colour,   in °kith there hē lenges.   *country*
Hēre the °fermes hē °fanges   of fifteen rewmes,   *revenues/siezes*
For ilke °Ẹstern ēven,   however that it fall,   *Easter Eve*
They send it him soothly   for °saught of the pople,   *peace*
Sēkerly at that sẹsoun   with certain knightes.
And hē has °asked Arthure   all this seven winter;   *asked for Arthur's (beard)*
1010 Forthy° hurdes hē hēre   tō °outraye his pople   *dwells/outrage*
Til the Britones king   have °burnisht his lippes   *i.e., shaved*
And sent his bẹrde tō that bọld   with his best bernes;
But thou have brọught that bẹrde   boun thee nọ further,
†For it is a bootless bāle   thou biddes ọught elles,
For hē has mọre trẹsure tō tāke when him līkes
Than ever °ọught Arthur   or any of his elders.   *owned*
If thou have brọught the bẹrde   hē °bēs mọre blīthe   *will be*
Than thou gāve him °Borgoine   or °Britain the mọre;   *Burgundy/Great Britain*
But look now, for charitee,   thou °chasty thy lippes   *discipline (close)*
1020 That thee nọ wordes escāpe,   whatsọ betīdes.
Look thy present bē °preste   and press him but little,   *ready*
For hē is at his °souper;   hē will bē °soon grēved.   *dinner/easily / annoyed*
And thou my counsēl dō,   thou °dọs off thy °clọthes   *take/i.e., armor / gown*
And kneel in thy °kirtle   and call him thy lọrd.
Hē °soupes all this sẹsoun   °with seven °knāve °chīlder,   *dines/on/male/ children*
Chopped in a °chargeur   of chalk-whīte silver,   *serving dish*
With pickle and powder   of precīous spīces,
†And pīment full plentēous   of °Portingāle wīnes;   *Portuguese*
Three °bāleful °birdes   his °brọches they turn,   *sad/maidens/ spits*
1030 That bīdes his °bedgatt,   his bidding tō °work;   *bedtime/do*
Such four sholde bē fey   within four houres
Ẹre his filth were °filled   that his flesh °yẹrnes."   *satisfied/yearns*

1014 For it will be a sorrow without remedy if you offer him anything
    else.
1028 [*Pīment*: wine mixed with honey and spices.]

"Yā, I have brought the berde," quod hē, "the better mē
     likes;
Forthy will I °boun mē and °bere it myselven   *go/bear*
But, °lēfe, wolde thou °lere mē where that °lēde lenges? *dear/teach/man*
I shall °alōwe thee, and I live, Our Lord so mē help!" *praise (reward)*

"°Ferk fast tō the fīre," quod shō, "that flāmes so high; *go*
†There filles that fēnd him, fraist when thee līkes.
But thou moste °seek more south, °sīdlings a little,   *go/sidewise*
1040 For hē will have scent himselve six mīle °large."   *away*

 Tō the source of the °reek hē °sought at the °gainest, *smoke/went/*
                    quickest
°Sained him sēkerly with certain wordes,   *crossed himself*
And °sīdlings of the °segge the sight had hē °reched;   *sidewise/man/*
                    reached
How unseemly that sot sat °soupand him one!   *dining*
Hē lay °lenand on long, °lodgand unfair,   *stretched out/*
                    lodging
The °thee of a mans °limm lift up by the haunch;   *thigh/limb*
His back and his °beuschers and his brode °lendes   *buttocks/loins*
Hē °bākes at the bāle-fire and °breekless him seemed; *warms/without*
                    trousers
There were °rostes full rūde and rewful °bredes,   *roasts/roast meats*
1050 Bernes and °bestail °broched tōgeders,   *beasts/spitted*
°Cowle full crammed of °crismed °chīlder,   *tub/baptized/*
                    children
Some as °bred °broched and °birdes them turned.   *roasts/spitted/*
                    maidens

 And then this °comlich king, because of his pople,   *comely*
His herte bleedes for bāle on °bente where hē standes; *ground*
Then hē dressed on his shēld, °shuntes no °lenger,   *holds back/*
                    longer
Braundisht his brode sword by the bright hiltes,
°Raikes tōward that °renk right with a rūde will   *goes/man*
And °hīely °hailses that hulk with °hautain wordes: *hastily/greets/*
                    proud
"Now, °All-wēldand God that worshippes us all   *all-ruling*
1060 Give thee sorrow and °sīte, sot, there thou °ligges, *grief/lie*
For the °foulsomest °frēke that formed was ever!   *foulest/man*
Foully thou feedes thee! The Fēnd have thy soul!
Hēre is °cury unclene, °carl, by my °trewth,   *cooking/churl/*
                    word
°Caff of crēatūres all, thou cursed wretch!   *chaff*
Because that thou killed has thēse °crismed °chīlder, *baptized/children*
Thou has martyrs māde and brought out of līfe
That hēre are °broched on °bente and °brittened with thy *spitted/earth/*
             handes,   *broken*
I shall °merk thee thy °meed as thou has much °served, *assign/reward/*
                    deserved

1038 There that fiend fills himself, to try when you please.

Through might of Saint Mīchel   that this mount °yēmes!   *possesses*
1070 And for this fair lādy   that thou has fey lẹved
And thus forced on °folde   for filth of thyselven,   *earth*
°Dress thee now, dog-son,   the devil have thy sọul!   *prepare yourself*
For thou shall dīe this day   through dint of my handes!"

Then °glōpined the glutton   and °glọred unfair;   *was terrified / glared*
Hē °grenned as a grayhound   with grisly tuskes;   *grinned*
Hē gāped, hē °grọned fast   with °grouchand °lātes   *groaned / grudging / expressions*
For grēf of the good king   that him with °grame greetes.   *anger*
His °fax and his °foretop   was °filtered tōgeders   *hair / forelock / matted*
And out of his fāce °fọm   an half foot °large;   *foam / long*
1080 His °front and his °forhẹved,   all was it ọver   *face / forehead*
As the °fell of a °frosk   and °frakned it seemed;   *skin / frog / freckled*

°Hook-nebbed as a hawk,   and a °họre bẹrde,   *hook-nosed / gray (hoar)*
And °hēred tō the °eyen-họles   with hangand browes;   *haired / eye-holes*

°Harsk as a hound-fish,   °hardly whọ-sọ lookes,   *harsh / intently*
Sọ was the hīde of that hulk   °họlly all ọver;   *wholly*
°Ẹrne had hē full hūge   and ugly tō °shew   *ears / be seen*
With °eyen full horrible   and °ardaunt for sooth;   *eyes / flaming*
Flat-mouthed as a °flūke   with °flerīand lippes,   *flounder / sneering*
And the flesh in his fore-teeth   °fouly as a °bẹre;   *foul / bear*
1090 His bẹrde was °brọthy and blak   that til his °brēste rẹched;   *fierce / breast*
°Grassed as a °mēre-swīne   with °carkes full hūge   *fat / dolphin / carcass*
And all °faltered the flesh   in his foul lippes,   *quivered*
†Ilke wrēthe as a wolf-hẹved   it wrāth out at ọnes!
Bull-necked was that berne   and brọde in the shoulders,
°Brok-brēsted as a °brawn   with bristeles full large,   *spotted-breasted / boar*
Rūde armes as an °ọke   with °ruskled sīdes,   *oak / wrinkled*
†Limm and leskes full lọthen,   lēve yē for sooth;
Shovel-footed was that °shalk   and °shāland him seemed,   *man / bowlegged*
With shankes unshāpely   °shovand tōgeders;   *shoving (i.e., knock-kneed)*
1100 Thick °thees as a °thurse   and thicker in the haunch,   *thighs / giant*
°Grẹẹs-grọwen as a °galt,   full °grillich hē lookes!   *fat / pig / horrible*
Whọ the °lenghe of the °lēde   °lẹly accountes,   *length / man / carefully*
Frọ the fāce tō the foot   was fīve °fadom lọng!   *fathoms*

Then °stertes hē up sturdily   on twọ stiff shankes,   *leaps*
And soon hē caught him a club   all of clẹne īron;

1093 Each fold (in the quivering skin of his lips) at once twisted out like
the head of a wolf.
1097 Limbs and loins very loathsome, believe you, truly.

Hē wǫlde have killed the king   with his °keen °wēpen,   *fierce/weapon*
But through the craft of Crīst   yet the °carl failed;   *churl*
The crest and the °coronal,   the claspes of silver,   *diadem*
Clęnly with his club   hē crashed down at ǫnes!

1110   The king castes up his shēld   and covers him fair,
And with his °burlich brand   a box hē °him ręches;   *stately/reaches to him*
Full butt in the °front   the °fromand hē hittes   *face/enemy*
That the burnisht blāde   tō the brain runnes;
Hē °feyed his °fysnamīe   with his foul handes   *wiped/face*
And °frappes fast at °his fāce   °fērsly there-after!   *strikes/Arthur's/fiercely*
The king chānges his foot,   °eschewes a little;   *retreats*
Ne had hē °eschāped that chop,   °chēved had ēvil;   *escaped/achieved (won)*
Hē follows in °fērsly   and fastenes a dint   *fiercely*
High up on the haunch   with his hard °wēpen   *weapon*
1120 That hē °hęled the sword   half a foot °large;   *buried/deep*
The hot blood of the hulk   untō the hilt runnes;
Ēven intō the °in-męte   the gīaunt hē hittes   *in-meat (intestines)*
Just tō the genitals   and °jāgged them °in sonder!   *cut/asunder*

Then hē °rōmed and °rǫred   and rūdely hē strīkes   *bellowed/roared*
Full °ęgerly at Arthur   and on the erthe hittes;   *eagerly*
A sword-°lenghe within the °swarth   hē °swappes at ǫnes   *length/ground/strikes*
That nęr swoones the king   for °swough of his dintes!   *sound*
But yet the king °sweperly   full °swīthe hē °beswenkes,   *swiftly/quickly/works*
°Swappes in with the sword   that it the °swang °bristed;   *strikes/loins/burst*
1130 Bǫth the guttes and the gore   gushes out at ǫnes,
That all °englaimes the grass   on ground there hē standes!   *makes slimy*

Then hē castes the club   and the king °hentes;   *seizes*
On the crest of the crāg   hē caught him in armes,
And enclǫses him clęnly   tō crushen his ribbes;
†Sǫ hard hǫldes hē that hende   that nęr his herte bristes!
Then the °bāleful °birdes   °bounes tō the erthe,   *sad/maidens/go*
Kneeland and cryand   and °clapped their handes: *clasped*
"Crīst comfort yon knight   and keep him frǫ sǫrrow,
And let never yon fēnd   fell him °o life!"   *out of*

1140   Yet is that °warlaw sǫ wight   hē °welters him under;   *warlock/rolls*
Wrǫthly they wrīthen   and wrestle tōgeders,
Welters and wallows ǫver   within thǫse wīld °buskes,   *bushes*

[1135] He holds that courteous one so hard that his heart nearly bursts!

°Tumbelles and turnes fast   and °teres their weedes, *tumble/tear*
Untenderly fro the top   they °tilten tōgeders, *topple*
°Whilom Arthur over   and other whīle under, *at times*
Fro the °heghe of the hill   untō the hard rock, *height*
They °feyne never ere they fall   at the °flood marches; *cease/edge of the sea*
But Arthur with an °anlace   egerly smītes *dagger*
And hittes ever in the hulk   up tō the hiltes.
1150 †The thēf at the ded-throwes   so throly him thringes
That three ribbes in his sīde   hē thrustes in sonder!

Then Sir Kayous the keen   untō the king °stertes, *leaps*
Said: "Alas! Wē are °lorn!   My lord is confounded, *lost*
°Over-fallen °with a fēnd!   Us is foul happned! *over-thrown/by*
Wē °mon bē forfeited, in faith,   and °flēmed forever!" *must/put to flight*

They °heve up his hawberk then   and °handelles there- *lift/handle*
                                under
His hīde and his haunch eek   °on height tō the shoulders, *up*
His flank and his °felettes   and his fair sīdes, *loins*
Both his back and his brēste   and his bright armes.
1160 They were °fain that they °fande   no flesh °entāmed *glad/found/injured*
And for that °journee made joy,   °thir gentle knightes. *day's fighting/these*

"Now certes," says Sir Bedvere,   "It seemes, by my Lord,
Hē seekes saintes but °selden,   the °sorer hē grippes, *seldom/more severely*
That thus °clēkes this °corsaint   out of °thir high cliffes, *drags/holy body/these*
Tō carry forth such a °carl   °at close him in silver; *churl/to enclose*
By Mīchel, of such a °mak   I have much wonder *fellow*
That ever our soveraign Lord   suffers him in heven!
And all saintes bē such   that serves our Lord
I shall never no saint bē,   by my °fader soul!" *father's*

1170   Then °bourdes the bold king   at °Bedvere wordes: *jokes/Bedevere's*
"This saint have I sought,   so help mē our Lord!
Forthy °braid out thy brand   and °broche him tō the herte; *draw/spit*
Be sēker of this °sergēaunt;   hē has mē sore grēved! *fellow*
I fought not with such a frēke   this fifteen winter;
†But in the mountes of Araby   I met such another;

1150-51 In his death throes the thief squeezes him so fiercely that he
   breaks asunder three ribs in his (Arthur's) side.
1175 [A reference to the giant Ritho, whom Arthur slew "in Aravio
   Montem" (in the mount of Araby), the Aran mountains in Wales.
   The story is told in Geoffrey of Monmouth, *Histories of the Kings of
   Britain*, Book X.]

†Hē was forcīer by fer   that had I nẹre founden;
Ne had my fortūne been fair,   fey had I lẹved!
†Anọn strīke off his hẹved   and stāke it thereafter;
Give it to thy °squīer,   for hē is well horsed,   *squire*
1180 Bẹre it tō Sir Howell   that is in hard °bọndes   *bonds of sorrow*
And bid him °herte him well;   his °enmy is destroyed!   *hearten/enemy*
Sēnn bẹre it tō °Barflēte   and brāce it in īron   *Barfleur*
And set it on the °barbican   bernes tō shew.   *main-gate tower*
My brand and my brọde shēld   upon the °bente °ligges,   *ground/lie*
On the crest of the crāg   there first wē encountered,
And the club there-by,   all of clẹne īron,
That many Cristen has killed   in °Constantīne landes;   *Peninsula of Cotentin*
°Ferk to the °fọre-land   and fetch mē that °wēpen   *go/promontory/ weapon*
And °let °found tō our fleet   in flood there it lenges.   *let us/go*
1190 If thou °will any °trẹsure,   tāke what thee līkes;   *want/treasure*
Have I the °kirtle and the club,   I covēt nọught °elles."   *gown/else*

       Now they kaire to the crag,   thēse °comlich knightes,   *comely*
And brọught him the brọde shēld   and his bright wēpen,
†The club and the cọte als,   Sir Kayous himselven,
And kaires with the conquerour   the kinges tō shew.
†That in covert the king hēld   clọse tō himselven
Whīle clẹne day frọ the cloud   clīmbed on loft.

       °By that tō court was comen   clamour full hūge,   *By that time*
And before the comlich king   they kneeled all at ọnes:
1200 "Welcome, our °lēge lord,   too lọng has thou dwelled!   *liege*
Governour under God,   °graithest and nọble,   *most active*
Tō whọm grāce is graunted   and given at His will,
Now thy comly °come   has comforted us all!   *coming*
Thou has in thy °rēaltee   revenged thy pople!   *royalty*
Through help of thy hand   thīne enmīes are °stroyed,   *destroyed*
That has thy renkes ọver-run   and °reft them their chīlder;   *bereft*
Was never °rewm out of array   so rẹdyly °relēved!"   *disordered realm/relieved*

       Then the conquerour °Cristenly   carpes tō his pople: *Christianly*
"Thankes God," quọd hē, "of this grāce   and nọ °gōme elles,   *man*
1210 For it was never mans deed,   but might of Himselven
Or mirācle of his Mōder,   that mīld is til all!"

1176 He was stronger by far than any I had ever found.
1178 Immediately strike off his head and put it on a stake thereafter.
1194 Sir Kay himself brings the club and the coat as well.
1196 Yet the king remained concealed, alone by himself.

Hē summond then the shipmen   sharply thereafter,
Tō °shāke forth with the °shīre-men   tō shift the goodes: *go/men of the shire*
"All the much tręsure   that traitour had wonnen
Tō commouns of the countree,   clergy and other,
Look it bē dōne and °dęlt   tō my dęre pople   *dealt out*
That nǫne °plain of their part   °o pain of your līves."   *complain/on*

Hē °commaunde his cosin,   with knightlich wordes,   *commanded*
Tō māke a °kirk on that crāg,   there the °corse ligges   *church/body*
1220   And a °covent there-in,   Crīst for tō serve,   *monastery*
In °mīnd of that °martyr   that in the mount restes.   *memory/i.e., the duchess*

When Sir Arthur the king   had killed the gīaunt,
Then blīthely frǫ Barflēte   hē °buskes on the morn,   *goes*
With his °batail on brede   by °thǫ blīthe stręmes;   *battalion spread out/those*
Tōward Castel Blank   hē °chēses him the way,   *chooses (i.e., goes)*
Through a fair °champain   under chalk hilles;   *open plain*
The king °fraistes a °furth   ǫver the fresh strandes,   *seeks/ford*
°Foundes with his fair folk   ǫver as him līkes;   *goes*
Forth steppes that °steren   and °strekes his tents   *stern (one)/ stretches out*
1230   On a °strenghe by a stręme,   in thǫse °strait landes.   *strong-hold/ narrow*

Anǫn after mid-day,   in the °męte-whīle,   *mealtime*
There comes twǫ messengers   of °thǫ °fer marches,   *those/far*
Frǫ the Marshal of Fraunce,   and °menskfully him greetes,   *honorably*
Besǫught him of succour   and said him thēse wordes:
"Sir, thy Marshal, thy minister,   thy mercy beseekes,
Of thy °mikel °magistee,   for °mendment of thy pople,   *great/majesty/ amendment*
Of these °marches-men   that thus are miscarrīed   *men of the marches*
And thus °marred amǫng   °maugree their eyen;   *harmed/in spite of*
I °witter thee the Emperour   is enterd intō Fraunce   *assure*
1240   With hǫstes of enmīes,   horrible and hūge;
°Brinnes in °Burgoine   thy °burges sǫ rich,   *burns/ Burgundy/cities*
And °brittenes thy baronāge   that °beldes there-in;   *beats down/ dwells*
Hē °encrǫches keenly   by craftes of armes   *invades*
Countrees and casteles   that tō thy crown °lǫnges,   *belong*
Confoundes thy commouns,   clergy and other;
°But thou comfort them, Sir King,   cover shall they never!   *unless*
Hē felles forestes °fęlę,   °forrays thy landes,   *many/plunders*
°Frithes nǫ °fraunchēs,   but °frayes the pople;   *spares/liberty/ affrights*
Thus hē felles thy folk   and °fanges their goodes;   *seizes*

1250 †Fremedly the French tonge   fey is belẹved.
    Hē drawes into °douce Fraunce,   as °Dutch-men telles,   *sweet/Germans*
    Dressed with his drāgons,   drēdful tō shew;
    All tō °dẹde they °dight   with dintes of swordes,   *death/put*
    Dūkes and douspeeres   that °dreches there-in;   *stay*
    Forthy the lọrdes of the land,   lādīes and other,
    Prayes thee for Pētere love,   the apostle of Rōme,
    Sēnn thou art present in plăce,   that thou will °proffer māke   *i.e., proffer battle*
    Tō that perilous prince   by prōcess of tīme.
    Hē °ayers by yon hilles,   yon high holtes under,   *goes*
1260 †Hōves there with họle strenghe   of hẹthen knightes;
    Help now for His love   That high in hẹven sittes
    And talk °tristly tō them   that thus us destroyes!"   *boldly*

    The king biddes Sir Bois: "°Busk thee °belīve!   *go/quickly*
    Tāke with thee Sir Berille   and Bedvere the rich,
    Sir Gawain and Sir Grime,   thēse °galīard knightes,   *jolly*
    And graith you tō yon green woodes   and °gọs on thir   *go/message*
        °needes;
    Says tō Sir Lūcīus   too unlọrdly hē workes
    Thus °litherly againes law   tọ °lẹde my pople;   *wickedly/treat*
    †I let him ẹre ọught lọng,   yif mē the life happen,
1270 Or many light shall lọw   that him ọver land followes;
    Commaund him keenly   with crūel wordes
    Kaire out of my °kingrik   with his kidd knightes;   *kingdom*
    In cāse that hē will nọt,   that cursed wretch,
    Come for his °courtaisy   and °counter mē ọnes;   *courtesy/ encounter*
    Then shall wē reckon full °rāthe   what right that hē claimes,   *quickly*
    Thus to rīot this rewm   and °ransoun the pople!   *ravage*
    There shall it °dẹrely bē °dẹlt   with dintes of handes;   *dearly/dealt*
    The °Drighten at Doomesday   °dẹle as Him līkes!"   *Lord/deal*

    Now they °graith them tō gọ,   thēse °galīard knightes,   *prepare/jolly*
1280 All glitterand in gold,   upon grẹte steedes,
    Tōward the green wood,   with °grounden wēpen,   *sharpened*
    Tō greet well the grẹte lọrd   that wọlde bē grēved soon.

    †Thēse hende hōves on a hill   by the holt ēves
    Behēld the housing full °high   of °hẹthen kinges;   *noble/heathen*

1250 By foreignẹrs the French tongue is destroyed.
1260 Waits there with (his) whole force of heathen knights.
1269 I shall stop him before much longer if life is granted to me (if I
    live).
1283 These courteous ones wait on a hill by the edge of the wood.

They herde in their °herberāge   hundrethes full many   *dwellings*
Hornes of °olyfantes   full °highlich blọwen;   *elephants/loudly*
†Palaises proudly pight,   that pāled were rich
Of pall and of purpure,   with precīous stọnes;
°Pensels and °pomells   of rich princes armes   *pennons/ tent-pommels*
290 °Pight in the plain °mẹde   the pople tō shew.   *placed/meadow*
And then the Rōmans sọ rich   had arrayed their tentes
On rọw by the river   under the round hilles,
The Emperour for honour   °ēven in the middes,   *exactly*
With °ẹgles all over   °ēnnelled sọ fair;   *eagles/decorated*
And saw him and the °Sowdan   and senatours many   *sultan*
°Seek tōward a °sale   with sixteen kinges   *go/hall*
°Syland softly in,   sweetly by themselven,   *gliding*
Tō °soupe with that soverain   full °selcouthe °mẹtes.   *dine/rare/foods*

Now they wend ọver the water,   thēse worshipful
                                              knightes,
300 Through the wood tō the °wonne   there the wyes restes;   *dwelling*
Right as they had °weshen   and went tō the tāble,   *washed*
Sir Wawain the worthy   °unwinly hē °spẹkes: *unfriendly/ speaks*
"The might and the majestee   that °menskes us all,   *honors*
That was °merked and māde   through the might of   *formed*
                                              Himselven,
Give you °sīte in your °sẹte,   Sowdan and other,   *grief/seat*
That hēre are sembled in sale;   °unsaught mot yē worthe!   *troubled may you be*
And the false heretik   that Emperour him calles,
That occūpīes in errour   the Empīre of Rōme,
Sir Arthure heritāge,   that honourāble king,
310 That all his °auncestres °ọught   but Uter him ọne,   *ancestors/owned*
That ilke cursing that °Caim   caught for his brōther   *Cain*
°Clēve on thee, °cuckewald,   with crown there thou lenges,   *cleave/cuckold*
For the unlọrdlīest lēde   that I on looked ever!
My lọrd marvēles him °mikel,   man, by my °trewth,   *much/word*
Why thou °murtheres his men   that nọ °misse °serves,   *murder/trouble/ deserve*
Commouns of the countree,   clergy and other,
That are nọught °coupable there-in,   ne knọwes nọught in   *guilty*
                                              armes,
Forthy the comlich king,   courtais and nọble,
Commaundes thee keenly   tō kaire °of his landes   *out of*
320 Or elles for thy °knighthēde   encounter him ọnes.   *knighthood*
Sēnn thou covētes the crown,   let it bē declared!

1287-88 Palaces (rich tents) proudly pitched that had rich walls of silk
    and purple cloth adorned with precious stones.

I have °discharged mē hēre,   challenge whǫ līkes,   *done my duty*
Before all thy chevalry,   chēftaines and other.
Shāpe us an answer,   and °shunt thou nǫ lenger,   *hold back*
That wē may °shift at the short   and shew tō my lǫrd."   *go quickly*

    The Emperour answerd   with °austeren wordes: *austere*
"Yē are with mīne enmy,   Sir Arthur himselven;
It is nǫne honour tō mē   tō °outraye his knightes,   *do violence to*
Though yē bē °īrous men   that °ayers on his °needes;   *angry/go/errands*
1330   Ne were it nǫt for reverence   of my rich tāble,
Thou sholde repent full °rāthe   of thy rūde wordes!   *quickly*
Such a °rebawd as thou   rebūke any lǫrdes   *low fellow*
With their retinūes arrayed,   full rēal and nǫble!
But say tō thy soveraign   I send him these wordes:
†Hēre will I sujourn,   whīles mē lēfe thinkes,
And sithen °seek in by Sēine   with solāce thereafter,   *go*
°Ensēge all the citees   by the salt strandes,   *besiege*
And sēnn rīde in by Rhōne   that runnes sǫ fair,
And of his rich casteles   rush down the walles;
1340   †I shall nǫught lęve in Paris,   by prōcess of tīme,
His part of a pecheline,   prōve when him līkes!"

    "Now certes," says Sir Wawain,   "much wonder have I
That such an °alfin as thou   dare spęke such wordes!   *foolish person*
I had °lēver than all Fraunce,   that °hęved is of rewmes,   *rather/head*
Fight with thee faithfully   on fēld by our ǫne!"

    Then answers Sir Gayous   full °gabbed wordes—   *foolish*
Was °eme tō the Emperour   and erl himselven: *uncle*
"Ever were thēse °Bretons   brāggers of old!   *Britons*
Lǫ, how hē brawles him   for his bright °weedes,   *garments (i.e., armor)*
1350   As hē might britten us all   with his brand rich!
Yet hē barkes much °bǫste,   yon °boy there hē standes!"   *boast/knave*

    Then grēved Sir Gawain   at his gręte wordes,
°Graithes tōward the °gōme   with °grouchand herte;   *goes/man/angry*
With his °steelen brand   hē strīkes off his hęved,   *steel*
And °stertes out tō his steed,   and with his °stale wendes.   *leaps/company*
Through the watches they went,   thēse worshipful knightes,

1335 Here will I stay, as long as it seems good to me.
1340-41 Within a short time I shall not leave him in Paris so much as a
    tiny spot; let him prove this when he pleases [and he will learn it is
    true].

And fíndes in their °fare-way   °wonderlich many;   *path/wondrously*
Qver the water they went   by wightness of horses,
And took wind as they wǫlde   by the °wood hemmes.   *edges of the wood*
1360 Then follows °frekly on foot   frēkes ynow,   *fiercely*
And of the Rōmans arrayed   upon rich steedes
Chāsed through a °champain   our chevalrous knightes   *open field*
Til a °chēf forest   on chalk-whīte horses.   *large (chief)*
But a frēke all in fīne gold   and °fretted in sāble   *adorned*
Cǫme furthermǫst on a °Frēson   in °flāmand weedes;   *Frisian horse/ glowing armor*
A fair flourisht spęre   in °fewter hē castes,   *spear-rest*
And followes fast on our folk   and °freshly °ascrīes.   *eagerly/cries*

Then Sir Gawain the good   upon a gray steed
Hē grippes him a gręte spęre   and °graithly him hittes;   *readily*
1370 Through the guttes into the gore   hē °girdes him ēven,   *smites him*
That the °grounden steel   glīdes tō his herte!   *sharpened*
The gōme and the gręte horse   at the ground °ligges,   *lies*
Full °grislich °grǫnand   for °grēf of his woundes.   *grisly/groaning/ grief*
Then presses a °priker in,   full proudly arrayed,   *rider*
†That bęres all of purpure,   pāled with silver
Bigly on a brown steed   hē proffers full large.
Hē was a °paynim of °Perse   that thus him °persewed;   *pagan/Persia/ pursued*
Sir Boys all °unabaist   hē buskes him againes;   *unabashed*
With a °bustous launce   hē bęres him through,   *wild*
1380 That the °brēme and the brǫde shēld   upon the °bente   *fierce (one)/ earth/lies*
°ligges!
And hē bringes forth the blāde   and °bounes tō his fellowes.   *goes*

Then Sir Feltemour, of might   a man °mikel praised,   *much*
Was mōved on his manner   and menāced full fast;
Hē graithes tō Sir Gawain   °graithly tō work,   *readily*
For grēf of Sir Gayous   that is on ground lęved.
Then Sir Gawain was glad;   again him hē rīdes;
With Galuth, his good sword,   °graithly him hittes;   *readily*
The knight on the courser   hē °clēved in sonder,   *cleaved in two*
°Clęnlich frǫ the crown   his °corse hē °devīsed,   *cleanly/body/ divided*
1390 And thus hē killes the knight   with his kidd wēpen.

Then a rich man of Rōme   °relīed tō his bernes: *rallied*
"It shall repent us full sǫre   and wē rīde further!

1375 That bears on his shield a heraldic device all of purple, striped
with silver.

Yon are bọld °bọsters   that such °bāle workes;   *boasters/evil*
It befell him full foul   that them sọ first nāmed!"

    Then the rich Rōmans   °returnes their brīdles,   *turn back*
Tō their tentes in °teen,   telles their lọrdes   *grief*
How Sir Marshall de Mowne   is on the °molde lẹved,   *ground*
°Forjousted at that journee   for his grẹte °jāpes.   *outjousted/jokes*
But there chāses on our men   chevalrous knightes,
1400 Fīve thousand folk   upon fair steedes,
Fast tō a forest   ọver a °fell water   *strong (i.e.,*
That filles frọ the fallow sẹ   fifty mīle °large.   *swift)*
                                                                       away
†There were Bretons enbushed   and banerettes noble,
Of the chevalry chēf   of the kinges chāmber;
Sees them chāse our men   and chāngen their horses
And chop down chēftaines   that they mọst charged.
Then the °enbushment of Bretons   brọke out at ọnes,   *ambush*
°Brọthly at banner   all °Bedvere knightes   *boldly/*
                                                                       Bedivere's
Arrested of the Rōmans   that by the °firth rīdes,   *wood*
1410 All the rēalest renkes   that tō Rōme °lọnges;   *belong*
They °ishe on the enmīes   and ẹgerly strīkes,   *rush*
Erles of England,   and "Arthur!" °ascrīes;   *cry*
Through °brenyes and bright shēldes   brēstes they °thirle,   *hawberks/pierce*
Bretons of the bọldest,   with their bright swordes.
There was Rōmans ọver-ridden   and rūdely wounded,
Arrested as °rebawdes   with rīotous knightes!   *low fellows*
The Rōmans out of array   remōved at ọnes
And rīdes away in a rout—   for °reddour it seemes!   *fear*

    Tō the Senatour Pēter   a °sandesman is comen   *messenger*
1420 And said: "Sir, sēkerly,   your °segges are °surprīsed!"   *men/seized*
Then ten thousand men   hē sembled at ọnes
And set °sodēnly on our °segges   by the salt strandes.   *suddenly/men*
Then were Bretons °abaist   and grēved a little,   *abashed*
But yet the °bannerettes bọld   and °bachelers nọble   *senior knights/*
                                                                       young knights
°Brẹkes that °batail   with brēstes of steedes;   *break/battalion*
Sir Bois and his bọld men   much °bāle workes!   *pain*
The Rōmanes °relīes then,   arrayes them better,   *rally*
And all °tō-rushes our men   with their °restẹ horses,   *dash asunder/*
                                                                       rested
Arrested of the richest   of the Round Tāble,
1430 Ọver-rīdes our °rẹre-ward   and grẹte °rewth workes!   *rear guard/*
                                                                       sorrow

1403 There were Britons laid in ambush, and noble senior knights.

Then the Bretons on the bente   abīdes nọ lenger,
But fled to the forest   and the fēld lẹved;
Sir Berille is borne down   and Sir Bois tāken,
The best of our bọld men   unblīthely wounded;
†But yet our stale on a strenghe   stotais a little,
All °tō-stonayed with the strọkes   of thọ steren knightes,   *astonished*
Mādе sọrrow for their soveraign   that sọ there was °nomen,   *taken*
Besọught God of succour,   send when him līked!

Then comes Sir Īdrus,   armed up °at all rightes,   *completely*
1440 With fīve hundreth men   upon fair steedes,
°Fraines fast at our folk   °freshly thereafter   *asks/eagerly*
Yif their frēndes were fer   that on the fēld °founded.   *went*
Then says Sir Gawain,   "Sọ mē God help,
We have been chāsed tōday   and °chulled as hares,   *driven like hares*
Rebūked with Rōmanes   upon their rich steedes,
And wē lurked under °lee   as °lowrand wretches!   *shelter/lowering*
†I look never on my lọrd   the dayes of my līfe
And wē sọ litherly him help   that him sọ well līked!"

Then the Bretons °brọthely   °brọches their steedes   *boldly/spur*
1450 And bọldly in batail   upon the bente rīdes;
All the °fērs men before   °frekly °ascrīes,   *fierce/boldly/cry*
°Ferkand in the forest   tō freshen themselven.   *going*
The Rōmanes then rẹdyly   arrayes them better,
On rọw on a °rowm fēld   °rightes their wēpens,   *broad/adjust*
By the rich river   and °rewles the pople;   *arrange the troops*
And with °reddour Sir Bois   is in arrest họlden.   *fear*

Now they °sembled unsaught   by the salt strẹmes;   *fiercely attacked*
Sadly these sēker men   settes their dintes,
With lovely launces on loft   they °lushen °tōgederes,   *dash/together*
1460 In Lorraine sọ lordly   on lẹpand steedes.
There were gōmes °through-gird   with °grounden wēpens   *pierced/sharpened*
Grisly °gaspand   with °grouchand °lātes.   *gasping/angry/expressions*
Grẹte lọrdes of Greece   grēved sọ high,
Swiftly with swordes   they °swappen thereafter,   *strike*
Swappes down full °sweperly   °sweltande knightes;   *swiftly/dying*
Sọ many sways in °swogh,   swoonand at ọnes,   *faint*

1435 But yet our company pauses a bit at a stronghold.
1447-48 May I never look on my lord the rest of my life if we serve him
    so poorly, we who once pleased him so well.

That all °sweltes on °swarth   that they °over-swingen.   *die/ground/cut down*

Sir Gawain the grācīous   full graithly hē workes;

The grętest hē greetes   with grisly woundes;

1470 With Galuth hē °girdes down   full °galīard knightes,   *strikes/jolly*

For grēf of the gręte lǫrd   sǫ grimly hē strīkes!

Hē rīdes forth °rēally   and rędyly thereafter   *royally*

°There this °rēal renk   was in arrest hǫlden;   *to where/ i.e., Bois*

He rīves the rank steel,   he °rittes their °brenyes,   *rips/hawberks*

And °reft them the rich man   and rǫde tō his °strenghes.   *bereft/ stronghold*

The Senatour Pēter   then °persewed him after,   *pursued*

Through the press of the pople   with his prīs knightes,

°Appertly for the prisonēr   prōves his strenghes,   *openly*

With °prikers the proudest   that to the press lǫnges;   *riders*

1480 °Wrǫthly on the °wrǫng hand   Sir Wawain hē strīkes,   *angrily/left*

With a wēpen of war   °unwinly him hittes;   *unpleasantly*

The °breny on the back half   hē °bristes in sonder;   *hawberk/breaks in two*

And yet °hē brǫught forth Sir Bois   for all their bāle bernes!   *i.e., Gawain*

Then the Bretons bǫldly   °brāggen their °trumpes,   *blow/trumpets*

And for bliss of Sir Bois   was brǫught out of bǫndes,

Bǫldly in batail   they bęre down knightes;

With brandes of °brown steel   they brittened °mailes;   *shining/armor*

They °steked steedes in °stour   with °steelen wēpens,   *stuck/battle/ steel*

And all °stewede with strenghe   that stood them againes!   *struck down*

1490 Sir Īdrus fitz Ēwain   then "Arthur!" °ascrīes,   *cries*

°Assembles on the senatour   with sixteen knightes   *attacks*

Of the sēkerest men   that tō our sīde lǫnged.

Sodēnly in a °soppe   they set in at ǫnes,   *small troop*

°Foines fast at the fore-brēste   with flāmand swordes   *strike*

And fightes fast at the front   °freshly thereafter,   *eagerly*

Felles °fęle on the fēld   upon the °ferrer sīde,   *many/farther*

Fey on the fair fēld   by thǫ fresh strandes.

But Sir Īdrus fitz Ēwain   °aunters himselven   *adventures*

And enters in °ǫnly   and ęgerly strīkes,   *alone*

1500 Seekes tō the senatour   and °sęses his brīdle;   *seizes*

°Unsaughtly hē said him   these °sittand wordes: *hostilely/fitting*

"°Yēlde thee, sir, °yāpely,   yif thou thy līfe °yęrnes;   *yield/quickly/ yearn for*

For giftes that thou give may   thou °yēme nǫt thyselven,   *save*

†For, drēdles, drech thou   or drop any wīles,

Thou shall dīe this day   through dint of my handes!"

1504 For, doubtless, if you delay or play any tricks.

"I assent," °quod the senatour,   "So mē Crīst help.   *said*
°So that I bē sāfe brought   before the king selven;   *providing that*
Ransoun me °reasonābely,   as I may °over-reche,   *reasonably/ obtain*
°After my rentes in Rōme   may redyly °further."   *as/furnish*

1510   Then answers Sir Īdrus   with austeren wordes:
"Thou shall have °condicīoun   as the king līkes,   *conditions*
When thou comes tō the kith   there the court holdes,
In cāse his counsēl bē   tō keep thee no longer,
Tō bē killed at his commaundement   his knightes before."

They led him forth in the rout   and °latched off his   *took/armor*
                         °weedes,
Left him with Līonel   and Lowell his brōther.
°O-low in the land then,   by the °līthe strandes,   *below/pleasant*
Sir Lūcīus lēge-men   lost are forever!
The Senatour Pēter   is prisonēr tāken!
1520 Of °Perse and Port °Jaffe   full many prīs knightes   *Persia/Jaffa*
                                       (formerly Joppa)
And much pople withal   perished themselven!
†For press of the passāge   they °plunged at ones!
There might men see Rōmans   rewfully wounded,
Over-ridden with renkes   of the Round Tāble.
†In the raike of the furth   they righten their brenyes
That ran all on red blood   redyly all over;
†They raght in the rere-ward   full rīotous knightes
For ransoun of red gold   and rēal steedes;
Redyly °rēlayes   and restes their horses,   *change horses*
1530 In route tō the rich king   they rode all at ones.

A knight kaires before,   and tō the king telles:
"Sir, hēre comes thy messengeres   with mirthes fro the
                               mountes;
They have been matched tōday   with men of the marches,
°Foremagled in the °morass   with marvēlous knightes!   *hacked/marsh*
Wē have foughten, in faith,   by yon fresh strandes,
With the °frekest folk   that tō thy fo longes;   *boldest*
Fifty thousand on fēld   of fērs men of armes
Within a furlong of way   fey are belēved!

₁₅₂₂ Because of the crowd at the ford they leaped into the water.
₁₅₂₅ On the path by the stream they adjust their hawberks.
₁₅₂₇ They placed the riotous (Roman) knights in the rear guard (as
    prisoners).

Wē have °eschewed this °check   through °chaunce of Our   *escaped/defeat/*
                                        Lọrd   *destiny*
1540 Of thọ chevalrous men   that charged thy pople.
     The chēf chaunceller of Rōme,   a chēftain full nọble,
     Will ask the charter of pęęs,   for charitee himselven;
     And the Senatour Pēter   tō prisonēr is tāken.
     Of Perse and Port Jaffe   °paynimes ynow   *pagans*
     Comes °prikand in the press   with thy prīs knightes,   *spurring*
     With povertee in thy prisoun   their paines tō °drīe. *suffer*
     I beseek you, sir,   say what you līkes,
     Whether yē °suffer them °saught   or soon delivered.   *grant/peace*
     Yē may have for the senatour   sixty horse °charged   *loaded*
1550 Of silver by Saterday   full sēkerly payed,
     And for the chēf chaunceller,   the chevalēr nọble,
     °Charottes chockful   °charged with gold.   *wagons/loaded*
     The °remenaunt of the Rōmanes   bē in arrest họlden,   *remnant*
     Til their rentes in Rōme   bē °rightwīsly knọwen.   *correctly*
     I beseek you, sir,   °certify yon lordes,   *make certain*
     Yif yē will send them ọver the sę   or keep them yourselven.
     All your sēker men, for sooth,   sound are belęved,
     Sāve Sir Ēwain fitz Henry   is in the sīde wounded."

     "Crīst bē thanked," quọd the king,   "and his clēre Mōder,
1560 That you comforted and helped   by craft of Himselven.
     †Skillfully skomfitūre   Hē skiftes as Him līkes.
     Is nọne sọ skāthly may scāpe   ne skew frọ His handes;
     °Destainy and doughtiness   of deedes of armes,   *destiny*
     All is deemed and dęlt   at °Drightenes will!   *God's*
     I can thee thank for thy °come;   it comfortes us all!   *coming*
     Sir knight," says the conquerour,   "sọ mē Crīst help,
     I give thee for thy °tīthandes   Toulouse the rich,   *tidings*
     The toll and the °tachementes,   tavernes and other,   *appurtenances*
     The town and the tenementes   with towres sọ high,
1570 †That touches to the temporaltee,   whīles my tīme lastes.
     But say tō the senatour   I send him thēse wordes:
     There shall nọ silver him sāve   °but Ēwain rēcover.   *unless*
     I had °lēver see him sink   on the salt strandes   *rather*
     Than the °segge were °sēke   that is sọ sọre wounded.   *man/sick*

1561-62 God skillfully handles trouble as He pleases; no one is so harmful
     that he can escape or slip away from His hands.
1570 All that concerns temporal life is yours while I live; [i.e., he is
     granted everything except Church property and that which is gov-
     erned by the Church.]

I shall °dissever that °sorte, so mē Crīst help, *separate/company*
And set them full solitary in °sēre kinges landes. *various*
Shall hē never sound see his °seinoures in Rōme, *lords*
Ne sit in the assemblee in sight with his °fēres, *comrades*
For it °comes to no king that conquerour is °holden *becomes/considered*
1580 Tō °cōmone with his captīves for °covētis of silver. *bargain/covetousness*
It come never of °knighthēd, know it if him līke, *knighthood*
Tō carp of °cosery when captīves are tāken; *business*
It °ought tō no prisonērs tō press no lordes *belongs (i.e., is proper)*
Ne come in presence of princes when °partīes are mōved. *i.e., business is discussed*
Commaund yon constāble, the castle that yēmes,
That hē bē clenlich keeped and in °close holden; *confinement*
Hē shall have °maundement °tō-morn ere mid-day bē *command/tomorrow*
                                        rungen
Tō what march they shall °merk with °maugree tō lengen." *go/spite*

    They convey this captīve with clene men of armes
1590 And °kend him to the constāble, °als the king biddes, *entrust/as*
And sēnn tō Arthur they ayer and egerly him °touches *tell*
The answer of the Emperour, °īrous of deedes. *angry*
Then Sir Arthur, on erthe °athelest of other *noblest*
At ēven, at his own bōrde °avaunted his lordes: *praised*
"Mē ought tō honour them in erthe over all other thinges,
That thus in mīne absence aunters themselven!
I shall them love whīles I live, so mē Our Lord help
And give them landes full large where them best līkes;
They shall not lōse on this °laik, yif mē līfe °happen, *game/is granted*
1600 That thus are °lāmed for my love by these °līthe strandes." *wounded/pleasant*

    But in the clēre °dawing the dere king himselven *dawn*
Commaunded Sir Cador, with his dere knightes,
Sir Clēremus, Sir Clēremond, with clene men of armes,
Sir Clowdmur, Sir Clēges, tō convey these lordes;
Sir Bois and Sir Berille, with banners displayed,
Sir Bawdwin, Sir Brīan, and Sir Bedvere the rich,
Sir Raynald and Sir Richer, Rowlaunde chīlder,
Tō rīde with the Rōmanes in route with their °fēres: *comrades*
"Prikes now privily tō Paris the rich
1610 With Pēter the prisonēr and his prīs knightes;
°Beteche them the provost in presence of lordes *entrust them to*
°O pain and o peril that °pendes there-tō, *on the/appends*
That they be wīsely watched and in ward holden,

Warded of °warantīses with worshipful knightes;   *sworn guards*
°Wāge him wight men   and °wǫnde for nǫ silver;   *hire/hesitate*
I have warned that wye;   bēware yif him līkes!"

    Now bounes the Britons   °als the king biddes,   *as*
Buskes their batailes,   their banners displayes,
Tōward Chartres they °chēse,   thēse chevalrous knightes,   *go*
1620 †And in the Champain land   full fair they eschēved,
For the Emperour of might   had ordained himselven
Sir Utolf and Sir Evander,   twǫ honourable kinges,
Erles of the Orīent   with austeren knightes,
Of the °auntrousest men   that tō his hǫst lǫnged   *most adventurous*
Sir Sextynour of °Lyby   and senatours many,   *Lybia*
The king of °Surry himself   with sarazens ynow;   *Syria*
The senatour of °Sūtere   with summes full hūge   *Sutri*
Was assigned tō that court   by °sente of his peeres,   *assent*
°Trays tōward °Troys   the trǫsoun tō work,   *goes/Troyes (in France)*
1630 Tō have betrapped with a °trayn   our °travēland knightes, *trick/travelling*
That had perceived that Pēter   at Paris sholde leng
In prisoun with the provost   his paines tō °drīe.   *suffer*
Forthy they °busked them boun   with banners displayed, *made themselves ready*
In the °buscaile of his way,   on blonkes full hūge,   *bushes*
Plantes them in the path   with powēr arrayed
Tō pick up the prisonērs   frǫ our prīs knightes.

    Sir Cador of Cornwall   commaundes his peeres,
Sir Clēgis, Sir Clēremus,   Sir Clēremond the noble:
"Hēre is the Clǫse of Clime   with °clēves sǫ high;   *cliffs*
1640 Lookes the countree bē clēre;   the corners are large;
°Discoveres now °sekerly   °skrogges and other,   *search/carefully/shrubs*
That nǫ °scāthel in the °skrogges   scorn us hēreafter;   *harmful person/shrubs*
Look yē °skift it sǫ   that us nǫ °scāthe °limpe,   *arrange/harm/befall*
†For nō scomfitūre in skulkery   is scomfit ever."

    Now they °hīe tō the °holt,   these °harāgēous knightes, *hasten/wood/violent*
Tō °herken of the °high men   tō helpen thēse lǫrdes, *hear/noble*
Fīndes them °helmed hǫle   and horsed on steedes,   *completely armed*
°Hōvand on the high way   by the °holt hemmes.   *waiting/wood's edges*
With knightly countenaunce   Sir Clēgis himselven

1620 And in the province of Champagne they succeeded very (*full*) well.
1644 No attack from ambush is ever defeated.

1650 Crīes tō the company   and carpes thēse wordes:
"Is there any kidd knight,   kaiser or other,
Will °kīthe for his kinges love   craftes of armes?   *show*
Wē are comen frọ the king   of this kith rich
That knọwen is for conquerour,   crownd in erthe;
His rich retinūes hēre,   all of the Round Tāble,
Tō rīde with that rēal   in rout when him līkes.
Wē seek jousting of war,   yif any will happen,
Of the jollïest men   ajudged by lọrdes;
If hēre bē any °hathel man,   erl or other,   *noble*
1660 That for the Emperour love   will aunter himselven."

     And an erl then in anger   answeres him soon:
"Mē angers at Arthur   and at his °hathel bernes   *noble*
That thus in his errour   occūpīes thēse rewmes,
And °outrayes the Emperour,   his erthly lọrd!   *outrages*
The array and the °rēaltees   of the Round Tāble   *royalty*
Is with rancour °rehẹrsed   in rewmes full many,   *told*
Of our rentes of Rōme   such revel hē họldes;
Hē shall give rẹsoun full °rāthe,   if us right happen,   *quickly*
That many shall repent   that in his rout rīdes,
1670 °For the reckless °roy   sọ rewles himselven!"   *because/king*

     "Ā!" says Sir Clēgis then,   "sọ mē Crist help!
I knọw by thy °carping   a °counter thee seemes!   *talking/*
                                                                   accountant
But bē thou auditour or erl   or Emperour thyselven,
Upon Arthures behalf   I answer thee soon,
The renk sọ rēal   that rewles us all,
The rīotous men and the rich   of the Round Tāble:
Hē has °araised his account   and °redde all his °rolles,   *drawn up/read/*
                                                                   records
For hē will give a reckoning   that °rew shall after,   *rue*
That all the °rich shall repent   that tō Rōme lọnges   *powerful (ones)*
1680 Ẹre the °rẹrage bē requīte   of rentes that hē claimes.   *debt be repaid*
†Wē crāve of your courtaisy   three courses of war,
And claimes of knighthood,   tāke keep tō yourselven!
Yē dō but °trayn us tōday   with °troufeland wordes;   *trick/trifling*
Of such °travēland men   trẹchery mē thīnkes.   *travelling*
Send out sadly   certain knightes
Or say mē sēkerly sooth;   °forsāke yif you līkes."   *surrender*

1681-82 [Clegis challenges the Romans to a formal tournament, with three
   courses of war (that is, three jousts with the lance) and the claims of
   knighthood (the winner to take the horse and arms of the loser)].

Then says the King of °Surry,   "°Als sāve mē Our Lord,   *Syria/as*
†Yif thou °lenge all the day   thou °bēs not delivered!   *delay/will be*
But thou sēkerly ensūre   with certain knightes
1690 That thy °cote and thy crest   bē knowen with lordes,   *coat of arms*
Of armes of auncestry   °enterd with landes."   *endowed*

"Sir King," says Sir Clēgis,   "full knightly thou askes;
†I °trow it bē for °cowardis   thou carpes thēse wordes;   *believe/*
                                                                        cowardice
Mīne armes are of auncestry   °envered with lordes,   *acknowledged*
†And has in banner been borne   sēnn Sir Brūt tīme;
At the citee of Troy   that tīme was °ensēged,   *besieged*
Oft seen in °assaut   with certain knightes;   *assault*
Forthy Brūt brought us   and all our bold elders
Tō Bretain the °brodder   °within ship-bōrdes."   *greater/aboard*
                                                                        ships

1700   "Sir," says Sir Sextynour,   "say what thee līkes,
And wē shall suffer thee,   als us best seemes;
†Look thy trumpes bē trussed   and troufle no lenger,
For though thou tarry all the day,   thee °tīdes no better,   *betides*
For there shall never Rōman   that in my rout rīdes
Bē with °rebawdes rebūked,   whīles I in world regne!"   *low fellows*

Then Sir Clēgis tō the king   a little °enclīned,   *bowed*
Kaires tō Sir Cador   and knightly him telles:
"Wē have founden in yon °firth,   flourished with leves,   *forest*
The flowr of the fairest folk   that tō thy fo longes,
1710 Fifty thousand of folk   of °fērs men of armes,   *fierce*
That fair are °fewtered on front   under yon free bowes;   *prepared for*
                                                                        battle
They are °enbushed on blonkes,   with banners displayed,   *in ambush*
In yon °beechen wood,   upon the way sīdes.   *beech*
They have the °furth °for-set   all of the fair water,   *ford/blockaded*
That °fayfully of force   fight us behooves,   *truly*
For thus °us shāpes tōday,   shortly tō tell;   *it befalls us*
†Whether wē shoun or shew,   shift as thee līkes."

1688-91 [The charge that Clegis is trying to delay things is only a *pro
   forma* insult. More important is the King of Syria's inquiry about
   Clegis' ancestry, since it would be beneath his dignity to joust with
   any but the highest noble.]
1693 [Clegis' insult, like the King of Syria's, is part of the formal *flyting*.]
1695 [See note on line 3376 of the *Stanzaic Morte Arthur*.]
1702 See that you pack up your trumpets and trifle no longer.
1717 Decide as you please whether we shun (battle) or show (fight).

    "Nay," quod Cador,   "so mē Crīst help,
It were shāme that wē sholde   °shoun for so little!   *shun (battle)*
1720 Sir Launcelot shall never laugh,   that with the king lenges,
That I sholde °let my way   for lēde upon erthe;   *give up*
I shall bē dēde and undōne   ēre I hēre °dreche   *delay*
For drēde of any °dogges-son   in yon dim °shawes!"   *dog's son/bushes*

    Sir Cador then knightly   comfortes his pople,
And with °corāge keen   hē carpes thēse wordes: *heart*
"Think on the valīant prince   that °vesettes us ever   *endows*
With landes and lordshippes   where us best līkes.
That has us °dūcherys delt   and dubbed us knightes,   *dukedoms*
Given us °gersoms and gold   and °guerdons many,   *gifts/rewards*
1730 Grayhoundes and grēte horse   and °alkīne gāmes,   *every sort of pleasure*
That °gaines til any gōme   that under God lives;   *profit any man*
Think on the rich renown   of the Round Tāble,
And let it never bē °reft us   for Rōman in erthe;   *taken from*
°Foyne you not faintly,   ne °frithes no wēpens,   *duel/spare*
But look yē fight faithfully,   frēkes yourselven;
†I wolde bē welled all quick   and quartered in sonder,
°But I work my deed,   whīles I in wrath lenge."   *unless*

    Then this doughty dūke   dubbed his knightes:
Īoneke and Askanere,   Aladūke and other,
1740 That °eieres were of Essex   and all those °este marches,   *heirs/eastern*
Howell and Hardolf,   °happy in armes,   *fortunate*
Sir Heryll and Sir Herygall,   thēse °harāgēous knightes.   *violent*
Then the soveraign assigned   certain lordes,
Sir Bawdwyne, Sir Uryelle,   Sir Bedvere the rich,
Raynald and Richere,   Rowlaundes chīlder:
"°Tākes keep on this °prince   with your prīs knightes,   *take care of/i.e., Peter*
And yif wē in the °stour   withstanden the better,   *battle*
Standes hēre in this °stede   and stirres no further;   *place*
And yif the chaunce fall   that wē bē over-charged,
1750 °Eschewes tō some castle   and °chēves yourselven,   *escape/save*
Or rīde tō the rich king,   if you °roo happen,   *respite*
And bid him come redyly   tō rescūe his bernes."

    †And then the Bretons brothely   enbrāces their shēldes,
°Braides on bacenettes   and buskes their launces;   *draw on helmets*

1736 I would be boiled alive and cut in quarters.
1753 And then the Britons boldly put their arms in the straps (*enbraces*)
    of their shields.

Thus hē °fittes his folk   and tō the fēld rīdes,   *arranges*
Fīve hundreth on a front   °fewtered at ǫnes!   *readied spears*
With °trumpes they °trīne   and trapped steedes,   *trumpets/go*
With cornettes and clarīouns   and °clergīal nǫtes;   *skillful*
Shockes in with a °shāke   and °shuntes nǫ lǫnger,   *sudden move-*
                                                                       ment/hold back
1760 †There shawes were sheen   under the shīre ēves.
And then the Rōmanes rout   remōves a little,
Raikes with a °rere-ward   thǫse rēal knightes;   *rear guard*
Sǫ °raply they rīde there   that all the rout ringes   *quickly*
Of °rives and rank steel   and rich gold mailes.   *nails*

     Then shot out of the °shaw °sheltrones many,   *bushes/troops*
With sharp wēpens of war   shootand at ǫnes.
The King of °Lyby before   the °avauntward hē lędes,   *Lybia/vanguard*
And all his °lēle °lēge-men   all on loud ascrīes.   *loyal/liegemen*
Then this crūel king   °castes in fewter,   *readies his spear*
1770 Caught him a °coverd horse,   and his course hǫldes,   *armored*
Bęres tō Sir Berille   and °brǫthely him hittes,   *stoutly*
Through the °golet and the °gorger   hē hurtes him ēven.   *gullet/neckpiece*
The gōme and the gręte horse   at the ground ligges,
And °grētes graithely tō God   and gives Him the sǫul.   *cries*
Thus is Berille the bǫld   brǫught out of līfe,
And °bīdes after the burīal   that him best līkes.   *awaits the burial*

     And then Sir Cador of Cornwall   is °careful in herte,   *sorrowful*
Because of his kinsman   that thus is miscarrīed;
°Umbeclappes the corse,   and kisses him oft,   *embraces*
1780 °Gart keep him °covert   with his clēre knightes.   *commanded/*
                                                                      protected
Then laughs the Lyby king,   and all on loud °męles: *speaks*
"Yon lǫrd is lighted!   Mē līkes the better!
Hē shall not °dęre us tōday;   the devil have his bǫnes!"   *harm*

     "Yon king," says Sir Cador,   "carpes full large,
Because hē killed this keen   —Crīst have thy sǫul!—
†Hē shall have corn-bōte,   sǫ mē Crīst help!
Ęre I kaire of this °cǫste,   wē shall encounter ǫnes: *place*
†Sǫ may the wind wheel turn,   I quīte him ęre ēven,
Soothly himselven   or some of his °fēres!"   *companions*

1760 Where shrubs were bright under the shining eaves of the forest.
1786 He shall repent, so help me Christ. [*Corn-bōte* is literally a fine
     paid in grain.]
1788 As (inevitably) as the wind can turn a wheel (windmill) I shall
     repay him before evening.

1790   Then Sir Cador the keen   knightly hē workes,
Crīes, "A Cornwall!" and °castes in fewter,   *readies his spear*
°Girdes °streke through the °stour on a steed rich;   *strikes/straight/ battle*
Many steren men hē °stirred by strenghe of him ǫne; *struck*
When his spere was °sprongen, hē sped him full °yęrne, *broken/eagerly*
Swapped out with a sword that °swīked him never, *failed*
Wrǫught wayes full wīde, and wounded knightes,
°Workes in his wayfare full °workand sīdes,   *makes/painful*
And hewes of the hardīest °halses in sonder,   *necks*
That all blendes with blood there his blonk runnes!
1800 Sǫ many bernes the bǫld brǫught out of līfe,
°Tittes tyrauntes down and °tēmes their saddles, *knocks/empties*
And turnes out of the toil when him tīme thinkes!

      Then the °Lyby king crīes full loud   *Lybian*
On Sir Cador the keen with crūel wordes:
"Thou has worship won and wounded knightes!
Thou °weenes for thy wightness the world is thīne ǫwn! *suppose*
I shall wait at thīne hand, wye, by my °trewth; *word*
I have warned thee well, bēware yif thee līkes!"

      With °cornus and clarīouns thēse new-mǎde knightes *horns*
1810 °Līthes unto the cry and °castes in fewter, *listen/ready their spears*
†Ferkes in on a front on feraunt steedes,
Felled at the first come fifty at ǫnes;
Shot through the °sheltrons and °shivered launces, *troops/split*
Laid down in the °lump lǫrdly bernes, *heap*
And thus nǫbly our new men °nōtes their strenghes! *use*
But new °nǫte is anǫn that °noyes mē sǫre: *business/annoys*
The King of Lyby has °laght a steed that him līked, *seized*
And comes in lǫrdly °in līones of silver, *i.e., on his shield*
°Umbelappes the °lump and °lettes in sonder; *surrounds/ group/drives*
1820 Many lēde with his launce the līfe has hē °rēved! *taken*
Thus hē chāses the chīlder of the kinges chāmber,
And killes in the °champaines chevalrous knightes; *open fields*
With a °chāsing spęre hē choppes down many! *hunting spear*

      There was Sir Aladūke slain and Achinour wounded,
Sir Origge and Sir Ermyngall hewen all tō °pēces! *pieces*
And there was Lewlin °laght and Lewlins brōther *taken*
With lǫrdes of Lyby and led tō their strenghes;

1811 Ride on iron-gray steeds at the front rank (of the Romans).

Ne had Sir Clēgis comen   and Clement the nǫble,
Our new men had gǫne tō nǫught   and °many mǫ other.   *many others*

1830   Then Sir Cador the keen   °castes in fewter   *readies his spear*
A crūel launce and a keen   and tō the king rīdes,
Hittes him high on the helm   with his hard wēpen,
That all the hot blood of him   tō his hand runnes!
The °hęthen °harāgēous king   upon the °hęthe ligges,   *heathen/violent/heath*
And of his °hertly hurt   °hęled hē never.   *mortal/healed*
Then Sir Cador the keen   crīes full loud:
"Thou has °corn-bōte, sir king,   there God give thee sǫrrow;   *penance*
Thou killed my cosin;   my care is the less!
°Kēle thee now in the clay   and comfort thyselven;   *cool yourself*
1840   Thou scorned us lǫng ęre,   with thy scornful wordes,
And now thou has chēved sǫ,   it is thīne own °scāthe;   *harm*
†Hǫld at thou hent has;   it harmes but little,
For hęthing is hǫme-hǫld,   ūse it whǫ-sǫ will!"

The King of °Surry then   is sǫrrowful in herte,   *Syria*
For sāke of his soveraign   that thus was °surprīsed;   *taken*
Sembled his sarazens   and senatours many;
°Unsaughtly they set then   upon our °sēre knightes.   *hostilely/various*
Sir Cador of Cornwall   hē °counters them soon   *encounters*
With his kidd company   clęnlich arrayed;
1850   In the front of the °firth,   as the way °forthes,   *forest/goes forth*
Fifty thousand of folk   was felled at ǫnes.
There was at the assemblee   certain knightes
Sǫre wounded soon   upon °sēre halves.   *every side*
The sēkerest sarazenes   that tō that °sorte lǫnged   *company*
†Behīnd the saddles were set   six foot large;
They °sheerd in the °sheltron   °shēlded knightes;   *cut down/troop/shielded*
Shalkes they shot through   °shrinkand mailes;   *wrinkled (plated)*
Through brenyes °brǫwden   brēstes they °thirled;   *braided/pierced*
°Brācers burnisht   °bristes in sonder;   *arm guards/burst*
1860   °Blāsons bloody   and blonkes they hewen,   *bloody shields*
With brandes of °brown steel,   °brankand steedes!   *shining/prancing*
The Bretons brǫthely   brittenes sǫ many
The bente and the brǫde fēld   all on blood runnes!
By then Sir Kayous the keen   a °capitain has wonnen;   *captain*

1842-43 Keep what you have taken; it does little harm, for scorn is
homegrown (comes home to roost), use it who will.
1855 [I.e., the Saracens are six feet from the waist up.]

Sir Clēgis °clinges in and °clekes another;	*rushes/clutches*
The Capitain of °Cornett, under the king selven,	*Corneto*
That was key of the °kith of all that cǫste rich	*country*
†Utolf and Ēvander Ioneke had nommen	
With the Erl of °Afrīke and other gręte lǫrdes.	*Africa*
1870 The King of Surry the keen tō Sir Cador is °yēlden,	*surrendered*
The Seneschal of °Sūtere tō Sāgramour himselven.	*Sutri*
When the chevalry saw their chēftaines were °nomen,	*taken*
Tō a chēf forest they °chǫsen their wayes,	*go*
And feeled them sǫ faint they fell in the °grēves,	*groves*
In the °feren of the °firth for °fęrd of our pople.	*ferns/forest/fear*
There might men see the rich rīde in the °shawes	*shrubs*
Tō rip up the Rōmanes °rūdlich wounded,	*rudely*
Shoutes after the hęthen men °harāgēous knightes,	*violent*
By hundrethes they hewed down by the °holt ēves!	*edge of the wood*
1880 Thus our chevalrous men chāses the pople;	
Tō a castel they °eschēved the few that °eschāped.	*achieved (got to)/escaped*
Then °relīes the renkes of the Round Tāble	*rally*
For tō °rīot the wood there the dūke restes;	*ride through*
Ransackes the °rindes all, °raght up their °fēres,	*woods/took/ companions*
That in the fighting before fey were °belęved.	*left*
†Sir Cador gart charre them and cover them fair,	
Carrīed them tō the king with his best knightes,	
And passes untō Paris with prisonērs himselven,	
°Betook them the provost, princes and other,	*entrusted them to*
1890 °Tas a °sope in the towr and tarrīes nǫ lǫnger	*takes/meal*
But turnes °tīte tō the king and him with °tonge telles:	*quickly/tongue*
"Sir," says Sir Cador, "a cāse is befallen;	
Wē have °countered tōday in yon cǫste rich	*encountered*
With kinges and kaiseres crūel and nǫble,	
And knightes and keen men clęnlich arrayed!	
They had at yon forest °for-set us the wayes,	*blockaded*
At the °furth in the °firth with fērs men of armes;	*ford/forest*
There fǫught wē in faith and °foined with spęres	*duelled*
On fēld with thy fǫmen and felled them °on live;	*alive (i.e., killed them)*
1900 The King of Lyby is °laid and in the fēld lęved,	*laid low*
And many of his lēge-men that yǫre tō him lǫnged;	
Other lǫrdes are °laght of °uncouthe °lēdes;	*taken/foreign/ countries*

¹⁸⁶⁸ [Ioneke captured Utolf and Ēvander. For word order see Introduction, p. xv.]
¹⁸⁸⁶ Sir Cador commanded they be put in wagons and covered with fair cloths.

Wē have led them °at lenge,   tō live whīles thee līkes.   *to remain here*
Sir Utolf and Sir Evander,   thēse honourable knightes,
By an aunter of armes   Īoneke has °nomen,   *taken*
With erles of Orīent   and austeren knightes,
Of auncestry the best men   that tō the host longed;
The Senatour Barouns   is caught with a knight,
The Capitain of °Cornette   that crūel is holden,   *Corneto*
1910 The Seneschal of °Sūtere,   unsaught with thēse other,   *Sutri*
The King of Surry himselven   and sarazenes ynow.
But fey of ours in the fēld   are fourteen knightes.
I will not °feyne ne °forbere   but faithfully tellen: *hold back/delay*
Sir Berille is one,   a bannerette noble,
Was killed at the first come   with a king rich;
Sir Aladūke of Towell   with his tender knightes,
Among the Turkes was °tint   and in tīme °founden;   *lost/found (dead)*
Good Sir Mawrelle of Mawnces   and Mawrene his brother,
Sir Menedūke of Mentoche   with marvēlous knightes."

1920   Then the worthy king wrīthes   and weeped with his eyen,
Carpes tō his cosin   Sir Cador thēse wordes:
"Sir Cador, thy °corāge   confoundes us all!   *courage*
Cowardly thou castes out   all my best knightes!
Tō put men in peril,   it is no °prīs holden,   *excellence*
But the partīes wēre °purveyed   and powēr arrayed;   *prepared*
When thou were °stedde on a strenghe   thou sholde have   *placed*
                                   with-stonden,
But yif ye wolde all my steren   °stroy for the nones!"   *destroy*

      "Sir," says Sir Cador,   "yē know well yourselven;
Yē are king in this kith;   carp what you līkes!
1930 Shall never berne upbraid mē   that to thy °bōrde longes,   *table*
That I sholde °blinn for their boste   thy °bidding tō work!   *cease/command*
When any °stertes tō °stale,   °stuff them the better,   *sets out/ company/supply*
Or they will be °stonayed and °stroyed   in yon strait landes.   *astonished/ destroyed*
†I did my deligence tōday   —I dō mē on lordes—
And in daungēr of °dede   for dīverse knightes,   *death*
I have no grāce tō thy °gree   but such grete wordes;   *reward*
Yif I °heven my herte,   my °hap is no better."   *speak my mind/ fortune*

      Though Sir Arthur was angered,   hē answers fair:
"Thou has doughtily dōne,   Sir Dūke, with thy handes,
1940 And has dōne thy °devēr   with my dere knightes;   *duty*

1934 I did my duty today—I put myself at the judgement of lords.

Forthy thou art deemed with dūkes and erles
For ọne of the doughtiest that dubbed was ever!
There is nọne °ischew of us on this erthe °sprongen;   *issue (child)/*
                                                          sprung
Thou art apparent tō bē °eier, or ọne of thy chīlder;   *heir*
Thou art my °sister son; forsāke shall I never!   *sister's*

Then °gart hē in his °ọwen tent a tāble bē set,   *commanded/own*
And °tryed in with °trumpes °travēled bernes,   *invited/trumpets/*
                                                   exhausted
Served them solemnly with °selcouthe °mẹtes,   *rare/foods*
°Swīthe seemly in sight with silveren dishes.   *very*

1950   When the senatours °herde say that it sọ happened,   *heard*
They said tō the Emperour: "Thy segges are °surprīsed!   *taken*
Sir Arthur, thīne enmy, has °outrayed thy lọrdes   *outraged*
That rọde for the rescūe of yon rich knightes!
Thou °dōs but °tinnes thy tīme and °tourmentes thy pople;   *do/lose/torment*
Thou art betrayed °of thy men that mọst thou on °traisted.   *by/trusted*
That shall turn thee tō °teen and °torfer forever!"   *pain/sorrow*

Then the Emperour °īrous was, angerd at his herte,   *irate*
For our valīant bernes such °prowesh had wonnen.   *prowess*
With king and with kaiser tō counsēl they wend,
1960 Soveraignes of sarazens and senatours many.
Thus hē sembles full soon certain lordes,
And in the °assemblee then hē says them thēse wordes: *assembly*
"My herte soothly is set, assent if you līkes,
Tō seek intō °Sessoine with my sēker knightes,   *Soissons*
Tō fight with my fọmen, if fortūne mē happen,
Yif I may fīnd the frēke within the four °halves;   *sides*
Or enter intō °Auguste aunters tō seek,   *Autun (province*
                                              in France)
And bīde with my bọld men within the °burg rich,   *town*
Rest us and revel and rīot ourselven,
1970 °Lende there in °delīte in lọrdshippes ynow,   *remain/delight*
°Tō Sir Lēo bē comen with all his °lēle knightes,   *until/loyal*
With lọrdes of Lumbardy tō let him the wayes."

But our wīse king is wary tō °waiten his renkes,   *look out for*
And wīsely by the woodes °voides his họst;   *withdraws*
†Gart felshen his fīres flāmand full high,
Trussen full traistely and trēunt there-after.

1975-76 Commands that his fires be fed so that they flame very high [to
   make the Romans think they are still in camp] and (commands them)
   to pack up securẹly and march away thereafter.

Sithen intō °Sessoine   hē °sought at the °gainest,   *Soissons/went/*
                                                                           quickest
And at the °sours of the sun   °disseveres his knightes,   *rising/separates*
°For-set then the citee   upon °sēre halves,   *blockaded/all*
                                                                           sides
1980   °Sodēnly on °eche sīde,   with seven grete °stales,   *suddenly/each/*
                                                                           troops
Only in the vāle   a °vaweward °enbushes.   *vanguard/lays in*
                                                                           ambush

Sir Valīant of Wāles   with valīant knightes
Before the kinges visāge   māde such avowes
Tō vanquish by victory   the Vīscount of Rōme;
Forthy the king °charges him,   what chaunce so befall,   *appoints*
Chēftain of the °check   with chevalrous   knightes,   *attack*
And sithen meles with mouth   °that hē most °traistes;   *to those that/*
                                                                           trusts
°Demenes the °middilward   °menskfully himselven,   *leads/middle*
                                                                           guard/honorably
°Fittes his footmen   als him fair thinkes;   *arranges*
1990 On front in the °fore-brēste   the flowr of his knightes;   *first rank*
His archers on either °half   hē ordained there-after   *side*
Tō °shāke in a °sheltron   tō shoot when them līkes;   *go/troop*
Hē arrayed in the rereward   full rēal knightes
With renkes renowned   of the Round Tāble,
Sir Raynald, Sir Richere   that °rade was never,   *fearful*
The rich Dūke of Rouen   with rīders ynow;
†Sir Kayous, Sir Clēgis,   and clene men of armes,
The king castes tō keep   by tho clēre strandes;
Sir Lot and Sir Launcelot,   thēse lordly knightes
2000 Shall lenge on his left hand   with lēgīones ynow,
Tō mōve in the °morn-whīle,   if the mist happen;   *morning*
Sir Cador of Cornwall,   and his keen knightes,
Tō °keep at the °karfuke,   tō close in °thir other;   *watch/*
                                                                           crossroads/these
Hē plantes in such plāces   princes and erles
That no power sholde pass   by no °privee wayes.   *secret*

But the Emperour anon   with honourāble knightes
And erles enters the vāle,   aunters tō seek,
And fīndes Sir Arthur   with hostes arrayed,
And at his °in-come,   tō °eeken his sorrow,   *entry/add to*
2010 Our burlich bold king   upon the bente hōves,
With his batail °on-brode   and banners displayed.   *spread out*
Hē had the citee °for-set   upon sēre halves,   *besieged*
Both the °clēves and the cliffes   with clene men of armes,   *gullies*

1997-98 The king decides Sir Kayous, Sir Clegis, and good men of arms
   should keep watch by those shining strands.

The moss and the °morass   with mountes sǫ high   *bogs*
With grẹte multitūde of men   tō °mar him in the wayes.   *harm*

When Sir Lūcīus him sees,   hē says tō his lǫrdes:
"This traitour has °treunt   this °trẹsoun tō work!   *marched here/*
                                                                         treason
Hē has the citee °for-set   upon sēre halves,   *blockaded*
All the °clēves and the cliffes   with clẹne men of armes!   *gullies*
2020 Hēre is no way, īwis,   ne nǫ °wit else,   *advice*
But fight with our fǫmen,   for flee may wē never!"

Then this rich man rāthẹ   arrayes his bernes,
Rewled his Rōmans   and rēal knightes;
Buskes in the °avauntward   the Vīscount of Rōme;   *vanguard*
Fro Viterbō tō Venice   thēse valīant knightes
°Dresses up drēdfully   the drāgon of gold,   *raises*
With °ẹgles all ǫver   °ēnamelled of sāble;   *eagles/adorned*
Drawen °dreghly the wīne   and drinken there-after,   *solemnly*
Dūkes and douspeeres,   dubbed knightes;
2030 For °dauncesing of °Dutch-men   and °dinning of pīpes,   *dancing/Germans/*
                                                                         sounding
All °dinned for °din   that in the dāle hōved.   *resounded/noise*
And then Sir Lūcīus on loud   said lǫrdlich wordes:
"Think on the much renown   of your rich faders,
And the °rīotours of Rōme   that regned with lǫrdes,   *ravagers*
And the renkes ǫver-ran,   all that regned in erthe,
°Ecrǫched all Cristendom   by craftes of armes;   *invaded*
In °everich a °vīage   the victory was hǫlden   *each/expedition*
°Inset all the sarazenes   within seven winter,   *overcame*
The part from Port °Jaffe   tō Paradīse gātes!   *Jaffa (formerly*
                                                                         Joppa)
2040 Thǫugh a rewm be rebel,   wē °reck it but little;   *reckon*
It is rẹsoun and right   the renk bē restrained!
°Dō dress wē therefore,   and bīde wē nǫ lǫnger,   *Let us prepare*
                                                                         ourselves
For °drēdles, withouten doubt,   the day shall be oures!"   *surely*

When thēse wordes was said,   the Welsh king himselven
Was ware of this °widerwin   that °warrayed his knightes;   *adversary/*
                                                                         made war on
Brǫthely in the vāle   with voice hē ascrīes:
†"Vīscount of Valence,   envīous of deedes,
The vassalāge of Viterbō   tōday shall bē revenged!
Unvanquisht frǫ this plāce   °void shall I never."   *leave*

²⁰⁴⁷ [The knights of the Round Table fulfill the vows they made; the
    King of Wales fulfills the vow he made in vv. 330–32.]

2050   Then the vīscount, valīant,   with a voice nǫble
      °Avoided the °avauntward,   °enveround his horse;   *left/vanguard/ turned*
      Hē dressed in a °derf shēld,   °endented with sāble,   *strong/edged*
      With a drāgon °engoushed,   drēdful tō shew,   *swollen*
      °Devourand a dolphin   with doleful lātes,   *devouring*
      In sign that our soveraign   sholde bē destroyed,
      And all dōne of dayes,   with dintes of swordes,
      For there is nǫught but °dęde   there the drāgon is raised!   *death*

      Then the comlich king   castes in fewter,
      With a crūel launce   °coupes full ēven   *strikes exactly*
2060 †Aboven the spayre a span,   amǫng the short ribbes,
      That the °splent and the spleen   on the spęre lenges!   *piece of armor plate*
      The blood °sprent out and °spredde   as the horse springes,   *spurt/spread*
      And hē °sprǫules full °spākely,   but spękes hē nǫ mǫre!   *sprawls/swiftly*
      And thus has Sir Valīant   hǫlden his avowes,
      And vanquisht the Vīscount   that victor was hǫlden!

      †Then Sir Ēwain fitz Ūrien   full °enkerly rīdes   *eagerly*
      Anǫn tō the Emperour   his °ęgle tō touch;   *eagle*
      Through his brǫde batail   hē buskes °belīve,   *quickly*
      °Braides out his brand   with a blīthe cheer,   *draws*
2070 †Reversed it rędily   and away rīdes,
      Ferkes in with °the fowl   in his fair handes,   *i.e., the eagle*
      And fittes in freely   on front with his fēres.

      †Now buskes Sir Launcelot   and braides full ēven
      To Sir Lūcīus the lǫrd   and lǫthly him hittes;
      Through °paunce and plātes   hē °pērced the mailes   *stomach guard/ pierced*
      That the proud °pensel   in his paunch lenges!   *pennon*
      The hęd °hailed out behīnd   an half foot large,   *came*
      Through hawberk and haunch   with the hard wēpen;
      The steed and the steren man   °strīkes tō the ground,   *i.e., he (Launcelot) strikes*
2080 °Strak down a standard   and tō his °stale wendes!   *struck/company*

2060 Six inches above the waist, between the short ribs.
2066 [Ewain fitz Urien fulfills the vow he made in vv. 357–63.]
2070 He quickly changed the direction of (*reversed*) the eagle; i.e., he carried it away.
2073 [Lancelot had vowed (vv. 372–77) to strike down the emperor himself, and accordingly he now strikes him down and leaves a spear stuck in his belly. The emperor evidently recovers very quickly, for he is soon back in battle.]

†Mē līkes well," says Sir Lot,   "yon lǫrdes are dēlivered!
The lot lenges now on mē,   with lęve of my lǫrd;
Tōday shall my nāme bē °laid,   and my līfe after,   *laid low*
But some °lępe frǫ the līfe   that on yon land hōves!"   *leap*

Then °strekes the steren   and straines his brīdle,   *stretches (in his
                                                                        stirrups)*
Strīkes intō the °stour   on a steed rich,   *battle*
°Enjoined with a gīaunt   and °jāgged him through!   *engaged/slashed*
Jollily this gentle knight   °for-jousted another,   *outjousted*
Wrǫught wayes full wīde,   °warrayand knightes,   *attacking*
2090 And woundes all °wāthely   that in the way standes!   *woefully*
Fightes with all the °frap   a furlǫng of way,   *troop*
Felled °fęle upon fēld   with his fair wēpen,   *many*
Vanquisht and has the victory   of valīant knightes,
And all °enverouned the vāle   and °void when him līked.   *rode around/left*

Then bǫwmen of Bretain   brǫthely there-after
†Bekered with brigandes   of fer in thǫ landes
With flǫnes fletterd they flit   full freshly thir frēkes,
°Fichen with °fętheres   through the fīne mailes;   *pierce/feathers*
Such °flytting is foul   that sǫ the flesh °dęres,   *contention/harms*
2100 That °flǫw °a ferrom   in flankes of steedes.   *flew/from afar*
Dartes the °Dutch-men   °dęlten °againes,   *Germans/dealt/
                                                                        in return*
With derf dintes of dęde   °dāgges through sheldes;   *cut*
†Quarrels quaintly   quappes through knightes
With īron sǫ °wekerly   that wink they never.   *swiftly*
Sǫ they shrinken for shot   of the sharp arrows,
That all the °sheltron shunt   and shuddered at ǫnes;   *troop*
The rich steedes °rependes   and °rashes on armes,   *buck/rush*
The hǫle hundreth °on hīe   upon °hęthe ligges;   *hastily/heath*
†But yet the hathelīest on hīe,   hęthen and other,
2110 All hourshes over hęde,   harmes tō work.
And all thēse gīauntes before,   engendered with fēndes,
°Joines on Sir Jonathal   and gentle knightes,   *attack*

[2081] [*Delivered*: have fulfilled their vows. Lot had vowed to be the
first to ride through the Roman ranks (vv. 386–94), which he now
does. When Lot has accomplished this, the vows are all fulfilled and
the battle proper begins.]
[2096-97] Fought with foot-soldiers (*brigands*) from afar in those lands;
with feathered arrows they very eagerly shoot those men.
[2103] Crossbow bolts skillfully whip through knights.
[2109-10] But yet the most noble hastily, heathens and others, all rush over
the heads (of the fallen) to do harms.

With clubbes of clẹne steel   clanked in helmes,
Crashed down crestes   and crashed braines,
Killed coursers   and °coverd steedes,   *armored*
Chopped through chevalērs   on chalk-whīte steedes;
Was never steel ne steed   might stand them againes,
But °stonays and strīkes down   that in the °stale hōves,   *astonish/troop*
Til the conquerour cọme   with his keen knightes.
2120 With crüel countenaunce   hē crīed full loud:
"I °wēnd nọ Bretons wọlde bē   °bashed for sọ little,   *supposed/ abashed*
And for bare-legged °boyes   that on the bente hōves!"   *knaves*

    Hē °clekes out °Caliburn,   full clẹnlich burnisht,   *draws/Excalibur*
Graithes him tō Golopas,   that grēved him mọst,
Cuttes him ēven by the knees   clẹnly in sonder;
"Come down," quọd the king,   "and carp tō thy fēres!
Thou art too high by the half,   I °hēte thee in trewth!   *promise*
Thou shall bē handsomer °in hīe,   with the help of my Lọrd!"   *hastily*
With that steelen brand   hē °strọke off his hẹd.   *struck*
2130 Sterenly in that stour   hē strīkes another.
Thus hē settes on seven   with his sēker knightes;
Whīles sixty were served sọ   °ne sẹsed they never;   *did not cease*
And thus at this °joining   the gīauntes are destroyed,   *encounter*
And at that journee °for-jousted   with gentle knightes.   *outjousted*

    Then the Rōmanes and the renkes   of the Round Tāble
°Rewles them in array,   rẹreward and other,   *arrange*
With wight wēpenes of war   they °wrọughten on helmes,   *worked*
°Rittes with rank steel   full rēal mailes   *rip*
But they °fit them fair,   thēse °frek bernes,   *ordered themselves/bold*
2140 °Fewters in freely   on °feraunt steedes   *fix lances/ iron-gray*
°Foines full °felly   with °flishand spẹres,   *duel/fiercely/ slashing*
°Fretten off °orfrayes   °fast upon shēldes;   *cut/gold ornaments/ fastened*
Sọ fẹlẹ fey is in fight   upon the fēld lẹved
That °ẹch a °furth in the °firth   of rẹd blood runnes.   *every/stream/ forest*
°By that swiftely on °swarth   the °swẹt is beleved,   *By then/ground/ lifeblood*
Swordes °swangen in twọ,   °sweltand knightes   *swung/dying*
Līes wīde ọpen °welterand   on °walopand steedes;   *rolling about/ galloping*
Woundes of °wāle men   °workand sīdes,   *choice/paining*
Fāces °fetteled unfair   in °feltered lockes,   *enclosed/matted*

2150 †All craysed, for-trodden   with trapped steedes,
        The fairest on °folde   that °figūred was ever,   *earth/created*
        As fer as a furlǫng,   a thousand at ones!

        By then the Rōmanes wēre   rebūked at little,
        Withdrawes them °drērily   and °dreches nǫ lenger;   *drearily/delay*
        Our prince with his powēr   °persewes them after,   *pursues*
        Prikes on the proudest   with his prīs knightes,
        Sir Kayous, Sir Clēgis,   Sir Bedvere the rich,
        Encounters them at the cliff   with clęne men of armes;
        Fightes fast in the firth,   °frithes nǫ wēpen,   *spares*
2160 Felled at the first come   fīve hundreth at ǫnes!
        And when they °fande them °for-set   with our fērs knightes,   *found/blockaded*
        †Few men again fęlę   mot fich them better,
        Fightes with all the °frap,   °foines with spęres,   *troop/duel*
        And fǫught with the frekkest   that tō Fraunce lǫnges.
        But Sir Kayous the keen   castes in fewter,
        Chāses on a courser   and tō a king rīdes;
        With a launce of °Lettow   hē °thirles his sīdes   *Lithuania/*
                                                                                                          pierces
        That the liver and the lunges   on the launce lenges;
        The shaft shuddered and shot   in the °shīre berne,   *shining*
2170 And °sǫught throughout the shēld   and in the °shalk restes.   *went/man*
        But Kayous at the °in-come   was keeped unfair   *entry*
        With a coward knight   of the kith rich;
        At the turning that tīme   the traitour him hit
        In through the °felettes   and in the flank after   *loins*
        That the °bustous launce   the °bewelles °entāmed,   *wild/bowels/*
                                                                                                          pierced
        That braste at the brawling   and brǫke in the °middes.   *middle*
        Sir Kayous knew well   by that kidd wound
        That hē was dęde of the dint   and dōne out of līfe;
        Then hē raikes in array   and °on rǫw rīdes,   *at the rank*
2180 On this rēal renk   his dęde tō revenge:
        "Keep thee, coward!"   and calles him soon,
        Clēves him with his clēre brand   clęnlich in sonder:
        "Had thou well dęlt   thy dint with thy handes,
        I had forgiven thee my dęde,   by Crīst now of hęven!"

        Hē wendes tō the wīse king   and °winly him greetes: *pleasantly*
        "I am °wāthely wounded,   °waresh °mon I never;   *woefully/*
                                                                                                          recover/may

²¹⁵⁰ All crushed, stamped to death by armored steeds.
²¹⁶² The few men must take better positions to fight against many.

Work now thy worship,   as the world °askes,   *requires*
And bring mē tō burīal;   °bid I nǫ mǫre.   *ask*
Greet well my lādy the queen,   °yif thee world happen,   *if you survive*
2190 And all the °burlich °birdes   that tō her bowr lǫnges;   *stately/maids*
And my °worthily wīfe,   that wrathed mē never,   *worthy*
Bid her for her worship   work for my sǫul!"

The kinges confessour cǫme   with °Crīst in his handes,   *i.e., the Host*
For tō comfort the knight,   °kend him °the wordes;   *told/i.e.,*
                                                                       absolution
The knight covered on his knees   with a °kaunt herte,   *stout*
And caught his Crēatour   that comfortes us all.
Then °rōmes the rich king   for rewth at his herte,   *bellows*
Rīdes intō the rout   his dęde tō revenge,
Pressed intō the °plump   and with a prince meetes   *crowd*
2200 That was °eier of Egypt   in thǫse ęste marches,   *heir*
Clēves him with Caliburn   clęnlich in sonder!
Hē brǫches ēven through the berne   and the saddle bristes,
And at the back of the blonk   the °bewelles °entāmed!   *bowels/pierced*
Manly in his °malencoly   hē meetes another;   *melancholy*
The middle of that mighty   that him much grēved
Hē °merkes through the mailes   the °middes in sonder,   *cuts/middle*
That the middes of the man   on the °mount falles,   *ground*
The °tother half of the haunch   on the horse °lęved;   *other/remained*
Of that hurt, as I °hǫpe,   hęles hē never!   *suppose*
2210 Hē shot through the °sheltrons   with his sharp wēpen,   *troops*
°Shalkes hē °shręde through   and °shrinked mailes;   *men/cut/*
                                                                       wrinkled
Banners hē bǫre down,   brittened shēldes;
Brǫthely with °brown steel   his °brēthe hē there wrękes;   *shining/anger*
°Wrǫthely hē wrīthes   by wightness of strenghe,   *wrathfully*
Woundes thēse °widerwinnes,   °warrayed knightes   *adversaries/*
                                                                       attacked
†Thrēped through the thickes   thriteen sīthes,
Thringes thrǫly in the throng   and thriches ēven after!

Then Sir Gawain the good   with worshipful knightes
Wendes in the °avauntward   by thǫ wood °hemmes,   *vanguard/edges*
2220 Was ware of Sir Lūcīus   on land there hē hōves
With lǫrdes and lēge-men   that tō himself lǫnged.
Then the Emperour °enkerly   askes him soon: *eagerly*
"What °will thou, Wawain?   Work for thy wēpen?   *do you want*
I wǫt by thy wāvering   thou °wilnes after sorrow;   *want*
I shall bē °wroken on thee, wretch,   for all thy gręte wordes!"   *avenged*

2216-17 Fought through the crowds thirteen times, presses hard in the
    throng and pushes straight through.

He laght out a long sword   and °lushed on fast,   *lashed*
And Sir Līonel in the land   lordly him strīkes,
Hittes him on the hed   that the helm bristes,
Hurtes his °herne-pan   an °hand-brēd large!   *skull/hand's*
                                                                     breadth deep
2230 Thus hē layes on the °lump   and lordly them served,   *crowd*
Wounded worthily   worshipful knightes,
Fightes with Florent,   that best is of swordes,
Til the °fomand blood   til his fist runnes!   *foaming*

Then the Rōmans °relēved   that ere were rebūked,   *rallied*
And all °tōrattes our men   with their °reste horses;   *scatter/rested*
For they see their chēftain   bē °chauffed so sore,   *bothered*
They chāse and chop down   our chevalrous knightes!
Sir Bedvere was borne through   and his brēste °thirled   *pierced*
With a burlich brand,   brode at the hiltes;
2240 The rēal rank steel   tō his herte runnes,
And hē rushes tō the erthe;   rewth is the more!

Then the conquerour took keep   and come with his
                                  strenghes
Tō rescūe the rich men   of the Round Tāble,
†Tō outraye the Emperour,   yif aunter it shew,
Ēven tō the egle,   and "Arthur!" ascrīes.
The Emperour then egerly   at Arthur hē strīkes,
°Awkward on the °umbrēre,   and egerly him hittes;   *slantwise/visor*
The nāked sword at the nose   °noyes him sore;   *annoys*
The blood of the bold king   over the brēste runnes,
2250 °Bebledde all the brode shēld   and the bright mailes!   *bloodied*
Our bold king °bowes the blonk   by the bright brīdle,   *turns*
With his burlich brand   a °buffet him °reches   *blow/reaches to*
                                                                     (gives)
Through the breny and brēste   with his bright wēpen;
†O slant down fro the slot   hē slittes him at ones!
Thus endes the Emperour   °of Arthure handes,   *by*
And all his austeren host   there-of were °affrayed.   *afraid*

Now they ferk tō the firth,   a few that are leved,
For °ferdness of our folk,   by the fresh strandes;   *fear*
The flowr of our fērs men   on °feraunt steedes   *iron-gray*
2260 Followes frekly on the frēkes   that °frayed was never.   *frightened*
Then the kidd conquerour   crīes full loud:

2244 To outrage the emperor if a chance should appear.
2254 Slantwise from the slot (at the base of the throat).

"Cosin of Cornwall,   tāke keep tō thyselven
†That nǫ capitain bē keeped   for nǫne silver,
Ęre Sir Kayous dęde   bē crūelly venged!"

"Nay," says Sir Cador,   "sǫ mē Crīst help!
There ne is kaiser ne king   that under Crīst regnes
That I ne shall kill cǫld-dęde   by craft of my handes!"

      There might men see chēftains   on chalk-whīte steedes
      Chop down in the chāse   chevalry nǫble,
2270 Rōmanes the richest   and rēal kinges,
      Braste with rank steel   their ribbes in sonder,
      Braines °forbrusten   through burnisht helmes,   *burst to pieces*
      With brandes °forbrittened   °on brǫde in the landes; *battered to*
                                                              death/abroad
      They hewed down hęthen men   with hilted swordes,
      By hǫle hundrethes °on hīe   by the °holt ēves;   *hastily/edges*
                                                              of the wood
      There might nǫ silver them sāve   ne succour their līves,
      Sowdan, ne sarazen,   ne senatour of Rōme.

      Then °relēves the renkes   of the Round Tāble,   *rally*
      By the rich river   that runnes sǫ fair;
2280 Lodges them lovely   by thǫ °līthe strandes,   *pleasant*
      All °on lǫwe in the land,   thǫse lǫrdlich bernes.   *on the ground*
      They kaire tō the carrīage   and took what them līkes,
      Camels and °cokadrisses   and coffers full rich,   *cockatrices*
                                                              (crocodiles)
      °Hackes and °hackenays   and horses of armes,   *kind of horse*
      Housing and °herberāge   of hęthen kinges;   *lodgings*
      They drew out dromedarīes   of dīverse lǫrdes,
      °Moilles milk-whīte   and marvēlous °bęstes,   *mules/beasts*
      †Olfendes and arrabys   and olyfauntes nǫble
      That are of the Orīent   with honourāble kinges.

2290   But Sir Arthur anǫn   ayeres thereafter
      Ēven tō the emperour   with honourāble kinges,
      Laght him up full lovelyly   with lǫrdlich knightes,
      And led him tō the °layer   there the king ligges.   *resting place*
      Then °harawdes °hīely   at °hest of the lǫrdes,   *heralds/quickly/*
                                                              command
      Huntes up the °haythemen   that on height ligges,   *heathens*

─────────

²²⁶³ That no captain be kept (alive) for any silver (i.e., no ransom be
    taken). [The practice of holding prisoners for ransom made medieval
    warfare a sometimes profitable business, and moralists frequently
    denounced the practice.]
²²⁸⁸ Camels and Arabian horses and noble elephants.

The Sowdan of Surry   and certain kinges,
Sixty of the chēf   senatours of Rōme.
Then they buskes and °bawmed   °thir burlich kinges,   *embalmed/these*
Sewed them in °sendell   sixty-fọld after,   *fine linen*
2300 †Lapped them in lęde,   less that they sholde
Chānge or chauffe   yif they might eschēve
°Clọsed in kēstes   clęne untō Rōme,   *enclosed in*
                                                                     chests
With their banners aboven,   their badges there-under,
In what countree they kaire,   that kightes might knọw
†Ęch king by his colours,   in kith where hē lenged.

Anọn ọn the second day,   °soon by the morn,   *immediately at*
                                                                     dawn
Twọ senatours there come   and certain knightes,
†Hoodless frọ the hęthe,   ọver the holt-ēves,
Bare-foot over the bente   with brandes sọ rich,
2310 Bowes tō the bọld king   and °biddes him the hiltes.   *offer*
Whether hē will hang them or °hędde   or họld them on life,   *behead*
Kneeled before the conquerour   in °kirtels alone,   *gowns (i.e.,*
                                                                     without armor)
With careful countenaunce   they carped thēse wordes:
"Twọ senatours wē are,   thy °subjettes of Rōme,   *subjects*
That has sāved our līfe   by thēse salt strandes,
Hid us in the high wood   through the helping of Crīst,
°Beseekes thee of succour,   as soveraign and lọrd;   *beseech*
Graunt us līfe and °limm   with liberal herte,   *limb*
For His love That thee °lente   this lọrdship in erthe!"   *granted*

2320   "I graunt," quọd the good king,   "through grāce of
                                                myselven;
I give you līfe and limm   and lęve for tō pass,
°Sọ yē dō my messāge   °menskfully at Rōme,   *providing/*
                                                                     honorably
That ilke charge that I you give hēre   before my chēf
                                                knightes."

"Yes," says the senatours,   "that shall wē ensūre,
Sēkerly by our °trewthes,   thy sayinges tō fulfill;   *pledged words*
Wē shall let for nọ lēde   that lives in erthe,
For pọpe ne for °potestate   ne prince sọ nọble,   *potentate*

2300-01 Wrapped them in lead, lest they spoil or rot before they could
    arrive.
2305 [The colors are the heraldic devices on the banners set above the
    caskets.]
2308-09 Bareheaded from the heath, by the edge of the wood, barefooted
    over the ground (as a sign of humility).

That wē ne shall lēly in land   thy letteres prōnounce,
For dūke ne for douspeer,   tō dīe in the pain!"

2330   Then the bannerettes of Bretain   brought them tō tents
There °barbours were °boun   with bāsins on loft;   *barbers/ready*
With warm water, īwis,   they wet them full soon;
They °shoven thēse °shalkes   °shāpely thereafter   *shaved/men/ suitably*
Tō °reckon thēse Rōmanes   recrēant and °yēlden;   *mark/surrendered*
Forthy °shove they them tō shew   for °skomfit of Rōme.   *shaved/ discomfiture*
They coupled the °kestes   on camelles °belīve,   *chests/quickly*
On asses and °arrabyes,   thēse honourāble kinges;   *Arabian horses*
The Emperour for honour   all by him one,
Ēven upon an °olyfaunt,   his egle out over;   *elephant*
2340 °Bekend them the captīves,   the king did himselven,   *entrusted them to*
And all before his keen men   carped these wordes:
"Hēre are the °kestes," quod the king,   "kaire over the   *chests*
                                 mountes,
°Mette full of the °monee   that yē have °mikel yerned,   *measured/ money/much*
The tax and the tribūte   of ten score winteres
That was teenfully °tint   in tīme of our elders;   *lost*
Say tō the senatour   the citee that yēmes
That I send him the sum;   assay how him līkes!
But bid them never bē so bold,   whīles my °blood regnes   *family*
°Eft for tō brawl them   for my brode landes,   *again*
2350 Ne tō ask tribūte ne tax   by °nokin tītle,   *no kind of*
But such tresure as this,   whīles my tīme lastes."

    Now they raik tō Rōme   the °rediest wayes   *quickest*
°Knelles in the Capitol   and commouns assembles,   *ring bells*
Soveraignes and senatours   the citee that yēmes,
°Bekend them the °carriāge,   °kestes and other,   *gave/baggage/ chests*
Als the conquerour commaunde   with crūel wordes:
"Wē have trustily °travailed   this tribūte tō fetch,   *worked*
The tax and the °trewage   of ten score winteres,   *tribute*
Of England, of Īreland   and all °thir °out-īles,   *those/outer isles*
2360 That Arthur in the Occident   occūpīes at ones.
Hē biddes you never bē so bold   whīles his blood regnes
Tō brawl you for Bretain   ne his brode landes,
Ne ask him tribūte ne tax   by °nokins tītle   *no kind of*
But such tresure as this,   whīles his tīme lastes.
Wē have foughten in Fraunce   and us is foul happened,
And all our much fair folk   fey are beleved;
°Eschāped there ne chevalry   ne chēftaines °nother,   *escaped/neither*
But chopped down in the chāse,   such chaunce is befallen!

Wē rẹde yē store you of stǫne   and stuffen your walles;
2370 You wākens wandreth and war;   bē ware if you līkes!"

In the °kalendes of May   this cāse is befallen;   *first day*
The roy rēal renowned   with his Round Tāble
On the cǫste of °Constantīne   by the clēre strandes   *Cotentine*
Has the Rōmanes rich   rebūked for ever!

When hē had foughten in Fraunce   and the fēld wonnen
And fērsely his fǫmen   °felld out of līfe,   *felled*
Hē bīdes for the burying   of his bǫld knightes,
That in batail with brandes   were brǫught out of līfe.
Hē burīes at Bayonne   Sir Bedvere the rich;
2380 The corse of Kayous the keen   at °Came is belẹved,   *Caen*
Covered with a crystal   clẹnly all ǫver;
His fader conquered that kith   knightly with handes.
Sēnn in °Burgoine he °badde   tō bury °mǫ knightes,   *Burgundy/ abided/more*
Sir Berade and Bawdwyne,   Sir Bedvere the rich,
Good Sir Cador at °Came,   as his °kīnd °askes.   *Caen/race/ requires*

Then Sir Arthur anǫn   in °Auguste thereafter,   *Autumn*
Enteres tō °Almaine   with hǫstes arrayed,   *Germany*
Lenges at °Lusheburgh   tō °lēchen his knightes,   *Luxembourg/ heal*
With his lēle lēge-men   as lǫrd in his °ǫwen;   *own (realm)*
2390 †And on Cristofer day   a counsēl hē hǫldes
With kinges and kaisers,   clerkes and other,
Commaundes them keenly   tō cast all their wittes
How hē may conquer by craft   the kith that hē claimes;
But the conquerour keen,   courtais and nǫble,
Carpes in the counsēl   thēse knightly wordes:
"Hēre is a knight in these °clēves,   enclǫsed with hilles,   *valleys*
That I have °covēt tō knǫw   because of his wordes,   *desire*
That is of Lorraine the °lēge,   I keep nǫt tō laine.   *lord*
The lǫrdship is lovely,   as lēdes mē telles;
2400 I will that dūchy °devīse   and °dẹle as mē līkes,   *divide/deal out*
And sēnn °dress with the dūke,   if °destainy °suffer;   *deal/destiny/ allow*
The renk rebel has been   untō my Round Tāble,
Rẹdy ay with Rōmanes   °at rīot my landes.   *to ravage*
Wē shall reckon full rāthẹ,   if rẹsoun sǫ happen,
Whǫ has right tō that rent,   by rich God of hẹven!
Then will I by Lumbardy,   °līkand tō shew,   *pleasing to see*
Set law in the land   that last shall ever,

2390 [*Cristofer day*: St. Christopher's day, July 25.]

The tyrauntes of °Tuskān   °tempest a little,   *Tuscany/trouble*

Talk with the °temporal,   whīles my tīme lastes;   *temporal lords (lay rulers)*

2410 I give my protection   tō all the pope landes,

My rich °pensel of °pęęs   my pople tō shew.   *pennant/peace*

It is a folly tō offend   our °fader under God   *father*

°Other Pēter or Paul,   thǫ °postles of Rōme;   *either/apostles*

If wē spare the spiritūal   wē °speed but the better;   *succeed*

†Whīles wē have for tō spęke,   spill shall it never!"

Now they speed °at the spurres   withouten spēche mǫre,   *with*

Tō the march of °Meyes,   thēse °manlich knightes,   *Metz/manly*

That is in Lorraine °alōsed   as London is hēre,   *praised*

Citee of that °seinour   that soveraign is hǫlden.   *lord*

2420 The king ferkes forth   on a fair steed

With Ferrer and Ferawnte   and other four knightes;

About the citee thǫ seven   they sǫught at the °next,   *nearest (way)*

Tō seek them a sēker plāce   tō set with °engines.   *siege engines*

Then they bended in °burgh   °bǫwes of vīse,   *town/cross bows*

°Bekers at the bǫld king   with °bustous lātes,   *shoot/hostile expressions*

°Allblawsters at Arthur   ęgerly shootes   *arbalasters (crossbowmen)*

For tō hurt him or his horse   with that hard wēpen.

The king shunt for nǫ shot   ne nǫ shēld askes,

But shews him sharply   in his sheen weedes,

2430 Lenges all at °leisere   and lookes on the walles   *leisure*

Where they were lǫwest   the lēdes tō assail.

"Sir," said Sir Ferrer,   "a folly thou workes,

Thus nāked in thy °nǫblay   tō nighe tō the walles,   *nobleness*

Singly in thy °surcǫte   this citee tō ręche   *surcoat (i.e., without armor)*

And shew thee °within   there tō °shend us all;   *to those within/shame*

Hīe us hāstily °hēnne   or wē °mon foul happen,   *hence/must*

For hit they thee or thy horse,   it harmes for ever!"

"If thou bē °rade," quǫd the king,   "I ręde thee rīde °ūtter,   *afraid/further back*

°Less that they °rew thee   with their round wēpen.   *lest/harm*

2440 Thou art but a °fauntekein,   nǫ °ferly mē thinkes!   *baby/wonder*

Thou will bē flayed for a fly   that on thy flesh lightes!

I am nǫthing °aghast,   sǫ mē God help!   *afraid*

Thǫugh such °gadlinges bē grēved,   it grēves mē but little;   *worthless men*

They win nǫ worship of mē,   but wāstes their °tackle;   *equipment*

2415 While I have power to speak, the Church's possessions shall never
be harmed.

They shall °want ęre I wend,   I °wāgen mine hęved!   *lack (equip-ment)/wager*
Shall never °harlot have °happe,   through help of my Lǫrd,   *rascal/fortune*
Tō kill a crownd king   with °crisom annointed!"   *holy oil*

Then come the °herbarīours,   °harāgēous knightes,   *scouts/violent*
The hǫle batailes °on hīe   °harraunt thereafter,   *in haste/shouting*
2450 And our °forrēours fērs   upon fęle halfes   *forragers*
Come flyand before   on °feraunt steedes,   *iron-grey*
°Ferkand in array,   °thir rēal knightes,   *going/these*
The renkes renowned   of the Round Tāble!
All the frek men of Fraunce   followed thereafter,
Fair fitted on front   and on the fēld hōves.
Then the shalkes sharply   shiftes their horses,
Tō shewen them seemly   in their sheen weedes;
Buskes in batail   with banners displayed,
With brǫde shēldes °enbrāced   and burlich helmes,   *on their arms*
2460 With °penouns and °pensells   of ilke prince armes,   *pennons/pennants*
Apparēlled with °perry   and precīous stǫnes;   *pearls*
The launces with °loraines   and °lēmand shēldes,   *pennons/shining*
°Lightenand as the °levening   and °lēmand all over;   *flashing/lightning/gleaming*
Then the prīs men prikes   and prōves their horses,
°Satilles to the citee   upon sēre halves;   *converge on*
°Ensęrches the suburbes   °sadly thereafter,   *search/carefully*
Discoveres of °shot-men   and skirmish a little,   *archers*
Scāres their °skotifers   and their °scout-watches   *shield bearers/guards*
Brittenes their °barrērs   with their bright wēpens,   *barriers*
2470 °Bętte down a °barbican   and the bridge winnes;   *beat/main gate tower*
Ne had the °garnison been good   at the gręte gātes,   *garrison*
They had won that °wonne   by their °ǫwen strenghe!   *dwelling/own*

Then with-drawes our men   and dresses them better,
†For drēde of the draw-bridge   dashed in sonder;
Hīes tō the °herberāge   there the king hōves   *lodging*
With his batail on high,   horsed on steedes.
Then was the prince purveyed   and their plāces nomen,
°Pight paviliouns of pall   and plantes in sēge.   *pitched tents of silk*
Then lenge they lǫrdly   °as them lēf thǫught,   *as seemed good to them*
2480 Watches in ilkę ward,   as tō the war falles,
Settes up sodēnly   certain °engines.   *siege engines*

2474 For fear of being dashed asunder by the draw bridge.

†On Sononday by the sun   has a flēthe yolden,
The king calles on Florent,   that flowr was of knightes:
†"The Fraunchmen enfeebleshes;   ne ferly mē thinkes!
They are °unfǫnded folk   in thǫ fair marches,   *untried (i.e.,*
                                                         weakened)
For °them wantes the flesh   and food that them līkes.   *is lacking to them*
Hēre are forestes fair   upon fęle halves,
And thider fǫmen are fled   with °freelich bęstes.   *noble beasts*
Thou shall °founde tō the °felle   and °forray the mountes; *go/mountains/*
                                                         forage
2490 Sir Ferawnte and Sir Floridas   shall follow thy brīdle.
°Us moste with some fresh męte   rēfresh our pople   *we must*
That are fed in the firth   with the fruit of the erthe.
There shall wend tō this °vīage   Sir Gawain himselven,   *journey*
Wardēn full worshipful,   and sǫ him well seemes;
Sir Wicher, Sir Walter,   thēse worshipful knightes,
With all the wīsest men   of the west marches,
Sir Clēgis, Sir Claribald,   Sir Clēremond the nǫble,
The Capitain of Cardiff,   clęnlich arrayed.
Gǫ now, warn all the watch,   Gawain and other,
2500 And wendes forth on your way   withouten mǫ wordes."

   Now ferkes tō the firth   thēse fresh men of armes,
Tō the °felle sǫ °fawe,   thēse °freshlich bernes,   *mountain/*
                                                         colorful/eager
                                                         valleys/
Through °hoppes and °hemland,   hilles and other,   *borderland*
Holtes and °hǫre woodes   with °hēslin shawes,   *gray/hazel copses*
Through mǫrass and moss   and mountes sǫ high,
And in the misty morning   on a °męde falles,   *meadow*
†Mǫwen and unmāde,   mainovred but little,
In swāthes sweppen down,   full of sweet flowres;
There unbrīdels thēse bǫld   and °baites their horses.   *graze*
2510 Tō the °gryging of the day   that birdes °gan sing   *dawning/did*
Whīles the °sours of the sun,   that °sande is of Crīst, *rising/messenger*
That solāces all sinful   that sight has in erthe.

   Then wendes out the wardēn,   Sir Gawain himselven,
Als hē that wīse was and wight,   wonders tō seek;
Then was hē ware of a wye,   wonder well armed,
°Baitand on a water bank   by the wood ēves,   *grazing his horse*
Busked in breny   bright tō behǫld,

2482 On Sunday by the time the sun shone brightly (lit., gave out a
    flood of light).
2484 The Frenchmen grow feeble; no wonder does it seem to me!
2507-08 (The hay) mown and unstacked, worked over but little, in rows
    of cuttings swept down, full of sweet flowers.

°Enbrāced a brōde shēld   on a blonk rich,   *holding on his arm*
Withouten any berne,   but a °boy ǫne   *servant*
2520 Hōves by him on a blonk   and his spęre hǫldes.
†Hē bǫre glessenand in gold   three grayhoundes of sāble,
With chappes and chaines   of chalk-whīte silver,
A charbocle in the chēf,   chāngand of hewes,
And a chēf aunterous,   challenge whǫ līkes.

Sir Gawain °gliftes on the gōme   with a glad will;   *looks*
A gręte spęre from his groom   hē grippes in handes,
°Girdes ēven ǫver the stręme   on a steed rich   *goes right*
Tō that steren in stour   on strenghe there hē hōves,
Ęgerly on English   "Arthur!" hē ascrīes.
2530 The °tother īrously   answers him soon   *other*
On the °lange of Lorraine   with a loud °steven   *language/voice*
That lēdes might listen   the °lenghe of a mīle: *length*
"Whider °prikes thou, °pilour,   that proffers sǫ large?   *spur/soldier*
Hēre pickes thou nǫ prey,   proffer when thee līkes,
°But thou in this peril   °put of the better,   *unless/i.e., fight better*
Thou shall bē my prisonēr   for all thy proud lātes!"

"Sir," says Sir Gawain,   "sǫ mē God help,
Such °glaverand gōmes   grēves mē but little!   *chattering*
But if thou °graithe thy °gęre   thee will grēf happen   *prepare/gear*
2540 Ęre thou gǫ °of this °grēve,   for all thy gręte wordes!"   *from/grove*

Then their launces they °latchen,   thēse lǫrdlich bernes,   *seize*
°Laggen with lǫng spęres   on °līard steedes,   *lay on/gray*
°Coupen °at aunter   by craftes of armes   *strike/at random*
Til both the crūel spęres   °brusten at ǫnes;   *break*
Through shēldes they shot   and °sheered through mailes,   *cut*
Bǫth sheer through shoulders   a °shaft-monde large.   *span (six inches) deep*
Thus worthily thēse wyes   wounded are bǫthen;
Ęre they wręke them of wrath   away will they never.
Then they °raght in the rein   and again rīdes,   *pulled*
2550 Rędily these °rāthe men   rushes out swordes,   *hasty*
Hittes on helmes   full hertilich dintes,

2521-24 He bore (as a heraldic device on his shield) glittering on (a)
gold background, three sable greyhounds, with jowls and collars of
chalk-white silver; a carbuncle (is placed) in the chief (upper third
of the shield) changing in colors (as it sparkles), and he (was) an
adventurous chief, challenge him who will.

Hewes on hawberkes   with full hard wēpens!
Full stoutly they strīke,   °thir steren knightes,   *these*
°Stokes at the stomach   with steelen pointes,   *stick*
Fighten and flourish   with flāmand swordes,
Til the °flawes of fīre   flāmes on their helmes.   *gusts*

    Then Sir Gawain was grēved   and °grouched full sọre;   *angered*
With Galuth his good sword   grimly hē strīkes,
°Clẹf the knightes shēld   clẹnlich in sonder.   *cleaved*
2560 †Whọ lookes to the left sīde,   when his horse launches,
With the light of the sun   men might see his liver.
Then °grọnes the gōme   for grēf of his woundes,   *groans*
And °girdes at Sir Gawain   as hē by °glentes,   *strikes/goes*
And °awkward ẹgerly   sọre hē him smītes;   *slantwise*
An °ālet ēnameld   hē °oches in sonder,   *shoulder plate/ hacks*
Bristes the °rẹrebrāce   with the brand rich,   *upper-arm plate*
Carves off at the °coutere   with the clẹne edge   *elbow piece*
†Anentis the avawmbrāce   railed with silver;
Through a double vestūre   of velvet rich
2570 With the venomous sword   a vein has hē touched
That °voides sọ vīolently   that all his wit chānged;   *empties*
The °vēsar, the °aventail,   his vestūres rich   *visor/lower face-guard*
With the valīant blood   was °verred all ọver.   *spotted*

    Then this tyraunt °tīte   turnes the brīdle,   *quickly*
Talkes untenderly and says: "Thou art touched!
†Us bus have a blood-band   ẹre thy blee chānge!
For all the °barbours of Bretain   shall not thy blood staunch,   *barbers (surgeons)*
For hē that is °blemist with this brọde brande   °blinne shall   *wounded/cease (bleeding)*
                                    hē never!"

    "Yā," quọd Sir Gawain,   "thou grēves mē but little.
2580 Thou weenes tō °glōpin mē   with thy grẹte wordes;   *terrify*
Thou °trowes with thy talking   that my herte °talmes;   *suppose/falters*
Thou betīdes °torfer   ẹre thou °hēnne turn   *trouble/hence*
But thou tell me °tīte   and tarry nọ lenger   *quickly*
What may staunch this blood   that thus fast runnes."

2560-61 The wound is so wide and deep that if one looked at the left side
    when the horse leaps up one could see his liver by the light of the sun.
2568 Near the lower arm plate, adorned with silver.
2576 We must have a bandage, ere your color changes (from loss of
    blood).

"Yis, I say thee soothly   and °sēker thee my trewth,   *pledge my word to you*
†Nǫ surgeon in Salerne   shall sāve thee the better,
°With-thy that thou °suffer mē   for sāke of thy Crīst   *providing/allow*
Tō shew shortly my °shrift   and °shāpe mē for mīne end,   *confession/ prepare*
[That I might be °cristened,   with °crisom annointed,   *baptized/holy oil*
Become meek for my misdeeds,   for °meed of my soul."]   *reward*

"Yis," quǫd Sir Gawain,   "sǫ mē God help,
2590 †I give thee grāce and graunt,   though thou have grēf served,
°With-thy thou say mē sooth   what thou hēre seekes,   *providing*
Thus singly and °sulain   all thyself ǫne,   *alone*
And what °lay thou °lēves on—°laine nǫt the sooth—   *religion/believe/ hide*
And what °lēgēaunce and land   and where thou art lǫrd."   *allegiance*

"My nāme is Sir Prīamus,   a prince is my °fader,   *father*
Praised in his °partyes   with °prōved kinges;   *country/ experienced*
In Rōme there hē regnes   hē is rich hǫlden;
Hē has been rebel tō Rōme   and ridden their landes,
°Warrayand wīsely   winters and yēres   *waging war*
2600 By wit and by wisdom   and by wight strenghe
And by worshipful war   his ǫwen has hē won.
Hē is of Alexander blood,   °ǫverling of kinges;   *overlord*
The uncle of his °aiele,   Sir °Ector of Troy.   *grandfather/ Hector*
And hēre is the °kinreden   that I am of come,   *family*
Of °Jūdas and °Josūe,   thēse gentle knightes;   *Judas Maccabaus/ Joshua*
I am °apparent his eier,   and eldest of other;   *his heir apparent*
Of °Alexandere and Afrīke   and all thǫ out-landes   *Alexandria*
I am in possessīon   and °plēnerly sǫsed.   *fully in possession*
In all the prīs citees   that tō the port lǫnges
2610 I shall have trewly   the trǫsure and the landes
And bǫth tribūte and tax   whīles my tīme lastes.
I was sǫ °hautain of herte   whīles I at hǫme lenged   *haughty*
I hēld nǫne °my hip-height   under hǫven rich;   *as tall as my hip*
For-thy was I sent hider   with seven scǫre knightes
Tō °assay of this war   by °sente of my fader;   *experience/assent*
And I am for °surquidrīe   °shāmely °surprīsed   *pride/shamefully/ captured*
And by aunter of armes   outrayed for ever!

2586 *Salerne*: Salerno. The University of Salerno was famous in the Middle Ages for its medical school.
2590 I give you grace and grant you your life, though you have deserved grief.

Now have I told thee the kin   that I of come,
Will thou for °knighthēde   ken mē thy nāme?"   *knighthood*

2620   "By Crīst," °quod Sir Gawain,   "knight was I never!   *said*
With the kidd conquerour   a °knāve of his chāmber   *servant*
Has wrought in his °wardrope   winters and yēres   *wardrobe*
On his long armour   that him best līked;
I °poine all his °paviliouns   that tō himselve °pendes,   *pitch/tents/*
Dightes his doublettes   for dūkes and erles,   *belong*
°Aketouns °avenaunt   for Arthur himselven   *padded jackets/*
That hē has ūsed in war   all these eight winter!   *seemly*
Hē māde mē °yōmen at °Yōle   and gāve mē grete giftes,   *yeoman (a free*
An hundreth pound, and a horse,   and °harnēss full rich."   *man)/Yule*
                                                              armour

2630   †"Yif I hap tō my hele   that hende for tō serve
I bē holpen in hāste,   I hēte thee for-sooth!
If his knāves bē such,   his knightes are noble!
There is no king under Crīst   may °kempe with him one!   *battle*
Hē will bē Alexander eier   that all the world °louted,   *bowed to*
Ābler than ever was   Sir Ector of Troy!
Now for the °crisom that thou caught   that day thou was   *holy oil*
                                               cristened,
Whether thou bē knight or knāve   °knowe now the sooth."   *acknowledge*

    "My nāme is Sir Gawain,   I graunt thee for-sooth,
Cosin tō the conquerour,   hē °knowes it himselven,   *acknowledges*
2640 Kidd in his °kalender   a knight of his chāmber,   *records*
And °rolled the richest   of all the Round Tāble!   *recorded as*
I am the douspeer and dūke   hē dubbed with his handes,
Daintily on a day   before his dere knightes;
°Grouch not, good sir,   though mē this grāce happen;   *grudge*
It is the gift of God;   the °gree is his owen!"   *reward*

    "Pēter!" says Prīamus,   "now °payes mē better   *pleases*
Than I of Provence were prince   and of Paris rich!
†For mē were lēver privily   bē priked to the herte
Than ever any priker   had such a prīse wonnen.

2630-31 If I have the good luck, for my recovery, to serve that noble
    (Arthur), I will be helped quickly (to recover), I tell thee truly.
2648-49 I would rather be stabbed to the heart in private (by such a one
    as Gawain) than to have some ordinary soldier win such a prize (as
    having the victory over me). [It would be dishonorable for Priamus
    to be defeated by an ordinary soldier; Gawain is such a great knight
    that even to be defeated by him is an honor that Priamus would prize
    even if no one were to learn of it. Compare Mador's words to Lancelot
    in the *Stanzaic Morte Arthur*, ll. 1616–19.]

2650 But hēre is °herberd at hand   in yon hūge holtes,   *lodged*
     Hole bataile on high,   tāke heed if thee līke!
     The Dūke of Lorraine the derf   and his dere knightes,
     The doughtīest of °Dolfinede   and °Dutch-men many,   *Dauphiné (in France)/Germans*
     The lordes of Lumbardy   that °leders are holden,   *leaders*
     The °garnison of °Goddard   gaylich arrayed,   *garrison/ Mt. Goddard*
     The wyes of the °Westfāle,   worshipful bernes,   *Westphalia*
     Of °Sessoine and °Suryland   sarazenes ynow;   *Saxony/Syria*
     They are numbered full nigh   and nāmed in rolles
     Sixty thousand and ten, for sooth,   of sēker men of armes;
2660 But if thou hīe fro this hethe,   it harmes us bothe,
     And but my hurtes bē soon °holpen,   °hole bē I never!   *helped/whole (healthy)*
     Tāke heed tō this °hansemen,   that hē no horn blow,   *servant (henchmen)*
     Or thou °hīely in hāste   °bēs hewen all tō °pēces,   *quickly/will be/ pieces*
     [For hēre hōves at thy hand   an hundreth good knightes].
     They are my retinūes   tō rīde where I will;
     Is none redīer renkes   regnand in erthe;
     °Bē thou raght with that rout,   thou rīdes no further,   *if you are seized by*
     Ne thou bēs never ransouned   for riches in erthe!"

     Sir Gawain went ere the °wāthe come   where him best   *trouble*
                   līked,
     With this worthilich wye   that wounded was sore,
2670 °Merkes to the mountain   there our men lenges   *goes*
     °Baitand their blonkes   there on the brode °mede,   *grazing/mead*
     Lordes °lenand low   on °lēmand shēldes,   *leaning/ gleaming*
     With loud laughters on loft   for līking of birdes,
     Of larkes, of °linkwhītes,   that lovelich songen;   *linnets*
     And some was °sleght on sleep   °with slight of the °pople   *slipped/by skill/ creatures*
     That sang in the °sesoun   in the sheen °shawes,   *season/shrubs*
     So low in the °laundes   so °līkand notes.   *hills/pleasing*
     Then Sir Wicher was °ware   their wardēn was wounded,   *aware*
     And went tō him weepand   and wringand his handes;
2680 Sir Wicher, Sir Walter,   thēse wīse men of armes
     Had wonder of Sir Wawain   and went him °againes,   *toward*
     Met him in the mid-way   and marvēl them thought
     How hē mastered that man,   so mighty of strenghes.
     By all the °welth of the world   so wo was them never: *wealth*
     "For all our worship, īwis,   away is in erthe!"

     "Grēve you not," quod Gawain,   for Goddes love of heven,
     †For this is but gosesomer   and given on erles;

2687 For this (wound) is but gossamer (a slight thing) and proper for earls (the sort of thing a nobleman should expect).

Thọugh my shoulder bē °shrẹde   and my shēld °thirled,   *cut/pierced*
And the °wēld of mīne arm   °workes a little,   *movement/hurts*
2690 This prisonēr, Sir Prīamus,   that has perilous woundes,
Says that hē has salves   shall soften us bọthen."

Then stertes tō his stirrup   °sterenfull knightes,   *stern*
And hē lọrdly alightes   and °laght off his brīdle,   *pulled*
And let his burlich blonk   °baite on the flowres,   *graze*
°Braides off his °bacenett   and his rich weedes,   *draws/helmet*
°Bounes tō his brọde shēld   and bowes tō the erthe;   *leans on*
In all the body of that bọld   is nọ blood lẹved!
Then presses tō Sir Prīamus   precīous knightes,
°Avīsely of his horse   °hentes him in armes   *carefully/take*
2700 His helm and his hawberk   they tāken off after,
And hāstely for his hurt   all his herte chānged;
They laid him down in the °laundes   and laght off his   *lawn*
                              weedes,
And hē °lẹned him on lọng   or how him best līked.   *leaned (stretched out)*
A foil of fīne gold   they °fande at his girdle,   *found*
†That is full of the flowr   of the four welle
That flọwes out of Paradīse   when the flood rīses,
That much fruit of falles   that feed shall us all;
Bē it °frette on his flesh   there sinews are °entāmed,   *rubbed/cut*
The frēke shall bē °fish-họle   within four houres.   *fit as a fish*
2710 They uncover that corse   with full clẹne handes,
With clēre water a knight   clẹnses their woundes,
°Kēled them kīndly   and comforted their hertes;   *cooled*
And when the °carves were clẹne   they °cledde them again.   *wounds/clad*
°Barrel-ferrers they °brọched   and brọught them the wīne,   *wine casks/broke open*
Both °brẹde and °brawn   and °brẹdes full rich;   *roast/lean meat/ breads*
When they had °eten   anọn they armed after.   *eaten*

Then °thọ auntrend men   "°As armes!" ascrīes,   *those adventuring/ To arms!*
With a °clarīoun clēre   °thir knightes tōgeder   *trumpet/these*
Calles tō counsēl   and of this cāse telles:
2720 "Yonder is a company   of clẹne men of armes,
The keenest in °contek   that under Crīst lenges;   *strife*
In yon °ọken wood   an họst are arrayed,   *oak*

---

²⁷⁰⁵ [The four wells of Paradise (which were thought to be in the East)
were celebrated for their magical qualities (one was the Fountain of
Youth) and thought to be the sources of the four great rivers of the
East—the Nile, the Ganges, the Tigris, and the Euphrates.]

°Under-tākand men   of thēse oute-landes,   *determined*
As says Sir Prīamus,   sọ help Saint Pēter!
Gọ men," quọd Gawain,   "and °grọpe in your hertes   *search*
Whọ shall graithe tō yon °grēve   tō yon grẹte lọrdes;   *wood*
If wē °get-less gọ họme,   the king will bē grēved   *empty-handed*
And say wē are °gadlinges,   aghast for a little.   *worthless men*
Wē are with Sir Florent,   as tō-day falles,
2730 That is flowr of Fraunce,   for hē fled never;
Hē was chọsen and charged   in chāmber of the king
Chēftain of this journee,   with chevalry nọble;
Whether hē fight or hē flee   wē shall follow after;
For all the °fẹre of yon folk   forsāke shall I never!"   *fear*

"°Fader," says Sir Florent,   "full fair yē it tell!   *Father (i.e., Sir)*
But I am but a °fauntekin,   °unfraisted in armes;   *infant/untested*
If any folly befall   the °faut shall be ours   *fault (loss)*
†And fremedly o Fraunce   bē flēmed for ever!
Woundes nọt your worship,   my wit is but simple,
2740 Yē are our wardēn, īwis;   work as you līkes."

"°Yē are at the °ferrest   nọt passand fíve hundreth,   *(Priamus*
                                                                   speaks)/most
And that is fully too few   tō fight with them all,
†For harlottes and hansemen   shall help but little;
They will hīe them °hēnn   for all their grẹte wordes!   *hence*
I rẹde yē work °after wit,   as wīse men of armes,   *according to*
And °warpes wīlily away,   as worshipful knightes."   *go with wile*

"I graunt," quọd Sir Gawain,   "sọ mē God help!
But hēre are some galīard gōmes   that °of the gree serves,   *deserve some*
                                                                   reward
The crūelest knightes   of the kinges chāmber,
2750 That can carp with the cup   knightly wordes;
Wē shall prōve tōday   whọ shall the °prīse win!"   *prize*

Now °forrēours fērs   untō the firth rīdes   *foragers*
And °fanges a fair feld   and on foot lightes,   *take*
Prikes after the prey,   as prīs men of armes,
Florent and Floridas,   with fíve scọre knightes,
Followed in the forest   and on the way foundes,
Flingand a fast trot   and on the folk drīves.

2738 And we shall be chased from France forever, like strangers.
2743 For rascals and servants (part of the five hundred) will help but
    little.

Then followes fast tō our folk   well a five hundreth
Of frek men tō the firth   upon fresh horses;
2760 Qne Sir Feraunt before,   upon a fair steed,
Was fostered in °Famacoste;   the fēnd was his fader;   *Famagosta (on Cyprus)*
Hē flinges tō Sir Florent   and °prestly hē cries: *quickly*
"Why flees thou, false knight?   The Fēnd have thy soul!"
Then Sir Florent was °fain   and in fewter castes,   *eager*
On °Fawnell of Frīsland   tō Feraunt hē rīdes,   *(his horse)*
And °raght in the rein   on the steed rich,   *pulled*
And rīdes tōward the rout,   restes hē no lenger!
Full butt in the °front   hē °flishes him ēven,   *forehead/pierces*
And all disfigūres his fāce   with his fell wēpen!
2770 Through his bright °bacenett   his brain has hē touched,   *helmet*
And °brusten his neck-bone   that all his °breth stopped!   *broke/breath*

     Then his cosin ascrīed   and crīed full loud:
"Thou has killed cold-dęde   the king of all knightes!
Hē has been °fraisted on fēld   in fifteen rewmes;   *tested*
Hē °fand never no frēke   might fight with him one!   *found*
Thou shall dīe for his dęde,   with my derf wēpen,
And all the doughty for dole   that in yon dāle hōves!"

     "Fy," says Sir Floridas,   "thou °fleryand wretch!   *sneering*
Thou weenes for tō flay us,   °flōke-mouthed shrew!"   *twisted-mouthed*
2780 But Floridas with a sword,   as hē by °glentes,   *glides*
All the flesh of the flank   hē flappes in sonder
That all the filth of the frēke   and fęle of his guttes
Followes his °fole foot   when hē forth rīdes!   *horse's*

     Then rīdes a renk   tō rescūe that berne;
That was Raynald of the °Rōdes,   and rebel tō Crīst,   *Rhodes*
†Perverted with paynims   that Cristen persewes,
Presses in proudly   as the prey wendes,
For hē had in °Prūssland   much °prīse wonnen;   *Prussia/praise (prize)*
For-thy in presence there   hē proffers so large.
2790 But then a renk, Sir Richere   of the Round Tāble,
On a rēal steed   rīdes him againes;
Through a round red shēld   hē rushed him soon
That the °rosseld spęre   to his herte runnes!   *tempered*
The renk reeles about   and rushes tō the erthe,
°Rores full °rūdly   but rode hē no more!   *roars/rudely*

2786 Perverted by pagans who persecute Christians.

Now all that is °fere and °unfey   of thēse fīve hundreth   *unhurt/alive*
Falles on Sir Florent   and fīve scǫre knightes,
Betwix a °plash and a flood,   upon a flat land;   *marshy place*
Our folk °fangen their fēld   and fǫught them againes;   *take*
2800 Then was loud upon loft   "Lorraine!" ascrīed,
When lēdes with lǫng spęres   °lashen tōgeders,   *rush*
And "Arthur!" on our sīde   when them ǫught ailed.

Then Sir Florent and Floridas   in fewter they cast,
°Frushen on all the °frap   and bernes affrayed,   *rush/company*
Felles fīve at the front   there they first entered
And, ęre they ferk further,   fęle of thēse other;
Brenyes °brǫuden they briste,   brittened sheldes,   *braided*
Bętes and bęres down   the best that them bīdes;
All that rewled in the rout   they rīden away,
2810 Sǫ °rūdly they °ręre,   thēse rēal knightes!   *rudely/move*

When Sir Prīamus, that prince,   perceived their °gāmen,   *sport*
Hē had pitee in herte   that hē ne °durste proffer;   *dared*
Hē went tō Sir Gawain   and says him thēse wordes:
"Thy prīs men for thy prey   put are all under;
They are with sarazenes ǫver-set,   mǫ than seven hundreth
Of the Sowdanes knightes,   out of sēre landes;
†Wǫlde thou suffer mē, sir,   for sāke of thy Crīst
With a °sop of thy men   °suppowel them ǫnes."   *small troop/*
                                                              support

"I °grouch nǫt," quǫd Gawain,   "the °gree is their ǫwen;   *grudge/reward*
2820 They °mon have guerdons full gręte   °graunt of my lǫrd;   *should/granted by*
°But the frek men of Fraunce   fraist themselven;   *But let*
Frēkes fǫught nǫt their fill   this fifteen winter!
I will nǫt stir with my stale   half a steed °lenghe,   *length*
But they bē °stedde with mǫre stuff   than on yon °stęde   *beset/place*
                                    hoves!"

Then Sir Gawain was ware,   withouten the wood-hemmes,
Wyes of the °Westfāle,   upon wight horses,   *Westphalia*
°Walopand °wōdely   as the way °forthes,   *galloping/madly*
                                                              goes forth
With all the wēpens, īwis,   that tō the war lǫnges;
The erl Antele the ǫld   the °avauntward hē buskes,   *vanguard*
2830 °Ayerand on either hand   eight thousand knightes;   *coming*

2817 I wish you would allow me, sir,

His °pelours and °pavisers   passed all in number   *bowmen/*
That ever any °prince lēde   purveyed in erthe!   *shield bearers*
                                                           noble

      Then the Dūke of Lorraine   dresses thereafter
With °double of the °Dutch-men   that doughty were hǫlden,   *double the*
°Paynims of Prüssland,   prikers full nǫble,   *number/Germans*
                                                               pagans
Come prikand before   with Prīamus knightes.
Then said the erl Antele   tō Algere his brōther:
"Mē angers ęrnestly   at Arthures knightes,
°Thus enkerly on an hǫst   aunters themselven!   *who thus eagerly*
2840 They will bē outrayed anǫn,   ęre °undron ring,   *undern (9 a.m.)*
Thus °foolily on a fēld   tō fight with us all!   *foolishly*
†But they bē fēsed, in fey,   ferly mē thinkes;
Wǫlde they purpose tāke   and pass on their wayes,
Prik hǫme tō their prince   and their prey lęve,
They might °lenghen their līfe   and °lōsen but little.   *lengthen/lose*
It wǫlde lighten my herte,   sǫ help mē our Lǫrd!"

      "Sir," says Sir Algere,   "they have little ūsed
Tō bē outrayed with hǫst;   mē angers the mǫre!
The fairest shall bē full fey   that in our flock rīdes,
2850 Als few as they °bēn,   ęre they the fēld lęve!"   *be*

      Then good Gawain,   grācīous and nǫble,
All with glorīous glee   hē gladdes his knightes:
"°Glōpins nǫt, good men,   for glitterand shēldes,   *fear*
Thǫugh yon °gadlinges bē gay   on yon gręte horses!   *worthless men*
Bannerettes of Bretain,   buskes up your hertes!
°Bēs nǫt °baist of yon °bǫyes   ne of their bright weedes!   *be/abashed by/*
                                                               knaves
Wē shall °blenke their °bǫste,   for all their bǫld proffer, *weaken/boast*
Als °buxom as °bird is   in bed tō her lǫrd!   *submissive/maid*
Yif wē fight tōday,   the fēld shall bē ours,
2860 The °fekil fey shall fail   and °falssēde bē destroyed! *false/falsehood*
†Yon folk is on frontēre,   unfraisted them seemes;
They māke faith and °faye   to the Fēnd selven!   *belief*
Wē shall in this °vīage   victores bē hǫlden   *engagement*
And °avaunted with voices   of valīant bernes,   *praised by*
Praised with princes   in presence of lǫrdes
And loved with lādīes   in dīverse landes!
°Ǫught never such honour   nǫne of our elders,   *possessed*

2842 If they are not defeated it would seem to me a great wonder.
2861 Those (yon folk) who are in the front rank seem untested.

†Unwine ne Absolon   ne nǫne of thēse other!
When wē are mǫst in distress   Marīe wē °mēne   *pray to*
2870 That is our māster's °saine   that hē much °traistes,   *saint/trusts*
Mẹles of that mīlde queen   that menskes us all;
Whǫ-sǫ mẹles of that maid,   miscarrīes hē never!"

°By thēse wordes were said   they were nǫt fer behīnd,   *by the time that*
But the °lenghe of a land   and "Lorraine!" ascrīes;   *length of the field*
Was never such a jousting   at journee in erthe
†In the vāle of Jōsephate,   as °gestes us telles,   *tales*
When Jūlīus and Jōatelle   were judged tō dīe,
As was when the rich men   of the Round Tāble
Rushed intō the rout   on rēal steedes,
2880 For sǫ rāthely they rush   with °rosseld spẹres   *tempered*
†That the rascāl was rade   and ran tō the grēves,
And kaired tō that court   as cowardes for ever!

"Pēter!" says Sir Gawain,   "this °gladdes mīne herte,   *gladdens*
That yon °gadlinges are gǫne   that māde grẹte number!   *worthless fellows*
I °hǫpe that thēse °harlottes   shall harm us but little,   *suppose/low fellows*
For they will hīde them in hāste   in yon holt ēves;
They are fewer on fēld   than they were first numbered
By fourty thousand, in faith,   for all their fair hǫstes."

But one Jolyan of Gene,   a gīaunt full hūge,
2890 Has joined on Sir Gerard,   a justice of Wāles;
†Through a jerowndē shēld   hē jāgges him through,
And a fīne °gesseraunt   of gentle mailes;   *coat of mail*
°Jointer and °gemous   hē jāgges in sonder!   *joint/clasp*
On a °jambē steed   this journee hē mākes;   *swift*
Thus is the gīaunt °for-jouste,   that °erraunt Jew,   *outjousted/wandering*
And Gerard is jocound   and joyes him the mǫre.

Then the °genatours of °Gene   enjoines at ǫnes   *horse soldiers/Genoa*
And ferkes on the °frontēre   well a five hundreth;   *front rank*
A frēke °hight Sir Frederik   with full fẹle other   *named*

2868 [*Unwine*: a legendary hero of the Goths, probably known to the
poet from a lost English romance. *Absolon*: Absalom (II Samuel xiii–
xix), celebrated in medieval romance for his personal beauty.]
2876 [The adventure in the Vale of Josephat, to which the *gestes* refer,
is an episode in the *Fuerre de Gaderes*, a story of the Crusades.]
2881 That the rascals (servants) were fearful and ran to the woods.
2891 He stabs him through a gyronny shield (a shield decorated with
two colors divided into triangles).

2900 Ferkes in on a °frush   and °freshlich ascrīes   *charge/eagerly*
     Tō fight with our °forrēours   that on fēld hōves;   *foragers*
     And then the rēal renkes   of the Round Tāble
     Rǫde forth full ęrnestly   and rīdes them againes,
     °Melles with the °middle-ward,   but they were ill-matched;   *meddles/middle guard*
     Of such a gręte multitūde   was marvēl tō hēre.
     Sēnn at the assemblee   the sarazenes discoveres
     The soveraign of Sessoine   that °salved was never;   *saved*
     Gīauntes are °for-jousted   with gentle knightes   *outjousted*
     Through °gesserauntes of Gene   jāgged tō the herte!   *hawberks*
2910 They hew through helmes   °hautain bernes,   *haughty*
     That the hilted swordes   tō their hertes runnes!
     Then the renkes renowned   of the Round Tāble
     Rīves and rushes down   °renayed wretches;   *renegade*
     And thus they drīven tō the dęde   dūkes and erles
     All the °dregh of the day,   with drēdful workes!   *length*

         Then Sir Prīamus the prince,   in presence of lǫrdes,
     Presses tō his °penoun   and °pertly it hentes,   *pennon/openly*
     °Reverted it rędily   and away rīdes   *reversed*
     Tō the rēal rout   of the Round Tāble;
2920 And °hīely his retinūe   raikes him after,   *quickly*
     For they his °ręsoun had °redde   on his shēld rich.   *reason (intent)/ read*
     Out of the sheltron they °shēd   as sheep °of a fǫld,   *poured/from*
     And steeres forth tō the stour   and stood by their lǫrd.
     Sēnn they sent tō the dūke   and said him these wordes:
     "Wē have been thy °soudēours   these six yęre and mǫre; *mercenaries*
     †Wē forsāke thee tōday   by sert of our lǫrd.
     Wē °sew tō our soveraign   in sēre kinges landes;   *follow*
     °Us defautes our fee   of this four winteres.   *we lack our pay*
     Thou art feeble and false   and nǫught but fair wordes;
2930 Our wāges are °węred out   and thy war ended;   *worn*
     Wē may with worship   wend whither us līkes!
     I ręde thou tręte of a °trewe   and °troufle nǫ lenger, *truce/trifle*
     ⸢Or thou shall °tinne of thy °tāle   ten thousand ęre ēven."   *lose/number (tally)*

         "°Fy a diables!" said the dūke,   "The Devil have your   *The Devil with you*
                                bǫnes!"
     The daungēr of yon dogges   drēde shall I never!
     Wē shall °dęle this day,   by deedes of armes,   *bargain for*
     My dęde and my °dūchery   and my dęre knightes;   *dukedom*

2926 [*Sert*: feudal service owed to one's lord.]

Such °soudēours as yē   I °set but at little,   *mercenaries/*
That sodēnly in defaut   forsākes their lǫrd!"   *reckon*

2940   The dūke dresses in his shēld   and °dreches nǫ lenger,   *delays*
Drawes him a dromedary   with drēdful knightes;
Graithes tō Sir Gawain   with full gręte number
Of gōmes of °Gernaide   that grēvous are hǫlden.   *Granada*
Thǫse fresh horsed men   tō the front rīdes,
Felles of our °forrēours   by fourty at ǫnes!   *foragers*
They had fǫughten before   with a fīve hundreth;
It was nǫ °ferly, in faith,   thǫugh they °faint waxen.   *wonder/grow
faint*
Then Sir Gawain was grēved   and grippes his spęre,
And girdes in again   with galīard knightes,
2950 Meetes the °matchles of °Meyes   and °melles him through,   *matchless (man)/
Metz/pierces*
As man of this middle-erthe   that mǫst had grēved!
But ǫne Chastelayne, a °chīld   of the kinges chāmber,   *i.e., young man*
Was ward to Sir Wawain   of the west marches,
Chāses tō Sir Cheldrik,   a chēftain nǫble;
With a °chāsing-spęre   hē °shockes him through!   *hunting spear/
drives*
This °check him °eschēved   by chaunces ǫf armes.   *defeat/achieved*
Sǫ they chāse that chīld   °eschāpe may hē never;   *escape*
But ǫne Swyan of °Swecy,   with a sword edge,   *Sweden*
The °swyers °swīre-bǫne   hē swappes in sonder!   *young noble's/
neck bone*
2960 Hē swoonand dīed   and on the swarth lenged,
Sweltes ēven swiftly   and °swank hē nǫ mǫre!   *worked*

        Then Sir Gawain °grētes   with his gray eyen;   *weeps*
The °guite was a good man,   beginnand of armes.   *youth*
For the °chęry child   sǫ his cheer chānged   *dear*
That the chilland water   on his cheekes runned!
"Wǫ is mē," quǫd Gawain,   "that I ne °witten had!   *known*
I shall °wāge for that wye   all that I wēld,   *spend*
But I bē °wroken on that wye   that thus has him wounded!"   *avenged*
Hē dresses him drērily   and tō the dūke rīdes,
2970 But ǫne Sir Dolphin the derf   dight him againes,
And Sir Gawain him gird   with a grim launce
That the grounden spęre   °glǫde tō his herte!   *glided*
And ęgerly hē °hent out   and hurt another,   *pulled*
An hęthen knight, Hardolf,   °happy in armes;   *fortunate*
†Slyly in at the slot   slittes him through
That the slīdand spęre   of his hand slippes!

²⁹⁷⁵ [*Slot*: see note on line 2254.]

There is slain in that slope   by °sleghte of his handes   *skill*
Sixty °slongen in a °slāde   of °sleghe men of armes!   *slung/ditch/*
                                                                              skillful
Though Sir Gawain were wǫ,   hē waites him by
2980 And was ware of that wye   that the child wounded,
And with a sword swiftly   hē swappes him through,
That hē swiftly swelt   and on the erthe swoones!
And then hē raikes tō the rout   and rushes on helmes,
Rich hawberkes hē rent   and °rāsed shēldes;   *destroyed*
Rīdes °on a randoun   and his °raik hǫldes;   *swiftly/course*
Throughout the rereward   hē hǫldes wayes,
And there raght in the rein,   this rēal the rich,
And rīdes °intō the rout   of the Round Tāble.   *i.e., back to*

Then our chevalrous men   chāngen their horses,
2990 Chāses and choppes down   chēftaines nǫble,
Hittes full hertely   on helmes and shēldes,
Hurtes and hewes down   hethen knightes!
°Kettle-hattes they clēve   ēven tō the shoulders;   *i.e., kettle-*
                                                                              shaped helmets
Was never such a clamour   of capitaines in erthe!
There was kinges sonnes caught,   courtais and nǫble,
And knightes of the countree   that knǫwen was rich;
Lǫrdes of Lorraine   and Lumbardy bǫthen
°Laght was and led in   with our lēle knightes.   *seized*
Thǫse that chāsed that day   their chaunce was better;
3000 Such a °check at a chāse   °eschēved them never!   *victory/achieved*

When Sir Florent by fight   had the fēld wonnen
Hē ferkes in before   with fīve scǫre knightes;
Their preyes and their prisonēres   passes on after,
With °pelours and °pavisers   and prīs men of armes;   *bowmen/shield*
                                                                              bearers
Then goodly Sir Gawain   guīdes his knightes,
°Gǫs in at the °gainest,   as guīdes him telles,   *goes/quickest*
                                                                              way
†For grēf of a garnison   of full grēte lǫrdes
Sholde nǫt grip up his °gere   ne such °gram work;   *booty/mischief*
For-thy they stood at the °straightes   and with his stale   *pass*
                                  hōved,
3010 Til his preyes were past   the path that hē drēdes.

When they the citee might see   that the king sēged
(Soothly the sāme day   was with °assaut wonnen),   *assault*
An °heraud hīes before   at °heste of the lǫrdes,   *herald/behest*

3007 For fear that a troop of very great lords.

Home °at the °herberāge,   ʼout of the high landes,   *to/lodgings*
Turnes tīte tō the tent   and tō the king telles
All the tāle soothly   and how they had sped:
"All thy °forrēours are °fere   that forrayed withouten,   *foragers/safe*
Sir Florent and Sir Floridas   and all thy fērs knightes;
They have forrayed and foughten   with full grēte number
3020 And fēle of thy fo-men   has brought out of līfe!
Our worshipful wardēn   °is well eschēved,   *has well
                                                                            succeeded*
For hē has wǫn tōday   worship for ever;
Hē has Dolphin slain   and the dūke tāken!
Many doughty is dęde   by dint of his handes!
Hē has prisonērs prīs,   princes and erles,
Of the richest blood   that regnes in erthe;
All thy chevalrous men   fair are eschēved,
But a chīld, Chastelain,   mischaunce has befallen."

"°Hautain," says the king,   "°Heraud, by Crīst,   *valiant man/
                                                                            herald*
3030 Thou has °hęled mīne herte,   I °hēte thee for-sooth!   *healed/promise*
†I give thee in Hampton   a hundreth pound large!"

The king then tō °assaut   hē sembles his knightes   *assault*
With °somercastel and °sowe   upon sēre halves,   *moveable
                                                                            towers/shelters*
°Shiftes his °skotiferes   and scāles the walles,   *moves about/
                                                                            shield bearers*
And ęch °watch has his °ward   with wīse men of armes.   *division/guard*
Then bǫldly they busk   and bendes °engines   *catapults*
°Paises in °pillotes   and °prōves their castes.   *heave/pellets/try*
°Minsteres and °māsondewes   they °mall tō the erthe,   *monasteries/
                                                                            hospitals/hammer*
Churches and chapels   chalk-whīte °blaunched,   *painted*
3040 Stǫne steeples full stiff   in the street ligges,
Chāmbers with °chimnees   and many chēf inns,   *chimneys*
°Paised and °pelled down   plastered walles;   *demolished/
                                                                            struck*
The °pīne of the pople   was pitee for tō hēre!   *pain*

Then the duchess her dight   with dāmesels rich,
The countess of Crasine   with her clēre maidens,
Kneeles down in the °kirnelles   there the king hōved,   *battlements*
On a °covered horse   comlyly arrayed.   *armored*
They knew him by countenaunce   and crīed full loud:
"King crowned °of kīnd,   tāke keep tō thēse wordes!   *by right*
3050 Wē beseek you, sir,   as soveraign and lǫrd,
That yē sāve us tōday,   for sāke of your Crīst!

3031 I give you freely in Hampton an estate worth a hundred pounds.

Send us some succour   and °saughte with the pople,   *make peace*
Ẹre the citee bē sodēnly   with °assaut wonnen!"   *assault*

Hē °vēres his °vēsar   with a °vout noble,   *turns up/visor/ expression*
With visāge virtūous,   this valīant berne,
Mẹles tō her mīldly   with full meek wordes:
"Shall nọne misdō you, mādāme,   that tō mē lọnges;
I give you charter of pẹẹs,   and your chēf maidens,
The chīlder and the °chāste men,   the chevalrous knightes;   *i.e., priests*
3060 The dūke is in daungēr;   °drēdes it but little!   *doubt*
Hē shall bē deemed full well,   °dout you nọught elles."   *fear*

Then sent hē on ẹch a sīde   tō certain lọrdes
For tō lẹve the assaut;   the citee was °yōlden   *yielded*
(With the erle eldest son   shō sent him the keyes)
And °sēsed the sāme night,   by °sent of the lọrdes.   *seized/assent*
The dūke tō Dọver is °dight   and all his dẹre knightes,   *sent*
Tō dwell in daungēr and dole   the dayes of his līfe.

When the king Arthur   had lēly conquered
And the castel covered   of the kith rich,
3070 All the crūel and keen,   by craftes of armes,
Capitains and constābles,   °knew him for lọrd.   *acknowledged*
Hē °devīsed and dẹlt   tō dīverse lọrdes   *divided*
A °dower for the duchess   and her dẹre chīlder;   *widow's estate*
Wrọught wardēnes by wit   tō °wēld all the landes   *rule*
That hē had wonnen of war   through his wīse knightes.
Thus in Lorraine hē lenges   as lọrd in his ọwen,
Settes lawes in the land   as him lēf thọught,
And on °Lammas day   tō Lūcerne hē wendes,   *August 1*
Lenges there at °leisere   with °līking ynow.   *leisure/pleasure*
3080 There his galleys were graithed,   a full grẹte number,
All glitterand as glass,   under green hilles,
With °cabanes covered   for kinges annointed   *cabins*
With clọthes of clēre gold   for knightes and other;
Soon stowed their stuff   and stābled their horses,
†Strekes streke ọver the strẹme   intō the strait landes.

Now hē mōves his might   with mirthes of herte
Ọver mountes sọ high,   thọse marvēlous wayes,

3085 Strikes straight over the stream into the narrow lands (mountain passes). [He crosses Lake Lucerne, in Switzerland.]

Gǫs in by °Goddard, the °garret hē winnes, — *Mt. Goddard/ watch tower*
°Graithes the °garnison grisly woundes! — *deals/garrison*
3090 When hē was passed the height, then the king hōves
With his hǫle batail behǫldand about,
Lookand on Lumbardy and on loud męles:
†"In yon līkand land lǫrd bē I think!"

Then they kaire tō °Cōmbe with kinges annointed, — *Como*
That was kidd of the °cǫste, key of all other. — *i.e., of Lake Como*
Sir Florent and Sir Floridas then foundes before
With freke men of Fraunce well a fīve hundreth;
To the citee unseen they sǫught at the °gainest, — *quickest way*
And set an °enbushment, als themselve līkes. — *ambush*
3100 Then °ishewes out of that citee, full soon by the morn, — *issue*
°Skāthel °discoverers °skiftes their horses; — *harmful/scouts/ manage*
Then skiftes thēse °scowerers and skippes on hilles, — *searchers*
†Discoverers for skulkers that they nǫ scāthe limpen.
°Poverāll and °pastorelles passed on after — *poor people/ shepherds*
With porkes tō pastūre at the prīs gātes;
°Boyes in the suburbes °bourden full high — *servants/jest*
At a °bǫre singlere that tō the bente runnes. — *wild boar*

Then °brękes our °bushment and the bridge winnes, — *breaks out/ ambush*
°Braides intō the burgh with banners displayed, — *rush*
3110 °Stekes and stabbes through that them °again-standes; — *stick/withstand*
Four streetes, ęre they stint, they stroyed forever!

There fled at the °ferrer gāte folk withouten number, — *farther*
For °fęrd of Sir Florent and his fērs knightes; — *fear*
Voides the citee and tō the wood runnes
With °vitail and °vessēl and vestūre sō rich; — *victuals/precious vessels*
†They busk up a banner aboven the brǫde gātes.
†Of Sir Florent, in fay, sǫ fain was hē never!
The king hōves on a hill, behēld the walles,
And said: "I see by yon sign the citee is oures!"
3120 Sir Arthur enters anǫn with hǫstes arrayed,
Ēven at the °undron °ettles tō lenge. — *undern (9 a.m.)/ intends*
In ęche °leverē on loud the king did cry — *division*
On pain of life and °limm and °lēsing of landes — *limb/loss*

3093 I intend to be lord of that pleasing land.
3103 Scout for those hiding (in ambush) so that no harm may befall them.
3116 [*They*: Florent and his men.]
3117 Of Sir Florent, in faith, so happy was he (Arthur) never.

That nǫ lēle lēge-man   that tō him lǫnged,
Sholde līe by nǫ lādīes,   ne by nǫ lēle maidens,
Ne by nǫ °burgēss wīfe,   better ne worse   *citizen's*
Ne nǫ bernes °misbid   that tō the °burgh lǫnged.   *mishandle/town*

Now is the conquerour in °Cōmbe   and his court hǫldes   *Como*
Within the kidd castel   with kinges annointed,
3130   °Recounsēles the commouns   that tō the kith lǫnges,   *advises*
Comfortes the care-full   with knightly wordes,
Māde a capitain keen   a knight of his ǫwen;
But all the countree and hē   full soon were accorded.

The Sīre of Milan herde say   the citee was wonnen,
And °send tō Arthur   certain lordes,   *sent*
Grǫte summes of gold,   sixty horses charged,
Besǫught him as soveraign   tō succour the pople,
And said hē wǫlde soothly   bē °subjet forever,   *subject*
And māke him °service and suīte   for his sēre landes;   *feudal homage*
3140   For °Plesaunce, for °Pawnce,   and for °Pownte Tremble,   *Piacenza/Ponte/*
                                                              Pontremoli
For °Pīse and for °Pavy   hē proffers full large   *Pisa/Pavia*
Bǫth °purpure and °pall   and precīous stǫnes,   *purple dye/silk*
Palfreyes for any prince   and prōved steedes
And ilk a yēre for Milan   a °melīon of gold,   *million*
†Meekly at Martinmas   tō menske with his hōrdes,
And ever, withouten asking,   hē and his eiers
Bē hommāgers tō Arthur   whīles his līfe lastes.
The king by his counsēl   a °condeth him sendes,   *safe conduct*
And hē is comen tō °Cōmbe   and °knew him as lǫrd.   *Como/*
                                                              acknowledged

3150   Intō Tuskānē hē turnes   when him tīme seemed,
Tākes townes full tīte   with towres full high;
Walles hē °welt down,   wounded knightes,   *knocked*
Towres hē °turnes,   and tourmentes the pople,   *overturns*
Wrǫught widowes full °wlonk   °wrotherayle °singen,   *bright/misery/*
                                                              to sing
Oft °wērye and weep   and wringen their handes;   *curse*
And all hē wāstes with war   there hē away rīdes;
Their wǫlthes and their °wonninges   °wandreth hē wrǫught!   *dwellings/*
                                                              sadness

Thus they springen and °sprǫde   and spares but little,   *spread*
°Spoiles °dispiteously   and °spilles their vīnes,   *plunder/*
                                                              pitilessly/destroy

---

3145 Meekly on St. Martin's Day (November 11) to pay homage with
   his treasures.

3160 Spendes °unsparely   that °spared was long,   *without stinting/*
                                                                            saved
      Speedes them tō °Spōlett   with speres ynow!   *Spoletto*
      Frō Spain intō °Spruysland   the word of him springes   *Prussia*
      And °spekings of his °spenses;   °despīte is full hūge.   *talk/spending/*
                                                                            bitterness
      Tōward Viterbō this valīant   °aveeres the reines;   *turns*
      °Avīsely in that vāle   hē °vitailes his bernes,   *wisely/victuals*
      With °Vernāge and other wīne   and venison °bāken   *white wine/baked*
      And on the °Vīscounte landes   hē °vīses tō lenge.   *viscount's/*
                                                                            determines
      °Vertely the avauntward   voides their horses   *quickly*
      In the Vertenonne vale   the vīnes °i-monges;   *among*
3170 There sujournes this soveraign   with solāce in herte,
      Tō see when the Senatours   sent any wordes,
      Revel with rich wīne,   °rīotes himselven,   *carouse*
      This °roy with his rēal men   of the Round Tāble,   *king*
      With mirthes and melody   and °manykin gāmnes;   *many sorts of*
                                                                            pleasures
      Was never merrīer men   māde on this erthe!

      But on a Saterday at noon,   a seven-night there-after,
      The cunningest Cardinal   that tō the court longed
      Kneeles to the conquerour   and carpes thēse wordes,
      Prayes him for the pees   and proffers full large
3180 Tō have pitee of the Pope,   that put was °at-under,   *at a disadvantage*
      Besought him of °suraunce   for sāke of our Lord   *a truce*
      But °a seven-night day   °tō they were all sembled   *a week from*
                                                                            today/until
      And they sholde sēkerly him see   the °Sononday there-after   *Sunday*
      In the citee of Rōme,   as soveraign and lord,
      And crown him kīndly   with °crismed handes   *annointed*
      With his sceptre, for sooth   as soveraign and lord.
      Of this °undertāking   hostāge are comen,   *agreement*
      Of eiers full °avenaunt,   eight score children,   *pleasant*
      In togges of °tars   full richly attīred,   *Chinese silk*
3190 And °betook them the king   and his clēre knightes.   *gave them to*

      †When they had treted their trewe,   with trumping
                                        thereafter
      They trīne untō a tent   where tābles were raised;
      The king himselven is set   and certain lordes
      Under a °sylure of silk,   °saught at the bōrdes.   *canopy/*
                                                                            reconciled
      All the senatours are set   °sēre by them one,   *each by himself*

3191-92 When they had discussed their truce, with trumpeting thereafter,
    they go into a tent where tables were set up (*on trestles*). [See note
    on line 457 of the *Stanzaic Morte Arthur.*]

Served solemnly   with selcouthe metes.
The king, mighty of mirth,   with his mīld wordes,
°Rehētes the Rōmanes   at his rich tāble,   *cheers*
Comfortes the Cardinal,   so knightly himselven,
3200 †And this roy rēal,   as romaunce us telles,
Reverences the Rōmans   in his rich tāble.
The taught men and the cunning,   when them tīme thought,
°Tās their leve at the king   and turned again;   *take*
Tō the citee that night   they sought at the gainest,
And thus the hostāge of Rōme   with Arthur is leved.

Then this roy rēal   °reherses these wordes: *rehearses (tells)*
"Now wē may revel and rest,   for Rōme is our owen!
Māke our hostāge at °ese,   thēse °avenaunt children,   *ease/pleasant*
And look yē holden them all   that in mīne host lenges,
3210 The Emperour of Almaine   and all thēse este marches;
Wē shall bē overling of all   that on erthe lenges!
†Wē will by the Cross-days   °encroch thēse landes   *invade*
And at the Cristenmass day   bē crowned there-after,
Regne in my rēaltees   and hold my Round Tāble,
With the rentes of Rōme,   as mē best līkes;
Sēnn graithe over the grete se   with good men of armes
Tō revenge the Renk   That on the °Rood dīed!"   *Cross*

Then this comlich king   as cronīcles telles,
Bounes brothly tō bed   with a blīthe herte;
3220 †Off hē slinges with sleght   and slākes his girdle,
And for °slewth of °slomour   on a sleep falles.   *sloth/slumber*
But by one after midnight   all his mood changed;
Hē °mette in the °morn-whīle   full marvēlous °dremes;   *dreamed/*
                                                             morning/dreams
And when his drēdful dreme   was driven tō the ende,
The king °dāres for doute,   dīe as hē sholde,   *cowers*
Sendes after philosophers,   and his °affray telles: *terror*
"Sēnn I was formed, in faith,   so ferd was I never!
For-thy °ransackes redily   and °rede mē my °swevenes,   *search/interpret/*
                                                             dreams
And I shall redily and right   °rehersen the sooth.   *rehearse (tell)*

3230   "Mē thought I was in a wood,   °willed mīne one   *wandered by*
                                                             myself
That I ne °wiste no way   °whider that I °sholde,   *knew/whither/*
                                                             should go

---

³²⁰⁰ [*Romaunce*: A story written in French or Latin.]
³²¹² Cross-days: Rogation days, three special days of prayer preceding
    Ascension Day (forty days after Easter).
³²²⁰ He throws himself quickly on the bed and loosens his belt.

For wolves and wīld swīne   and wicked bęstes
Walked in that °wāstern   °wāthes tō seek,   *waste place/ prey*
There līons full °lǫthly   licked their tuskes   *loathly*
All for lapping of blood   of my lēle knightes!
Through that forest I fled   there flowres were high,
For tō °fēle mē for fęrd   of thǫ foul thinges,   *hide*
Merked tō a °mędow   with mountaines enclǫsed   *meadow*
The merrīest of middle-erthe   that men might behǫld.

3240   The °clǫse was in °compass   °casten all about   *enclosed place/ extent/covered*
With clǫver and °clēvewort   °cledde even over;   *small grass/clad*
The vāle was °enveround   with vīnes of silver,   *encircled*
All with grāpes of gold,   gręter were never,
°Enhorild with °arbory   and °alkins trees,   *surrounded/ groves/all kinds of gardens*
°Erberes full honest,   and herdes there-under;
All fruites °foddemed was   that flourished in erthe,   *produced*
†Fair frithed in fraunk   upon the free bowes;
Was there nǫ danking of dew   that ǫught dęre sholde;
With the drought of the day   all dry were the flowres.

3250   "Then descendes in the dāle,   down frǫ the cloudes,   *expensively/ patterned*
†A duchess °dęreworthily dight   in °dīapered weedes,
In a °surcǫte of silk   full °selcouthly hewed,   *surcoat/rarely*
All with °loyotour overlaid   lǫw tō the hemmes   *otter fur*
And with °lādily °lappes   the lenghe of a yard,   *ladylike/lappets*
And all rędily °rēversed   with °rebanes of gold,   *trimmed/ribbons*
†With °brouches and besauntes   and other bright stǫnes;   *brooches*
Her back and her brēste   was °brǫched all over,   *adorned*
With °kell and with °coronal   clęnlich arrayed,   *hair net/diadem*
†And that sǫ comly of colour   ǫne knǫwen was never.

3260   "About shō whirled a wheel   with her whīte handes,
°Overwhelm all quaintly   the wheel, as shō sholde;   *skillfully turned*
The °rowel was ręd gold   with rēal stǫnes,   *wheel*

3247-48 Beautifully enclosed (lit. protected in an enclosure) upon the
noble boughs; There was no moisture of dew that could harm anything.
3251 [Dame Fortune, with her Wheel of Fortune, is a familiar figure in
late Medieval poetry, as are the Nine Worthies whom Arthur sees in
his dream. The Nine Worthies first appear in fourteenth-century
works such as *The Parlement of the Three Ages* and reappear as late
as Shakespeare's *Midsummer Night's Dream*.]
3256 [*Besauntes*: coins (originally from Byzantium), here coin-shaped
golden discs.]
3259 And one so comly of complexion was never known.

°Railed with riches and rubīes ynow;	*adorned*
The °spēkes was °splented all with °speltes of silver,	*spokes/plated/bars*
The spāce of a °spere-lenghe springand full fair;	*spear length*
There-on was a chair of chalk-whīte silver	
And checkered with °charbocle chānging of hewes	*carbuncle*
Upon the °compass there °clēved kinges on row,	*outer edge/clung*
With crowns of clēre gold that cracked in sonder;	
3270 Six was of that °settle full sodēnlich fallen,	*seat*
Ilk a segge by himself and said thēse wordes:	
'That ever I regned on this °roo mē rewes it ever!	*wheel*
Was never roy so rich that regned in erthe!	
When I rode in my rout °rought I nought elles	*I thought of*
But °rivaye and revel and raunson the pople!	*to hunt*
And thus I drīve forth my dayes whīles I °drīe might,	*endure*
And therefore °derflich I am damned for ever!'	*direly*

"The last was a little man that laid was °beneth;	*beneath*
His °leskes lay all °lene and lothlich tō shew,	*loins/lean*
3280 His lockes °līard and long the lenghe of a yard,	*gray*
His °līre and his °ligham °lāmed full sore,	*face/body/crippled*
The °tone eye of the berne was brighter than silver	*one*
The °tother was yellower than the yolk of a °nay.	*other/egg*

" 'I was lord,' quod the lēde, 'of landes ynow,	
And all lēdes mē °louted that lenged in erthe.	*bowed to me*
And now is left mē no °lap my °ligham tō hele	*rag/body*
But °lightly now am I lost, °lēve eche man the sooth.'	*quickly/believe*

"The second sir, forsooth, that °sewed them after	*followed*
Was °sēkerer tō my sight and °sadder in armes;	*stronger/more determined*
3290 Oft hē sighed unsound and said thēse wordes:	
'On yon °see have I sitten als soveraign and lord,	*throne*
And lādīes mē loved tō °lap in their armes,	*fold*
And now my lordshippes are lost and laid for ever!'	

"The third thoroughly was °thro and thick in the shoulders,	*stout*
A thro man tō °thret of there thirty were gadered;	*threat*
His dīadem was dropped down, °dubbed with stones,	*adorned*
°Endented all with °dīamaundes and dight for the °nones;	*adorned/diamonds/occasion*
'I was °dredde in my dayes,' hē said, 'in dīverse rewmes,	*dreaded*
And now damned tō the dede, and dole is the more!'	

3300 "The °fourt was a fair man   and °forcy in armes,   *fourth/forceful*
The fairest of figūre   that formed was ever.
'I was frek in my faith,' hē said,   'whīles I on folde regned,
Fāmous in fer landes   and flowr of all kinges;
Now is my fāce defāded   and foul is mē happened,
For I am fallen frọ fer   and frēndles belęved.'

"The °fift was a fairer man   than fęle of these other,   *fifth*
A °forcy man and a fērs,   with °fọmand lippes;   *forceful/foaming*
Hē °fanged fast on the °feleighes   and fọlded his armes   *gripped/rim*
But yet hē failed and fell   a fifty foot large;
3310 But yet hē sprang and °sprent   and °spradden his armes,   *leaped/spread*
And on the spẹre-lenghe °spēkes   hē spẹkes thēse wordes: *spokes*
'I was in Surry a Sīre   and set by mīne ọne
As soveraign and °seinyour   of sēre kinges landes;   *lord*
Now of my solāce I am   full sodēnly fallen
And for sāke of my sin   °yon sẹte is mē rewed.'   *yon seat is denied me*

"The °sixt had a °sawter   seemlich °bounden   *sixth/psalter/bound*
With a °surepel of silk   °sēwed full fair,   *surplice (cover)/sewn*
A harp and a hand-sling   with hard flint-stones;
What harmes hē has hent   hē °hallowes full soon: *announces*
3320 'I was deemed in my dayes,' hē said,   'of deedes of armes
Ọne of the doughtīest   that dwelled in erthe;
But I was °marred on molde   in my mọst strenghes   *injured*
With this maiden sọ mīld   that mōves us all.'

"Twọ kinges were clīmband   and °claverand on high,   *clambering*
†The crest of the compass   they covēt full yẹrne.
'This chair of °charbocle,' they said,   'wē challenge hēreafter,   *carbuncle*
As twọ of the chēfest   chọsen in erthe.'

"The chīlder were chalk-whīte,   cheekes and other,
But the chair aboven   °chēved they never.   *achieved*
3330 The furthermọst was °freely   with a °front large   *noble/forehead*
The fairest of °fisnamy   that formed was ever,   *physiognomy*
And hē was °busked in a °blee   of a °blew nọble   *dressed/color/blue*
With °flourdelys of gold   flourished all ọver;   *fleur-de-lis (lilies)*
The °tother was °cledde in a cọte   all of clēne silver,   *other/clad*
With a comlich cross   °cọrven of gold;   *carved*

3325 The top of the wheel they eagerly covet.

Four °crosselettes crafty   by the cross restes   *little crosses*
And thereby knew I the king,   that cristened him seemed.

   "Then I went tō that °wlonk   and °winly her greetes,   *bright (one)/*
                                                                     graciously
   And shō said: 'Welcome, īwis,   well art thou °founden;   *come*
3340 Thou ǫught tō worship my will,   and thou well °couthe,   *knew how*
   Of all the valīant men   that ever was in erthe,
   For all thy worship in war   by mē has thou wonnen;
   I have been frēndly, frēke,   and °fremmed til other.   *strange (hostile)*
                                                                     to others
   That thou has founden, in faith,   and fęle of thy bernes,
   †For I felled down Sir Frolle   with °frǫward knightes;   *hostile*
   For-thy the fruits of Fraunce   are freely thīne ǫwen.
   Thou shall the chair °eschēve,   I chēse thee myselven,   *achieve*
   Before all the chēftaines   chǫsen in this erthe.'

   "Shō lift me up lightly   with her °lęne handes   *lean*
3350 And set mē softly in the °see,   the °septer mē °ręched;   *throne/sceptre/*
                                                                     gave
   Craftily with a cǫmb   shō °kembed mīne hęved,   *combed*
   That the °crispand °krok   tō my crown °raught;   *curling/lock/*
                                                                     reached
   Dressed on mē a dīadem   that dight was full fair,
   And sēnn proffers mē a °pome   °pight full of fair stǫnes,   *orb/set*
   Ēnameld with azūre,   the erthe there-on depainted,
   Circled with the salt sę   upon sēre halves,
   In sign that I soothly   was soveraign in erthe.

   "Then brǫught shō mē a brand   with full bright hiltes
   And bade mē braundish the blāde: 'The brand is mīne ǫwen;
3360 Many swain with the swing   has the °swęt leved,   *lifeblood*
   For whīles thou °swank with the sword   it °swīked thee   *labored/failed*
                                           never.'

   "Then raikes shō with °roo   and rest when her līked,   *quiet*
   Tō the °rindes of the wood,   richer was never;   *trees*
   Was nǫ °pomerīe sǫ pight   of princes in erthe,   *orchard*
   Ne nǫne apparēl sǫ proud   but paradīse ǫne.
   Shō bade the °bowes sholde bow down   and bring tō my   *boughs*
                                           handes

3345 [Frollo was the ruler of France whom Arthur killed in single com-
bat when he conquered that country as part of the conquests that
immediately precede the action of this poem and that are summarized
in the opening lines. The story is told in Geoffrey of Monmouth's
Histories of the Kings of Britain, Book IX, chapter 11, where Arthur's
adversary is called Flollo, and in Wace's *Brut* (which our poet may
have known), where he is called Frolle or Frollo.]

Of the best that they bǫre   on braunches sǫ high;
Then they °helded tō her °hest,   all hǫlly at ǫnes,   *bowed/command*
The highest of ęch a °hirst,   I °hēte you forsooth.   *grove/promise*
3370 Shō bade mē °frith nǫt the fruit,   but °fǫnde whīles mē līked: *spare/try*
'°Fǫnde of the fīnest,   thou °freelich berne,   *try/noble*
And °ręche tō the rīpest   and °rīot thyselven.   *reach/enjoy*
Rest, thou rēal roy,   for Rōme is thīne ǫwen,
And I shall rędily roll   the °roo at the gainest   *wheel*
And ręche thee the rich wīne   in rinsed cuppes.'

"Then shō went to the well   by the wood ēves,
That all welled of wīne   and wonderlich runnes,
Caught up a cup-full   and covered it fair;
Shō bade mē °dęrelich °draw   and drink tō herselven;   *dearly/take a draught*
3380 And thus shō led mē about   the lenghe of an hour,
With all līking and love   that any lēde °sholde.   *should want*

"But at the mid-day full ēven   all her mood changed,
And māde much menāce   with marvēlous wordes.
When I crīed upon her,   shē cast down her browes:
'King, thou carpes for nǫught,   by Crīst that mē māde!
For thou shall lōse this °laik   and thy līfe after;   *pleasure*
Thou has lived in °delīte   and lǫrdshippes ynow!'   *delight*

"About shō whirles the wheel   and whirles mē under,
Til all my quarters that °whīle   were °quasht all tō pēces,   *time/crushed*
3390 And with that chair my chin   was chopped in sonder;
And I have shivered for °chele   sēnn mē this chaunce   *chill*
                        happened.
Thus wakened I, īwis,   all wēry °fordręmed,   *wearied from dreaming*
And now wǫt thou my wǫ;   °worde as thee līkes."   *speak*

"Frēke," says the philosopher,   "thy fortūne is passed,
For thou shall find her thy fǫ;   fraist when thee līkes!
Thou art at the highest,   I °hēte thee forsooth;   *promise*
Challenge now when thou will,   thou chēves nǫ mǫre!
Thou has shed much blood   and °shalkes destroyed,   *men*
°Sakeles, in °surquidrīe,   in sēre kinges landes;   *innocent/pride*
3400 °Shrīve thee of thy shāme   and °shāpe for thīne end.   *confess/prepare*
Thou has a °shewing, Sir King,   tāke keep yif thee līke,   *revelation*
For thou shall fērsly fall   within fīve winters.
Found abbeyes in Fraunce,   the fruites are thīne ǫwen,

†For Frolle and for Feraunt   and for thir fērs knightes
†That thou fremedly in Fraunce   has fey belęved.
Tāke keep yet of other kinges,   and °cast in thīne herte,   *consider*
That were conquerours kidd   and crowned in erthe.

　†"The eldest was Alexander   that all the world °louted,   *bowed to*
The °tother Ector of Troy,   the chevalrous gōme;   *other*
3410　The third Jūlīus Cēsar,   that gīaunt was họlden,
In ęche journee gentle,   ajudged with lọrdes.
†The fourth was Sir Jūdas,   a jouster full nọble,
The masterful Macabee,   the mightīest of strenghes;
The °fift was Josūe,   that jolly man of armes,   *fifth*
That in Jerusalem họst   full much joy °limped;   *befell*
The °sixt was David the dęre,   deemed with kinges   *sixth*
Ọne of the doughtīest   that dubbed was ever,
For hē slew with a sling   by °sleight of his handes   *skill*
°Golīas the gręte gōme,   grimmest in erthe;   *Goliath*
3420　Sēnn °endīted in his dayes   all the dęre psalmes   *composed*
That in the °sawter are set   with selcouthe wordes.   *psalter*

　"The °tọne clīmband king,   I knọw it forsooth,   *one*
†Shall Karolus bē called,   the °kinge son of Fraunce;   *king's*
Hē shall bē crūel and keen   and conquerour họlden,
°Cover by conquest   countrees ynow;   *obtain*
He shall °encrọch the crown   that Crīst bọre himselven,   *capture*
And that lovelich launce   that °lępe tō His herte   *leaped*
When He was crūcified on cross,   and all the keen nailes
Knightly hē shall conquer   °tō Cristen men handes.   *i.e., for*

3430　"The °tother shall bē Godfray,   that God shall revenge   *other*
On the Good Frīday   with °galīard knightes;   *jolly*
Hē shall of Lorraine bē lọrd   by lęve of his fader
And sēnn in Jerūsalem   much joy happen,
†For hē shall cover the cross   by craftes of armes

3404 [For Frollo see note on line 3345; Feraunt is a Roman noble, one of
　Lucius' knights, first mentioned in line 2760.]
3405 Whom you unkindly (as a stranger) left dead in France.
3408-10 [Alexander the Great, Hector of Troy, and Julius Caesar are the
　three Pagan Worthies.]
3412-16 [Judas Maccabeus, Joshua, and King David are the three Jewish
　Worthies.]
3423 [Carolus (Charlemagne) is the first of the three Christian Worthies.
　The second is Godfrey of Bouillon (3430), and the third is Arthur
　himself.]
3434 He shall recover the Cross (when he conquers Jerusalem). [God-
　frey's deeds, like Charlemagne's, and prophesied, since historically
　Arthur comes before both.]

And sēnn bē crowned king   with °crisom annointed.   *holy oil*
Shall nǫ dūkes in his day   such °destainy happen,   *destiny*
Ne such mischief °drīe   when trewth shall bē °trīed.   ·   *suffer/proved*

"For-thy Fortūne thee fetches   tō fulfill the number,
Als °nīnde of the nǫblest   nāmed in erthe;   *ninth (of the Nine Worthies)*
3440 This shall in romaunce bē redde   with rēal knightes,
Reckoned and rēnownd   with rīotous kinges,
And deemed on Doomesday   for deedes of armes,
For the doughtīest that ever   was dwelland in erthe;
°Sǫ many clerkes and kinges   shall carp of your deedes   *thus*
And keep your conquestes   in cronīcle for ever.

"But the wolves in the wood   and the wīld bęstes
Are some wicked men   that °werrayes thy rewmes,   *attack*
Is entered in thīne absence   tō werray thy pople,
And ālīenes and hǫstes   of °uncouthe landes.   *foreign*
3450 Thou °gettes tīdandes, I trow,   within ten dayes,   *i.e., will get*
That some °torfer is °tidde   sēnn thou frǫ hǫme turned.   *trouble/ happened*
I ręde thou reckon and °rehęrse   unręsonāble deedes   *tell (i.e., confess)*
Ęre thee repentes full rāthe   all thy °rewth workes.   *sad*
Man, amend thy mood,   ęre thou °mishappen,   *have misfortune*
And meekly ask mercy   for °meed of thy sǫul."   *reward*

Then rīses the rich king   and raght on his weedes,
A ręd °acton of rǫse,   the richest of flowres,   *quilted jacket*
†A pesan and a paunson   and a prīs girdle;
And on hē °hentes a hood   of scarlet full rich,   *draws*
3460 A °pavis pillion-hat   that pight was full fair   *large cloth hat*
With °perry of the Orīent   and precīous stǫnes;   *pearls*
His glǫves gaylich gilt   and °grāven by the hemmes   *decorated*
With °graines of rubīes   full grācīous tō shew.   *small stones*
°His °bedē greyhound and his brand   and nǫ berne else   *(He takes)/ saucy*
And bounes ǫver a brǫde °męde   with brēthe at his herte.   *meadow*
Forth hē stalkes a °sty   by tho still ēves,   *path*
†Stotays at a high street,   studyand him ǫne.

At the °sours of the sun   hē sees there comand,   *rising*
°Raikand tō Rōme-ward   the °rędīest wayes,   *going/quickest*
3470 †A renk in a round clǫk   with right rowme clǫthes

3458 An armor neckpiece, a stomach guard, and an excellent belt.
3467 Pauses at a main road, thinking by himself.
3470 A man in a round (full cut) cloak, with right roomy (full cut)
    clothes. [Fully cut clothes were very fashionable in the late four-
    teenth century.]

With hat and with high °shoon   °homely and round;   *shoes/ comfortable*
With flat °farthinges the frēke   was °flourished all over   *coins/adorned*
†Many shreddes and shragges   at his skirtes hanges
†With scrip and with sclavin   and scallopes ynow
Both pīke and palm,   als pilgrim him sholde;
The gōme graithly him °grette   and bade good °morwen;   *greeted/morning*
The king, lordly himself,   of °lāngāge °of Rōme,   *language/i.e.,*
                                                              Italian
Of Latin °corrumped all,   full lovely him °menes: *corrupted/speaks*
"°Wheder °wilnes thou, wye,   walkand thīne one?   *whither/seek*
3480 Whīles this world is °o war,   a °wāthe I it hold;   *at war/danger*
Hēre is an °enmy with host,   under yon vīnes;   *enemy*
And they see thee, forsooth,   sorrow thee betīdes;
But if thou have °condeth   of the king selven,   *safe-conduct*
Knāves will kill thee   and keep °at thou haves,   *what*
And if thou hold the high way,   they °hent thee also,   *take*
But if thou hāstily have help   of his hende knightes."

Then carpes Sir Craddok   tō the king selven:
"I shall forgive him my dede,   so mē God help,
Any gōme under God   that on this ground walkes!
3490 Let the keenest come   that tō the king longes,
I shall encounter him as knight,   so Crīst have my soul!
For thou may not °reche mē   ne °arrest thyselven,   *seize/stop (me)*
Though thou bē richly arrayed   in full rich weedes;
I will not °wonde for no war   tō wend where mē līkes   *hesitate*
Ne for no wye of this world   that wrought is on erthe!
But I will pass in pilgrimāge   this °pās tō Rōme   *way*
Tō purchāse mē pardon   of the Pope selven,
And of the paines of Purgatory   bē °plēnerly °assoilled;   *fully/forgiven*
Then shall I seek sēkerly   my soveraign lord,
3500 Sir Arthur of England,   that °avenaunt berne!   *seemly*
For hē is in this empīre,   as °hathel men mē telles,   *noble*
†Hostayand in this Orīent   with awful knightes."

"Frō °whethen come thou, keen man,"   quod the king then, *whence*
"That knowes King Arthur   and his knightes also?

3473 [The "shreds" and "shragges" are scalloped edges, a fashionable
   touch (see note on line 905).]
3474-75 With wallet and with pilgrim's mantle and many scallop shells,
   both staff and palm branch, as if he were a pilgrim. [The scallop shells
   were the mark of a pilgrimage to St. James of Compostella in Spain,
   the palm branch of a pilgrimage to the Holy Land.]
3502 Warring in this eastern land, with awesome knights.

Was thou ever in his court　whīles hē in kith lenged?
Thou carpes sǫ kindly　it comfortes mīne herte!
Well °węle has thou went　and wīsely thou seekes,　　　　　　*nobly*
For thou art °Breton berne,　as by thy brǫde spēche."　　　　*British*

　　"Mē ǫught tō knǫw the king;　hē is my kidd lǫrd,
3510　And I was called in his court　a knight of his chāmber;
Sir Craddok was I called　in his court rich,
Keeper of Caerlīon,　under the king selven;
Now I am chāsed out of kith,　with care at my herte,
And that castel is caught　with °uncouthe lēdes."　　　　　　*foreign*

　　Then the comlich king　caught him in armes,
Cast off his kettle-hat　and kissed him full soon,
Said: "Welcome, Sir Craddok,　sǫ Crīst mot mē help!
Dęre °cosin of kind,　thou cǫldes mīne herte!　　　　　　　*blood relative*
How fares it in Bretain　with all my bǫld bernes?
3520　Are they brittened or °brint　or brǫught out of līfe?　　　*burned*
°Ken thou mē kindly　what cāse is befallen;　　　　　　　　*tell*
†I keep nǫ crēdens tō crāve;　I knǫw thee for trew."

　　"Sir, thy wardēn is wicked　and wīld of his deedes,
For hē wandreth has wrǫught　sēnn thou away passed.
Hē has castels °encrǫched　and crownd himselven,　　　　　*captured*
Caught in all the rentes　of the Round Tāble;
Hē °devīsed the rewm　and dęlt as him līkes;　　　　　　　*divided*
Dubbed of the °Denmarkes dūkes and erles,　　　　　　　　*i.e., Danes*
†Dissevered them sonderwīse,　and citees destroyed;
3530　Of Sarazenes and °Sessoines　upon sēre halves　　　　　*Saxons*
Hē has sembled a sorte　of °selcouthe bernes,　　　　　　　*foreign*
Soveraignes of Surgenale　and °soudēours many　　　　　　*mercenaries*
Of °Peghtes and °paynims　and prōved knightes　　　　　　*Picts/pagans*
Of Īreland and Argyle,　outlawed bernes;
All thǫ laddes are knightes　that lǫng tō the mountes,
And °lęding and lǫrdship has all,　als themselve līkes;　　　*command*
And there is Sir Childrik　a chēftain hǫlden,
That ilke chevalrous man,　hē °charges thy pople;　　　　　*burdens*
They rob thy °religīous　and ravish thy nunnes　　　　　　　*monks*
3540　And rędy rīdes with his rout　tō °raunson the poor;　　　*rob*

3522 I need ask for no credentials; I know you are true.
3529 Scattered them in every direction (throughout the realm).

†Fro Humber tō Hawyk   hē holdes his owen,
And all the countree of Kent   by covenant °entailled,   *in his possession*
The comlich castles   that tō the crown longed,
The holtes and the °hore wood   and the hard bankes,   *hoar (gray)*
†All that Hengest and Hors   hent in their tīme;
At Southampton on the se   is seven score shippes,
°Fraught full of fērs folk,   out of fer landes,   *filled*
For tō fight with thy °frap   when thou them assailes.   *company*
But yet a word, °witterly,   thou wot not the worst!   *certainly*
3550 He has wedded Waynor   and her his wīfe holdes,
And °wonnes in the wīld boundes   of the west marches,   *dwells*
And has wrought her with chīld,   as witness telles!
Of all the wyes of this world,   °wo mot him worthe,   *woe be to him*
Als wardēn unworthy   women tō yēme!
Thus has Sir Mordred   °marred us all!   *injured*
For-thy I °merked over these mountes   tō °mene thee the   *came/tell*
                                     sooth."

    Then the burlich king,   for brēthe at his herte
And for this °booteless bāle   all his °blee chānged;   *without remedy/*
"By the Rood," says the roy,   "I shall it revenge!   *color*
3560 Him shall repent full rāthe   all his rewth workes!"
All weepand for wo   hē went tō his tentes;
°Unwinly this wīse king   hē wākenes his bernes,   *unhappily*
°Clēped in a clarīoun   kinges and other,   *called with a*
Calles them tō counsēl   and of this cāse telles: *trumpet*
"I am with tresoun betrayed,   for all my trew deedes!
And all my travail is tint,   mē tides no better!
Him shall °torfer betīde   °this tresoun has wrought,   *trouble/i.e., who*
                                                                           this
And I °may °traistely him tāke,   as I am trew lord!   *can/surely*
This is Mordred, the man   that I most traisted,
3570 Has my castels encroched   and crownd himselven
With rentes and riches   of the Round Tāble;
Hē māde all his retinūes   of °renayed wretches,   *renegade*
And devīsed my rewm   tō dīverse lordes,
Tō soudēours and Sarazenes   out of sēre landes!

3541 From the Humber river (at the southern border of Yorkshire) to the
    town of Hawick (in southern Scotland; i.e., the whole North Coun-
    try).
3545 [Hengest and Horsa were traditionally the first Germanic (that is,
    Anglo-Saxon) invaders of Britain; Geoffrey of Monmouth (*Histories
    of the Kings of Britain*, Book VI, chapter 11) gives the traditional
    account.]

He has wedded Waynor   and her tō wīfe hǫldes,
And a chīld is y-shāped,   the chaunce is nǫ better!
They have sembled on the sę   seven scǫre shippes,
Full of °ferrom folk   tō fight with mīne ǫne!   *foreign*
†For-thy tō Bretain the brǫde   buske us behooves,
3580 For tō britten the berne   that has this bāle raised.
There shall nǫ freke men fare   but all on fresh horses
That are fraisted in fight   and flowr of my knightes.
Sir Howell and Sir Hardolf   hēre shall °belęve   *remain*
Tō bē lǫrdes of the lēdes   that hēre tō mē lǫnges;
†Lookes intō Lumbardy   that there nǫ lēde chānge,
And tenderly tō Tuskānē   tāke °tent als I bid;   *attention*
Receive the rentes of Rōme   when they are reckoned;
Tāke °sēsin the sāme day   that last was assigned,   *possession*
Or elles all the hostāge   withouten the walles
3590 Bē hanged high upon height   all hǫlly at ǫnes."

      Now bounes the bold king   with his best knightes,
†Gars trumpe and trusse   and trīnes forth after,
Turnes through Tuskānē,   tarrīes but little,·
Lights nǫt in Lumbardy   but when the light failed;
Merkes ǫver the mountaines   full marvēlous wayes,
Ayers through Almaine   ēven at the gainest
°Ferkes ēven intō °Flandresh   with his fērs knightes.   *goes/Flanders*
Within fifteen dayes   his fleet is assembled,
And then hē °shǫpe him tō ship   and °shounes nǫ lenger,   *prepared himself/delays*
3600 °Sheeres with a sharp wind   ǫver the shīre waters;   *cuts*
By the °roche with rǫpes   hē rīdes on °anker.   *rocks/anchor*
There the false men °flēted   and on flood lenged,   *floated*
†With chēf chaines of charre   chocked tōgeders,
Charged ēven chock-full   of chevalrous knightes;
Hatches with hęthen men   hęled were there-under,
And in the °hinter on height,   helmes and crestes   *rear*
Proudlich °pourtrayed   °with painted clothes,   *painted/on*
Ęch a pēce by pēce   °prikked til other,   *sewed*
°Dubbed with °dagswainnes   doubled they seem;   *adorned/heavy cloth*

3579 Therefore it behooves us to hasten to Great Britain.
3585 See that in Lombardy no man change his allegiance (which has
     been pledged to Arthur).
3592 Commands them to blow bugles and pack up and goes forth there-
     after.
3603 Pressed together with great wagon chains (apparently to form a
     defensive line).

3610 And thus the derf °Denmarkes   had dight all their shippes,   *Danes*
　　　†That nọ dint of nọ dart　　°dẹre them sholde.   *harm*

　　　　Then the roy and the renkes   of the Round Tāble
　　　All rēaly in rẹd   arrayes his shippes;
　　　That day dūcherīes hē dẹlt   and dubbed knightes,
　　　Dresses °dromoundes and °dragges   and drawen up stọnes;   *galleys/barges*
　　　The top-castels hē stuffed   with °toiles, as him līked;   *slings*
　　　Bendes °bọwes of vīse   brọthly there-after;   *crossbows*
　　　°Toloures °tently   tackle they righten,   *sling attendants/ carefully*
　　　°Brāsen hẹdes full brọde   busked on °flọnes,   *bronze/missiles*
3620 Graithes for °garnisons,   gōmes arrayes,   *garrisons*
　　　Grim °gọdes of steel,   °gīves of īron;   *goads/fetters*
　　　†Stighteles steren on steren   with stiff men of armes;
　　　Many lovelich launce   upon loft standes,
　　　Lēdes on °lēburd,   lọrdes and other,   *lee (sea side of ship)*
　　　°Pight °pavis on °port,   painted shēldes,   *arranged/ shields/port side*
　　　On °hīnder °hurdace on height   helmed knightes.   *rear/barrier*
　　　Thus they °shiften for °shottes   on thọse shīre strandes,   *maneuver/ shooting*
　　　Ilke shalk in his °shroud,   full sheen were their weedes.   *garment*

　　　　The bọld king is in a barge   and about rọwes,
3630 †All bare-hẹvede for besy   with bẹveren lockes,
　　　And a berne with his brand   and an helm °bẹten,   *adorned (beaten)*
　　　°Menged with a °mauntelet   of mailes of silver,   *adorned/little mantle*
　　　°Compast with a °coronal   and °covered full rich;   *encircled/diadem/ decorated*
　　　Kaires tō ẹch a °cogge   tō comfort his knightes;   *ship*
　　　Tō Clēgis and Clēremond   hē crīes on loud:
　　　"Ọ Gawain! Ọ Galyran!   Thēse good mens bodīes!"
　　　Tō Lot and tō Līonel   full lovely hē mẹles,
　　　And tō Sir Launcelot de Lāke   lọrdlich wọrdes:
　　　"Let us cover the kith,   the cọste is our ọwn,
3640 And °gar them °brọthelich °blenk,   all yon blood-houndes!   *make/violently/ blanch*
　　　Britten them °within bōrde   and brin them there-after!   *aboard*
　　　Hew down hertily   yon hẹthen °tīkes!   *dogs*
　　　†They are harlotes half,   I hēte you mīne hand!"

　　　3611 [Apparently the painted cloths (sewn together and doubled) are
　　　　　meant to serve as protection against arrows.]
　　　3622 Supplies stern after stern (i.e., ship after ship) with stout men of
　　　　　arms.
　　　3630 All bareheaded because of business, with beaver-colored locks.
　　　3643 They are on the rascal's side, I swear by my hand.

Then hē coveres his °cogge   and catches on °anker,   *ship/anchor*
Caught his comlich helm   with the clēre mailes;
Buskes banners on brọde,   °bẹten of gules,   *adorned with red*
With crowns of clēre gold   clẹnlich arrayed;
†But there was chọsen in the chēf   a chalk-whīte maiden,
And a chīld in her arm   that Chēf is of hẹven;
3650 †Withouten chānging in chāse   thēse were the chēf armes
Of Arthur the avenaunt,   whīles hē in erthe lenged.

Then the mariners mẹles   and masters of shippes;
Merrily īch a mate   °mẹnes til other;   *speaks*
†Of their termes they talk,   how they were tidd,
Tọwen °trussel on trete,   trussen up sailes,   *bundles on trestles*
°Bẹte bonnetes on brọde,   °bettred hatches;   *set small sails/ adjusted*
Braundisht brown steel,   °brāgged in trumpes;   *blew in trumpets*
Standes stiff on the °stamin,   steeres on after,   *prow*
°Streken over the strẹme,   there strīving beginnes.   *strike*
3660 °Frọ the °wāggand wind   out of the west rīses,   *when/swaying*
Brọthly °bessomes with °birr   in bernes sailes,   *rushes/force*
†Wẹther bringes on bōrde   burlich cogges,
Whīles the °biling and the °bẹme   bristes in sonder;   *bilge/beam*
Sọ stoutly the °fore-stern   on the °stam hittes   *stern/prow*
That °stockes of the °steer-bōrde   strīkes in pēces!   *planks/starboard side*
By then °cogge upon cogge,   °crayers and other,   *ship/small ships*
Castes °crēpers °on-cross,   als tō the craft lọnges;   *grappling hooks/ across*
Then was hẹd-ropes hewen,   that hēld up the mastes;
There was °contek full keen   and cracking of shippes!   *strife*
3670 Grẹte cogges of °kemp   crashes in sonder!   *war*
Many °cabane clēved,   cābles destroyed,   *cabins*
Knightes and keen men   killed the bernes!
Kidd castels were °cọrven,   with all their keen wēpen,   *carved*
Castels full comlich   that coloured were fair!
°Up-tīes °edgeling   they °ochen there-after;   *mast-stays/ edgewise/hack*
With the swing of the sword   sways the mastes,
Ọver-falles in the °first   frēkes and other;   *i.e., first blow*

3648 But there was placed in the chief (the upper third of the shield) a
    chalk-white maiden (i.e., the Virgin Mary).
3650 [Arthur will not change his arms to disguise himself even when
    hard-pressed, as Mordred later does (ll. 4181–85).]
3654 They talk in their jargon (*termes*) about what has happened.
3662-63 Weather (i.e., wind) brings stout ships against planks (*on
    bōrde*), so that the bilge and the beam burst apart. [Ramming and
    boarding were the principal tactics in fourteenth-century sea battles,
    since cannon had only recently been introduced.]

Many frēke in the fore-ship   fey is belęved!
Then brǫthly they °beker   with bustous °tackle;   *fight/equipment*
3680 †Brushes bǫldly on bōrde   brenyed knightes,
Out of bǫtes on bōrde,   was busked with stǫnes,
Bęte down of the best,   bristes the hatches;
Some gōmes °through-gird   with °gǫdes of īron,   *pierced/goads*
Gōmes gaylich °cledde   °englaimes wēpenes;   *clad/make slimy*
Archers of England   full ęgerly shootes,
Hittes through the hard steel   full °hęrtly dintes!   *mortal*
Soon °ochen in hǫlly   the hęthen knightes,   *completely cut down*
Hurt through the hard steel,   °hęle they never!⁻   *heal*
Then they fall to the fight,   °foines with spęres,   *duel*
3690 All the frekkest on °front   that tō the fight longes,   *front rank*
And °ilkon freshly   fraistes their strenghes,   *each one*
°War tō fight in the fleet   with their fell wēpenes.   *to fight the battle*
Thus they dęlt that day,   thir dubbed knightes,
Til all the Dānes were dęde   and in the deep throwen!
Then Bretons brǫthly   with brandes they hewen;
†Lępes in upon loft   lǫrdlich bernes;
When lēdes of out-landes   lępen in waters,
All our lǫrdes on loud   laughen at ǫnes!

By then spęres were °sprongen,   °spalded shippes,   *broken/split*
3700 °Spanīoles speedily   °sprented °ǫver-bōrdes;   *Spaniards/ leaped/overboard*
All the keen men of °kemp,   knightes and other,   *battle*
Killed are cǫld-dęde   and casten ǫver-bōrdes;
Their °swyers swiftly   has the °swęt lęved;   *young men/ lifeblood*
Hęthen °hęvand on hatch   in °thir hawe rīses,   *heaving/these gray waves*
Sinkand in the salt sę   seven hundreth at ǫnes!
Then Sir Gawain the good,   hē has the °gree wonnen,   *prize*
And all the cogges gręte   hē gāve tō his knightes.
Sir Garin, Sir Griswold,   and other gręte lordes;
†Gart Galuth, a good gōme,   gird off °their hędes!   *i.e., the captives'*
3710 Thus of the false fleet   upon the flood happened,
And thus thēse °ferin folk   fey are belęved!   *foreign*

Yet is the traitour on land   with trīed knightes,
And all °trumped they trip   on trapped steedes   *accompanied with trumpets*

3680-81 Armored knights rush boldly on board, (coming) out of small
    boats on board, (and) were pelted with stones (thrown by defenders
    in the top-castles).
3696 Lordly men leap into the water from the decks.
3709 [Galuth is Gawain's sword, here personified as *a good gōme*.]

Shews them under shēld   on the shīre bankes;
Hē ne shuntes for nǫ shāme   but °shewes full high!   *shows himself*
Sir Arthur and Gawain   °avyed them bǫthen   *set out*
Tō sixty thousand of men   that in their sight hōved.
†By this the folk was felled,   then was the flood passed;
Then was it silke a slowde   in slackes full huge
3720 That let the king for tō land   in the lǫw water.
For-thy hē lenged on laye   for lēsing of horses,
Tō look of his lēge-men   and of his lēle knightes,
Yif any were lāmed or lost,   live yif they sholde.

      Then Sir Gawain the good   a galley hē tākes
And glīdes up at a °gole   with good men of armes;   *small bay (gully)*
When hē °grounded, for grēf   hē °girdes in the water   *ran aground/*
                                                             leaps
That tō the girdle hē gǫes   in all his gilt weedes,
°Shootes up upon the sand   in sight of the lǫrdes,   *rushes*
°Singly with his °soppe,   my sǫrrow is the more!   *alone/small*
                                                             troop
3730 With banners of his °badges,   best of his armes,   *heraldic devices*
Hē braides up on the bank   in his bright weedes;
Hē biddes his °bannēour: "Busk thou °belīve   *banner bearer/*
                                                             quickly
Tō yon brǫde batail   that on yon bank hōves,
And I ensūre you °soothe   I shall you °sew after;   *truly/follow*
Look yē °blenk for nǫ brand   ne for nǫ bright wēpen,   *blanch*
But bǫres down of the best   and bring them °o-dawe!   *out of daylight*
°Bēs nǫt °abaist of their bǫste,   abīde on the erthe;   *be/abashed*
Yē have my banneres borne   in batailes full hūge;
Wē shall fell yon false,   the fēnd have their sǫules!
3740 Fightes fast with the °frap,   the fēld shall bē oures! *company*
°May I that traitour ǫver-tāke,   torfer him tīdes   *If I can*
That this trǫsoun has °timbered   °tō my trew lǫrd!   *built/for*
†Of such a °engendūre   full little joy happens,   *engendering*
And that shall in this journee   bē judged full ēven!"

      Now they seek over the sand,   this °soppe at the gainest, *small troop*
°Sembles on the soudēours   and °settes their dintes;   *attack/set on*
Through the shēldes sǫ sheen   shalkes they touch

3718-21 By the time the battle was finished the high tide had passed; then
     was the water near the shore such a slush, in very large pools, that the
     king could not land in the low water. Therefore he remained on the
     deep water for fear of losing his horses (if he landed).
3743 [*Engendure* may be a reference to Mordred's incestuous begetting
     (see *Stanzaic Morte Arthure*, ll. 2955–56), though there is no direct
     reference to it in this poem.]

With shaftes °shivered short   of those sheen launces;   *broken*
Derf dintes they delt   with °dāggand speres;   *piercing*
3750 On the dank of the dew   many dede ligges,
Dūkes and douspeeres   and dubbed knightes;
The doughtïest of Danemark   undōne are forever!
Thus those renkes in rewth   °rittes their brenyes   *rip*
And °reches of the richest   °unrecken dintes,   *give/countless*
There they throng in the thick   and thrustes tō the erthe
Of the throest men   three hundreth at ones!
But Sir Gawain for grēf   might not °again-stand,   *withstand*
°Umbegrippes a spere   and tō a gōme runnes,   *grasps*
That bore of °gules full gay   with °goutes of silver;   *arms of red/ droplets*
3760 Hē girdes him in at the °gorge   with his grim launce   *throat*
That the grounden °glaive   graithes in sonder;   *point*
With that bustous blāde   hē bounes him tō dīe!
The King of °Gotheland it was,   a good man of armes.   *Gothland (South Sweden)*
Their avauntward then all   voides there-after,
Als °vanquist °verrayly   with valïant bernes;   *vanquished/ verily*
Meetes with °middle-ward   that Mordred ledes;   *middle guard*
Our men merkes them tō,   as them mishappened,
For had Sir Gawain the grāce   tō hold the green hill,
Hē had worship, īwis,   wonnen forever!

3770   But then Sir Gawain, īwis,   hē waites him well
Tō wreke on this °warlaw   that this war mōved,   *warlock*
And merkes tō Sir Mordred   among all his bernes,
†With the Montagūes   and other grete lordes.
Then Sir Gawain was grēved   and with a grete will
Fewters a fair spere   and freshly ascrīes:
"False fostered °fōde,   the fēnd have thy bones!   *creature*
Fy on thee, felon,   and thy false workes!
Thou shall bē dede and undōne   for thy derf deedes,
Or I shall dīe this day,   °if destainy worthe!"   *if it be my destiny*

3780   Then his enmy with host   of outlawed bernes
All °enangles about   our excellent knightes   *surround*
That the traitour by tresoun   had °trīed himselven;   *experienced*
Dūkes of Danemark   hē dightes full soon,

3773 [The Montagues were a famous Northern English family. The head
of the family was a supporter of Richard II and a suspected heretic.
He rebelled against Henry IV in 1400; he was beheaded and his head
was displayed on London Bridge as a warning to other potential
traitors.]

And lęders of °Lettow   with lēgīons ynow,   *Lithuania*
°Umbelapped our men   with launces full keen,   *surrounded*
Soudēours and Sarazenes   out of sēre landes,
Sixty thousand men,   seemlyly arrayed,
Sēkerly assembles there   on seven score knightes,
Sodēnly in °dischaite   by thǫ salt strandes.   *deceit*
3790 Then Sir Gawain °grette   with his grey eyen   *wept*
For grēf of his good men   that hē guīde sholde.
Hē wiste that they wounded were   and °wēry for-fǫughten,   *exhausted with fighting*
And what for wonder and wǫ,   all his wit failed.
And then sighand hē said   with °syland °tęres: *flowing/tears*
"Wē are with Sarazenes beset   upon sēre halves!
I sigh nǫt for myself,   sǫ help mē our Lǫrd,
But for tō see us °surprīsed   my sǫrrow is the mǫre!   *captured*
°Bēs doughty tōday,   yon dūkes shall bē yours!   *be*
For dęre Drighten this day   drēdes nǫ wēpen.
3800 Wē shall end this day   als excellent knightes,
Ayer tō endless joy   with āngeles °unwemmed;   *spotless*
Thǫugh wē have °unwittyly   wāsted ourselven,   *unwisely*
Wē shall work all well   in the worship of Crīst!
Wē shall for yon Sarazenes,   I °sēker you my trewth,   *pledge*
°Soupe with our Sāvīour   solemnly in hęven,   *dine*
In presence of that Precīous,   Prince of all other,
With prophetes and patrīarkes   and apostles full nǫble,
Before His freelich face   That formed us all!
Yonder tō yon °yaldsones!   Hē that yēldes him ever   *mare's sons*
3810 Whīles hē is °quick and in °quert,   unquelled with handes,   *alive/sound health*
Bē hē never mǫ sāved,   ne succoured with Crīst,
†But Sātanase his sǫul   mowe sink intō Hell!"

Then grimly Sir Gawain   grippes his wēpen;
Again that gręte batail   hē graithes him soon,
°Radly of his rich sword   hē rightes the chaines;   *quickly*
In hē °shockes his shēld,   shuntes hē nǫ lenger,   *pushes*
But all unwīse, °wōdewīse,   hē went at the gainest,   *madly*
Woundes of thǫse °widerwinnes   with °wrakful dintes;   *enemies/wrathful*
All welles full of blood   there hē away passes;
3820 And thǫugh him were full wǫ,   hē wǫndes but little,
But vwrękes at his worship   the wrath of his lǫrd!
Hē stickes steedes in stour   and °sterenfull knightes,   *stern*
That steren men in the stirrupes   stǫne-dęde they ligge!

3812 But may Satan sink his soul into Hell!

Hē rīves the rank steel,   hē rittes the mailes;
There might nǫ renk him arrest;   his ręsoun was passed!
Hē fell in a °frensy   for fērsness of herte;   *frenzy*
Hē fightes and felles down   that him before standes!
Fell never °fey man   such fortūne in erthe!   *to a fated man*
Intō the hǫle batail   °hędlings hē runnes   *headlong*
3830 And hurtes of the hardīest   that on the erthe lenges;
°Lętand as a līon   hē °launches them through,   *acting like/stabs*
Lǫrdes and lęders   that on the land hǫves.
Yet Sir Wawain for wǫ   °wǫndes but little,   *hesitates*
But woundes of those °widerwinnes   with wonderful dintes,   *enemies*
Als hē that wǫlde wilfully   wāsten himselven,
And for °wondsome and °will   all his wit failed,   *fierceness/*
                                                                                  wilfulness
That °wōde als a wīld bęste   hē went at the gainest;   *crazy*
All wallowed on blood   there hē away passed;
†Ich a wye may bē ware   by węreke of another!

3840   Then hē mōves tō Sir Mordred   amǫng all his knightes,
And met him in the mid-shēld   and °malles him through,   *hammers*
But the shalk for the sharp   hē shuntes a little;
He °share him on the short ribbes   °a shaftmond large.   *cut/six inches*
                                                                                  deep
The shaft shuddered and shot   in the °shīre berne   *shining*
That the sheddand blood   ǫver his shank runnes
And shewed on his °shin-bawde   that was °shīre burnisht!   *shin plate/*
                                                                                  brightly burnished
†And sǫ they shift and shove   hē shot tō the erthe,
With the °lūsh of the launce   °hē light on his shoulders   *blow/i.e.,*
                                                                                  Mordred
°An ācre-lenghe on a °laund   full lǫthly wounded.   *full length/hillock*
3850 Then Gawain gird tō the gōme   and °on the grouf falles;   *on his face*
All his grēf was graithed;   his grāce was nǫ better!
Hē °shockes out a short knīfe   °shęthed with silver   *draws/sheathed*
And sholde have °slotted him in   but nǫ slit happened;   *stabbed*
His hand slipped and °slǫde   °o-slant on the mailes   *slided/aslant*
And the °tother °slēly   slinges him under;   *other/slyly*
With a °trenchand knife   the traitour him hittes   *cutting*
Through the helm and the hęd   on high on the brain;
And thus Sir Gawain is gǫne,   the good man of armes,
Withouten rescūe of renk,   and rew is the mǫre!
3860 Thus Sir Gawain is gǫne   that °guīed many other;   *guided*
Frǫ Gower tō °Gernesay,   all the gręte lǫrdes   *Guernsey*

3839 Each man can be ware (be warned) by vengeance wreaked on
      another.
3847 And so (stoutly) did they move and shove.

Of °Glamour, of °Gālys land,   thēse galīard knightes   *Glamorgan/*
†For glent of glōpining   glad bē they never!   *Wales*

King Frederik of Frīsland   °faithly there-after   *Frisia/faithfully*
Fraines at the false man   of our fērs knight:
"Knew thou ever this knight   in thy kith rich?
Of what °kīnd hē was comen   beknow now the sooth;   *family*
What gōme was hē,   this with the gay armes,
†With this griffon of gold,   that is °on grouf fallen?   *on his face*
3870 Hē has gretly grēved us,   so mē God help,
Gird down our good men   and grēved us sore!
Hē was the sterenest in stour   that ever steel °wered, *wore*
For hē stonayed our stale   and stroyed for ever!"

Then Sir Mordred with mouth   meles full fair:
"Hē was °makless on molde,   man, by my trewth.   *matchless*
This was Sir Gawain the good,   the gladdest of other,
And the grāciousest gōme   that under God lived,
Man hardīest of hand,   °happīest in armes,   *most fortunate*
And the hendest in hall   under °heven-rich,   *the kingdom of*
                                                         heaven
3880 And the lordlīest in °lēding   whīles hē live might, *leadership*
†For hē was līon alōsed   in landes ynow;
Had thou knowen him, Sir King,   in kithe there hē lenged,
His cunning, his knighthood,   his kīndly workes,
His dōing, his doughtiness,   his deedes of armes,
Thou wolde have dole for his dede   the dayes of thy līfe."

Yet that traitour als tīte   teres let hē fall,
Turnes him forth tīte   and talkes no more,
Went weepand away   and °wēryes the °stounde   *curses/time*
That ever his °wērdes were wrought   such wandreth tō   *fates*
                                           work!
3890 When hē thought on this thing   it °thirled his herte; *pierced*
†For sāke of his sib-blood   sighand hē rīdes;
When that °renayed renk   remembered himselven   *renegade*
Of reverence and rīotes   of the Round Tāble,
Hē °rōmed and repent him   of all his rewth workes,   *moaned*

3863 Because of this sight of terror (this terrible sight) they will never
    be glad (again).
3869 [The golden griffin (a winged dragon) is Gawain's usual heraldic
    device.]
3881 For he was praised as a lion in many lands.
3891 [*Sib-blood*: family relationship. Mordred and Gawain are cousins;
    their mothers were Arthur's sisters.]

Rọde away with his rout,   restes hē nọ lenger,
†For rade of our rich king,   rīve that hē sholde.

   Then kaires hē tō Cornwall,   care-full in herte,
Because of his kinsman   that on the cọste ligges;
Hē tarrīes trembland ay,   tīdandes tō herken.
3900 Then the traitour °treunted   the Tuesday there-after,   *set forth*
°Trīnes in with a °trayn   trẹsoun tō work,   *goes/trick*
And by the °Tamber that tīde   his tentes hē rẹres,   *the River Tamar*
And then in a °mett-whīle   a messānger hē sendes   *short time*
And wrọte untō Waynor   how the world chānged
And what comlich cọste   the king was arrīved,
On flood fọughten with his fleet   and felled them °o līfe;   *from*
Bade her ferken °o-fer   and flee with her chīlder   *afar*
†Whīles hē might wīle him away   and win tō her spēche,
Ayer intō Īreland,   into thọse °oute-mountes,   *outer mountains*
3910 And °wonne there in wilderness   within thọ °wāste landes.   *live/deserted*

   Then shō °yermes and °yeyes   at York in her chāmber,   *cries/sobs*
Grọnes full grisly   with °grētand tẹres,   *weeping*
Passes out of the palais   with all her prīs maidens,
Tōward Chester in a °charre   they chẹse her the wayes,   *carriage*
Dight her ēven for tō dīe   with dole at her herte;
Shō kaires tō Caerlīon   and °caught her a veil,   *i.e., became a nun*
Askes there the °habit   in honour of Crīst   *nun's garment*
And all for °falshēd and fraud   and °fẹre of her °lọrd!   *falsehood/fear/ husband*

   But when our wīse king wiste   that Gawain was landed,
3920 Hē all °tō-wrīthes for wọ,   and wringand his handes,   *writhes violently*
Gars launch his bọtes   upon a lọw water,
Landes als a līon   with lọrdlich knightes,
Slippes in in the °sloppes   °o-slant tō the girdle,   *pools/aslant*
°Swafres up swiftly   with his sword drawen,   *staggers*
Bounes his batail   and banners displayes,
Buskes over the brọde sand   with brēthe at his herte,
Ferkes frekly on fēld   there the fey ligges;
Of the traitours men   on trapped steedes,
Ten thousand were tint,   the trewth tō account,
3930 And, certain, on our sīde   seven score knightes,
°In suīte with their soveraign   °unsound are belẹved.   *together/not whole (dead)*

3896 For fear that our powerful king should arrive.
3908 Until he could get away by stealth and manage to come to speak
  to her.

The king comly °ǫvercast   knightes and other,   *turned over*
Erles of Afrīke   and °Estriche bernes,   *Austrian*
Of Argyle and Orkney   the Īrish kinges,
The nǫblest of Norway,   numbers full hūge,
Dūkes and Danemarkes   and dubbed knightes;
And the °Guthēde king   in the gay armes   *Gothic*
Līes grǫnand on the ground   and gird through ēven.
The rich king °ransackes   with rewth at his herte   *searches*
3940 And up °rippes the renkes   of all the Round Tāble,   *pulls*
Sees them all in a °soppe   °in suīte by them ǫne   *little group / together*

With the Sarazenes °unsound   encircled about,   *not whole (i.e., dead)*
And Sir Gawain the good   in his gay armes,
†Umbegripped the gers   and on grouf fallen,
His banners braiden down,   °bęten of gūles,   *adorned with red*
His brand and his brǫde shēld   all bloody °berunnen.   *run over*
Was never our seemlich king   sǫ sǫrrowful in herte,
†Ne that sank him sǫ sad   but that sight ǫne.

Then °gliftes the good king   and °glōpins in herte,   *stares / is terror-struck*
3950 Grǫnes full grislich   with °grētande tęres,   *weeping*
Kneeles down tō the corse   and caught it in armes,
Castes up his °umbrere   and kisses him soon,   *visor*
Lookes on his eye-liddes   that locked were fair,
†His lippes līke tō the lęde   and his līre fallowed.
Then the crownd king   crīes full loud:
"Dęre °cosin of kind   in care am I lęved,   *blood relative*
For now my worship is went   and my war ended!
Hēre is the hǫpe of my °hęle,   my °happing in armes,   *well-being / good fortune*
My herte and my hardīness   hǫlly on him lenged!
3960 My counsēl, my comfort,   that keeped mīne herte!
Of all knightes the king   that under Crīst lived!
Thou was worthy tō bē king,   thǫugh I the crown bare!
My °węle and my worship   of all this world rich   *wealth*
Was wonnen through Sir Gawain   and through his wit ǫne!
"Alas," said Sir Arthur,   "Now °eekes my sǫrrow!   *increases*
I am utterly undōne   in mīne ǫwen landes!
Ā °doutous, derf dęde,   thou dwelles too lǫng!   *fearful*
†Why drawes thou sǫ on dregh?   Thou drownes mīne herte!"

3944 Clutched the grass, and fallen on his face.
3948 Nor was there anything that sank (his spirits) so sadly as that sight
   alone.
3954 His lips like lead and his complexion turned pale.
3968 Why do you draw back so (delay so long)?

Then °sweltes the sweet king   and in swoon falles,   *faints*
3970 °Swafres up swiftly   and sweetly him kisses   *staggers*
Til his burlich bęrde   was °bloody berunnen,   *covered with blood*
Als hē had °bęstes brittened   and brọught out of līfe;   *beasts*
Ne had Sir Ēwain comen   and other gręte lọrdes,
His bọld herte had bristen   for bāle at that °stounde!   *time*

"°Blinn," says thēse bọld men,   "thou °blunders thyselven!   *stop/harm*
This is °bootless bāle,   for better °bēs it never!   *without remedy/ will be*
It is nọ worship, īwis,   tō wring thīne handes;
Tō weep als a woman   it is nọ wit họlden!
Bē knightly of countenaunce,   als a king sholde,
3980 And lęve such clamour,   for Crīstes love of hęven!"

"For blood," says the bọld king,   "blinn shall I never
Ęre my brain °tō-brist   or my brēste °ọther!   *shatter/either*
Was never sọrrow sọ soft   that sank to my herte;
It is full °sib tō myself;   my sọrrow is the mọre.   *closely related*
Was never sọ sọrrowful a sight   seen with mīne eyen!
Hē is °sakless surprīsed   for sin of mīne ọne!"   *innocent*

Down kneeles the king   and crīes full loud,
With care-full countenaunce   hē carpes thēse wordes:
"Ọ °rightwīse rich God,   this rewth thou behọld,   *righteous*
3990 This rēal ręd blood   run upon erthe!
It were worthy tō bē °shrēde   and shrīned in gold,   *clothed*
For it is °sakless of sin,   sọ help mē our Lọrd!"   *innocent*

Down kneeles the king   with care at his herte,
Caught it up kindly   with his clęne handes,
Cast it in a kettle-hat   and coverd it fair,
And kaires forth with the corse   in kithe there hē lenges.

"Hēre I māke mīne avow,"   quọd the king then,
"Tō °Messīe and tō Mary,   the mīld Queen of hęven: *Messiah*
I shall never °rivaye   ne °ratches °uncouple,   *hunt/hounds/ unleash*
4000 At rọe ne °rein-dēre   that runnes upon erthe,   *reindeer*
Never greyhound let glīde,   ne °gossehawk let fly   *goshawk*
Ne never fowl see felled   that °flighes with wing,   *flies*
°Faucon ne °formēl   upon fist handle   *falcon/female hawk*
Ne yet with °gerefaucon   rejoice mē in erthe,   *gerfalcon*
Ne regne in my royaltees,   ne họld my Round Tāble,
Til thy dęde, my dęre,   bē dūly rēvenged!"

But ever droop and °dare   whiles my life lastes,   *lie still*
Til °Drighten and derf dede   have dōne what them likes!"   *the Lord*

Then caught they up the corse   with care at their hertes,
4010 Carried it on a courser   with the king selven;
The way untō Winchester   they went at the gainest,
Wēry and °wandsomly   with wounded knightes;   *sorrowfully*
There come the prīor of the plāce   and professed monkes,
°A-pās in processīon,   and with the prince meetes,   *quickly*
And °hē °betook them the corse   of the knight noble: *entrusted to*
"Lookes it bē clenly keeped," hē said,   "and in the °kirk   *church*
                                            holden;
†Dōn for him diriges,   as tō the dede falles,
Mensked with masses   for °meed of the soul;   *reward*
°Look it °want no °wax,   ne no worship elles,   *see that/lack/*
                                                                     candles
4020 And that the body bē °baumed   and on °bēre holden;   *embalmed/bier*
†Yif thou keep thy covent,   encroch any worship
At my coming again,   yif Crīst will it °thōle;   *allow*
°Abīde of the burying   til they bē brought under   *wait for*
That has wrought us this wo   and this war mōved."

Then says Sir Wichere the wye,   a wīse man of armes:
"I rede yē warily wend   and workes the best,
Sujourn in this citee   and semble thy bernes,
And bīde with thy bold men   in the burgh rich;
†Get out knightes of countrees   that castels holdes,
4030 And out of garrisons grete   good men of armes,
For wē are faithly too few   tō fight with them all
That wē °see in his sorte   upon the se bankes."   *saw*

With crūel countenaunce then   the king carpes thēse
                                            wordes:
"I pray thee care not, sir knight,   ne °cast thou no drēdes!   *imagine*
Had I no segge but myself   one under sun,
And I may him see with sight   or on him set handes,
I shall ēven among his men   °malle him tō dede,   *hammer*
Ēre I of the °stede stir   half a steed lenghe!   *place*
I shall strīke him in his stour   and stroy him forever,
4040 And there-tō māke I mīne avow   °devōtly tō Crīst   *devoutly*

4017 Do dirges for him, as befits the dead.
4021 If you keep your part of the bargain (i.e., bury him honorably),
   claim any reward.
4029 Get knights who hold your castles from their countries.

And tō his mōder Mary,   the mīld Queen of hęven!
I shall never sujourn sound,   ne °saught at mīne herte,.   *have peace*
In citee ne in suburb   set upon erthe,
Ne yet °slomour ne sleep   with my slǫw eyen,   *slumber*
†Til hē bē slain that him slogh,   if any sleight happen,
But ever °persew the pāganes   that my pople destroyed   *pursue*
Whīles I may °pare them and °pinne   in plāce there mē   *hurt/imprison*
                  līkes."

     There durst nǫ renk him °arrest   of all the Round Tāble,   *stop*
Ne nǫne °pay that prince   with °plęsand wordes,   *please/pleasing*
4050 Ne nǫne of his lēge-men   look him in the eyen,
Sǫ lǫrdly hē lookes   for loss of his knightes!
Then drawes hē tō Dorset   and dreches nǫ lenger,
°Derf-ful, °drēdless,   with droopand tęres,   *sorrowful/ doubtless*
Kaires intō Cornwall   with care at his herte;
The trāce of the traitour   hē °trīnes full ēven,   *follows*
And turnes in by the °Trentis   the traitour tō seek,   *River Trent*
Fīndes him in a forest   the Frīday there-after;
The king lightes on foot   and freshly ascrīes,
And with his freelich folk   hē has the fēld °nomen!   *taken*

4060   Now °isshewes his enmy   under the wood ēves   *issues out*
With hǫstes of ālīenes   full horrible tō shew!
Sir Mordred the °Malbranche,   with his much pople,   *i.e., ill-begotten*
Foundes out of the forest   upon fęle halves,
In seven gręte batailes   seemlich arrayed,
Sixty thousand men   —the sight was full hūge—
All fightand folk   of the fer landes,
Fair °fitted on front   by thǫ fresh strandes.   *arranged*
And all Arthurs hǫst   was °āmed with knightes   *reckoned by*
But eighteen hundreth of all,   enterd in rolles.
4070 This was a match °un-męte,   °but mightes of Crīst,   *unequal/save for*
Tō °melle with that multitūde   in thǫse main landes.   *fight*

     Then the royal roy   of the Round Tāble
Rīdes on a rich steed,   arrayes his bernes,
Buskes his avauntward,   als him best līkes;
Sir Ēwain and Sir Errak,   and other gręte lǫrdes
°Demęnes the middle-ward   menskfully there-after,   *command*
With Merrak and Menedūke,   mighty of strenghes;

4045 Until he be slain who slew him (Gawain), if any chance should
     appear.

Īdrous and Alymer,   thir avenaunt children,
Ayers with Arthur   with seven-score of knightes;
4080 Hē rewles the rereward   redyly there-after,
The °rekenest redy men   of the Round Tāble;   *most active*
And thus hē fittes his folk   and freshly ascrīes,
And sēnn comfortes his men   with knightlich wordes:
"I beseek you, sirs,   for sāke of our Lord,
That yē dō well tōday   and drēdes no wēpen!
Fightes fērsly now   and °fendes yourselven,   *defend*
Felles down yon fey folk,   the fēld shall be ours!
They are Sarazenes, yon sorte,   unsound °mot they worthe!   *may they be*
Set on them sadly,   for sāke of our Lord!
4090 Yif us bē °destained tō dīe   tōday on this erthe,   *destined*
Wē shall bē °heved unto heven   ere wē bē half cold!   *lifted*
Look yē let for no lēde   lordly tō work;
Layes yon laddes low   by the °laike end;   *end of the game*
°Tāke no tent untō mē,   ne tāle of mē °recke;   *pay no attention/believe*
†Bēs busy on my banners   with your bright wēpens,
That they bē °strenghely °stuffed   with steren knightes   *strongly/provided*
And holden lordly on-loft   lēdes tō shew;
Yif any renk them °arāse,   rescūe them soon;   *take them away*
Workes now my worship;   tōday my war endes!
4100 Yē wot my wele and my wo;   workes as you līkes!
Crīst comly with crown   comfort you all
For the kīndest crēatūres   that ever king led!
I give you all my blessing   with a blīthe will,
And all Bretons bold,   blīthe °mot yē worthe!"   *may you be*

    They pīpe up at °prīme tīme,   °approches them °ner,   *9 a.m./ approach/nearer*
Prīs men and °preste   prōves their strenghes;   *ready*
†Brēmly the brethe-men   brāgges in trumpes,
In °coronettes comlyly,   when knightes assembles;   *horns*
And then jollyly °enjoines   thēse gentle knightes;   *join battle*
4110 A jollīer journee   ajudged was never,
When Bretones boldly   °enbrāces their shēldes,   *put on (their arms)*
And °Cristen °encrossed them   and castes in fewter!   *Christians/ crossed themselves*

    Then Sir Arthur host   his enmy °escrīes,   *sees*
And in they °shock their shēldes,   shuntes no lenger,   *thrust*

4095 Be busy with your bright weapons around my banners. [The
banners must be defended not only for the sake of honor but because
signals made with the banners are the only means of communication
during a battle.]
4107 Boldly the buglers (breath-men) blow on trumpets.

Shot tō the sheltrones   and shoutes full high;
Through shēldes full sheen   shalkes they touch!
Rędily thǫse °rydde men   of the Round Tāble   *fierce*
With rēal rank steel   °rittes their mailes;   *rip*
Brenyes °brǫuden they brist   and burnisht helmes,   *woven*
4120 Hewes hęthen men down,   °halses in sonder!   *necks*
Fightand with fīne steel   the fey blood rinnes;
Of the frekkest on front   °un-fērs are belęved.   *unfierce (i.e.,*
                                                                 defeated)
Hęthenes of Argyle   and Īrish kinges
°Enverounes our avauntward   with venomous bernes,   *surround*
°Peghtes and paynimes   with perilous wēpens,   *Picts*
With spęres °dispitously   despoiles our knightes   *pitilessly*
And hewed down the hendest   with °hertly dintes!   *mortal*
Through the hǫle batail   they hǫlden their wayes;
Thus fērsly they fight   upon fęle halves,
4130 That of the bǫld Bretons   much blood spilles;
There °durst none rescūe them   for riches in erthe,   *dared*
†The steren were there sǫ stedde   and stuffed with other;
°Hē durst nǫt stir a step,   but stood for himselven,   *i.e., Arthur*
Til three stales were stroyed   by strenghe of him ǫne!

    "Īdrous," quǫd Arthur,   "ayer thee behooves!
I see Sir Ēwain ǫver-set   with Sarazenes keen!
Rędy thee for rescūes,   array thee soon!
Hīe thee with hardy men   in help of thy fader!
Set in on the sīde   and succour yon lǫrdes!
4140 But they be succoured and °sound,   °unsaught bē I ever!" *safe/troubled*

    Īdrous him answers   ęrnestly there-after:
"Hē is my fader, in faith,   forsāke shall I never—
Hē has mē fostered and fed   and my fair brethern—
But I forsāke this °gāte,   sǫ mē God help,   *going (to his aid)*
And soothly all °sibrēden   but thyself ǫne.   *kinship*
I brǫke never his °bidding   for berne on līfe,   *command*
But ever °buxom as bęste   blīthely tō work.   *(was) obedient*
                                                                 as a beast
Hē commaund mē kindly   with knightly wordes,
That I sholde lēly on thee lenge,   and on nǫ lēde elles;
4150 I shall his commaundment hǫld,   if Crīst will mē °thōle! *allow*
Hē is elder that I,   and end shall wē bǫthen;
Hē shall ferk before,   and I shall come after;
Yif him bē °destained tō dīe   tōday on this erthe,   *destined*
Crīst, comly with crown,   tāke keep tō his sǫul!"

4132 The stern men were so beset and hard-pressed by others.

Then °rōmes the rich king   with rewth at his herte,   *cries*
°Hęves his handes on height   and tō the Hęven lookes: *lifts*
†"Why then ne had Drighten   destained at His dęre will
That Hē had deemed mē tōday   tō dīe for you all?
That had I lēver than bē lǫrd   all my līfe-tīme
4160 Of all that Alexander ǫught   whīles hē in erthe lenged!"

Sir Ēwain and Sir Errak,   thēse excellent bernes,
Enters in on the hǫst   and ęgerly strīkes;
The hęthenes of Orkney   and Īrish kinges
°They °gobone of the grętest   with grounden swordes,   *i.e., Ewain and*
                                                                    Errak/chop
Hewes on thǫse hulkes   with their hard wēpens,
°Layed down thǫse lēdes   with lǫthly dintes;   *laid*
Shoulders and shēldes   they shręde tō the haunches,
And middles through mailes   they °merken in sonder!   *cut*
Such honour never ǫught   nǫne erthly kinges
4170 At their ending day   but Arthur himselven!

Sǫ the drought of the day   dryed their hertes
That bǫth drinkless they dīe;   dole was the mǫre!
Now °melles our middle-ward   and °mengen tōgeder.   *attacks/mingles*
Sir Mordred the °Malbranche   with his °much pople,   *ill-begotten/*
                                                                    great army
Hē had hid him behīnd   within thēse holt ēves,
With hǫle batail on °hęthe,   harm is the mǫre!   *heath*
Hē had seen the °contek   all clęne tō the end,   *conflict*
How our chevalry °chēved   by chaunces of armes;   *fared*
Hē wiste our folk was °for-fǫughten   that there was fey   *outfought*
                                       lęved;
4180 Tō encounter the king   hē °castes him soon,   *plans*
†But the churlish chicken   had chānged his armes;
†Hē had soothly forsāken   the sauturour engrēled,
And laght up three līons   all of whīte silver,
Passand in purpure   of perry full rich,
For the king sholde nǫt knǫw   the °cautelous wretch.   *cunning*
†Because of his cowardice   hē cast off his attīre;

4157-58 Why did the Lord not destine (me to die) at His dear will? (I
    wish) that He had ordered me today to die for you all.
4181 [Mordred adopts the cowardly strategem of changing his heraldic
    devices, which Arthur would never do (see note on l. 3650).]
4182-84 Truly, he had forsaken the saltire (two bands forming an "X")
    engrailed (with wavy edges) and taken up three lions all of white
    silver, passant (shown from the side, walking) on a purple back-
    ground of very rich jewels.
4186 [*Attīre*: his customary heraldic device, which is worn on the cloth
    garment (*gipon*) that goes over the armor as well as on the shield.]

But the comlich king   knew him full swīthe,
Carpes tō Sir Cador   thēse kīndly wordes:
"I see the traitour come yonder   °trīnand full yerne;   *going*
4190 Yon lad with the līons   is līke tō himselven;
Him shall torfer betīde,   °may I touch ones,   *if I can*
For all his tresoun and °trayn,   als I am trew lord!   *trickery*
Tōday Clarent and °Caliburn   shall °kīthe them tōgeders   *Excalibur/*
                                                             make known
°Whilk is keener of °carfe   or harder of edge!   *which/carving*
Fraist shall wē fīne steel   upon fīne weedes.
°It was my darling °daintēous   and full dere holden,   *the sword*
                                                              Clarent/dainty
Keeped for °encrownmentes   of kinges annointed;   *coronations*
On dayes when I dubbed   dūkes and erles
It was burlich borne   by the bright hiltes;
4200 I durst never °dere it   in deedes of armes   *harm*
But ever keeped clene   because of myselven.
For I see Clarent °uncledde   that crown is of swordes,   *i.e., drawn*
My °wardrope at Walingford   I wot is destroyed.   *wardrobe*
°Wiste no wye of °wonne   but Waynor herselven;   *knew/the*
                                                            dwelling place
Shō had the keeping herself   of that kidd wēpen,
Of coffers enclosed   that tō the crown longed,
With ringes and relickes   and the °rēgālē of Fraunce   *regalia*
†That was founden on Sir Frolle   when he was fey leved."

      Then Sir Marrak in °malencoly   meetes °him soon,   *melancholy/*
                                                            Mordred
4210 With a °malled māce   mightyly him strīkes;   *hammered*
The °bordour of his °bacenett   hē bristes in sonder,   *border/helmet*
That the shīre red blood   over his breny runnes!
The berne °blenkes for bāle   and all his °blee changes,   *blanches/*
                                                           complexion
But yet hē bīdes as a °bore   and °brēmly hē strīkes!   *boar/fiercely*
°Hē braides out a brand   bright als ever any silver   *Mordred*
That was Sir Arthur owen,   and Utere his faders,
In the °wardrope at Walingford   was wont tō bē keeped;   *wardrobe*
Therewith the derf dog   such dintes hē reched
The °tother withdrew °on dregh   and durst dō none other   *other/back*
                                                            i.e., weakened
                                                            by age
4220 For Sir Marrak was man   °marred in elde,
And Sir Mordred was mighty   and in his most strenghes;
Come none within the compass,   knight ne none other,
Within the swing of sword,   that hē ne the °swet leved.   *lifeblood*

      That perceives our prince   and presses °tō fast,   *i.e., to battle*
Strīkes intō the stour   by strenghe of his handes,

4208 [Frollo: see note on l. 3345.]

Meetes with Sir Mordred;   hē mẹles unfair:
"Turn, traitour untrew,   thee tīdes nọ better;
By grẹte God, thou shall dīe   with dint of my handes!
Thee shall rescūe no renk   ne riches in erthe!"

4230   The king with Caliburn   knightly him strīkes;
The °cantel of his clēre shēld   hē carves in sonder,   *cornerpiece*
Intō the shoulder of the shalk   °a shaftmonde large   *six inches deep*
That the shīre rẹd blood   shewed on the mailes!
Hē shuddered and shrinkes   and shuntes but little,
But shockes in sharply   in his sheen weedes;
The felon with the fīne sword   freshly hē strīkes,
The °felettes of the °ferrer sīde   hē flashes in sonder,   *rib plates/farther*
Through °jupon and °gesseraunt   of gentle mailes,   *gipon (tunic)/ hawberk*
The frēke °fiched in the flesh   an half-foot large;   *pierced*
4240 That derf dint was his dẹde,   and dole was the mọre
That ever that doughty sholde dīe   but at Drightens will!

    Yet with Caliburn his sword   full knightly hē strīkes,
Castes in his clēre shēld   and coveres him full fair,
Swappes off the sword hand,   als hē by °glentes—   *goes*
An inch frọ the elbọw   hē °oched it in sonder   *chopped*
That hē swoones on the swarth   and on °swim falles—   *swoon*
Through °brācer of brown steel   and the bright mailes,   *armguard*
That the hilt and the hand   upon the hẹthe ligges.

    Then freshlich °the frēke   the °fente °up-rẹres,   *Arthur/vent/ raises*
4250 Brọches him in with the brand   tō the bright hiltes,
And hē °brawles on the brand   and bounes for tō dīe.   *struggles*
†"In faye," said the fey king,   "sọre mē for-thinkes
That ever such a false °thēf   sọ fair an end haves."   *thief*

    When they had finisht this fight,   then was the fēld
                        wonnen,
And the false folk in the fēld   fey are belẹved!
Til a forest they fled   and fell in the grēves,
And fērs fightand folk   followes them after,
Huntes and hewes down   the hẹthen °tīkes,   *dogs*
°Murtheres in the mountaines   Sir Mordred knightes;   *murder*
4260 There °chāped never nọ chīld,   chēftain ne other,   *escaped*
But choppes them down in the chāse;   it °charges but little!   *troubles*

    4252 "In faith," said the fated (to die) king, "I sorely repent."

But when Sir Arthur anon   Sir Ēwain hē findes,
And Errak the avenaunt   and other gręte lordes,
Hē caught up Sir Cador   with care at his herte,
Sir Clēgis, Sir Clēremond,   thēse clēre men of armes,
Sir Lot and Sir Līonel,   Sir Launcelot and Lowes,
Marrak and Menedūke,   that mighty were ever;
With langour in the land   there hē layes them tōgeder,
Looked on their °lighames,   and with a loud °steven,   *bodies/voice*
4270 †Als lēde that list nǫt live   and lost had his mirthes—
Then hē °stotays for °mad   and all his strenghe failes,   *staggers/dizziness*
Lookes up tō the °lift   and all his °līre chānges,   *sky/face*
Down hē sways full swīthe,   and in a swoon falles,
Up hē coveres on knees   and crīes full often—
"King, comly with crown,   in care am I lęved!
All my lǫrdship lǫw   in land is laid under,
†That mē has given guerdones,   by grāce of Himselven,
Maintained my °manhēd   by might of their handes,   *manhood*
Māde mē manly on molde   and māster in erthe,
4280 In a °teenful tīme   this torfer was °ręred,   *sad/raised*
That for a traitour has tint   all my trew lǫrdes!
Hēre restes the rich blood   of the Round Tāble,
Rebūked with a °rebaud,   and rewth is the mǫre!   *scoundrel*
I may helpless on hęthe   house by mīne ǫne,
Als a wǫful widow   that wantes her berne!
I may °wērye and weep   and wring mīne handes,   *curse*
For my wit and my worship   away is forever!
Of all lǫrdshippes I tāke   lęve tō mīne end!
Hēre is the Bretones blood   brǫught out of līfe,
4290 And now in this journee   all my joy endes!"

Then °relīes the renks of the   Round Tāble;   *rally*
To the rēal roy   they rīde them all;
Then assembles full soon   seven scǫre knightes
In sight tō their soveraign   that was unsound lęved;
Then kneeles the crowned king   and crīes on loud:
"I thank thee, God, of thy grāce,   with a good will,
That gāve us vertūe and wit   tō venquish these bernes,
And us has graunted the gree   of thēse gręte lǫrdes!
Hē sent us never nǫ shāme   ne °shenship in erthe   *disgrace*

4270 Like a man that had no desire to live.
4277-78 Those who have given me rewards, earned by the help of God,
    maintained my manhood (honor) by the might of their hands. [Com-
    pare Arthur's words in lines 399–402.]

4300 But ever yet the °ǫver-hand   of all other kinges;   *i.e., upper hand*
      Wē have nǫ °leisere now   thēse lǫrdes tō seek,   *leisure*
      For yon lǫthly lad   mē lāmed sǫ sǫre!
      †Graith us tō Glashenbury;   us gaines nǫne other;
      There wē may rest us with °roo   and °ransack our woundes.   *peace/search (treat)*
      Of this dęre dayes work   the Drighten bē °lowed,   *praised*
      That us has destained and deemed   tō dīe in our °ǫwen."   *i.e., own land*

         Then they hǫld at his °hest   hǫlly at ǫnes,   *command*
      And graithes tō °Glashenbury   the °gāte at the gainest;   *Glastonbury/ way*
      Entres the °Īle of Avalon   and Arthur hē lightes,   *Isle*
4310 Merkes tō a manor there,   for °might hē nǫ further;   *could go*
      †A °surgen of Salerne   °ensęrches his woundes;   *surgeon/treats*
      The king sees by °assay   that sound °bēs hē never,   *examination/will be*
      And soon tō his sēker men   hē said thēse wordes:
      "Dō call mē a confessor   with °Crīst in his armes;   *i.e., the Eucharist*
      I will bē °houseld in hāste   what hap sǫ betīdes.   *given the Sacrament*
      Constantīne my cosin   hē shall the crown bęre,
      Als becomes him of kīnd,   if Crīst will him thōle!
      Berne, for my °benison,   thou bury yon lǫrdes   *blessing*
      That in batail with brandes   are brǫught out of līfe,
4320 And sithen merk manly   tō Mordred children,
      That they be °slēly slain   and °slongen in waters;   *wisely/slung*
      Let nǫ wicked weed °wax   ne °wrīthe on this erthe;   *grow/flourish*
      I warn, for thy worship,   work als I bid!
      I forgive all grēf,   for Crīstes love of hęven!
      If Waynor have well wrǫught,   well her betīde!"

         †Hē said "*In manus*" with main   on molde where hē ligges,
      And thus passes his spirit   and spękes hē nǫ mǫre!

         The baronāge of Bretain then,   bishoppes and other,
      Graithes them tō Glashenbury   with °glōpinand hertes   *dismayed*
4330 Tō bury there the bǫld king   and bring tō the erthe
      With all worship and węlth   that any wye °sholde.   *should have*
      †Thrǫly belles they ring   and *Requiem* singes,
      °Dōs masses and matins   with mōrnand nǫtes;   *do*
      °Religīous °reveste   in their rich cǫpes,   *monastics/ dressed*

      ⁴³⁰³ Let us go to Glastonbury (where Arthur is said to be buried);
            nothing else avails.
      ⁴³¹¹ [*Salerne:* Salerno. See note on l. 2586.]
      ⁴³²⁶ [*In manus:* Into your hands (O Lord, I commend my soul).]
      ⁴³³² [*Requiem:* Office for the dead.]

°Pontificalles and prēlātes   in precīous weedes,   *bishops*
Dūkes and douspeeres   in their °dole-cǫtes,   *mourning*
                                                                       garments
Countesses kneeland   and claspand their handes,
Lādīes languishand   and °lowrand tō shew;   *frowning*
All was busked in black,   birdes and other,
4340 That shewed at the °sepultūre   with °syland tęres;   *sepulcher/*
                                                                       flowing
Was never sǫ sǫrrowful a sight   seen in their tīme!

      Thus endes King Arthur,   as °auctors allege,   *written*
                                                                       authorities tell
That was of °Ectores kin,   the kinge son of Troy   *Hector's*
And of Sir °Prīamous, the prince,   praised in erthe;   *Priam*
Frǫ °thethen brǫught the Bretons   all his bǫld elders   *thence (i.e.,*
                                                                       Troy)
†Intō Bretain the brǫde,   as the Brūt telles.

        ††Hic jacet Arthurus, rex quondam rexque futurus.
          (*Here lies Arthur, king once and king to be.*)
    Here endes Morte Arthure, written by Robert of Thornton
    R. Thornton dictus qui scripsit sit benedictus. Amen.
          (*May the said R. Thornton, who wrote this, be blessed. Amen.*)

4346 [*Brūt*: The History of Britain (which begins with Brutus, who
    settled the country). "Brūt" refers to any history of Britain, though
    the poet may have meant some specific work, such as the popular
    English prose *Brut*.]

---

    †† This and the following lines are not by the original author of our
    poem. This line, which is the inscription on Arthur's tomb (dating from
    1278), was added by a later reader of the manuscript. The next lines
    concern the scribe rather than the author of the poem. Robert Thornton,
    who lived in Yorkshire, around 1440, wrote out the manuscript that
    contains this and a number of other romances. The final Latin line, ask-
    ing that Robert be blessed for his work, was written by a grateful reader
    in the later fifteenth century.

Glossary of Common Words

This glossary contains only those words that appear at least five times in either poem and that differ in form, meaning, or usage from Modern English. A few words that differ only slightly and obviously in spelling have been omitted: words ending in -*our* where Modern English has -*or* (such as *confessour*), words ending in -*oun* where Modern English has -*on* (such as *prisoun*), words ending in -*ee* where Modern English has -*y* (such as *citee*), and words with *aun* where Modern English has *an* (such as *commaund, auncestry,* or *gīaunt*). Present participles (such as *flāmand*) are omitted, and ordinarily variant uses of final -*e* are not noted. Entries are brief, and the glossary is intended primarily as a check-list of some of the most common Middle English words, a knowledge of which will make the study of more advanced texts a good deal easier. Etymologies are included simply for the general information of readers with some interest in the history of the language. Etymologies are not provided for the few common place-names included. The following abbreviations are used: O.E., Old English; O.F., Old French; O.N., Old Norse.

A

Afrīke   Africa.

again, againes   against (O.E. *on-gēan*).

Almaine   Germany.

als, alsǫ, as   as; often an intensifier, as in *alsǫ swīthe, as swīthe* (O.E. *alswā*).

and, and yif   if (O.E. *and, gif*).

anǫn   immediately (O.E. *on* + *ane*, in one).

array   *noun* and *verb*, order, arrange(ment) (O.F. *arrei*).

as   see *als* (above).

ascrīe   shout, cry (O.F. *escrie*).

at   from, at; to (when used with infinitive, as in *at close*, to enclose); that, what (as in *Hǫlde at thou hent has*, Keep what you have taken); only the first meaning ("from") is common in these texts (O.N. *at*, to; O.E. *æt*, from, at).

239

aunter   *noun* and *verb*, chance, fortune, adventure (O.F. *aventure*).
austeren   bold, stern (O.F. *austere*).
avauntward   forward guard (O.F. *avantward*).
avenaunt   seemly, noble (O.F. *avenant*, suitable).
avow   *noun* and *verb*, vow (O.F. *avoer*).
ay   ever, always (O.N. *ey*, O.E. *ā*).
ayer   go (O.F. *errer*, *oirrer*, to journey).

B

bachelor   young knight (as opposed to *banneret*, below) (O.F. *bacheler*, candidate for knighthood).
bāle   evil, pain, sorrow (O.E. *bealu*, sorrow, destruction).
banneret   senior knight, one entitled to his own banner (O.F., *baneret*, knight entitled to carry a banner).
batail   division of an army, battle (O.F. *bataile*).
bēde   offer, proclaim (O.E. *bēodan*, bid, announce).
belęve, *past* belęved, beleft   leave behind, remain behind (O.E. *belǣfan*, remain, relinquish).
bēn   *infinitive*, to be; *past participle*, been; *present plural indicative*, are (O.E. *bēon*).
bente   field, ground (O.E. *beonet*, a sort of grass).
bęrde   beard (O.E. *beard*).
bęre   bear, carry (O.E. *beran*).
berne   man (O.E. *beorn*, warrior).
bęte   beat (O.E. *bētan*).
bīde   abide, remain (O.E. *bīdan*).
bird(e)   maiden (O.E. *brȳd*, betrothed or newly married woman).
blinn(e)   cease, stop (O.E. *blinnan*).
blonk   horse (O.E. *blanca*, [white?] horse).
bōrde   board, table; *on bōrde*, aboard ship (O.E. *bord*, board).
bǫre   wild boar (O.E. *bār*).
bǫte   boat (O.E. *bāt*).
boun   *verb*: prepare, go; *adjective*, ready, prepared (O.N. *búinn*, ready).
bowr   bedroom, bower (O.E. *būr*).
boy   knave, servant, a low-born person (origin uncertain).
braid   hasten, go, draw out (as a sword) (O.E. *bregdan*).
brand   sword (O.E. *brand*).
braste   broke, burst (*past* of *brist*, below).
bręde   bread; roast, baked meat (O.E. *brēad*).
brēme   fierce, wild (O.E. *brēme*, valiant).
bren(ne), *past* brent   burn; this is the form preferred by the stanzaic poet; see *brin(ne)*, below.
breny   hauberk, mail corslet (O.E. *byrne*).
brēste   breast (O.E. *brēost*).
brēthe   anger (O.N. *brǣðe*).
brin(ne), *past* brint   burn; the form preferred by the alliterative poet; see *bren(ne)*, above (O.N. *brinnen*, O.E. *bærnan*).

brist, *past* braste   break, burst (O.E. *berstan*).
britten   beat down (O.N. *brytja*, break up).
brǫche   pierce, stab, spit (O.F. *broche*).
brǫde   broad (O.E. *brad*).
brōder, *plural:* brethern   brother (O.E. *brōder*).
brǫthely   fiercely, boldly (O.N. *bráðligr*, violent).
brown   shining, brown (O.E. *brūn*, brown, shining).
burgh   town, fortress (O.E. *burh*, fortified place).
burlich, burly   stately, strong (? O.E. **bur-lic*, fit for the bower, i.e., the
    court?).
busk   go, hasten, prepare; often reflexive, as in *him buskes* (O.N. *búask*, get
    ready).
bustous   wild, strong (? O.F. *boisteus*, rude, lame).
but, but yif   unless, except, save for (O.E. *būton*).
by   by the time that, by (O.E. *bī*).
bydēne   together, as well; *all bydēne*, at once, immediately (? origin un-
    known).

C

capitain   captain (O.F. *capitain*).
carp   speak, say (O.N. *karpa*).
castel   castle (O.F. *castel*).
certes   certainly (O.F. *certes*).
charge   load, burden (O.F. *chargier*).
cheer   countenance, expression (O.F. *chère*, face).
chēf   chief (O.F. *chef*).
chēftain   chieftain (O.F. *chevetain*).
chēse; *past:* chęse, chǫse   choose, go; often reflexive, as in *chēse him the*
    wayes (O.E. *cēosan*).
chevalry   chivalry (O.F. *chevalerie*).
chēve   achieve, attain, arrive at (O.F. *chevir*, succeed).
chīld, *plural:* chīlder   young man, child (O.E. *cild*, child).
cledde   clad (*past participle* of *clǫthe*).
clęne   *adjective:* clean, bright, pure; *adverb:* completely (O.E. *clǣne*).
clęnlich, clęnly   cleanly, completely (O.E. *clǣne + līch*).
clēpes   calls, summons (O.E. *clēopian*).
clēre   *adjective:* bright, clean, pure; *adverb:* completely (O.F. *cler*).
clēve   cut, cleave (O.E. *clēofian*).
cog(ge)   ship (O.N. *kuggr*, Middle Low German, *kogge*).
comlich, comly   comely (O.E. *cȳmlīc*).
coronal   diadem, the circular ornament on a helmet (Latin *coronalis*, dia-
    dem).
corse   body (O.F. *cors*).
cosin   relative; *cosin of kind*, blood-relative (O.F. *cosīn*).
cǫste   coast (O.F. *coste*).
coude   could, knew how, variant of *couthe*, below.
courtais   courteous (O.F. *courtois*).

courtaisy courtesy (O.F. *courtesie*).

couthe could, knew how (O.E. *cūðe*, preterite of *cunnan*, know how).

cover attain, recover, take; *cover up*, get up on, as in *cover up on knees* (O.F. [*re*]*covrer*, regain).

covered armored, as in *covered steedes* (O.F. *covrir*, cover).

cūrīous skillfully made (O.F. *curious*, made with care).

D

dẹde *adjective*: dead; *noun*, death (O.E. *dēad*).

dẹle, *past*: delt deal out, give (O.E. *dǣlan*, divide, separate).

dẹre costly, dear (O.E. *dēore*).

dẹre harm, injure (O.E. *derian*).

derf strong, dire (O.E. *dearf*, firm, valiant).

destayn destine (O.F. *destiner*).

dẹth(e) death (O.E. *dēaþ*).

devīse divide (O.F. *deviser*, divide, give).

dight, past: dight prepare, place, adorn (O.E. *dihtan,* prepare).

dō, *past:* did, *infinitive:* dōn cause, order (O.E. *dōn*).

douspeer high nobleman; originally one of Charlemagne's twelve peers (O.F. *duzpers*).

doute fear, doubt (O.F. *douter*).

drayn drawn, dragged (O.E. *dragan*, draw, carry).

dreche delay, wait (O.E. *dreccan*).

drēde, *past:* dredde dread, fear; as *noun,* dread, doubt (O. E. *ondrǣdan*).

drẹme dream (O.E. *drēam*, joy).

drĕrily drearily, sadly (O.E. *drēorig* + *līce*).

drēry dreary (O.E. *drēorig*).

drīe suffer, endure (O.E. *drēogan*, accomplish, suffer).

Drighten God (O.E. *drihten*, lord).

drīve go (O.E. *drīfan*, drive, go).

drow drew, dragged (past of *drayn*).

dūchery, *plural*: dūcheries duchy, dukedom (O.F. *duché*).

durste dare (O.E. *dorste*, dared).

E

ẹch each (O.E. *ǣghwilc, ǣlc*).

ẹchon each one, every (Middle English *ech* + *ọne*).

eek also (O.E. *ēac*).

ẹger eager (O.F. *aigre*, ardent).

ẹgle eagle (Lucius' Roman standard, adorned with an eagle) (O.F. *aigle*).

eier heir (O.F. *heir*).

elles else (O.E. *elles*, otherwise).

encrọche invade, encroach (O.F. *acrocher*, approach).

enmy, *plural*: enmies enemy (O.F. *enemis*).

erl earl (O.E. *eorl*).

ẹrly early (O.E. *ǣrlīce*).

erthe earth (O.E. *eorðe*).

eschēve   achieve, obtain, get to (O.F. *achever*, succeed, conclude).
ęste   east (O.E. *ēast*).
ēven   exactly, directly; even (O.E. *efen*).
ēves   edge of a wood; the eaves formed by its branches (O.E. *efese*, eaves).
eyen   eyes (O.E. *ēagen*).

F

fader   father; sir (O.E. *fader*).
fain   eager, glad; *he wolde full fain*, he eagerly desired (O.E. *fægen*, joyful).
fand(e)   found, *past* of find (O.E. *fand*, past singular of *findan*).
fēld   field (O.E. *feld*).
fęle   many (O.E. *fela*).
fell   fierce (O.E. *fel*, cruel).
fēnd   fiend (O.E. *fēond*, enemy).
fer   far (O.E. *feorr*, distant).
fęrd   frightened, afeared (O.E. *fǣr*, danger).
fęre   fear (O.E. *fǣr*, danger).
fēre   companion; *in fēre*, together (O.E. *ȝefēra*).
ferk   go (O.E. *fercian*, carry, go).
ferly, ferlich   *noun*: wonder; *adverb*: wondrously (O.E. *fǣrlīc*, sudden).
ferrom   distance; *o ferron*, from afar (O.E. *feorran*, from afar).
fērs   fierce (O.F. *fiers*).
fērsly, fērslich   fiercely (O.F. *fiers* + *liche*).
fęste   feast (O.F. *feste*).
fewter   *noun*: the spear-rest on the saddle; *cast in fewter*, put the spear in the
   spear-rest, i.e., prepare for battle; *verb*: prepare for battle (O.F. *feutre*,
   spear-rest ?).
fey   dead, fated to die (O.E. *fǣge*, fated, dead).
firth   wood, forest (O.E. *fyr[h]ð*, wooded country).
flowr   flower (O.F. *fleur*).
fǫ   foe (O.E. *fāh*, hostile).
foine   duel, stab (? O.F. *foine*, a spear).
folde   earth, ground (O.E., *folde*, land).
fǫmen   foemen (O.E. *fāh*, hostile + *men*).
fǫnde   try, prove (O.E. *fandian*).
fonge   take, seize (O.E. *fangen*, *past participle* of *fōn*, grasp).
forjousted   outjousted (O.E. *for-*, an intensifier implying destruction or loss
   + O.F. *jouster*, joust).
forray   plunder (O.F. *forrer*).
forset   besiege, attack (O.E. *forsettan*, bar, impede).
for-thy   therefore (O.E. *for*, for + *þy*, instrumental of *sē*).
found(e)   go, advance (O.E. *fundian*, seek, go, try).
frain   ask (O.E. *fregnan*).
fraist   try, seek, prove (O.N. *freista*, ask, examine).
frap   company, troop (? O.F. *frape*, troop).
free   noble (O.E. *frēo*).
freelich, freely   *adjective*: noble; *adverb*: nobly (O.E. *frēo* + *līce*).

frek   bold (O.E. *frec*, insolent, daring).
frēke   man (O.E. *freca*, warrior).
freklich, frekly   boldly (O.E. *frec* + *līce*).
frēnd   friend; *plural* is often without ending: *frēnd*, friends (O.E. *frēond*).
frēndlich, frēndly   friendly (O.E. *frēond* + *līce*).
fresh   eager, strong (O.F. *frais*, eager).
freshliche, freskly   eagerly, strongly (*fresh*, above + *liche*).
frǫ   from (O.E. *fra*).
furth   ford, stream (O.N. *fjorðr*, fiord).

G

gab   tell lies, gossip (O.N. *gabba*, accuse).
gader   gather (O.E. *geador*, together).
gain, gainest   quick; *at the gainest*, by the quickest way (O.N. *gegn*, ready).
galīard   jolly, bold (O.F. *gaillard*).
gāme   pleasure, mirth (O.E. *gāmen*, pleasure).
gan, *plural:* gonne   did (often merely the sign of the past) (O.E. *ginnan*,
    onginnan, begin, endeavor).
gar, *past:* gart   cause, order (O.N. *ger[v]a*, make, do).
gesseraunt   hauberk, corslet (O.F. *gesseraunte*).
gird   go, go to; strike, attack (O.E. *gyrdan*).
give, gave   cause, in expressions such as *gave him ill*, made himself sick
    (O.E. *gifan*, give).
glōpin   be terrified, amazed (O.N. *glepja*, reflexive: *be confounded*).
gōme   man (O.E. *gūma*).
gonfanoun   banner (O.F. *gonfanon*, standard).
gonne   did (*plural* of *gan*, above).
graith   go, prepare (O.N. *greiða*, prepare).
graithelich, grathely   readily, vigorously (O.N. *greiðr*, prepared + O.E. *līce*).
gree   victory, prize (O.F. *gré*, degree).
grēf   grief (O.F. *grief*).
grēt, *past:* grette   weep (O.E. *grētan*).
grǫte   great (O.E. *grēat*).
grēve   woods, grove (O.E. *græfe*).
grēve   grieve (O.F. *grēver*).
grǫn   groan (O.E. *grānian*).
guīe, *past:* guīed, guīde   guide (O.F. *guier*).

H

half   side, half (O.E. *healf*, side).
harageous   bold, violent (O.F. *aragier*, to become enraged).
harlot   rascal, scoundrel (usually male) (O.F. *herlot*).
hathel   noble, bold (O.E. *æþel*, noble; O.E. *hæleþ*, warrior).
hautain   *adjective:* proud; *noun:* pride (O.F. *hautain*).
hęd   head (O.E. *heafod*).
hęle   heal (O.E. *hǣlan*).
hęle   hide, conceal (O.E. *helan*).

hende   courteous, skillfull, handy (O.E. *hende*, convenient, near).
hendely   courteously, skillfully (O.E. *hende* + *līce*).
hent(e)   seized, took (*past* of O.E. *hendan*, to seize).
heraud   herald (O.F. *heraud*).
herberāge   lodging (O.F. *herbergāge*).
hēre, *past*: herde   hear (O.E. *hīeran*).
herken   hearken, listen (O.E. *heorcnian*, listen).
herte   heart (O.E. *heorte*).
hertily, hertilich   heartily; mortally; cheerfully (O.E. *herote* + *līce*).
hest   command; promise (O.E. *hæs*, command).
hēte, *past*: hette   command, promise (O.E. *hātan*, command).
hęthe   ground, heath (O.E. *hǣþ*).
hęve   heave, lift up (O.E. *hebban*).
hęved   head (O.E. *heofod*).
hęven   heaven (O.E. *hēofan*).
hew   hue, color (O.E. *hīw*).
hider   hither (O.E. *hider, hiðer*).
hīe   hasten; *on hīe*, hastily (O.E. *hīgian*, hurry).
hīely   quickly (*hīe*, above + *-liche*).
hight   called, promised (O.E. *heht*, past of *hatan*, command, call).
hight   height; *on hight*, on high (O.E. *hīehþu*).
hǫld, *past*: hēld, *past participle*: hǫlden   consider, regard (O.E. *healdan*, hold).
hole   whole, sound (O.E. *hāl*).
hǫllich, hǫlly   wholly (O.E. *hāl* + *līce*).
holt   wood, forest (O.E. *holt*).
hǫpe   suppose, expect (O.E. *hopian*, expect, trust).
hōve   wait, remain, stand (Derivation unknown; may be connected with *hęve*).
hundreth   hundred (O.E. *hundreð*).

I

īch, īch a   each, every; *variant* of *ech*, above.
īchon   each one, every; *variant* of *echon*, above.
ilk(e), ilkon   each, every; same (O.E. *ilca*, the same).
īrous   angry, irate (O.F. *irus*, angry).
īvel   evil (O.E. *yfel*, wicked).
īwis   certainly (O.E. *gewiss*, certain, sure).

J

jāg   pierce, stab (derivation unknown).
join   attack; often with *on*, as in *joines on* (O.F. *joindre*, join).
journee   day's work, day's fight, journey (O.F. *journee*, a day).

K

kaire   go (O.N. *keyra*).
keep   watch, heed, wait (O.E. *cēpan*, keep).

kidd   famous, well known (*variant* of past of *cȳðan,* below).
kith   native land (O.E. *cȳðu,* acquaintance, knowledge).
kīthe   make known, declare (O.E. *cȳðan*).
knǫw, *past*: knew   acknowledge, recognize (O.E. *cnāwan,* know).

L

laght   seized, took (O.E. *lǣht,* past of *lǣccan,* to seize).
laine   conceal, hide (O.N. *løyna,* conceal, O.E. *lignan,* deny).
large   distance; in expressions of measurement, such as *six inches large* or *a shaftmonde large,* the word is an intensifier meaning "deep," "long," "away," or whatever is appropriate to the measurement; in expressions such as *at my large,* meaning "freely," the word means "freedom" or "freedom from control of oneself or his possessions," as in Modern English *at large* (O.F. *large,* abundant, ample).
lāte   expression, countenance (O.N. *lāt,* face, O.E. *lǣte,* manner).
lēche   *noun*: physician; *verb*: to give medical attention (O.E. *lǣce,* physician).
lęde   lead (O.E. *lǣdan*).
lēde   man; prince (rarely); nation (rarely) (O.E. *lēod*).
lęęs   lies, falsehood (O.E. *lēas,* falsehood).
lēf   dear, good; *as him lēf thinkes,* as seems good to him (O.E. *lēof*).
lēge-men   liege-men (O.F. *liege* + O.E. *man*).
lēle   loyal (O.F. *leal*).
lēly   loyally (O.F. *leal* + O.E. *liche*).
lēman   sweetheart, lover (O.E. *leof* + *man*).
lende, *past*: lente   stay, remain; grant, give (O.E. *lendan,* to endow).
lęne   lean (O.E. *lǣne,* frail).
lenge   stay, remain (O.E. *lengan,* delay).
lenger   longer (O.E. *leng,* long + *-er*).
lenghe   length (O.E. *lengð*).
lępe   leap (O.E. *hleapan*).
let   *verb*: hinder, prevent, delay; *noun*: hindrance, delay (O.E. *lettan*).
lęve, *past*: lęved, left   leave (O.E. *lǣfan*).
lēve   dear (O.E. *lēof*).
lēver   rather; *him were lēver,* he would rather (*comparative* of *lēve,* above).
ligges   lies, reclines (O.E. *licgan*).
līke   please; as impersonal verb, *him līkes,* it pleases him, i.e., he likes (O.E. *līcian,* please).
līking   *noun*: pleasure, desire; *adjective*: pleasing (*participle* and *gerund* of *līke,* above).
limm   limb (O.E. *lim*).
limpe   befall, take place (O.E. *limpan,* happen).
līthe   listen, hear (O.N. *hlȳða*).
līthe   pleasant, graceful (O.E. *līðe,* gentle).
lǫng   belong to; as *impersonal verb,* to long for, desire, as in *her longes,* she longs for (O.E. *langian,* yearn for; O.E. *gelang,* belonging to).

lǫrdinges   lords (O.E. *hlaford*, lord + *-inga*).
lorn   lost (O.E. *loren*, vanished, lost).
lǫthly, lǫthliche   loathly, hateful (O.E. *lāþlīc*).
lǫugh   laughed (O.E. *hlōh*, past of *hliehhan*, laugh).
Lumbardy   Lombardy (a province in Northern Italy).
Lyby   *Noun*: Lybia; *adjective*: Lybian.

M

main   *adjective:* strong, important; *noun:* strength (O.E. *mægen*, strength).
mall   hit, hammer (O.F. *mall*, hammer).
march   country, border, borderland (O.E. *mearc*, border district).
may, *past:* might   can, be able (O.E. *magan,* past: *meaht*).
mẹde   meadow, mead (O.E. *mǣd*).
mẹle   speak, say (O.E. *mǣlan*).
mẹne, *past:* mẹned, ment   say, tell, speak; mean, intend (O.E. *mǣnan*).
mensk   courtesy, honor (O.N. *mennsk*, humanity; O.E. *mennisc*, mankind).
menskfully   honorably, courteously (*mensk*, above + *fully*).
merk   go, march (O.E. *mearcian*, mark a boundary; O.F. *marcher*, go).
mẹte   food, meal (O.E. *mæte*).
mikel   much, large (O.E. *micle*).
mǫ   more (O.E. *mā*).
mōd   mind, disposition (O.E. *mōd*).
mōder   mother (O.E. *mōdor*).
molde   earth, ground (O.E. *molde*, soil, ground).
mon   must (O.E. *mon*, singular of *munan*, think, remember).
mǫne   moan, speak (O.E. *mǣnan*).
mōrne   mourn (O.E. *murnan*).
morrow   morning (O.E. *morgen*).
moste   must (old past of *mot*).
mot   may; *mot yē worthe*, may you be (O.E. *motan*).

N

ne   not; *ne . . . ne*, not . . . nor, neither . . . nor (O.E. *ne*).
needes   message, errand (O.E. *nēod*, need).
nẹr   near, nearer (O.E. *nēara, comparative* of *nēah*, near).
neven   name, tell (O.N. *nefna*, name).
nǫlde   would not, did not want to (*ne* + *wǫlde*, below).
nomen   took, seized (O.E. *nōmen,* past of *niman*, take).

O

of   by, from; of (O.E. *of*).
ǫne   one, alone; *him one*, him alone; *his one*, himself alone (O.E. *ān*).
ǫnes   once (O.E. *ānes*).
ǫught   owned, possessed (past of *owe,* below) (O.E. *ahte*, owned, past of *agan*).
outray   injure, outrage (O.F. *outrage*, injure).

ǫverling   overlord (O.E. *ofer*, over + *ling*).
ǫwe; *past*: ǫught   own, possess (O.E. *agan*).
ǫwen   *possessive pronoun and adjective*, own; *in his ǫwen*, in his own right, as he pleases (O.E. *agen*).
ower   our (O.E. *ūre*).

P

palais   palace, castle (O.F. *palais*).
paynim   pagan (O.F. *paenisme*, paganism).
pēce   piece (O.F. *piece*).
pight   adorned, placed, arranged (O.E. *piht, past of *piccean, adorn; O.N. *pikka*, adorn).
pople   people (O.F. *pople*).
press   crowd, company (O.F. *presse*).
press   go, hasten (O.F. *presser*, hurry).
prik   ride, spur (O.E. *prica*).
priker   rider (from above + *-er*).
prīs   excellent (O.F. *pris*).
proffer   offer oneself for battle, attack (O.F. *proferer*).
purpure   purple; purple cloth, dye (O.F. *purpre*).

Q

quǫd   said (O.E. *cwæð*, past of *cwiððan*, to say).

R

raght   drew, pulled, took (O.E. *raht*, past of *rǣcan*, reach, get).
raik   go (O.N. *reika*).
rank   strong, stout (O.E. *ranc*).
rāthe   *adjective*: quick; *adverb*: quickly (O.E. *hræðe*).
raunson   *noun*: ransom; *verb*: ransom, plunder (O.F. *raençon*).
rēal   royal (O.F. *real*).
rēally   royally (above + O.E. *-līce*).
rēaltee   royalty (O.F. *realtē*).
rǫche   reach, offer, give (O.E. *rǣcan*, reach, get).
reddour   fear (O.N. *hrǣddr*, afraid).
rǫde, *past*: redde   advise, read (O.E. *rǣdan*).
rǫdily   readily, quickly (above + *-līce*).
rǫdy   ready (O.E. *hrǣd*, quick).
regn(e)   reign (O.F. *reigne*).
rēme   realm (form preferred by stanzaic poet; see *rewm* below).
renk   man (O.E. *rinc*, warrior).
rent   revenue, tax (O.F. *rente*).
rǫre   rear (O.F. *riere*).
rǫreward   rearguard (O.F. *rerewarde*).
rǫse   attack, rush (O.E. *rǣs*).
rǫsoun   reason (O.F. *raison*).
rǫve   plunder, take (O.E. *rēafian*).

rew rue; as impersonal verb, *him rewes,* it saddens him, i.e., he rues (O.E. *hrēowian*).

rewle rule (O.F. *reule*).

rewm realm (form preferred by the alliterative poet) (O.F. *reaume*).

rewth sorrow, pity, pain (? O.N. *hrygð,* sorrow).

rich strong, noble; wealthy (O.E. *rice*).

right *adjective:* straight, direct; *adverb:* directly; *verb:* adjust, set right (O.E. *riht,* right).

rīot *verb:* amuse oneself, plunder; *noun:* amusement, plunder (O.F. *riote,* debate, quarrel).

rit tear, slash (? possibly related to OHG *ritten,* split).

rīve rip, tear (O.N. *rīfa*).

roy king (O.F. *roi*).

rout company, troop (O.F. *route*).

S

sale hall (O.E. *sæl*).

salūe greet, salute (O.F. *saluer*).

sarazen saracen (O.F. *sarazin*).

sayn to say (O.E. *secgan*).

sę sea (O.E. *sǣ*).

seek, *past:* sought go (O.E. *sēcan,* seek).

seem *impersonal verb: him seems,* it seems concerning him, i.e., he seems (O.N. *soema,* honor).

sēge *noun:* siege; *verb:* besiege (O.F. *sege,* siege, *assegier,* besiege).

segge man (O.E. *secg*).

sēke ill, sick (O.E. *sēoc*).

sēker *adjective:* sure, trusty, certain; *verb:* trust, swear (O.E. *sicor*).

sēkerly certainly (O.E. *sicorlīce*).

selcouthe rare (O.E. *seldcūþ*).

semble assemble; *semble on,* attack (O.F. *assembler*).

sēnn since, then (O.E. *siþþan*).

sēre various, many; *on sere halves,* on all sides (O.N. *sér,* many).

sęse cease (O.F. *cesser*); seize (O.F. *saiser*).

sęsoun season (O.F. *saison*).

shalk man (O.E. *scealc*).

sheer shear, cut (O.E. *scieran*).

shēld shield (O.E. *scild*).

sheltron troop, phalanx (O.E. *scildtruma,* shield-troop).

shend, *past:* shent put to shame, destroy (O.E. *scendan,* shame).

shew appear, show, to be seen (O.E. *sceawian*).

shift arrange, order, move about (O.E. *sciftan,* move).

shō she (form preferred by the alliterative poet) (? O.E. *sīo,* feminine demonstrative article).

sholde should, must (O.E. *sceolde, past* of *sculan,* must).

shręd shredded, cut with scalloped edges (O.E. *scrēadian*).

sinne since (O.E. *siþþan*).

sithe   since, then, afterwards (O.E. *siþþan*).
slee, *past*: slogh, slew   slay, kill (O.E. *slēan*, strike, past: *slāh*).
slǫ   slay, kill (variant of *slee*, above).
sǫ   as (O.E. *swa*).
sodēnly   suddenly (O.F. *soudain*, sudden, + *liche*).
solāce   pleasure, rest (O.F. *solas*, amusement).
somoun   summon (O.F. *sumoner*).
sonder   apart, asunder; *in sonder*, asunder, in pieces (O.E. *sundor*).
soon   immediately (O.E. *sōna*).
sooth   truth (O.E. *sōð*).
soper, souper   dinner, meal (O.F. *super, souper*).
sorte   company, troop (O.F. *sorte*, kind).
soudēour   mercenary soldier (O.F. *soudier*).
sǫught   went; *past of seek*, above (O.E. *sōht*, past of *sēcan*, seek).
sowdan   sultan (O.F. *soldan*).
spēche   speech (O.E. *spæc*).
speed   succeed (O.E. *spēdan*).
spęke, *past*: spāke, spǫke   speak (O.E. *spēcan*).
spęre   spear (O.E. *spere*).
spręde, *past*: spredde   spread (O.E. *sprædan*).
sprent   leaped (O.N. *spretta*, from older **sprenta*?).
sprǫng   sprung, broken (as of a spear) (O.E. *sprang*, past of *springan*, leap).
squīer   squire (O.E. *escuir*).
stale   troop, company (O.E. *steall*, place, position).
steren   strong, stern (O.E. *styrn*).
sterte   leap, go (? O.E. **styrtan*, influenced by O.N. *sterta*).
steven   voice (O.E. *stefn*).
stiff   strong, stout (O.E. *stif*).
stonay   astonish (O.F. *estouner*).
stounde   space of time, while (O.E. *stund*, time).
stour   battle (O.F. *estour*).
stręme   stream (O.E. *strēam*).
strenghe   strength, stronghold, strong position (O.E. *strengð*, strength).
stroy   destroy (O.F. *destruire*).
suīte   group, company; *in suite*, together (O.F. *suite*, company).
sujourn   rest, sojourn (O.F. *sojorner*, spend the day).
surprīsed   captured, taken (O.F. *surpris*, past participle of *surprendre*, seize).
Surry   Syria.
swap   cut, slash (O.E. *swapan*, sweep).
swarth   grassy ground (O.E. *sweard*, outer covering).
swelt   die, faint (O.E. *sweltan*, die).
swīthe   fast, quick; sometimes as an intensifier meaning "very"; *also swīthe, as swīthe*, quickly (O.E. *swīð*, strong, active).

T

tāke, *past*: took   give, offer; take (O.N. *taka*).
teen   *noun*: sorrow, grief; *verb*: grieve (O.E. *tēona*, injury, wrong).

tere tear (O.E. *tēar*).
there where, there; *there as*, there (O.E. *þær*, there).
thider thither (O.E. *þider*).
thir these (? O.N. *þeir*, they).
thirl stab, pierce (O.E. *ðyrlian*).
tho then (O.E. *ðā*).
tho those (O.E. *ðā*, plural of demonstrative).
thōle allow, suffer (O.E. *ðolian*).
thret threaten (O.E. *ðrēatian*).
thro bold, strong (O.N. *þrár*).
throly boldly, strongly (O.N. *þráligr*).
tīdandes tidings, news (O.E. *tīdande*, happening).
tīde *noun*: time (O.E. *tīd*); *verb*: happen, betide (O.E. *tīdan*).
til to, until (O.E. *til*, to).
tinne, *past*: tint lose (O.N. *týna*).
tīte quickly; *also tite, als tite*, quickly (O.N. *títt*).
tithinges, tithandes tidings, news, variant of *tīdandes*, above (influenced by
     O.N. *tíðendi*, events, news).
tōgeder together (O.E. *tōgædere*).
torfer trouble, sorrow (O.N. *torføra*, trouble).
towr tower (O.F. *tour*).
traist trust (O.N. *traustr*).
trechery treachery (O.F. *tricherie, trecerie*).
tresoun treason (O.F. *traison*).
tresure treasure (O.F. *tresor*).
trete deal, treat with, bargain (O.F. *treter, traitier*, treat).
trew true (O.E. *trēow*).
trewe, trewes truce (*plural* of *trew*, above).
trewlich, trewly truly (O.E. *trēowlīc*).
trewth truth, troth, pledged word (O.E. *trēowþ*, truth).
trīne go, move (? cf. Swedish *trina*, go).
tristly boldly, surely (*traist*, above + *-liche*).
troufle *noun* and *verb*: trifle (O.F. *trufle*, from *trufe*, deceit).
trouth troth, pledged word; truth (variant of *trewth*, above).
trow suppose, expect (O.E. *trēowian*, believe, hope).
trump *noun*: trumpet; *verb*: blow on a trumpet (O.F. *trompe*).
Tuskānē Tuscany (a province of northwestern Italy).

U

unsaught hostile (O.E. *unseht*).
unsaughtly with hostile intent (*unsaught*, above + *liche*).
unsound injured, ill, not healthy (*un* + *sound*, from O.E. *gesund*, solid,
     healthy).
unwinly sadly, joylessly (*un* + O.E. *wynlīc*, joyful).

W

wandreth trouble, sorrow (O.N. *vandrǣði*).–

ware   aware (O.E. *wær*).
warlaw   warlock, wizard (O.E. *wǣrloga*, liar, devil).
weed   garment, clothing (O.E. *wǣd*).
ween   expect, suppose; as *noun*: doubt (O.E. *wēnan*, expect).
wēld   rule, control, wield (O.E. *wēaldan*).
wẹle   prosperity, joy (O.E. *wela*).
wẹlth   wealth (*wẹle*, above + *-að*, abstract suffix).
wend   turn, go (*wendan*).
wēnd   supposed, thought (past of *ween*).
wēpen   weapon (O.E. *wǣpn*).
wērily   wearily (*wery*, above + *liche*).
werray   make war on, attack (O.F. *guerroier*).
wēry   weary (O.E. *wērig*).
wex, wexed   grew, became (past of *wax*; O.E. *weaxan*).
widerwinne   enemy (O.E. *wiðerwinna*).
wight   *adjective*: strong; *noun*: person; *no wight*, not at all (O.N. *vígt*, skilled in arms; O.E. *wiht*, creature, thing).
wightly   strongly (*wight*, above + *liche*).
wightness   strength, boldness (*wight*, above + *ness*).
wilne   want, desire (O.E. *wilnian*).
wite, *present*: wọt; *past*: wiste   know (O.E. *witan, wāt, wiste*).
with   by means of, with (O.E. *wið*, against, with).
wọ   woe (O.E. *wā*).
wōde   mad, crazy (O.E. *wōd*, wild).
wọlde   would, desired (past of *will*; O.E. *wolde*, past of *willan*).
wọnde   hesitate, doubt (O.E. *wandian*).
wonne   dwell (O.E. *wunian*).
work, *past*: wrought   do, make, effect (O.E. *wyrcan*, work).
worship   honor (O.E. *weorðscipe*).
worthe   become, be (O.E. *weorðan*).
wọt   knew (past of *wite*).
wrake   trouble, ruin (O.E. *wracu*).
wrẹken, *past*: wroke   avenge, wreak (O.E. *wrecan*).
wye   man (O.E. *wiga*, warrior).

Y

yare   ready (O.E. *gearu*).
yēde   went; past of *go* (O.E. *ēode*, past of *gān*, go).
yēld, *past*: yēlden, yolden   yield (O.E. *gieldan*, pay).
yēme   control, possess (O.E. *gīeman*).
yēre   year (O.E. *gēar*).
yerne   *verb*: yearn, desire; *adverb*: eagerly (O.E. *giernan*).
yif   if (O.E. *gif*).
ynow   many, enough; often redundant with a vague sense of "many," as in *knightes ynow*, many knights (O.E. *geneah*, enough).
yōde   went (past of *go*, variant of *yede*, above).
yonge   young (O.E. *geong*).

Textual Notes

THE STANZAIC MORTE ARTHUR

The manuscript of the *Stanzaic Morte Arthur* was very carefully written; the scribes made few errors and frequently corrected those that they did make. Bruce's edition corrects the obvious errors, and I have followed his emendations, including the addition of a line (supplied by Furnivall) between lines 1413 and 1414. I have departed from Bruce's text only in the following cases (the readings of Bruce and of the manuscript follow in parentheses those of this text):

 309   Hit him (*hitte*)
1105   Ender (*ʒender*)
1377   Aguilt (*gilte*)
2345   Joyous Gard then they (Bruce: *Ioyus gard they*; Manuscript: *Ioyus gard the they*)
3121   His (*hye*)
3628   Nun (*man*)
3709   Black and whīte (*whyte and blak*)
3815   Ring a bell (*a bell ring*)
3896   Fifth (*fyfty*).

THE ALLITERATIVE MORTE ARTHURE

The manuscript of the *Alliterative Morte Arthure* is apparently a hastily written and uncorrected copy, and it contains many words and lines that make little or no sense. Consequently, even the most conservative editions contain many conjectural emendations. As the following notes will show, I have freely emended the text. These notes contain only significant variants and do not include corrections of obvious scribal errors (repeated words, missing letters). Each entry consists of the reading adopted in the present edition followed by an indication of the source of the emendation (where no such abbreviation follows the conjecture is my own) and, in parentheses, the manuscript reading as represented, usually, in Brock's text.

Abbreviations are as follows (see Bibliography for full identification): Br = Brock; Ba = Banks; Bj = Björkman; Fi = Finlayson; GV = Gordon and Vinaver; OL = O'Loughlin; OED = *Oxford English Dictionary*.

42	Overgne Ba (*Eruge*)
134	There is Br (*Thare*)
142	Crowned was Bj (*corounde*)
178	Togges OL (*togers*)
187	When Bj (*whame*)
256	Disūse (*deffuse*)
301	Months Bj (*eldes*)
305	Congee beseekes Bj (*besekys*)
334	Of wightest GV (*of Wyghte and*)
458	Lēfe Bj (*lette*)
471	Sixteen Bj (*sex sum of*)
513	Sandesman Bj (*sandes*)
515	Wye OL (*waye*)
587	Boyes (*Bayous*)
674	Worldes Bj (*werdez*)
716	Sways Bj (*Twys*)
769a	Supplied by GV
771a	Suggested by GV
785	At (*it*)
804	Thring Bj (*bring*)
812–813	Second half of 812 appears in the manuscript as the second half of 813, and vice versa; rearranged by Bj.
821	Tattered Bj (*taschesesede*)
910	Ēnamelled Bj (*enarmede*)
946	Them (*thus*)
1083	Eyen-hǫles Bj (*hole eyghne*)
1123	Genitals Br (*genitates*)
1142	Wīld buskes Bj (*buskez*)
1231	Mẹte-whīle GV (*mene while*)
1248	Frayes Bj (*fraisez*)
1281	With Bj (*That with*)
1302	Worthy Bj (*worthethy*)
1334	Appears in MS as line 1330; Bj.
1364	Sāble Bj (*salle*)
1378	All unabaist Bj (*vnabaiste alle*)
1408	All Bj (*and*); Bedvere (*Bedwyne*)
1427	relīes (*redyes*)
1466–67	Appear in MS in reverse order.
1503	Nǫt Bj (*now*)
1567	Tīthandes Bj (*thyȝandez*)

1653   Kith Bj (*lythe*)
1688   Leng Bj (*hufe*)
1690   Crest Bj (*breste*)
1698   Forthy (*ffro the*); Brūt Bj (*Borghte*)
1732   On the Bj (*one*)
1744   Bawdwyne Bj (*Wawayne*)
1745   Rowlaundes Bj (*and Rowlandez*)
1768   All on loud Bj (*o laundone*)
1797   In his Bj (*his ine*)
1866   Cornett (*Cordewa*)
1878   Hęthen men Bj (*mene*)
1904   Utolf Bj (*Vtere*)
1911   Sarazenes ynow Bj (*Sarazenes*)
1912   Are Bj (*a*)
1930   Never berne Bj (*neuer*)
1938   Though (*ʒofe*)
1979   Then Bj (*theme*)
1980   Sīde Bj (*halfe*)
1982   Wāles Bj (*Vyleris*)
2016   Him sees Bj (*sees*)
2066   Ēwain fitz Ūrien Bj (*Ewayne sir Fitz Vriene*)
2108   Hęthe Bj (*heyghe*)
2112   Jonathal OL (*Ienitalle*)
2151   On Folde Bj (*fygured folde*)
2157   Sir Bedvere the rich Fi (*with clene mene of armez*)
2180   Rēal renk Bj (*ryalle*)
2198   Intō the Bj (*into*)
2217   Thriches Bj (*chis*)
2250   All Bj (*at*)
2280   Līthe Bj (*lyghte*)
2286   Dromedaries of Bj (*of dromondaries*)
2288   Olfendes Bj (*Elfaydes*)
2305   Hē lenged Br (*lengede*)
2328   Wē ne Bj (*ne*)
2343   Full of Bj (*fulle*); the monee (*monee*)
2358   Ten Bj (*fowre*)
2386   Auguste OL (*the Auguste*)
2398   Of Lorraine the lēge Bj (*Lorayne the lele*)
2403   At (*and*)
2408   Tuskān Ba (*Turkayne*)
2418   Is in Bj (*es*)
2419   Citee Br (*Pety*)
2424   Bended Bj (*beneyde*)
2438   Rade Bj (*ferde*)
2478   Plantes Bj (*plattes*)
2495   Wicher (*Wecharde*)

2519   Withouten any berne Bj (*With birenne ony borne*)
2521   Glessenand OL (*gessenande*)
2522   And Bj' (*a*)
2531   The lange Bj (*a launde*)
2568   Railed Bj (*vrayllede*)
2588a–2588b   Suggested by GV
2594   Lēgēaunce and land OL (*legyaunce*)
2663a   Supplied by GV
2664   They are (*For they are*)
2675   Slight Bj (*slaughte*)
2771   Brethe Bj (*breste*)
2797   And Bj (*a*)
2854   Though Bj (*ʒofe*)
2890   Gerard Bj (*Ierante*)
2900   Ferkes in Bj (*fferkes*)
2908   Gīauntes are Bj (*gyawntis*)
2940   Dūke dresses Bj (*duke*)
2950   Matchless (*maches*)
2977   Sleghte Bj (*elagere*)
3013   At heste Bj (*the beste*)
3057   Nǫne GV (*no*)
3061   Be deemed Bj (*idene the*)
3064   Shō Bj (*he*)
3112–3127   These lines appear after 3067 in the MS. GV suggests the move on
             the evidence of Malory.
3101   Skāthel Bj (*Slale*)
3118   King GV (*knyghte*)
3140   For Pawnce, and for Bj (*of Pawnce and of*)
3150   Him tīme seemed GV (*thus wele tymede*)
3186   Sceptre, for sooth GV (*ceptre*)
3209   Hǫlden Bj (*hondene*)
3220   Slākes his Bj (*slakes*)
3241   Clēvewort Bj (*clerewort*)
3256   With brouches Bj (*Bruchez*)
3257   Her back Bj (*With hir bake*)
3263   Riches Bj (*reched*)
3272   This roo Bj (*thir roʒ*)
3282   tǫne eye Bj (*two eyne*)
3308   Fǫlded Bj (*fayled*)
3352   Crispand Bj (*krispane*)
3356   Circled Bj (*Selkylde*)
3422   Tǫne clīmband kyng Bj (*two clymbande kynges*)
3427   Lovelich Bj (*lifelich*)
3439   Nīnde Bj (*nynne*)
3474   Sclavin Bj (*Slawyne*)
3480   Wāthe Bj (*wawhte*)

3510   I was Bj (*I*)
3530   Of Bj (*To*)
3592   Trumpe Bj (*trome*)
3605–06   Appear in MS in reverse order
3662   Węther (*With hir*)
3672   Bernes Bj (*braynes*)
3675   Uptīes (*Vpcynes*); see *OED*, s.v. upties.
3678   Many frēke Bj (*ffrekke*)
3796   Help mē (*helpe*)
3797   Tō see us Br (*to vs*)
3864   Frederick of Frīsland Bj (*ffroderike of Fres*)
3911   yeyes Bj (*ʒee*)
3924   Swafres Bj (*Swalters*)
3929   Trewth Bj (*trewghe*)
3937   Guthēde Bj (*guchede*)
3942   Encircled Bj (*enserchede*)
3996   Kithe Bj (*kyghte*)
4010   Carrīed it Br (*Karyed*)
4017   Dōn for him Bj (*Done for*)
4020   Bēre Bj (*erthe*)
4129   Fele Bj (*sere*)
4157   Why then ne (*Qwythen*)
4181   Churlish OL (*churles*)
4221   And in Br (*And*)
4223   Hēne Bj (*ne he*)
4305   Dayes (*day*)
4343   Kin Bj (*blude*)